Georgina O'Hara Callan
is the author of *The Encyclopaedia
of Fashion* (1986) and *The World of the Bride* (1991).
She is at present engaged on a biography of the
designer Edward Molyneux. British born, she lives
in the United States with her husband
and two children.

WORLD OF ART

This famous series
provides the widest available
range of illustrated books on art in all its aspects.
If you would like to receive a complete list
of titles in print please write to:
THAMES AND HUDSON
30 Bloomsbury Street, London WC1B 3QP
In the United States please write to:
THAMES AND HUDSON INC.
500 Fifth Avenue, New York, New York 10110

Printed in Italy

The Thames and Hudson

DICTIONARY
OF FASHION
AND FASHION
DESIGNERS

Georgina O'Hara Callan

352 illustrations
73 in color

THAMES AND HUDSON

This revised, expanded and updated edition published in
the World of Art in 1998
© 1986, 1989 and 1998 Thames and Hudson Ltd, London
Text © 1986, 1989 and 1998 Georgina O'Hara Callan

The previous edition was published as *The Encyclopaedia of Fashion*
This edition first published in the United States of America in
paperback in 1998 by Thames and Hudson Inc., 500 Fifth Avenue,
New York, New York 10110

Library of Congress Catalog Card Number 97-61609
ISBN 0-500-20313-X

Printed and bound in Italy

CONTENTS

PREFACE

The Dictionary of Fashion and Fashion Designers covers the period from around 1840 – when the sewing machine came into use, setting the cornerstone of the ready-to-wear industry – until the end of the 1990s. It concentrates on that period's major fashion capitals: Paris, London, New York, Rome and Milan, for it was from these cities that the main thrust of fashion direction emerged, though other places, such as Hollywood, also made their contribution.

Biographies of designers – the innovators, creators and interpreters, even those whose contribution was no greater or smaller than producing good work during a specific period of time – form an important part of this book. The first designer of consequence was Charles Worth. An Englishman in Paris, he was a celebrity in his own right, whose marketing and publicity stunts, coupled with indisputable talent, extended his influence far beyond the wardrobes of the well-dressed. In him we can see the beginnings of the modern-day fashion designer. Worth led the way for other great names of the early twentieth century: Doucet, Paquin, Poiret, Lanvin . . .

Travel and communications spread the word. Patou brought models from the USA to show his clothes in Paris – sporty American women who suited the jaunty clothes of the 1920s. Two women picked up the reins in the 1920s and 1930s: Chanel and Schiaparelli. Chanel's ideas are still alive today: her look was as casual, unstructured and uncomplicated as she herself was complex. Schiaparelli, with her witty and irreverent clothes, brought humour to fashion, taking the art world's most avant-garde ideas to use in her designs. Through her, fashion and art fused and fashion no longer took itself so seriously.

During World War II the USA fell out of touch with Paris and began to go its own way. In the French capital itself fashion marked time until 1947, when Dior caught everyone's attention. Although as early as 1939, and certainly through the war years, many Parisian designers had been working towards a new shape which was to become known, in 1947, as the New Look, it was Dior who launched it, and it is with his name that it will be irrevocably linked.

The haute couture of Balmain and Balenciaga dominated in the 1950s but that was to change when Saint Laurent showed street fashion on the runway, and many fashion taboos were broken in the wake of 'pop' culture. Mary Quant became the heroine of the 1960s. What has been called the 'sober seventies' saw the establishment in the USA of two highly influential designers, Ralph Lauren, who captured the essence of gentrified America by romanticizing its pioneering past, and Calvin Klein, whose simplified shapes spoke of an unadorned, minimal look. After the clothing revolution of the 1960s, the 1970s settled into a modernization of classic looks, or at the other extreme, to theme dressing, disco dressing, ethnic fashion, and 'executive dress' for women. At the end of the decade the Japanese held court: Miyake, Kawakubo and Kansai Yamamoto built a bridge not only from the East to the West but also from the 1970s to the 1980s. They introduced layer dressing and with it an entirely new attitude to clothing. Their legacy lingered into the 1990s with the 'minimalist' look, and their ideas were re-explored by the 'deconstructionists'.

The end of the century was hallmarked by a mood that had begun during the youth culture of the 1960s. Increasingly designers looked to the street and to the multicultural urban scene for inspiration. Designers such as Vivienne Westwood linked fashion to aggressive sex and an anarchic youth culture. It was from the street that 'grunge' emerged. In its way, this was a revolution as important as the one that took place in the 1960s. The 'deconstructionists' – designers such as the Belgians Martin Margiela and Ann Demeulemeester – challenged the whole concept of clothing by paring garments down to their basic components, ripping and shredding cloth, repositioning sleeves, zips and collars, and experimenting with unlikely fabrics. At the same time there was a renewed interest in haute couture, as the crowns of the great Paris houses passed into the younger hands of John Galliano and Alexander McQueen.

Fashion has also been influenced by designers of cinema costume, especially in the early part of the twentieth century. And though the influence of television has been more general, the power of its images – spacemen in bodysuits, armies in battle fatigues, hippies, and even little known African tribes – has helped to spread or even start a trend.

Illustrators are also included here. At the turn of the nineteenth century there were over one hundred fashion periodicals published in Paris. The artists of the *Gazette du bon ton* created their own. Bakst's theatre designs influenced pre-World War I fashions while Barbier and Lepape epitomized the female of the period as Eric was to do thirty years later. When photography became the dominant visual form, Steichen, Hoyningen-Huene and Horst, followed by Avedon, Penn, Parkinson and, later, Bailey, brought their own interpretations of mood and style. Bruce Weber took the artifice out of the genre.

Fashion would have no focus without the publishers and editors whose eyes select the styles of tomorrow and whose hands sign up the talent and skill of the day to the avatars of fashion, the magazines. Condé Nast, John Fairchild, Edna Woolman Chase, Diana Vreeland, Carmel Snow – their names are as revered today as the designers they featured in *Harper's Bazaar*, *Vogue* and *Women's Wear Daily*. Artists are also listed: Christian Bérard, who worked with Schiaparelli; Raoul Dufy, who designed fabric for Bianchini-Férier; Mondrian, whose paintings inspired Saint Laurent; and Bridget Riley of Op Art fame.

There are also those who march with – and sometimes lead – fashion: Cartier, Schlumberger and Kenneth Jay Lane, for example, in the world of jewelry; Ferragamo, Vivier and Blahnik in shoes; Paulette, Reboux, Daché and Treacy as milliners; Hermès and Gucci for accessories. Jackie Kennedy Onassis, Brigitte Bardot, Jawaharlal Nehru, Dwight D. Eisenhower and Madonna are found here too, for they are among the people who have influenced fashion or have given their name to a fashion garment or style.

Fashion is also the result of designers and brilliant industrial, commercial and scientific minds interacting together. Developments in exercise wear, for example, are directly related to progress in the manufacture of fibres and fabrics. In the field of underwear, too, the advancement of textiles has been significant. The numerous and cumbersome items of the nineteenth century were eventually replaced by lighter (and fewer) pieces. More than one item of underwear has eventually become outerwear; the peignoir became a tea gown and eventually a day dress; the bra and panties became a bikini; the corset prepared the way for the swimsuit; the chemise, earlier worn as a nightshirt or under a corset, became a dress shape; and the slip and bustier emerged as eveningwear.

Fashion is a mobile, changing reflection of the way we are and the times in which we live. Clothes reveal our priorities, our aspirations, our liberalism or conservatism. They go a long way towards satisfying simple or complex emotional needs, and they can be used consciously or unconsciously to convey subtle or overt sexual messages. Clothes contribute colour and shape to our environment and give form to our feelings. As this book reveals, clothes, and the designers who create them, are the first and last words of the language that is fashion.

A READER'S GUIDE TO THE USE OF THIS BOOK

This dictionary covers fashion in all its aspects, with entries on fashion designers, couture houses, manufacturers, makers of accessories and jewelry, hairdressers, and costume designers for theatre and film. It includes all the chief types of garment, as well as fabrics and furs. Artists and art movements which have influenced fashion have a place here, as do fashion magazines and fashion editors, photographers and illustrators. Fashion movements, including street styles, are also covered. In addition, a brief look through these pages will reveal entries such as 'Madonna', 'boutique', 'Twiggy' and 'Seventh Avenue', which fall into none of the categories mentioned above but which are nevertheless part of the story of fashion.

Cross-references are indicated by the use of SMALL CAPITALS and have been kept to a minimum in order to make the entries as readable as possible. Though the names of designers are always cross-referenced, those of garments and fabrics are not, since they appear too frequently to make cross-referencing useful.

Illustrations are usually on the same page or double-page as the entries they illustrate. Where they appear under a different heading, the cross-reference is preceded by an asterisk: thus, in the 'Space Age' entry, * COURREGES.

Alphabetization of entries works according to the word-by-word method: thus 'bra' is followed by 'bra slip' rather than 'braces'. Where fashion terminology occasionally differs between the UK and the US, both terms are given.

The bibliography is divided into categories which sometimes overlap. It covers the most fundamental and informative sources on the subject of fashion.

A

Abraham Textile manufactory founded in Switzerland in the 19th century. In 1943 it became a limited company with headquarters in Zürich. Known for the manufacture and distribution of silks to the international haute couture and ready-to-wear industries, Abraham also produces plain and printed cottons, wools, rayons, jacquard and jersey. A major supplier to France, the company manufactured SAINT LAURENT's popular shawls during the 1970s.

accordion pleats Fine, narrow, regular pleating created by sewing or pressing minute DARTS into the fabric of dresses and skirts, usually from the waistband towards the hem. Accordion pleating was used in the construction of ball gowns during the late 19th century. By the turn of the century it was an integral part of many styles and became especially popular during the 1920s and 1950s. *See also* BOX PLEAT *and* SUNRAY PLEATS.

acetate Man-made cellulose acetate fabric or yarn created in Germany in 1869. Work on the fibre was continued by Swiss chemists Camille and Henri Dreyfus of Basle in the 1900s, but their research was interrupted by the outbreak of World War I when acetate was used to make waterproof varnishes for French and British fabric-covered aeroplanes. In 1920 British Celanese Ltd made a commercially viable acetate fibre using the Dreyfus method. Acetate has since been used to make lingerie, blouses, dresses and knitwear as well as other garments requiring lightweight, silky fabrics.

acrylic Synthetic fibre often used as a substitute for wool. It was first launched commercially in 1947 but not produced in any great volume until the 1950s. Acrylic is a strong, warm fabric that drapes well. It is used to make sweaters and tracksuits, and is also made into linings for boots, gloves, jackets and slippers. Common tradenames for acrylic are Acrilan and Orlon.

Adolfo 1933–. Milliner, designer. Born Adolfo Sardiña in Havana, Cuba. Adolfo emigrated to New York in 1948 and worked as an apprentice millinery designer at Bergdorf Goodman. In 1951 he moved to Paris to work at BALENCIAGA before returning to New York to rejoin Bergdorf Goodman where he designed hats under the name Adolfo of Emme. During the 1950s, he was recognized for his technique of shaping hats by stitching, without the use of wiring or inner stuffing. In 1962 he started his own business. His innovations include jersey visor caps, hats with removable goggles and huge fur BERETS. In the 1960s he showed a 'Panama Planter's Hat' made of straw and trimmed with striped ribbon or jersey, shaggy COSSACK hats made of velour or fur, and variations on BOWLERS and PILLBOXES. The clothes he designed to wear with his hats had a costume feel: a long melton officer's coat with EPAULETS and gold buttons, gingham DIRNDL skirts, organdy jumpers, GIBSON GIRL blouses and PATCHWORK skirts. In the 1970s he abandoned the theatrical design elements that had been his hallmark in the previous decade, basing his collection instead on knitted suits and tailored dresses which appealed to an upmarket conservative clientele. Adolfo closed his workroom in 1993.

Adri 1934–. Designer. Born Adrienne Steckling in St Joseph, Missouri, USA. Adri attended the School of Fine Arts at Washington University in St Louis, Missouri, and in the summer of 1955 became guest editor of *Mademoiselle*'s college issue. The following year she studied at Parsons School of Design in New York, where she was strongly influenced by designer Claire MCCARDELL, then a lecturer at the school. Adri worked for the wholesale house of B. H. Wragge for many years and for Anne FOGARTY. In 1972 she began producing her own line of clothes, including accessories. Her clothing is functional, practical and easy to wear. She believes in building a wardrobe piece by piece with interchangeable separates.

Adrian 1903–59. Costume designer. Born Gilbert Adrian in Naugatuck, Connecticut, USA. Adrian studied at the School for Fine and Applied Arts, New York, and in Paris. He designed costumes for Broadway shows until 1925, when he went to Hollywood to make clothes for Rudolph Valentino. From 1926 to

This example of **Aesthetic Dress**, advertised in Liberty's catalogue *c.* 1909, harmonizes well with the Art Nouveau furnishings.

1928 he worked for De Mille Studios, but shortly afterwards joined Metro-Goldwyn-Mayer, where he became chief costume designer. At MGM he designed for Greta GARBO for many years. For her role in *A Woman of Affairs* (1928), he created a SLOUCH HAT that influenced fashion for at least a decade. In *Romance* (1930) he dressed her in a velvet, ostrich-feather-trimmed hat, the 'Eugénie', which partially obscured one eye. This was a much copied style. The PILLBOX hat for Garbo in *As You Desire Me* (1932) was another trendsetter, as was the SNOOD created for Hedy Lamarr in *I Take This Woman* (1939). For actress Joan Crawford in *Letty Lynton* (1932), Adrian made a wide-shouldered white organdy dress with ruffled sleeves and a narrow waist. This was widely copied throughout the USA;

Macy's department store in New York reported selling 500,000 similar styles. Adrian gave Crawford her visual hallmark: wide, padded shoulders that made her hips look smaller. For Jean Harlow he produced slinky, figure-hugging dresses, cut on the BIAS. His designs were characterized by bold silhouettes and patterns, DOLMAN and KIMONO SLEEVES, long tapering waistlines, and diagonal fastenings. He favoured asymmetric lines and frequently used black crepe for slim, bias-cut evening gowns. In 1942 Adrian retired from the cinema and opened a shop in Beverly Hills, California, though he continued to make original garments for films until his death.

Aertex Cotton cellular fabric introduced in England during the late 19th century by Lewis Haslam, one-time Member of Parliament for Newport, Monmouthshire, England, and two doctors: Sir Benjamin Ward Richardson and Richard Greene. In 1888 the three men formed the Aertex Company. By 1891 the company was manufacturing women's underwear in Aertex fabric. Aertex has always been popular for undergarments and sportswear. Since the 1970s, it has also been made into shirts, blouses and skirts for summer wear. It was the forerunner of the cotton thermal knit worn as casual wear – LEGGINGS, jackets, T-SHIRTS – in the 1990s.

Aesthetic Dress Dress associated with the Aesthetic Movement of the 1880s to the 1900s, which took inspiration from the garments depicted in the work of Millais, Holman Hunt, Rossetti and other Pre-Raphaelite painters. The Aesthetic Movement applied to painting, graphics and the decorative arts. Aesthetic dress for women consisted of medieval-like robes – loose, unstructured and with little detail and few accessories or trimmings. The aim of the movement was to encourage a more natural style than the tiny waists and full bosoms decreed by the fashions of the period. Women who wore Aesthetic Dress loosened their CORSETS (some abandoned them altogether) and wore garments that created a smoother, more fluid, outline. The style appealed to intellectuals and those involved in the art world and it was linked to the general movement for women's emancipation. *See also* RATIONAL DRESS SOCIETY *and* BLOOMER.

Azzedine **Alaïa**'s bare-backed sheath dress from his Summer 1981 collection, part of a series which used zips with jersey. The zips allowed the wearer to expose different parts of the body. Drawing by Thierry Perez.

Afro Naturally grown, bushy hairstyle popular among African-Americans since the 1960s.

Agha, Mehemet Fehmy c.1896–1950. Art director. Born in Kiev, Russia. Agha studied at the Ecole des Beaux-Arts in Paris during the 1920s and later gained a doctorate in political science. He worked in Paris as a studio chief for the Dorland Advertising Agency before joining German VOGUE in Berlin, where he was discovered by Condé NAST. In 1929 Agha moved to *Vogue* in New York where he altered the visual style of the magazine by introducing sans-serif typefaces and revolutionizing layouts and front covers. He was responsible for presenting the work of the photographers BEATON, HORST, HOYNINGEN-HUENE and STEICHEN. Agha also contributed written features to the magazine. In 1943 Alexander LIBERMAN, his heir-apparent, took over.

Agnès B 1941–. Designer. Born Agnès Troublé in Paris, France. Agnès B joined *Elle* magazine as a junior editor at the age of seventeen. Two years later she moved to DOROTHEE BIS as a designer but left in 1964 to work freelance. She opened her own store in 1975 in Paris, where her affordable, relaxed, wearable clothes catered to a wide age group. Many of her early designs were adapted from French workers' uniforms. She specialized in separates, notably a snap-button CARDIGAN. Much of the charm of her clothes lies in the fact that they have a worn-in look.

aigrette Tall FEATHER, often from the osprey or egret, which adorned the CHIGNON hairstyle or trimmed a hat in the late 19th century. Aigrette plumes were worn on hats until the 1940s.

Alaïa, Azzedine 1940–. Designer. Born in Tunisia. Alaïa studied at the Ecole des Beaux-Arts in Tunis before moving in 1957 to Paris, where he worked for DIOR, LAROCHE and MUGLER. During the 1970s demand from private clients for Alaïa's designs increased and in 1981 he launched his first collection. An early collection (1986/87), made mostly of leather, included garments punched with metal-ringed eyelets, studded muslin skirts and leather GAUNTLETS. His early designs concentrated on idealizing the female form with body-hugging, curvaceous shapes made of soft glove leather, jersey and silk. The success of his modern-day HOURGLASS silhouettes was due to his purity of line and his understanding and advancement of fabric technology. His stretch outfits made of Lycra and wool allowed him to cut and shape fabric as though it peels round the body, creating almost a second skin of complexly constructed clothes. His inventive use of zips is both practical and an integral part of the design. A widely influential designer, he continues to experiment with fabric, especially boiled wool, as well as with stretch materials and new weaving techniques.

Albini, Walter 1941–83. Designer. Born in Busto Arsizio, Italy. Albini studied fashion and costume design in Italy before moving to France where he worked as an illustrator for various Italian magazines. He returned to Italy in 1960 and joined KRIZIA for three years.

Alençon lace

Queen **Alexandra** (*centre*), wearing the famous choker, or dog collar, which she popularized. It reached from the neck to low on the bodice. At the left is the Duchess of Fife, at the right Princess Victoria.

Albini also produced several ready-to-wear collections for BASILE before opening his own business in 1965. Heavily influenced by Chanel, and inspired by the glamorous clothes of the movies of the 1930s and 1940s, he successfully translated these ideas into subtle, cleverly cut garments which won considerable acclaim in Europe. He often worked with silk and handled other luxurious fabrics in a sensitive manner. His influence was cut short by an early death.

Alençon lace Alençon is a town in Normandy, France, famous for its needlepoint lace-making from the mid-17th century until the late 19th century. Needlepoint lace originated in Venice, and early Alençon versions were classically designed with carefully arranged swags and flowers on a fine net background outlined with a heavy, raised outer edge.

Alexandra, Queen 1844–1925. Born Alexandra Caroline Charlotte Louisa Julia, daughter of Christian IX, in Copenhagen, Denmark. In 1863 Alexandra married the Prince of Wales, (later Edward VII). As the Princess of Wales, she was responsible for several fashion innovations.

She wore a full-length, double-breasted PELISSE which buttoned to the hem – a practical coat, which was widely copied. She also initiated a vogue for wearing a CHOKER of jewels. Her famous DOG COLLAR, as it was sometimes known, consisted of rows of PEARLS from the neck to low on the BODICE. She also wore round her neck a wide band of velvet onto which a brooch or clasp was pinned. During the late 19th century, a petticoat – the Alexandra – was named after the Princess.

Alexandre 1922–. Hairdresser. Born Alexandre Louis de Raimon in Saint-Tropez, France. Alexandre trained in Cannes at one of the salons belonging to master hairdresser ANTOINE. He joined Antoine's principal salon in Paris in 1939 and shortly after World War II became its artistic director. He formed his own company in 1952. Over the following twenty-five years, Alexandre created more than five hundred hairstyles. He is credited with the revival of wigs during the 1960s and he influenced fashions for CHIGNONS, short backcombed hair and BEEHIVES. He is also known for his technique of decorating intricate styles with ribbons and jewels. His clients have included Greta GARBO, Elizabeth Taylor, Sophia Loren and Maria Callas. For many years he was personal hairdresser to Princess Grace of Monaco. Alexandre collaborated with many designers to create hairstyles for their seasonal collections.

Alfaro, Victor 1965–. Designer. Born in Mexico. Emigrating to the USA in 1981, Alfaro graduated from New York's Fashion Institute of Technology in 1987. His own business was established in the early 1990s and he quickly achieved a reputation as an eveningwear designer whose clothes suggest sex and power. His body-clinging garments in leather and sheer fabrics are worn by many prominent women. Alfaro's designs are influenced by STREET STYLE and though they are sleek in cut and line, and made up in luxurious fabrics, they are ultimately considered avant-garde.

Alice band Band of material, often ribbon or velvet, worn across the top of the head to keep hair off the forehead. It is named after the hairband worn by the heroine of Lewis Carroll's book *Through the Looking Glass* (1872). Alice bands have been popular for girls and young women since the end of the 19th century.

A-line Dress shape dating from *c.*1955. The A-line dress or skirt flares from the bust or waist to form two sides of a triangular 'A'. The hem is the third side. *See* DIOR.

Alix *See* GRES.

alpaca Wool of the alpaca, a member of the camel family native to the Andes mountain regions of South America. In 1836 Sir Titus Salt introduced alpaca cloth, which at that time was a blend of alpaca and silk. Cheaper than pure silk, alpaca had many of the lustrous qualities of the heavy types of silk available during the 19th century. Alpaca was popular during the 1840s when the health cult of that period created an upsurge of interest in woollen materials. It was used to make outer garments and to line coats. From the late 19th century, alpaca was blended with cotton. During the 1900s the cloth was made into dresses and suits. Since the 1950s the word alpaca has referred to a rayon crepe fabric with a wiry texture, which is mainly used for outerwear.

A-line suit from Christian Dior, for Spring 1955.

Classic Hardy **Amies** tweed suit from his 1953–54 collection.

Amies, Hardy 1909–. Designer. Born in London, England. Amies left England at the age of eighteen to work in France and Germany. He returned to London in 1930 as the representative of a British weighing machine company. Four years later he was introduced to the fashion house of LACHASSE, where he became managing director and designer. The house specialized in tweed suits for women and in 1937 Amies created a suit called 'Panic' which attracted a great deal of attention because of its fine tailoring and fit. During World War II, he contributed to the UTILITY SCHEME operated by the British Board of Trade. In 1945 Amies opened his own house selling couture and ready-to-wear clothes, particularly classically tailored suits and dresses which were often made of tweed and woollen fabrics. He designed day dresses for the Queen (then Princess Elizabeth) and was awarded a Royal Warrant in 1955. He is also known for his PUFF-SLEEVED evening dresses and lavish ball gowns. In 1962 he became the first women's couturier to design for men. He has an international reputation as both a womenswear and a menswear designer. See LINTON TWEED.

Andrevie, France 1950–84. Designer. Born in Montauban, France. Andrevie opened her own line in a boutique in St Tropez in 1976.

The following year she was hailed as an innovative new designer in both France and the USA. Her clothes were classic in style but modern in manner, cut into large, bold shapes and with unusual colour combinations.

angora Hair of the angora goat, which originates in Turkey. Angora is also the hair of the angora rabbit, which is native to the island of Madeira and now farmed in the USA, Europe and Japan. In both cases, angora is characterized by long, smooth, soft fibres. It is mixed with rayon and wool for dresses, knitwear and sweaters. See also MOHAIR.

aniline dye Dyestuff produced from plants of genus *Indigofera* by Sir William Perkin in England in 1850. A violet-blue (the colour known as indigo) was produced first, followed by bright purple, green and magenta. The plant provides a chemical base for many dyes. Coal tar has replaced the extensive use of indigo.

animal prints Fabrics with patterns and colours imitating the skins of animals have been made up into blouses, coats and scarves since the 1930s. They became widely popular in the 1970s and 1980s, made into dresses, LEGGINGS and accessories.

ankle socks During World War II, when clothes were rationed and nylon STOCKINGS in short supply in the UK, British women wore lisle stockings or went bare-legged. British *VOGUE* promoted the use of ankle socks, which were usually white and made of cotton or wool. Some styles were produced in tweed to match suits. White ankle socks have been worn as a casual style of clothing since the 1960s. See also BOBBY SOCKS.

ankle straps Worn by women for many centuries both as decoration and as a means of securing the foot inside the shoe, ankle straps have been popular at some point in almost every decade, on both high-heeled and flat shoes.

Anna Karenina 1. The heroine of Tolstoy's 1876 novel of the same name. Several films based on the book were made: in 1927, US title *Love* (costumes by Gilbert Clark); in 1935 (costumes by ADRIAN); and in 1947 (costumes by

Cecil BEATON). Anna Karenina became a term, loosely used, for various dress styles that were glamorous, romantic and fur-trimmed. *2.* In the mid-1960s the Anna Karenina coat was a popular style. It was cut to any length, decorated with FROGGING and had a circlet of fur on the neckline.

Annie Hall UNISEX style of dress popularized by the American actress Diane Keaton in the film *Annie Hall* (1977), for which Ralph LAUREN designed the costumes. Keaton dressed in oversize garments, notably baggy trousers, an extra-large man's shirt, and a man's pinstriped waistcoat. A tie and floppy hat completed the outfit. Other interpretations of the Annie Hall style included mixing expensive designer-label garments with second-hand RETRO clothes.

anorak Hip-length, hooded garment worn by Inuits. The word is believed to come from the Aleutian Islands. The anorak was originally made of sealskin. Until the latter part of the 20th century it was made of nylon and insulated with other man-made fibres and worn exclusively as outerwear. Zipped or buttoned from hip to neck, it is worn both for sporting activities and as casual attire. During the 1980s designers produced anoraks in satin and luxurious fabrics for eveningwear. The garment, depending on the fabric, is worn as outdoor wear or as a decorative jacket. *See also* PARKA *and* WINDCHEATER.

Antoine 1884–1976. Hairdresser. Born Antek Cierplikowski in Sieradz, Poland. Antoine was first apprenticed to a barber and then worked for Pawel Lewandowski, the leading Polish hairdresser. Between 1902 and 1906 he was employed in salons in Biarritz, Cannes, Deauville, Nice, Paris and London. He then settled in Paris and became a private hairdresser who paid house calls on his clients. Some years later he opened a salon which was patronized by many socialites and actresses, including Sarah Bernhardt. He bobbed the hair of French actress Eve Lavallière in 1910, cutting it short in a style normally worn by children. This fashion was not widely adopted in Europe until 1912. During World War I, Antoine introduced brightly coloured wigs. He experimented with

hair dyes in non-natural colours and in 1924 dyed Lady Elsie Mendl's grey hair blue, creating a popular trend. From 1925 until 1939 he commuted between Paris and New York, where he ran a beauty establishment for Saks Fifth Avenue's Manhattan store. He is credited with the SHINGLE cut of the late 1920s, the upswept hairstyles of the 1930s, the design of both Greta GARBO's long bob and Claudette Colbert's fringe (bangs), and the introduction of a blonde or white lock into an otherwise dark head of hair.

Antonio 1943–87. Illustrator. Born Antonio Lopez in Puerto Rico. Antonio, the son of a couturier, moved to New York at the age of eight. He studied at the High School of Industrial Art and the Fashion Institute of Technology. In the early 1960s he worked as a sketch artist on SEVENTH AVENUE, until in 1964 he met the designer Charles JAMES, who was to be an enormous influence on him. Antonio worked with James, drawing all the designer's clothes, for a number of years. In the early 1970s he moved to Paris where he established himself as the foremost fashion illustrator on both sides of the Atlantic. His clever drawings of sculptured women are positive, vital and modern. His style is highly distinctive: bold, sweeping brush strokes show both garments and accessories in clear, attentive detail. This close attention in no way slows down the pace

Antoine's famous blond or platinum streak on a dark head of hair in a style for 1931.

appliqué

Aquascutum field coat, from 1923. This style, like those of today, has its origins in the trenchcoat of World War I. It was to change remarkably little during the course of the 20th century.

of the illustration. It can be said of Antonio that his work helped create a return to the almost forgotten art of fashion illustration in magazines. He exerted a strong influence on many younger artists. *See* ★MISSONI.

appliqué Ornamental pieces of fabric sewn or glued onto another piece of fabric or onto a garment. Petal, leaf and flower designs or animal motifs are commonly applied to cotton, lace and satin. Appliqué was popular during the 1950s, when simple felt motifs were used to adorn CIRCULAR SKIRTS, and in the 1970s, when more elaborate designs were sewn onto padded satin jackets.

Aquascutum The firm of Aquascutum (from the Latin, literally 'water-shield') was established in 1851 as a tailor's shop in London, England. Aquascutum coats were among the first showerproof coats to be made from wool and were worn by British soldiers in the trenches

during World War I. These ankle-length TRENCHCOATS had a military appearance, emphasized with EPAULETS and brass rings on the belt, a style that has remained popular. Between the wars, while supplying coats for the military, the company also sold fashionable showerproof coats for men and women who required suitable attire for their increasingly active, outdoor lives. In the early 1950s Aquascutum RAINCOATS were made exclusively from Wyncol D.711, a cotton and nylon poplin. In 1955, a cotton gabardine in iridescent shades was introduced. Up to this point, rainwear had been made chiefly in grey, blue and beige. These new coats were lined with satin and woven fabrics. In the same year, the company broke with tradition and shortened the raincoat to the knees. The need for reproofing raincoats after dry-cleaning was eliminated in 1959 with a process, introduced by the company, called Aqua 5. During the 1976–77 season, the 'Club-Check' was launched as a lining for men's rain-

coats. This pattern was subsequently used for accessories and in the 1980s for a clothing range for men and women.

Aran Style of knitting associated with the Aran Islands, off the west coast of Ireland. Coarse, handspun wool, usually in its natural, off-white colour, is knitted in cables, twists and bobbles into a centre front and two side panels, creating an embossed effect. Aran knitting was traditionally used for sweaters but since the mid-20th century has also been used for cardigans, coats, scarves, TAM O'SHANTERS and mittens. It is always associated with casual attire.

Argentan lace Lace produced in the town of Argentan in Normandy, France, from the mid-16th century until the late 19th century. It resembles ALENÇON LACE but has a larger hexagonal net background and characteristic variety in the corded threads which connect the lace patterns.

Argyle Multicoloured diamond pattern – an approximation of the TARTAN of the Scottish clan Argyle – formerly hand-knitted in Britain but now machine-made throughout the world. The Argyle pattern is most often seen on socks, scarves and sweaters.

Armani, Giorgio 1934–. Designer. Born in Piacenza, Italy. Armani studied medicine at Milan University. After military service he joined the Italian department store chain La Rinascente as a window dresser. He first worked as a menswear designer with manufacturer Nino CERRUTI from 1961 until 1970, when he turned freelance. His own menswear collection was launched in 1974, with a womenswear collection the following year. In 1981 he launched Emporio Armani and Armani Jeans. Armani was one of the most influential designers of the 1980s. His success is based on his understanding of menswear and its adaptation to both womenswear and a more relaxed,

Jacket by Giorgio **Armani**, 1977. The most radical menswear designer of the late 20th century, Armani created a new look for men, with softer tailoring and more relaxed lines.

Men such as these touched the hearts of American women in the late 19th and early 20th centuries. Joseph Leyendecker's drawings and paintings for the **Arrow** shirt company, in Troy, New York, provoked the kind of fan mail a pop star might receive today. Although Arrow were specialists in men's shirts, it is easy to see how women's blouses evolved from these turn-of-the-century designs.

contemporary aesthetic. By reconstructing the suit jacket – for both men and women – he has created an elegant, understated garment that retains a timeless quality. The easy, supple lines of his tailoring, the clear uncluttered minimalist look of his clothes, often made of fine alpaca, wool, leather and suede, result in clothes that are equally sought after by both men and women, and have assured him of international acclaim. A world leader in menswear design, Armani also designs clothes for women which follow many of the principles of male dress, with exaggerated but controlled proportions. In the late 1970s and 1980s he showed suits for women with extra-wide shoulders that contributed to the POWER SUIT look of that period. By the mid-1980s he progressively relaxed the suit shoulders and his clothes became sleeker and less pronounced. Invariably designing in muted colours, Armani has produced large, loose BLAZER jackets and well-cut trousers, all tailored on generous but supple lines. Much of his womenswear has an androgynous quality that appeals to working women who favour a quietly empowered style that suggests as much about a lifestyle as a working life.

army surplus Ex-Forces surplus gear, such as DUFFLE COATS, flying jackets, trousers and boots, were made available to the public during the 1950s. These items became part of the fashion scene in the 1960s and have remained in style ever since. They were worn initially as street clothes by young people who undermined the seriousness and practicality of the garments themselves by teaming them with boldly coloured skirts and tailored trousers. BATTLE JACKETS, BOMBER JACKETS and duffle coats have subsequently become part of everyday clothing made up in fabrics and colours suited to casual wear. *See also* STREET STYLE.

Arrow collars and shirts The detachable, starched collar on men's shirts is believed to have been invented in the USA in the 1820s. Forty years later these collars were in great demand. A manufacturing plant was established around this time by Messrs Maullin and Blanchard in Troy, New York. The company merged with Coon & Company in 1889 and shortly after launched the Arrow trademark. In 1913 the company became Cluett, Peabody & Co., Inc. Artist J. C. LEYENDECKER was engaged to illustrate Arrow shirt collars for advertisements. At the end of World War I, Arrow were manufacturing more than four hundred different kinds of shirt collars. In the following years, as the demand for detachable collars declined, Arrow produced a shirt with the collar as an integral part, which was preshrunk and tailored to fit the lines of the body. After World War II, Arrow helped popularize coloured shirts. Designers have adapted men's shirts to womenswear since the early part of the 20th century, closely following fashionable alterations in cut and fit. Arrow shirts are typical of the styles imitated.

Art, goût, beauté French, high-fashion monthly magazine published between 1920 and 1933. It became *Voici la Mode: art, goût, beauté* until 1936. It was mostly printed by the *pochoir* method, which produced a high standard of colour reproduction. Contributing artists to the magazine were, notably, George BARBIER, Paul IRIBE, Georges LEPAPE, Charles MARTIN and André MARTY.

Art Nouveau Decorative art form which spread across Europe during the 1890s. It took its name from L'Art Nouveau, a shop opened in Paris in 1895 by Siegfried Bing. Other proponents of the movement were Julius Meier-Graefe, also in Paris, and Arthur Lasenby LIBERTY in London. Although Art Nouveau was mainly expressed in architecture, interior decoration and furniture design, it also found its way into the design of jewelry and fabrics. It is distinguished by graceful, if exaggerated, lines, elongated strokes ending in curlicues, and flower and leaf motifs. Art Nouveau textiles were revived by Liberty in the 1960s. *See also* *FOUQUET, KLIMT *and* MUCHA.

artificial silk *See* RAYON.

ascot Man's mid-19th-century cravat with wide ends, worn around the neck and looped under the chin. Part of formal dress, it was usually made of a plain fabric, often silk, and unfringed. The loop, or double knot, was sometimes held in place by a jeweled pin. As part of the general trend towards menswear, women wore versions of ascots during the latter part of the 20th century.

Ashley, Laura 1925–1985. Designer and manufacturer. Born Laura Mountney in Merthyr Tydfil, Wales. In 1953, with her husband, Bernard, Laura Ashley formed a company for the production of printed headscarves and tea towels. In 1959 she designed a shortsleeved SMOCK top, based on a gardener's smock, made of 100 percent cotton. During the 1960s she created voluminous dresses with PATCH POCKETS and, toward the end of that decade, ankle-length printed cotton dresses. Her long PINAFORE dresses were worn over high-necked blouses. In the early 1970s, some of her best-known designs appeared, including EDWARDIAN-STYLE dresses, many with high, frilly collars and LEG-OF-MUTTON SLEEVES, or SCOOP NECKS and short PUFF SLEEVES. Most of her fabrics were printed with simple floral motifs based on 18th- and 19th-century patterns: tiny geometric prints, flowers, trailing sprigs, and fine spots and stripes. Until the early 1980s the company designed and manufactured garments in cotton only, but later collections included clothes in cotton mixtures and jersey fabrics.

astrakhan Originally the fleece of the karakul lamb which is found in Russia. Astrakhan was popular until the late 19th century, used as a trimming on the collars and cuffs of coats and made into hats. In the 20th century the name was given both to the fleece itself and to a heavy fabric, knitted or woven, with a deep-pile surface of curled loops which imitates the fleece. Also known as persian lamb.

Augustabernard dates unknown. Designer. Born Augusta Bernard in Provence, France. Augustabernard opened her house in 1919. She made tasteful, well-cut garments on elegant lines and was highly successful until 1934, when she retired.

Avedon, Richard 1923–. Photographer. Born in New York, USA. Avedon's philosophy studies at Columbia University were interrupted in 1942, when he was assigned for two years to the US Merchant Marine's photography branch, where he took pictures of personnel. In 1944, back in civilian life, he began to study photography at New York's New School for Social Research. In the same year he persuaded the New York branch of the department store

Azagury, Jacques

Bonwit Teller to lend him some high-fashion apparel for a photographic session. The resulting photographs earned him commissions from the store. In 1945 Alexey BRODOVITCH, art director of HARPER'S BAZAAR, hired Avedon as staff photographer to take pictures of celebrities and cover the fashion scene. Twenty years later he moved to VOGUE. Avedon used a wide-angle lens, exaggerated camera angles, and strobe lighting to capture the unusual, often disassociated, expressions on the faces of his subjects. In his early fashion pictures he chose unfamiliar settings, such as zoos, circuses, the NASA launch pads at Cape Kennedy, and junkyards, and he encouraged his models to move about while he took the shots. The resulting pictures were original and dramatic. In the late 1950s and 1960s, Avedon concentrated most of his work in a studio.

Azagury, Jacques 1958–. Designer. Born in Casablanca, Morocco. Educated in England, Azagury left school early to work in a clothing factory. After he had spent two years at the London College of Fashion and one year at St Martin's School of Art in London, *Harpers & Queen* magazine featured his 1978 diploma show, and orders for his garments soon followed. His knitted three-piece outfit – a strapless TUBE worn with a long pleated skirt and a long sleeveless coat with a draped back – was a great success. He specializes in glamorous evening clothes for an international market.

B

baby doll Nightwear introduced during the late 1950s, popularized by the film *Baby Doll* (1956). Often short and trimmed with synthetic lace, bows and tiny ribbons, baby-doll garments are reminiscent of children's underwear of the 19th century.

backpack A utilitarian bag, worn on the back and attached to the body by shoulder straps. Miuccia PRADA introduced nylon backpacks in the early 1980s, but the accessory did not become fashionable until later in the decade. During the 1990s the backpack became a staple accessory, made in various sizes and designs, in leather, suede, nylon or luxurious cloths.

Badgley, Mark *See* BADGLEY MISCHKA.

Badgley Mischka Design team. James Mischka (b. 1960, Burlington, Wisconsin, USA) enrolled in 1982 at Parsons School of Design in New York, where he met classmate Mark Badgley (b. 1961, East Saint Louis, Illinois, USA). After graduation and separate apprenticeships, with Badgley as assistant designer to Donna KARAN and Mischka as assistant designer to Willi SMITH, the pair formed their own company in 1985. Their 1987 show attracted buyers from major department stores who were drawn to their elegant, contemporary versions of classic designs. In recent years they have attracted a Hollywood clientele for their DECOLLETE COCKTAIL DRESSES and TUNICS encrusted with beads, and off-the-shoulder bridal gowns made of ivory lace and silk crepe.

bagheera Fine, uncut pile velvet used for evening gowns until the early part of the 20th

David **Bailey**'s photograph of top model Jean Shrimpton, taken in 1965.

Josephine **Baker** shocked and enthralled the world with her exotic dancing and various states of undress. She could be seen at the Folies-Bergère in outfits such as this ostrich feather dress.

century. In later years imitation bagheera was made from rayon crepe.

Bailey, David 1938–. Photographer. Born in London, England. After leaving school Bailey spent a brief period in the RAF before taking up photography. In 1959 he worked as an assistant to John FRENCH. The following year he began his career as a fashion photographer, working for numerous magazines, including *VOGUE*, *Elle* and *GLAMOUR*, and for many British newspapers. He was hailed as one of the most innovative photographers of the 1960s. His lively, fresh style successfully captured the prevailing youthful outlook of the decade. He worked consistently with one model, in the 1960s Jean Shrimpton and later Marie Helvin, concentrating on the relationship between the woman and the clothes, emphasizing the freedom of fashion with clear, striking, uncomplicated pictures. In the 1970s he began directing films and since that time has produced many books of his photographs. *See also *QUANT.

Baker, Josephine 1906–75. Music-hall artist. Born in St Louis, Missouri, USA. Baker was attracted to the theatre and to music and dance from an early age and left home at sixteen to join a touring theatrical troupe from Philadelphia. After appearing in the choruses of shows in Boston and on Broadway in the early 1920s, she joined the *Revue Nègre*, with which she travelled to London and Paris. During the late 1920s she worked in Paris at the Folies-Bergère and the Casino de Paris. Baker made black skin fashionable and promoted beads, necklets, bracelets, anklets, brightly dyed gloves, fringes (bangs) and colourful costumes. She often appeared on stage naked or wearing only a feathered loincloth. A MAILLOT of tulle, decorated with DIAMANTE, was designed for one of her performances.

Bakst, Léon 1866–1924. Artist. Born Lev Rosenberg in St Petersburg, Russia. Bakst attended the Imperial Academy of Arts in St Petersburg and worked for many years as both a court painter and a costume and scenery designer. In 1906 he went to Paris to prepare the Russian section of the annual art exhibition, the Salon d'Automne. He returned to France two years later with Sergei DIAGHILEV as a scenery painter and costume designer for the *BALLETS RUSSES. Working between two cities, Bakst founded a liberal school of painting in St Petersburg and produced plays for the Paris Opéra. His contribution to fashion derives from his association with the Ballets Russes, for which he designed vivid, brilliantly coloured sets and costumes which had a direct influence on clothing of the period. *See *HOBBLE SKIRT.

balaclava Helmet-like head covering, either knitted or crocheted, named after the village in the Crimea where the Charge of the Light Brigade took place in 1854. For soldiers in the two world wars, British and US women knitted balaclavas in khaki, a colour used for camouflage. The cuff around the neck of a balaclava may be drawn up over the chin and mouth. The balaclava was seen as a fashion item on the runways of Paris during the 1960s.

Balenciaga, Cristobal 1895–1972. Designer. Born in Guetaria, near San Sebastian, Spain. Balenciaga's talents revealed themselves early. By the age of fourteen he was already able to copy couturier clothes. He trained as a tailor

Balenciaga suit in dark grey wool ottoman, worn with a red velvet beret. Winter collection, 1950.

and in 1916 opened a dressmaking and tailoring establishment in San Sebastian. By the early 1930s he had earned a reputation as Spain's leading couturier. He moved to Paris in 1937. His tailoring background enabled him to design, cut, put together and sew a gown. Balenciaga was not an advocate of popular trends; his clothes were often formal: uncluttered, balanced and restrained. He frequently used sombre colours, such as shades of dark brown, though he later gained a reputation as a colourist and in a collection of the late 1950s showed lambswool that had been dyed bright yellow and pink. Balenciaga emphasized the stark elegance of his designs by using blocks of white against darker tones. In 1939 he introduced a dropped shoulder line with a nipped-in waist and rounded hips, a style that prefigured the 1947 NEW LOOK. After the war he showed jackets with more natural waistlines and large sleeves. Ten years later Balenciaga created a distinctive line by raising the hemlines of his dresses and coats at the front and dropping them sharply at the back. In the same year, 1956, he presented a loose CHEMISE DRESS, known as the SACK. During the 1960s he showed loose, full jackets with DOLMAN SLEEVES. Models at his 1963 shows wore harlequin tights and he was

one of the first designers to put his models into BODYSTOCKINGS. His name is still associated with large buttons and a collar which, raised on a band, stands away from the throat and neck. Considered to be purist and classicist, Balenciaga made garments that were instantly identifiable. He retired in 1968.

balkan blouse Low-waisted blouse with full sleeves which became fashionable in Europe after the Balkan Wars (1912–13).

ball gown Traditionally a full-skirted gown reaching at least to the ankles, made of a luxurious fabric, delicately and exotically trimmed. Most versions are cut off the shoulder with DECOLLETE necklines. The ball-gown shape has changed little since the mid-19th century. Although man-made fabrics are now sometimes used, the most common fabrics are satin, silk, taffeta and velvet with trimmings of lace, pearls, sequins, embroidery, ruffles and ruching. *See* ★BALLERINA SKIRT *and* CRINOLINE.

ballerina skirt Full skirt that reaches to just above the ankles. A popular style during the 1950s.

Ballerina skirts have been a consistently popular length for ball gowns, especially for young women.

Programme for Sergei Diaghilev's **Ballets Russes**, designed by Léon Bakst.

Ballets Russes Series of ballets devised by Sergei DIAGHILEV in Russia in the early years of the 20th century. For the first time the decor, costumes and music were integral parts of the dance itself, which relied on mime. The colours, fabrics and designs of the costumes had a strong influence on fashion. Inspired by the Orient, the costumes were unrestrained, fluid and brightly coloured, in contrast to the rigidly constructed shapes and pale, delicate hues of the late 19th century. Many designs were painted on to linen, or APPLIQUE was used on various cloths, particularly velvet. Trends were created for richly embroidered satins and silks, HAREM PANTS, AIGRETTES, TURBANS and brilliant jewels. The Ballets Russes first appeared in Paris in 1909, performing one year later in London. Their productions included *Firebird* (1910); *Schéhérazade* (1910) in which Nijinsky, painted black, danced the role of a slave; *Daphnis and Chloe* (1912); *L'Après-midi d'un faune* (1912); and *Jeux* (1913). *See also* BAKST *and* POIRET.

Right: 'For the Ballets des Champs-Élysées', drawing by René Gruau of a design by Pierre **Balmain**, Spring/Summer 1946.

balloon skirt Introduced after World War II, the balloon skirt was full, gathered at the waist, and seamed to curve in towards the knees where it was held in place by a circular band on the hem. In the 1980s a similar design, known as a 'POUF skirt', was popularized by Christian LACROIX.

balloon sleeve Nineteenth-century sleeve shape that was full over the upper arm and narrowed from elbow to wrist.

balmacaan Loose-fitting, calf-length, tweed overcoat with RAGLAN sleeves. Balmacaans were worn by men in the 19th century and had been adapted to womenswear by the end of the century.

Balmain, Pierre 1914–82. Designer. Born in St Jean de Maurienne, France. Balmain's family owned a wholesale drapery business. Balmain studied architecture at the Ecole des Beaux-Arts in Paris but did not complete his studies. He worked for MOLYNEUX between 1934 and 1939

'For an Embassy Dinner', drawing by René Gruau of a design by Pierre **Balmain**, Spring/Summer 1946.

Balmoral boot In the mid-19th century Queen VICTORIA's devotion to her Scottish estate at Balmoral helped popularize in the UK fashions for TARTAN and garments named after Scottish towns. The Balmoral boot covered the ankle, had a thick sole, and was suitable for walking. Made of leather, it was decorated with brass eyelet holes and elaborate stitching.

Balmoral petticoat White or grey horsehair PETTICOAT worn instead of a cage frame CRINOLINE from the mid-19th century. *See also* BALMORAL BOOT.

Banana Republic Store opened in San Francisco in 1978 by Mel and Patricia Ziegler, specializing in casual SAFARI styles and ARMY SURPLUS clothing. Many of the utilitarian items had sturdy zips and snaps and were double-stitched and reinforced. The store sold desert army hats, sheepskin vests, shorts and other items of travel clothing to armchair travellers. Banana Republic inspired contemporary casual styles based on loose-fitting shorts, shirts, jackets and trousers in muted shades. The company was purchased by THE GAP in the 1980s.

bandanna Probably from the Hindu word 'bandhnu', which describes a primitive method

The Warehouse chain under the influence of Jeff **Banks** brought inexpensive fashion to the streets of London during the 1970s. This Autumn 1984 photograph shows the fashionable waistcoat worn over long, loose shirts. Note the vogue for the creased look.

and then spent two years at LELONG, where he met DIOR. He opened his own house in 1945. In that year he showed long, bellshaped skirts with small waists – a line that became popular in 1947 as part of Dior's NEW LOOK. In 1951 he opened branches in the USA selling ready-to-wear clothes. His success in the USA has been attributed to the fact that he was able to translate French fashion into clothes for the American woman's generally larger frame, without compromising style. Balmain designed many SPORTSWEAR collections for this ready-to-wear market. His talent as a designer lay in his ability to make simple, tailored suits as well as grand evening gowns, in the same slender, supple and elegant lines. During the 1950s he popularized the stole for day as well as evening wear and created a vogue for SHEATH dresses beneath jackets. His coats were generously cut to give a full back and were sometimes half-belted. In the same period, his COSSACK-like wraps and capes were trendsetters. Balmain was noted as a designer for the international set.

of tie-dyeing. The name was given to the large, brightly coloured HANDKERCHIEFS produced by this process. The bandannas used by cowboys in the American West were often quite simple pieces of cloth, dyed one colour, which could be worn around the neck or pulled up over the chin, mouth and nose as protection against dust. During the 1950s and 1960s, when American clothes were popular, bandannas were worn tucked into denim shirts, particularly in the USA. *See also* COWBOY *and* TIE-DYE.

bandeau *1.* A headband worn around the forehead to keep hair out of the eyes during sporting activities, popularized by Suzanne LENGLEN in the 1920s, by HIPPIES of the 1960s, and by US tennis player John McEnroe in the late 1970s. *2.* A piece of fabric, often elasticated, which is worn around the bust, as in a BIKINI. *3.* A bandeau-style dress is one with a horizontal band across the bust.

Banks, Jeff 1943–. Designer. Born in Ebbw Vale, Wales. Banks studied textile and interior design at Camberwell School of Art, London, from 1959 to 1962. In 1964 he opened a shop called Clobber, in London, where he sold both his own designs and those of others. In 1974 he became involved with the establishment of the Warehouse Utility chain of shops which provides inexpensive fashions in bold colours for a predominantly young market. He has also worked freelance for a number of companies, including LIBERTY of London. Throughout the 1970s Banks was completely in tune with contemporary fashions. With an imaginative use of inexpensive fabrics he was able to provide young women with access to fashion without compromising taste.

Banlon Tradename of the US firm Joseph Bancroft & Sons for a process that texturalizes yarn, adding crimp and stretch to synthetic fabrics. Banlon fibre was popular in the 1960s, made up into socks, sweaters and dresses.

Banton, Travis 1894–1958. Costume designer. Born in Waco, Texas, USA. Banton was educated at Columbia University and the Art Students League, New York. His early design career took place in New York with a dress manufacturer and he did not go to Hollywood until 1924. Paramount Pictures employed Banton as a costume designer for the film *The Dressmaker from Paris* (1925) which starred Leatrice Joy. During the 1920s Banton created costumes for many actresses, including Bebe Daniels, Pola Negri and Clara Bow. In the 1930s he designed for other Paramount stars – Claudette Colbert, Marlene Dietrich, Kay Francis, Greta GARBO, Carole Lombard and Mae West – and set the Paramount hallmark of elegant, sensuous clothes, which were often cut on the BIAS. Banton joined 20th Century-Fox in 1939 and stayed for several years. He worked for Universal Studios from 1945 to 1948. During his film career, Banton designed costumes for more than two hundred productions. In the 1950s he returned to the retail trade.

barathea Worsted or woollen fabric used in the 19th century for outer garments. Since the early 20th century it has been used for making suits.

Barbier, George 1882–1932. Illustrator, costume designer. Born in Nantes, France. Barbier studied at the Ecole des Beaux-Arts in Paris from 1908 to 1910. He spent many years designing theatrical costumes and sets and worked as an illustrator for the GAZETTE DU BON TON, LE JOURNAL DES DAMES AT DES MODES, FEUILLETS D'ART, FEMINA and VOGUE. He was interested in both 18th-century art and ART NOUVEAU and the strong influence of the latter can be seen in the curlicues and flowing shapes of his supple, fashionable women. Bar-bier also illustrated albums of ballet dancers and made wood engravings.

Bardot, Brigitte 1934–. Actress. Born in Paris, France. Bardot modelled for *Elle* and *jardin des modes* until 1952, when she became an actress. In 1956 she was photographed wearing a gingham BIKINI decorated with frills. At her second wedding in 1959, she wore a pink gingham lace-trimmed dress, with a SCOOP NECK, nipped-in waist, full skirt and three-quarter-length sleeves. This dress, with a more modest neckline, was widely copied in Europe and the USA.

barège *1.* Lightweight, semi-transparent dress fabric made of silk and wool, with an open-mesh weave. Barège was most often used as a

VEIL or headdress during the 19th century. It was first produced in the valley of the same name in France, though Paris later became the centre of production. 2. A printed SHAWL which was popular in France during the mid-19th century.

barrel shape Skirt shape created by banding fabric from the waist into a narrowed hem. First seen in the HOBBLE SKIRTS of the early 1900s and, later, in a much shorter version, in skirts of the early 1960s.

Barthet, Jean 1930–. Milliner. Born in the Pyrenees, France. Barthet arrived in Paris in 1947 and launched his first collection of hats in 1949. By 1965 he was one of France's most prominent milliners, with a clientele that included film stars and jet-setters. He provided MONTANA, RYKIEL and UNGARO with hats for their collections. Although Barthet's hats are often highly structured, his signature hat is a man's FEDORA, scaled down for women.

Basile Company founded in Milan, Italy, in 1969 by businessman Aldo Ferrante, who had previously been employed by KRIZIA and MISSONI. Basile started as a small company manufacturing menswear. In Ferrante's hands it became known for its luxury daywear and eveningwear and its tailored suits and jackets, which are both retailed and wholesaled. ALBINI, TARLAZZI and VERSACE are just three designers who have worked at Basile on womenswear designs.

basque Short skirt addition sewn onto the BODICE of a dress or jacket. The basque is pleated or gathered onto the hem of the bodice. Also known as a peplum.

Bass Weejuns Slipper-type MOCCASIN made by the G. H. Bass Company, which was founded in Wilton, Maine, USA, in 1876. Originally known as 'Norwegian moccasins', Bass Weejuns have been popular for casual wear since 1936. Also known as penny loafers.

bateau neckline Shallow, boat-shaped neckline which runs from one shoulder to the other and is the same depth front and back. A popular style for dresses and blouses since the early 1920s.

John **Bates**'s famous backless evening dress of 1973.

Bates, John 1938–. Designer. Born in Ponteland, Northumberland, England. In the 1950s Bates worked alongside Gérard PIPART at the design house of Herbert Siddon. Two years later he became a freelance fashion illustrator. After a brief period with a wholesale design company, he was invited in 1964 to form the company Jean Varon. Under this label Bates contributed a wide range of youthful designs to the 1960s and 1970s fashion picture. He introduced some of the shortest MINI-DRESSES in the early 1960s; TROUSER SUITS in 1962; STRING-VEST dresses in 1963; a bridal CATSUIT, striped tube dresses, and stockings with matching dresses in 1964. Bates also designed costumes for Diana Rigg in the role of Emma Peel in the British television series *The Avengers*. By 1965 copies of these clothes were on sale; the leather outfits and the white vinyl coat were enormously popular. Although he experimented widely with daring OP ART print fabrics and bold shapes, he adhered to a clear, simple silhouette and acquired a reputation for EMPIRE-LINE evening dresses which were often elaborately embroidered. Eveningwear played a major part in his collections.

bathing suit The late-19th-century bathing suit was composed of two pieces: a long TUNIC and knickers which together almost completely covered the body. It was usually made of serge or wool and was therefore unsuitable for bathing. Around the turn of the century, the cumbersome combination of tunic and knickers began to be replaced by one-piece garments. These were popularized by the swimmer Annette Kellerman, who competed against men in events held in the River Thames in London, the Seine in Paris and the English Channel. The first rib-knit, elasticized, one-piece bathing suit was made in the USA in 1920 by the Jantzen company and in 1924 Jean PATOU introduced bathing suits with Cubist-inspired designs. CHANEL was also instrumental in promoting bathing suits. In the 1920s most bathing suits were designed for beachwear, rather than for swimming. In the following decade backless costumes became popular. After World War II, the invention of fast-drying, lightweight fabrics helped further to popularize swimwear. By the mid-20th century, 'bathing suit', 'swimsuit'

and 'bathing costume' were interchangeable names for the same garment. Swimsuits in the 1950s were often boned and corsetted to emphasize the bust and minimize the waist, and they resembled foundation garments of the period. Briefer costumes began to appear during the 1960s, cut away around the tops of the thighs and around the arms and shoulders. This trend continued throughout the 1970s and at the end of that decade the one-piece swimsuit was back in fashion. Swimsuits in the 1980s and 1990s were often sculpted around the lines of the body, following its natural form. Increasingly elaborate materials included sophisticated stretch and metallic fabrics. Shapes were cut out in the fabric to accentuate the body. *See also* ★BIKINI, BRIGANCE, ★BRUCE, ★GERNREICH *and* LASTEX.

batik East Indian method of wax printing whereby wax is applied to certain areas of a

Bathing dress from *Harper's Bazar*, 1876. It would be replaced by a one-piece garment around the turn of the century,

fabric to prevent those areas from being dyed. A popular form of printing fabrics for dresses, blouses and men's shirts during the 1960s and 1970s, batik clothing will always be associated with the HIPPIE generation, whose visits to India and fascination with Hindu culture influenced their clothing styles. *See also* ETHNIC.

batiste Originally a sheer, finely woven cloth of cotton or linen which was named after an 18th-century French linen weaver, Jean Baptiste. It has become the generic name for a sheer, fine, mercerized cotton which is used for blouses, dresses and lingerie; a fine wool which is lighter than challis; a sheer silk; and a polyester, rayon or cotton blend fabric.

Battelle, Kenneth 1927–. Hairdresser. Born in Syracuse, New York, USA. After being discharged from the US Army at the end of World War II, Battelle attended the University of Syracuse. He completed his studies at the Wanamaker Academy of Beauty Culture in New York and, after an apprenticeship in Syracuse and Miami, Florida, joined the Helena Rubinstein salon in New York in the mid-1950s. Battelle's fame came in the early 1960s when he joined the beauty establishment set up by milliner Lilly DACHE. His hairstyles for Jacqueline Kennedy (ONASSIS) earned him a huge following.

battle jacket Waist-length, single-breasted jacket used by the US Army during World War II. It was adapted to civilian use by both sexes after the war. A battle jacket is generously cut, especially over the shoulders, with long sleeves and pockets. It is fastened up the front with buttons or zips. *See also* BOMBER JACKET *and* EISENHOWER JACKET.

batwing sleeve *See* DOLMAN SLEEVE.

beanie Small, round skullcap, once known as a calotte, which originated in Ancient Greece. It later became an ecclesiastical headdress. During the 1930s it was a briefly popular hat style for women.

Beaton, Cecil 1904–80. Photographer, designer, illustrator, writer. Born in London, England. Beaton was educated at St John's College, Cambridge. He went to London in 1925 to work as a clerk and typist, teaching himself photography in his spare time. His photographic experiments and designs for theatre sets soon led to commissions. When Beaton sailed for New York in 1929, he was already a successful society and fashion photographer. He worked for British and American *VOGUE* until 1936. The style of photography for which Beaton was noted involved the use of artificial backdrops of mirrors, cellophane and ruched silver fabrics, against which he would pose his subjects as if they were part of an elaborate tableau. In the mid-1930s he moved to Hollywood, where he took portraits of actresses and designed scenery and costumes for the theatre. A prolific illustrator, he contributed to numerous magazines in England and the USA. He published several books of observations on fashion and fashionable people, some of which were illustrated with photographic studies and caricatures. After World War II, he worked mostly on theatre, film and opera design. He created the costumes for thirteen films, notably *Anna Karenina* (1947), *Gigi* (1958) and *My Fair Lady* (1964).

beaver Light-brown fur of a water rodent previously found all over Europe but now mainly confined to Canada and the USA. Beaver fur is thick, soft, warm and hard-wearing. Beaver coats were fashionable during the late 19th century, but were subsequently considered practical rather than glamorous.

bed jacket Jacket of 19th-century origin worn in bed over a nightgown. Usually made of lightweight synthetic fabrics, it can be of any length between bust and waist.

beehive Tall, dome-shaped hairstyle achieved by backcombing. Popular during the 1950s. *See* ALEXANDRE.

Beene, Geoffrey 1927–. Designer. Born in Haynesville, Louisiana, USA. Beene left Tulane Medical School in New Orleans before taking a degree and started work in the display department of the Los Angeles branch of the clothing store chain I. Magnin. In 1947 he moved to New York and studied at the Traphagen School of Fashion. He spent 1948 to 1951 in

Reversible organdy and quilted charmeuse evening jacket of 1984, cut on a basic T-shape, shows Geoffrey **Beene**'s skill at geometry and at balancing different weights of fabrics.

Paris, attending the Académie Julian and the tailoring studio of MOLYNEUX. He returned in 1952 to New York and worked for several ready-to-wear companies before leaving the last one, Harmay, in 1954 to join major manufacturer Teal Traina. In 1963 Beene set up his own company. In the 1960s he gained a reputation for high-waisted, braid-edged EMPIRE dresses, simple SHIFTS, and dresses produced on a T-line. He stressed the simplicity of this last shape by including detail on the collars and cuffs. One of the first US ready-to-wear designers to show short skirts with long jackets, Beene also attracted much attention in 1967 with a long black evening dress constructed like a cassock and worn with a curé's hat. In another collection he showed long, sequined evening dresses resembling oversize football sweaters, complete with numbers on the back. Beene's clothes are structured but never rigid, and rely on the craftsmanship of careful detail. Many of his designs contain an element of fantasy. He has a casual approach to opulent fabrics, successfully blending them with less expensive materials, for example flannel trimmed with RHINESTONES, quilted ticking with chiffon, jersey with taffeta.

Beer Owned by a German designer, Beer was the first couture house to open on the fashionable Place Vendôme in Paris, in 1905. The house produced feminine dresses and lingerie for a conservative clientele. It merged with DRECOLL in 1929.

bell bottoms Traditionally, sailors' trousers that were cut into a bell shape from knee to ankle. In the late 1960s a version of bell bottoms, with the fabric clinging tightly to the thigh and flaring out from the knee, was popular with both men and women. The HIPSTER pants of the same period were similarly styled.

Bellville Sassoon Belinda Bellville, the daughter of a famous London dressmaker, Cuckoo Leith, founded her own couture firm in 1953. David Sassoon (b. 1932 in London, England) joined the firm after graduating from the Royal College of Art, London, in the 1950s. During the 1960s and 1970s the firm's name was synonymous with quality eveningwear – especially ball gowns and COCKTAIL DRESSES of chiffon, organdy and tulle – and bridal clothes. The company continues to design and produce glamorous eveningwear.

belt The belt has its origins in the military GIRDLE or band which was worn around the waist to support clothes or hold weapons. In

A crinoline ball gown of 1982 by the London house of **Bellville Sassoon**.

women's fashion, the popularity of the belt has always been dependent on the positioning of the waistline and on the style of dress. Belts did not feature prominently until the 1850s, when they were often made in the same fabric as the dress or skirt. Later in the century, influenced by the ART NOUVEAU movement, belts with decorative buckles became popular. In the 1920s, as the waistline dropped, belts disappeared from fashion, but a decade later their popularity was restored and self-fabric belts were again common. After World War II, belts became wider, to focus attention on the narrow waist and full hips of the NEW LOOK, and this trend extended well into the 1950s. The 1960s saw widespread use of leather, plastic and gilt-chain belts and there was a brief trend for a version of the wide-buckled COWBOY belt. In the 1970s masculine-style belts were worn, usually of leather, and in different widths and styles. Brightly coloured belts were especially popular. Towards the end of the 1970s the JAPANESE influence on fashion created a trend for extra-long belts which wrapped around the body several times. Belts are now made from rubber, plastic, suede, metal, leather and fabric. *See* CUMMERBUND, OBI *and* SASH.

Benetton Family firm, established in North Italy in the early 1960s by Luciano Benetton, which specializes in inexpensive but fashion-conscious knitwear. Benetton has used wool, lambswool, Shetland wool, and a wool and angora mix for casual, simply designed sweaters and cardigans in a wide spectrum of colours. It also sells T-shirts, jeans and trousers in cotton and cotton mix fabrics. Its worldwide chain of stores is distinguished by its low-cost, brightly coloured garments and knitwear. Luciano's two brothers, Gilberto and Carlo, and his sister, Giuliana, joined the firm in the late 1960s.

Benito, Edouard 1891–1953. Illustrator. Born Eduardo García Benito in Valladolid, Spain. At the age of twelve Benito was apprenticed to a painter. Seven years later he moved to Paris and established himself as a portrait painter, decorative artist and illustrator. Benito worked for numerous magazines and periodicals, including the *GAZETTE DU BON TON*, *LE GOUT DU JOUR*, *LA GUIRLANDE* and *LES FEUILLETS D'ART*. During the 1920s he illustrated for *VOGUE*, producing many stylish and memorable covers. His strokes were strong, simple and economical but very supple. With swift lines he captured the taut, smooth women who epitomized the 1920s.

Bérard, Christian 1902–49. Artist, illustrator. Born in Paris, France. As a child, Bérard was fascinated by the theatre and ballet and compiled albums of costume and scenery designs. By the end of the 1920s, he was an influence on and inspiration to several designers, notably DIOR and SCHIAPARELLI. Though painting was his first love, he concentrated during the 1930s on fabric and interior design, and book and fashion illustration. His work appeared in *HARPER'S BAZAAR* and later in *VOGUE* and was instantly recognizable by his free, elliptical style, indicating elegant shape and form without severe delineation. He was an adventurous colourist. His use of light/dark combinations, though initially considered avant-garde, later became acceptable and even fashionable.

Berardi, Antonio 1968–. Designer. Born in Grantham, England, of Italian parentage. While still a student at St Martin's School of Art, Berardi worked for three years as an assistant to John GALLIANO. He started his own label on leaving college in 1994 and showed his debut collection in 1995. His designs combine sensuality with fine tailoring, quality materials and attention to detail. He is known for sexy, provocative, highly feminine clothes, which often incorporate elements of STREET STYLE.

beret Soft, circular cap of ancient Greek or Roman origin. The two most common beret styles are the basque, often worn with the band showing, and the modeleine, which has no band. The tiny spike on the top of the beret was originally sewn on to cover the eye of the weave. Berets were fashionable in the 1880s, trimmed with flowers, FEATHERS and ribbons. Since then, they have mostly remained unadorned. They were popular during both World War I and World War II, when elastic for millinery purposes was scarce. The most noted revival of berets took place during the late 1960s and 1970s, prompted, in part, by the actress Faye Dunaway's beret in the film *Bonnie and Clyde* (1967). *See* ★KANGOL.

Elio **Berhanyer**, one of Spain's finest designers, produced this confident black wool crepe trouser suit inspired by the Spanish toreador in 1970.

Beretta, Anne-Marie 1937–. Designer. Born in Béziers, France. Beretta arrived in Paris at the age of twenty and was encouraged by Roger Bauer at Jacques GRIFFE to pursue a career in fashion. In the 1950s she worked for Antonio CASTILLO, designing for the theatre in spare moments. In 1965 she joined manufacturer Pierre d'Alby and launched a highly successful line of brown linen garments. She went on to work for Georges Edelman, Ramosport – who manufactured her rainwear line in the 1980s – and Bercher. She established her own ready-to-wear label in 1974. She has a serious, sombre style and sees her clothes as mobile sculptures. She also designs ski-wear and contributes to Max Mara's stylishly tailored suits.

bergère Straw hat with a low crown and wide brim, first popular during the 18th century and revived during the 1860s. Associated with the shepherdess fashions of the late 19th century.

Berhanyer, Elio 1931–. Designer. Born Eliseo Berenguer in Córdoba, Spain. At the age of seventeen, Berhanyer left home for Madrid to seek work as a manual labourer. Ten years later he was employed by the fashion magazine La Moda and in fashion shops, painting in his spare time. In 1959 he opened his own salon. Berhanyer grew to be one of Spain's leading designers, a self-taught specialist in tailoring. He created smartly cut black dresses, which he teamed with BOLEROS and ruffled blouses in the traditional Spanish manner. He also made coats, suits and stately evening gowns. Berhanyer's handling of fabric and seaming gave a formal, somewhat austere, line to some of his creations. He is also noted for his menswear.

This lace **bertha** of *c.* 1843 emphasizes the bust and narrows the waist. The elaborate jewels add focus, against the background of a completely bare neck and a deceptively simple-looking hairstyle.

Berlei Berlei was founded in 1907 as Grover & Company, a corsetry business in Sydney, Australia, by a Mr Grover and a Miss Mobberly. In 1912 the company was taken over by Fred R. Burley. The trademark 'Berlei' was registered in 1917. Berlei specialized in making CORSETS and BRASSIERES for the wholesale trade and from 1926 based its designs for underwear on statistics and information from an anthropometric survey conducted by Sydney University. In 1934 a branch of the company was established in London. Berlei maintains an international reputation and leading brand status for its retail and wholesale foundationwear.

bermuda shorts During the 1930s and 1940s Bermuda became a popular holiday resort. Since local laws did not allow women to reveal their legs, a fashion developed for SHORTS which reached almost to the knee. Bermuda shorts have since become popular with both sexes as summerwear. Some versions are cuffed.

bertha Mid-19th-century cape-like collar, usually made of lace.

Bettina blouse Introduced by GIVENCHY in 1952, the Bettina blouse was named after Bettina Graziani, one of Paris's top models, who worked exclusively for Givenchy in the 1950s. The blouse was made of shirting, with a wide, open neck and full, ruffled broderie-anglaise sleeves. Popular for several years, it was widely copied in Europe and the USA.

Biagiotti, Laura 1943–. Designer. Born in Rome, Italy. Biagiotti graduated in archaeology from Rome University. She first joined her mother's small clothing company but left in 1972 to set up a design business in Florence. She is celebrated in Italy as a classic knitwear designer, specializing in cashmere and wools. Her designs are restrained, soft and fluid, the main interest being provided by the detail and fabric. She also creates daywear and eveningwear.

Bianchini-Férier Firm established in Lyons, France, by Charles Bianchini, an Italian textile manufacturer who settled in Paris in the 1890s. At the turn of the century he joined forces with a Monsieur Férier to form the company Bianchini-Férier. The firm produces its own fabrics, mainly silks, but it also purchases fabrics from other companies and sells them under its own name. In the early 1900s Bianchini-Férier launched a crepe georgette which became very popular. *See also* ★DUFY *and* POIRET.

Givenchy's **Bettina blouse**, named after Bettina Graziani, one of the designer's favourite models.

The 'string' **bikini** of the mid-1970s.

bias cut A cut across the grain of a fabric, which causes the material to fall into a smooth, vertical drape and allows it to be easily manipulated into clinging folds. Bias-cut dresses were worn during the 1920s and 1930s, frequently featuring in films of that era. *See* ADRIAN *and* VIONNET.

Biba *See* HULANICKI.

big hair Elaborate, tall hairstyles, artificially created to increase the height of the wearer, were popular in the 18th century. Women's hairstyles during the 19th and early 20th century were concentrated close to the head. During World War II, Frenchwomen piled their hair on top of their heads as a protest against the Occupation of Paris. In the 1950s a style known as the BEEHIVE became popular. During the 1970s, partly in response to the wide, padded shoulders of the POWER SUIT, women began teasing and spraying their hair up and out to the sides, creating a large, thick mass. This style became outmoded with the sleeker looks of the 1980s.

big shirt Oversize shirt for women, often cut along the lines of a man's casual shirt. This style has been popular since the 1950s, and became known as a big shirt in the 1980s, when it was accepted as a fashion garment shape for day and evening as well as for casual wear.

bike shorts *See* CYCLING PANTS.

bikini Abbreviated two-piece BATHING SUIT. The bikini was launched simultaneously in France in 1946 by Louis Réard, a little-known designer, and the more famous Jacques HEIM. Heim called his bikini the *atome*, but when in the same year the USA conducted atomic bomb tests on a site called Bikini Atoll, the garment was renamed the 'bikini'. Early bikinis were often trimmed and decorated with animal motifs and artificial flowers or were made of crochet. The bikini was already popular in France by the 1950s but it was not accepted in the USA until *c*.1965. In the 1970s a very brief version – the string – appeared, consisting of two minuscule triangles of fabric held together by ties at each hip, and a bra-like top that was attached by ties around the neck and back. *See also* BARDOT.

Bikkembergs, Dirk 1962–. Designer. Born in Flavorsheim, Germany. After studying fashion at the Royal Academy of Arts in Antwerp, Bikkembergs served with the Royal Belgian Army in Germany. He spent several years as a freelance designer for European fashion houses, before forming his own company in 1985, specializing in menswear. He designed separates in dark, muted tones and heavily ribbed sweaters paired with matching LEGGINGS. His footwear included variations on infantryman, football and biker boots. In 1993 he presented his first womenswear collection in Paris. His street-chic, futuristic designs for women included floor-length flared trousers, sheer HALTER tops, and leather trousers with studding.

biretta Originally ecclesiastical headgear, a biretta is a square cap with three or four projections radiating from the centre. It was first seen as a fashion item for women after World War II and enjoyed a brief vogue.

bishop sleeve Long sleeve on a dress or blouse which is full below the elbow and gathered or left loose at the wrist. Popular since the mid-19th century, it faded from the fashion scene in the early 1970s.

Manolo **Blahnik**'s fantastical shoe designs spanning two decades. *Above:* style 'Paloma', cobalt blue reptile skin, Summer 1977; *top:* thong with wood boules covered in soft nappa, Summer 1982; *top right:* ottoman silk evening pump, Winter 1997.

Blahnik, Manolo 1943–. Shoe designer. Born in Santa Cruz, Canary Islands. Blahnik studied law and literature at the University of Geneva before moving to Paris, where he spent 1968 studying art at the Ecole du Louvre. He moved to London in 1970. On a visit to New York, Blahnik showed his portfolio of sketches to several fashion editors, including Diana VREELAND, who encouraged him to concentrate on shoe design. Blahnik was put in touch with an Italian shoe manufacturer. In 1973 he opened his first BOUTIQUE in London. He also designed shoes for Ossie CLARK. Since that time, Blahnik has become one of the world's most famous shoe designers and has contributed to the collections of many clothing designers and couturiers, including Perry ELLIS, Calvin KLEIN, Jean MUIR, Zandra RHODES, Yves SAINT LAURENT, Rifat OZBEK and Isaac MIZRAHI. He has also created simple plastic JELLIES for FIORUCCI. The styles sold through his London and New York stores are highly sophisticated. Blahnik is noted for his use of coloured leather, often decorated with graceful, fluid designs. Most of his shoes have a signature tapered vamp. He is an influential designer with a loyal international clientele who appreciate his ebullient but refined creations.

Blass, Bill 1922–. Designer. Born William Ralph Blass in Fort Wayne, Indiana, USA. Blass studied fashion design at Parsons School of Design in New York in 1939. From 1940 to 1941 he worked as a sketcher for David Crystal, a SPORTSWEAR manufacturer, before being drafted into the army. After World War II, he moved to Anna Miller & Co., as a designer. When Miller merged with manufacturers Maurice RENTNER Ltd in 1950, Blass stayed on and, in 1962, became vice president. In 1970 he

bought the company, renaming it Bill Blass. Blass is best known as a designer of American daywear. He takes traditional garments, such as the HACKING JACKET, and by softening the lines creates a more fluid, less severe, design. His suits are tailored but consciously curved to imitate the female body. Even his most structured garments are softened by gentle bends at the hem, lapels or fastenings. Blass is inventive in his mixing of texture and pattern. He uses tweeds and shirtings, and often designs his garments with a discreet splash of colour, such as a bright frill of lace or a fur trim. His use of ruffles has been particularly effective. His simple summer dress of 1963, which had a small ruff at the neck and hem, was a bestseller. In 1966 Blass showed a PEA JACKET made of white mink. Two years later the model Jean Shrimpton appeared in an advertisement wearing a beige, chantilly lace dress of Bill Blass design, with ruffled collar and cuffs. Public demand for this garment was so great that Maurice Rentner Ltd immediately put the design into mass production. Blass is also an established eveningwear designer, creating dresses which, like his daywear, trace sinuous lines but tend toward exaggeration. He has been highly successful in mixing tailored jackets and FLOUNCES for eveningwear.

Bill **Blass** from the 1960s to the 1980s: *Above:* a summer evening gown in green organza trimmed with ribbon and white lace, 1968; *top:* a lace-trimmed mini-dress of 1968; *top left:* a mixture of tailoring and ruffles for 1982.

Mrs Amelia **Bloomer**, *c.* 1850, wearing the outfit that she advocated for all sensible women.

Late 19th-century **bloomers** in action: the complete cycling outfit, with jacket, ruffled blouse, bloomers, boater and flat shoes.

blazer Loose-fitting, lightweight sports jacket worn by men since the turn of the 20th century. Blazers were originally made of flannel with either bold regimental stripes of solid colour or thin stripes. During the 1920s, the style was appropriated by women and worn with pleated skirts, shirts and TIES. The navy-blue naval-style blazer with gilt buttons has also been interpreted as a fashion garment. The classic length for a blazer is to the top of the thigh. Blazers were popular with women during the 1970s, when they became an important ingredient of female EXECUTIVE dress, teamed with a tailored skirt and a blouse or a man's shirt. *See* CHANEL *and* KLEIN, CALVIN.

Bloomer, Amelia Jenks 1818–94. In the mid-1850s Dexter Bloomer, proprietor and editor of a New York weekly journal, *The Seneca County Courier*, published an article suggesting that the short skirts and ankle-length trousers worn by Turkish women were far more practical than the voluminous long-skirts and petticoats of their European and American counterparts. Mr Bloomer's wife, Amelia, took up the theme and printed an article in her own feminist paper, *The Lily*, calling for functional clothing for women. Several women thereupon abandoned the KNICKERBOCKERS and NORFOLK JACKET worn at the time for sporting activities and dressed instead in an outfit consisting of a fitted BODICE; a full, knee-length skirt; and TURKISH TROUSERS, or BLOOMERS, which reached to the ankle, where they were frilled and gathered. In England this outfit was known as a Camilla costume. It was not adopted by significant numbers of women until the 1880s and 1890s, when cycling became popular. The wearing of bloomers was initially the object of public outrage, amusement and ridicule.

bloomers Since the late 19th century, the word bloomers describes any loose, full, trouser-like garment which is gathered at some point between the knee and ankle and worn under long skirts. *See* BLOOMER.

blouse Loose, long- or short-sleeved upper garment for women, usually made of cotton, linen, lawn or silk, and traditionally worn tucked into a skirt. The introduction of trousers in the early 20th century created the need for a more tailored blouse, and designers produced fitted versions along the lines of a man's shirt.

blouson *1.* Hip-length outer jacket with a drawstring through the bottom hem which, when pulled, creates soft GATHERS around the hips. The garment's shape originated in the ANORAK worn by Inuits and in the waterproof and windproof clothing of Arctic explorers. In the second half of the 20th century, the blouson shape came to be generally associated with casual attire for both sexes. *2.* BLOUSE of lightweight fabric, which is gathered to fall in soft folds on a band about the hips.

Blumenfeld, Erwin 1897–1969. Photographer. Born in Berlin, Germany. In 1913 Blumenfeld started a three-year apprenticeship with a womenswear manufacturer. After World War I, he moved to Holland where he worked for seventeen years as a bookseller, art dealer and leather goods merchant, while teaching himself photography. In 1936 he set himself up in Paris as a professional photographer. Two years later he received commissions from *VOGUE*, shortly followed by a contract with *HARPER'S BAZAAR*. He spent several of the World War II years interned in a French prisoner-of-war camp and after the war went to New York, where he took US nationality. He continued to work freelance for French and American *Vogue, Harper's Bazaar* and numerous other magazines. Blumenfeld's early work was distinguished by surreal images. He experimented with solarization, double-exposure and optical distortion. His use of damp cloth to drape and swathe the female form was widely copied by younger photographers. During the 1940s and 1950s, Blumenfeld successfully adapted his technique to colour photography and produced many bold, striking, often slightly erotic, pictures.

boa Long, fluffy, tubular scarf made of FEATHERS or fur. During the late 19th and early 20th centuries, feather boas, particularly those made from ostrich feathers, were very popular. Boas enjoyed further vogues during the 1930s and 1960s.

boat neck *See* BATEAU NECKLINE.

boater Circular straw hat with a flat top and straight brim. The crown is trimmed with a band or ribbon. Boaters are so named because,

teamed with striped BLAZERS and flannel trousers, they made up the male uniform for the summer sport of boating from the late 19th century until *c*.1940. They were popular with women during the 1920s.

boating shoes Shoe developed in the early 20th century with a traction rubber sole for gripping the deck of a boat. The original boating shoes were made with brown leather uppers but these were later replaced by canvas. Variations have subsequently been worn as casual attire.

bobby socks Short, usually white, socks, reaching above the ankle, worn since the mid-1940s by US teenagers. They were particularly popular in the 1950s, and were often teamed either with flat or high-heeled shoes, CIRCULAR SKIRTS over layers of petticoats, and tight sweaters, or with flat BROGUES and long KILTS. *See also* ANKLE SOCKS.

bodice *1.* Portion of a dress or coat between the shoulders and waist. In the 15th century the bodice was a close-fitting garment made of two layers of linen which were sewn or pasted together for greater stiffness. In the 16th century WHALEBONE was used to create a severe, rigid, front panel. By the 19th century, the bodice was tight-fitting and boned. Bodices have varied in length depending on the position of the waistline at any particular period. *2.* In the 20th century, the bodice is a dressmaker's term for the top front and back section of a garment which is joined at a high waistline to a skirt section. *See* BUST BODICE *and* CORSET.

During the 1860s the **bodice** was a fitted top section of a dress, treated as a fashion item in itself. It was only during the 20th century that the word began to refer to the top section of a garment, shown here with darts.

Youthful 1980s designs in black and white from the London firm of **Body Map**.

Body Map Company formed in 1982 by David Holah and Stevie Stewart (both born in London, England, in 1958), after the two designers studied together at Middlesex Polytechnic between 1979 and 1982. Body Map specialized in unstructured, layered clothing for a young market. The two designers frequently worked with black, cream and white, redefining traditional body shapes by layering different textures and prints.

bodystocking/bodysuit The bodystocking has its origins in the LEOTARD and the early-19th-century MAILLOT. It was introduced in the 1960s to wear under the semi-transparent dresses then in vogue. It is a fine, knitted garment, usually flesh coloured, with a low neck, no back, and narrow shoulder straps. For complete body cover, it can be teamed with matching tights or made in one piece. It is designed without buttons or bows in order to follow smoothly the line of the body. In 1985

The classic lacy **bodystocking** of the 1960s.

American designer Donna KARAN launched a line of black bodysuits which she showed worn with jeans, fitted and WRAPAROUND skirts, and under suits. Made of Lycra or other stretch fabric, or of fine wool and cashmere, the bodysuit snapped together under the legs, and had either long or short sleeves.

Bohan, Marc 1926–. Designer. Born Roger Maurice Louis Bohan in Paris, France. Bohan's mother was a milliner. Bohan obtained a certificate in art and philosophy from the Lycée Lakanal in Paris. He gained his early design experience between the years 1945 and 1958 working for three houses in succession: PIGUET, MOLYNEUX and PATOU. During these years he was also briefly employed by Madeleine DE RAUCH and worked as a freelance designer for a New York wholesale clothing company. In 1958 the house of DIOR sent Bohan to London as director of its English operation. He was recalled two years later to take on the position of chief designer and artistic director of Dior, succeeding SAINT LAURENT. During his first decade at Dior, Bohan gained a reputation as a designer who could turn pop fashion into haute couture without sacrificing the youthful spirit of the clothes. In 1961 he presented a narrow silhouette with long, slim BODICES and narrow skirts. His most widely influential collection, in 1966, featured garments based on the film *Doctor Zhivago* (1965): full, fur-trimmed, belted coats, swirling calf-length dresses, and boots. Bohan designed famously elegant ball gowns and evening dresses in exotic fabrics. Many styles had bows, like BUSTLES, attached to the back. In 1989 Bohan left the house of Dior and the following year became fashion director of Norman HARTNELL in London, where his sophisticated styles invigorated the couture house. He resigned in 1992.

boilersuit Once worn by manual labourers, the boilersuit became compulsory wear for women in munitions factories during World War II. Made of heavy cotton or denim, it is an all-in-one garment with long sleeves; a long BODICE section that is zipped or buttoned from the navel to the collar; trousers and pockets. *See also* SIREN SUIT.

Women putting on make-up at a Royal Ordinance Factory in the UK during World War II, before going back to the business of shell production. For added protection while working, they have been provided with **boilersuits** of fire-resistant serge and fireproof turbans.

bolero Open, sleeveless or sleeved, BODICE-like jacket, reaching almost to the waist; of Spanish origin. In the early 20th century boleros were worn with high-necked frilly blouses and sweeping skirts. During the 1960s and 1970s they were revived and worn with either skirts or trousers. Boleros in black velvet were popular for eveningwear. For daywear, boleros have been made of many fabrics, including various cottons, brocade, felt, denim and leather. Some versions are trimmed with braid.

bombazine Fine, plain or twilled weave fabric of silk warp and worsted weft, usually black. First produced in ancient China and later in Europe, bombazine was a popular fabric for MOURNING DRESS from the 16th until the late 19th century.

bomber jacket Waist-length woollen garment adapted from the jackets worn by fighter pilots in the British Royal Air Force during World War II. It is generously cut with wide but fitted sleeves which are gathered or elasticated at the waist. A zip fastens the jacket at the front from the waist to the neck, where the collar can be turned up. Since World War II bomber jackets have been worn as casual attire by both sexes and can be made of almost any fabric. *See also* BATTLE JACKET *and* EISENHOWER JACKET.

bonnet Headgear with or without a front brim, which covered the top, sides and back of the head and tied under the chin. In the 19th century bonnets were usually made of straw and trimmed with crepe, lace, satin, silk or velvet. Some styles exposed the face while others concealed it. At least one variation formed an oval frame around the face with the curved brim pulled down over the ears. Ties, usually ribbon, were attached to the brim or sewn to the insides of the bonnet. By the early 20th century bonnets were rarely worn as fashion items.

boots In the 19th century women wore boots with daywear in both summer and winter. They were usually low-heeled, made of leather or finer materials, and laced or buttoned to reach the lower calf. In the first half of the 20th century they became mainly utilitarian items – worn mostly in bad weather. Fashion boots, designed purely for effect, first appeared in the 1960s. They were shown in all lengths, from the ankle to high on the thigh. Materials ranged from plastic and vinyl to leather. In the 1970s fashion boots constructed to encase the foot and leg to the knee became popular winter wear in a range of colours. In the same decade other styles also became popular, such as small, cuffed ankle boots or leather COWBOY boots with elaborate tooling. The heavy utilitarian workmen's boots known as Dr Martens (DOC MARTENS) were worn by skinheads during the 1960s and

Despite the immensely elaborate hairstyles of the 19th century, **bonnets** were essential dress accessories. Round or oval, they generally concealed the profile. They were decorated with ribbons and lace.

The walking **boot** of the late 19th century, a version of which became the popular 'granny boot' of the 1960s.

in the 1980s they reappeared on the fashion scene in a more refined form. They have subsequently become part of casual wear. *See* COUR-REGES BOOT, GERNREICH *and* PUNK.

botany Fine wool originally obtained from the MERINO sheep of Botany Bay, New South Wales. In the 19th century botany wool was made up into outer garments but during the 20th century its use was mainly limited to sweaters.

Bouché, René 1906–63. Artist, illustrator. Born in France. A successful painter and portraitist, Bouché contributed to *VOGUE* throughout the 1940s as a fashion illustrator and observer of fashionable society. He worked in pen and ink or crayon, skilfully blending the character of the dress with that of the wearer. His drawings of women were elegant, vibrant and often amusing, though he was able to vary his style to produce a less defined, more abstract, form.

bouclé From the French *boucler*, 'to curl'. Bouclé fabric is woven or knitted from looped yarn which gives it a highly napped surface.

Jackets and sweaters made from bouclé fabric have been popular since the 1950s. It is also the name of a knitting yarn.

boudoir cap Nineteenth-century cap, worn to protect the coiffure when dressing, which was made redundant by the 20th century's short hairstyles. Made of muslin or cambric, it was threaded with ribbons that could be pulled and tied to encircle the head and keep the cap in place. The boudoir cap was sometimes shirred and often had a lace border.

Bouët-Willaumez, René 1900–79. Illustrator. Born in Brittany, France. Bouët-Willaumez was a frequent contributor to *VOGUE* during the 1930s and 1940s. His work was soft and fluid, usually pen and ink drawings of fashions and fashionable women.

Bourdin, Guy 1928–1991. Photographer. Born in Paris, France. After his demobilization, Bourdin spent time with Man RAY. During the 1960s he established himself as an artist and photographer. In the 1970s he frequently worked for French *VOGUE*. Bourdin's pictures are hard, distant and distinctly cold. Sex, violence and SURREALISM were integral parts of his work. He became famous in 1976 when he produced a provocative catalogue of lingerie, 'Sighs and Whispers', for Bloomingdale's. His surreal photographs for Charles JOURDAN shoes were equally well known.

Boutet de Monvel, Bernard 1884–1949. Painter, illustrator. Born in Paris, France. Fellow Zouave officer of Jean PATOU, Boutet de Monvel was a talented painter and illustrator. Lucien VOGEL commissioned him to work on the *GAZETTE DU BON TON* until the publication folded in 1925. After World War I, Boutet de Monvel contributed fashion illustrations to *FEM-INA*, *VOGUE* and *HARPER'S BAZAAR*. His economic, controlled style was in great demand and he was responsible for the design of many of Patou's advertisements.

boutique Boutiques started in the 1920s as small shops within couture houses. They sold the by-products of couture – a SPORTSWEAR line at PATOU, jewelry at CHANEL. During the 1930s other designers followed suit: Lucien

Boutiques proliferated in the 1960s, especially in 'Swinging London'. Biba was so popular and successful that it expanded into a department store, shown here decorated in nostalgic 1930s style.

LELONG opened a boutique to sell his 'editions' (less expensive versions of model clothes requiring only one fitting or none at all). After World War II, boutiques opened worldwide, showing a selection of merchandise from various designers or an exclusive designer label. During the 1960s, boutiques specializing in young, inexpensive fashions or second-hand clothes proliferated, the most famous being in London's CARNABY STREET, KING'S ROAD and Kensington. Two of the most popular were Lee Bender's Bus Stop, and Biba, Barbara HULANICKI's famous store. *See also* SCHIAPARELLI.

bow tie Man's necktie in the shape of a stiff bow, often made of grosgrain ribbon or velvet

Carnaby Street, in London's West End, was home to the city's most famous 1960s **boutiques**, including the small menswear shop I Was Lord Kitchener's Valet, which sold clothing with Union Jack designs and ex-military uniforms.

and usually part of formal dress. A popular accessory with women during the UNISEX vogue in the 1960s.

bowler (US: derby) Man's late-19th century hard hat with a round crown and a brim well curved at the sides. After World War I, bowler hats became acceptable formal wear in Britain, replacing top hats. Until the 1950s and 1960s they were associated with City of London businessmen. They are rarely seen today. Women wore bowlers during the UNISEX vogue of the 1960s, but they have never been a major female fashion item.

box pleat Pleat made of two flat folds turned inward towards each other.

bra See BRASSIERE.

bra slip Bra section with narrow straps which is attached to a waist slip below the bust. A form

of bra slip was first seen in the 1930s but it was not until the 1960s, when changes taking place in fashion created a need for lingerie to be more functional and less obtrusive, that the garment became popular.

braces (US: suspenders) Designed to hold up men's breeches in the 18th century, braces were originally made of cord or webbing. By the late 19th century, canvas, cotton, rubber and velvet were all used in the making of braces. Around 1900 braces became two bands joined at the back and attached to trousers by buttons and, later, by metal clips. In the 20th century they were usually made of elastic. Women appropriated braces during the 1960s and 1970s as part of the UNISEX trend.

braid Narrow band of fabric created by weaving or braiding threads together in a decorative manner. Commonly used on uniforms, braid became fashionable in the 1930s, when CHANEL used it to trim the edges of suits.

Braque, Georges 1882–1963. Artist. Born in Argenteuil, France. Braque was part of the Fauvist movement until he met PICASSO in 1907, when the two painters developed the art form that came to be known as CUBISM. Braque's work influenced textile designers of the 1920s and 1930s. See FAUVISM.

brassiere Brassieres date from the early 1900s. A design for a brassiere made from two handkerchiefs and narrow ribbon was patented in the USA in 1914 by Mary Phelps Jacob (Caresse Crosby). Until the mid-1920s, brassieres were boneless and were designed to flatten the bust and push it downwards. They were widely adopted during the 1920s when fashionable at-home dresses and, later, COCKTAIL DRESSES were often made of revealing, semi-transparent fabrics. By 1925, brassieres had adjustable front straps and a division between the breasts in the BANDEAU front. During the late 1920s the Kestos Company of America produced a brassiere made of two triangular pieces of fabric secured to elastic that was pulled over the shoulders, crossed at the back, and buttoned at the front under a darted 'cup'. During the late 1920s and 1930s corsetry companies began manufacturing brassieres which were boned

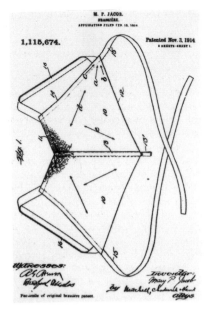

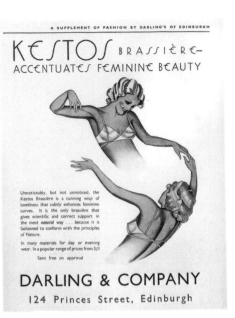

The first **bra**: the original patent granted to Mary Phelps Jacob (Caresse Crosby) in 1914.

The Kestos **bra**, from a 1935 advertisement, described as a 'cunning wisp of loveliness'.

and stitched into different cup sizes. A boned strapless brassiere appeared in the late 1930s and it was during this decade that the word 'bra' came into popular usage. In the 1940s the use of foam pads gave additional shape to many bras. Their outline was most exaggerated during the 1950s, when bras were both wired and stitched in circular patterns to further stiffen the fabric. The strapless bra was popular during the 1950s, when it was worn under off-the-shoulder, strapless dresses. The same decade saw manufacturers beginning to produce bras for teenagers. With the 1960s came greater flexibility of design and further liberation and comfort for women through the introduction of fabrics containing Lycra. Since the 1970s, mouldings of thermoplastic fibres at high temperatures have produced one-piece seamless bras. In 1964 a Canadian company, later purchased by Sara Lee Intimates, designed a 'Wonderbra', a padded, underwired, push-up bra that made a more pronounced breast shape. This style gained wide popularity from 1994, in the wake of adverse publicity for artificial breast implants. *See* BERLEI, GERNREICH *and* WARNER BROS CO.

breton hat Originally worn by French peasants, the breton hat has a brim that rolls up all the way round. It has been popular since the end of the 19th century.

Brigance, Tom 1913–90. Designer. Born in Waco, Texas, USA. Brigance studied at Parsons School of Design in New York and later at the Sorbonne in Paris. He worked as a designer for the New York department store Lord & Taylor before joining the US Army. After his demobilization in 1944 he resumed design work and established his own business in 1949. He was known as a specialist beachwear designer.

British warm Overcoat worn by British officers during World War I which later became popular for civilian use. The British warm was made of a heavy cloth – camel, cashmere, melton or wool – and slightly shaped to fit the body. It was knee-length or longer, single- or double-breasted, with large pockets, deep REVERS and leather buttons. It has inspired many subsequent designs for men's and women's wear.

broadcloth Generic term for a variety of cloth. Originally, broadcloth was a woollen shirting fabric cut wider than any other cloth. The term also refers to a closely woven wool suiting cloth with a smooth nap and lustrous appearance, or a tightly woven cotton cloth with a fine crosswise rib.

brocade Rich, jacquard-weave fabric which has a raised design, usually flowers or figures, woven into it, often in silk, gold or silver threads. Brocade has been associated with eveningwear since the mid-19th century.

broderie anglaise Also known as Swiss or Madeira embroidery, broderie anglaise is a form of embroidery initially created with a needle and thread. It is characterized by a white thread on a white background (usually cotton) into which a pattern of round or oval holes is pierced. The edges of the holes are then overcast with stitches. Known in Europe since the 16th century, broderie anglaise was particularly popular from 1840 to 1880, when it was made up into nightwear and underwear, most often for children. From the 1870s a Swiss machine successfully copied the styles. Since the beginning of the 20th century, broderie anglaise has been used for dress trimmings and summer attire and is still in use for underwear.

Brodovitch, Alexey 1898–1971. Photographer, art director, teacher. Born in St Petersburg, Russia. Brodovitch went to Paris as a refugee around 1918. In the early 1920s he painted scenery for the BALLETS RUSSES, as well as designing fabrics, posters, books and magazines. Emigrating to the USA in 1930, he became director of the Philadelphia Museum School of Industrial Art. In 1934 he was appointed art director of *HARPER'S BAZAAR* and for twenty-four years his ideas dominated the visual side of the magazine. He encouraged young photographers and used the magazine as a platform for new ideas in fashion photography and graphic design. He resigned from *Harper's Bazaar* in 1958 but continued teaching and lecturing until 1967, when he retired to France.

brogue Stout shoe that originated in Scotland and Ireland as a single piece of untanned leather held together by a tie lace. The modern brogue is a laced, flat-heeled, stitched leather shoe decorated with a perforated design. The word brogue also describes an OXFORD shoe that has been punched and stitched in the same manner.

Brooks, Donald 1928–. Costume and fashion designer. Born in New York, USA. Brooks was educated in New Haven, Connecticut; the Fine Arts School of Syracuse University, New York; and Parsons School of Design, which he left to work for the first of many ready-to-wear companies. In 1958 he began designing under his own label and in the mid-1960s was one of the first designers to include luxurious evening pants and voluminous PYJAMAS in his collections. In 1959 he began working as a costume designer. His plays include *Barefoot in the Park* (1962), and his films *The Cardinal* (1963) and *Star!* (1968). He is recognized for his promotion of the CHEMISE and his creation of simple, unadorned dresses, trimmed coats and STOLES.

Brooks Brothers Established in New York in 1818 as Brooks Clothing Company, Brooks Brothers was a pioneer of ready-to-wear clothes for men. In 1896 a Brooks Brothers representative was impressed by the button-down shirt collars worn by polo players in England, and four years later the store introduced the button-down shirt to the USA. It was one of

The classic **Brooks Brothers** button-down shirt, still one of the most popular and fashionable styles in the USA today.

Bikini for Spring/Summer 1996 from the American-born designer Liza **Bruce**.

several Brooks Brothers specialities, many of which originated in England. Others include the foulard TIE, madras fabric for shirts (originally designed for British officers in India), Harris tweed (from Scotland), Shetland sweaters and the POLO COAT, which was originally white with pearl buttons and a full belt but was later made in camel and grey with various belt styles. These fashions were introduced between the 1890s and the outbreak of World War I. In 1949, Brooks Brothers began selling pink cotton button-down shirts for women. Cashmere polo shirts, introduced in the 1950s, were also appropriated by women.

Bruce, Liza 1955–. Designer. Born in New York, USA. Bruce started her own company in New York in 1981 after attracting attention with the sophisticated swimwear she designed for herself and her friends. Although by 1988 she had expanded her collection to include daywear, her subsequent work reflects her earliest

pieces, with streamlined silhouettes and an extensive use of Lycra, mixed with crepe, mohair and silk. Known for minimalist designs, she specializes in body-hugging garments. She created stretch lustre crepe LEGGINGS which eventually became a wardrobe staple.

Brunelleschi, Umberto 1879–1949. Illustrator and costume designer. Born in Montemurio, near Pistoia, Italy. After completing his studies in Florence, Brunelleschi moved to Paris where he worked as a caricaturist and illustrator, often under the name Harun-al-Rashid. By 1912 he was illustrating books, designing posters and working for the JOURNAL DES DAMES ET DES MODES and FEMINA. He also designed costumes, creating many outfits for Josephine BAKER's revues. In his early years his work was recognizable by its clearly executed, delicate lines and fanciful flourishes.

Brussels lace Needlepoint lace, famous since the 17th century, which was most popular in the 19th century. Made in several Belgian towns, Brussels lace characteristically incorporates ornate designs of leaves and flowers.

bubble cut Short, curly hairstyle, resembling bubbles, usually achieved by permanent waving. Popular from the late 1950s until the 1970s.

bubble dress In 1957, French designer Pierre CARDIN introduced short-skirted, bubble-shaped dresses and skirts, produced by BIAS cutting over a stiffened base.

Burberry See BURBERRY, THOMAS.

Burberry, Thomas 1835–1926. Shopowner. Born in Dorking, Surrey, England. Burberry trained as an apprentice to a draper. In 1856 he opened his own drapery business, T. Burberry & Sons, in Basingstoke, Hampshire. In collaboration with the owner of a cotton mill, he produced a waterproof coat based on the close weave and loose style of an agricultural SMOCK. The cotton cloth, called GABARDINE, was proofed in the yarn before weaving, then closely woven and proofed again. In 1891 Burberry established a wholesale business in London. He specialized in making gabardine clothes for active leisure pursuits and for the sports field. Most popular was the smock-like 'Walking Burberry', cut on straight, easy-fitting lines with a fly-front fastening and RAGLAN sleeves. In 1902 Burberry established 'Gabardine' as a trademark and in 1909 'The Burberry' was registered as a trademark for the company's coats. During World War I Burberry designed coats for the British Royal Flying Corps (later the RAF). The military style model of the Burberry became the TRENCHCOAT of that war. It has a deep back YOKE, EPAULETS, buckled cuff straps, a button-down storm flap on one shoulder, and storm pockets. Metal D rings on belts were intended for the attachment of military accoutrements. After the war, the trenchcoat was absorbed into civilian life. Known as a 'Burberry', it has been copied worldwide.

burnous Full, hooded CLOAK of Arab origin, often embroidered and trimmed with tassels. The burnous shape formed the basis of the 19th-century MANTLE.

Burrows, Stephen 1943–. Designer. Born in Newark, New Jersey, USA. After studying at the Philadelphia Museum College of Art and the Fashion Institute of Technology in New York, Burrows went to work for the New York department store Henri Bendel. With partner Roz Rubenstein, he left in 1973 to open a design house. At the beginning of his career, Burrows was noted for his adventurous approach to clothing design and construction. He created garments in leather, notably a nail-studded black jacket and PATCHWORK trousers. His hallmark was the highly visible use of machine-made stitching, often zigzags, which he used on the hemlines of skirts, creating a fluted, crinkled effect that was often described as a lettuce-edge. He top-stitched in contrast colours and inlaid patches of colour. Burrows is also known for comfortable, supple leisure clothing and for bright, body-conscious garments for the DISCO scene.

busk Strip of WHALEBONE or shell which was inserted into a CORSET or STAYS during the late 19th century to create the S-BEND SILHOUETTE of the period. Shaped like a long paper knife, thicker at the top than at the bottom, the busk was held in place by laces. It extended from the bust to the waist or hips.

bust bodice Undergarment popular until the 1920s. Based on the CAMISOLE, it was heavily boned, padded and taped to give a full, bow-fronted, rounded appearance to the bust. It either fitted around the bust or was slightly longer, reaching to the waist. The bust bodice was replaced by the BRASSIERE.

buster brown collar Broad, round, starched collar first worn by small boys in the early 20th century. It was named after 'Buster Brown' – hero of a US comic strip popular from c.1909 – who wore a tweed suit of knee-length trousers and double-breasted belted jacket, with a round-collared shirt. This style of collar has been adapted to womenswear.

bustier Item of underwear known in various forms from the early 19th century. It is a deep, waisted garment based on a BRASSIERE and CAMISOLE which embraces the ribs and hip

Vivienne Westwood **bustier**-type corset, Spring/Summer, 1991. Many designers promoted the underwear as outerwear look in the 1980s and early 1990s.

bones. The shoulder straps are set far apart to enable the bustier to be worn with a BATEAU NECKLINE. It was popular in the 1950s and emerged in the 1980s in exotic fabrics as outerwear for evening. International singer and film star MADONNA promoted the bustier in a contemporary, exaggerated form – with conically stitched cups – designed by Jean-Paul GAULTIER. Such bras and bustiers, reminiscent of the high, pointed shape of the 1950s, became, in less exaggerated form, a popular component of eveningwear.

bustle Pad of cork, down or other type of stuffing worn under a skirt, which is attached to the back below waist level and which serves as a base over which the skirt's material is pleated or looped. The bustle was the prevailing skirt shape during the 1860s and 1870s. A wood, steel or WHALEBONE basket which tied at the waist and curved down to the hips was also worn under skirts. Some bustles were made of spring metal bands. *See also* CRINOLINE *and* WORTH.

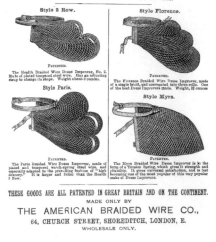

HEALTH BRAIDED WIRE
DRESS IMPROVERS.

The eminent Physician, Dr H. E. LONGSHORE, says: "If ladies will wear DRESS IMPROVERS, I advise them to confine themselves to those made by the American Braided Wire Company, as they are less heating to the spine than any others."

SOLD BY DRAPERS AND LADIES' OUTFITTERS.

Style 2 Row.   Style Florence.

PATENTED.
The Health Braided Wire Dress Improver, No. 2. Made of plated tempered steel wire. Has an adjusting strap to change its shape. Weight about 2 ounces.

PATENTED.
The Florence Braided Wire Dress Improver, made of a single braid, and corrugated into three rolls. One of the best Dress Improvers made. Weight, 2¼ ounces.

Style Paris.   Style Myra.

PATENTED.
The Paris Braided Wire Dress Improver, made of plated and tempered watch-spring steel wire, and especially adapted to the prevailing fashion of "high" drapery. It is larger and fuller than the Health 2 Row.

PATENTED.
The Myra Braided Wire Dress Improver is the form of a Torsion Spring, which gives it strength and pliability. It gives universal satisfaction, and is fast becoming one of the most popular of this very popular Dress Improvers.

THESE GOODS ARE ALL PATENTED IN GREAT BRITAIN AND ON THE CONTINENT.
MADE ONLY BY
THE AMERICAN BRAIDED WIRE CO.,
64, CHURCH STREET, SHOREDITCH, LONDON, E.
WHOLESALE ONLY.

Known as dress improvers, late-19th-century **bustles** were designed in many different shapes.

Busvine House founded in London in 1863 by a Mr Busvine, who had trained under Henry CREED the Younger. Busvine supplied riding outfits and other tailored garments to members of the British royal family. By the turn of the century, Busvine had become a household name among the aristocracy. Branches were established in Paris and Berlin. In the 1920s Richard Busvine, grandson of the founder, opened a branch in New York. He became chief designer of the London branch in the 1930s. In 1939 Busvine merged with REDFERN.

butcher's boy cap Large cap with a broad brim, based on a 19th-century tradesman's cap. It was popular during the 1960s, made of tartan, velvet, vinyl and other fabrics.

Butterick, Ebenezer New England tailor who, in 1863, made paper patterns of a gingham dress designed by his wife. He graded the patterns so that dresses of different sizes could be made. Shortly after, Butterick began making shirt patterns and by the 1880s he had several thousand agencies in the USA and Canada selling his patterns. First established in New York, he set up in London's Regent Street in 1873 and published his patterns for men's, women's and children's fashions in reviews and magazines. He also founded a publishing empire of more than thirty magazines.

buttons Buttons have been used as decorative items of dress since the 14th century, though their prominence is entirely dependent on fashion trends. By the early 19th century, machine-made fabric buttons and buttons made of ceramics, glass and papier-mâché were in existence but they were not strongly featured in fashions of the period. From the mid-19th century, shell, mother-of-pearl, black glass, stamped steel and brass, and moulded horn were often used for buttons, which by this time had become integral parts of fashion design. Dresses and blouses were made with many tiny buttons. In the 1880s there was a revival in the use of enamel (previously popular in the 18th century), and buttons were also made of glass or porcelain, or covered with embroidery. These trends continued until World War I, when there was a marked decline in the number of buttons used. The Art Deco movement of the

Elsa Schiaparelli's famous pink silk jacket from her 'Circus' collection of 1938 is decorated with metallic **buttons** in the shape of acrobats. Schiaparelli often used unusual buttons in her designs.

1920s brought buttons once more into fashion's focus and this interest continued throughout the 1930s and stimulated the production of buttons made from wood, cork, plexiglass and synthetic plastics. Novelty buttons enjoyed a vogue in this decade. Used as strategic parts of clothing designs, they often resembled baskets of fruit or cigarette packets. MAINBOCHER presented silver clasp buttons, ROCHAS showed buttons in the shape of open books, and PATOU adorned his outfits with flower pots, foxes, mermaids and snake buttons. SCHIAPARELLI also used unusual buttons in her designs, notably the acrobat buttons of her 'Circus' jacket. After World War II, buttons became less decorative and more functional.

Byblos Fashion house, founded in 1973 in Italy. Early designers included Gianni VERSACE and Guy PAULIN. In 1981, the British team of Alan Cleaver and Keith Varty took over as principal designers. Between 1981 and 1996 they consistently produced collections of young, sophisticated clothes, often thematic, based on their travels in North Africa and Southeast Asia. In 1996, Richard TYLER was appointed design director.

C

cable knit Raised decorative pattern resembling twisted cables, used in knitted sweaters.

Cacharel, Jean 1932–. Designer. Born in Nîmes, France. Cacharel began his design career as an apprentice tailor. In 1956 he moved to Paris and two years later opened a small atelier where he made men's shirts. This

Ocelot coat with sleeves of blue fox by the British fur company **Calman Links**, c. 1935.

sleeves, which was usually bound with a SASH and made from silk or cotton. In the 1950s DIOR showed versions of the caftan, without the sash, worn over floor-length evening dresses. During the 1960s HALSTON and SAINT LAURENT were just two designers who utilized this basic shape. In the 1970s caftans became popular as eveningwear and, generously cut, as at-home gowns. Some versions were zipped from neck to ankle. Most were worn without sash. The caftan shape is also used for night gowns. Caftans can be made from almost any fabric. Synthetic materials which trace the body's lines are frequently chosen, as are satin and heavily embroidered fabrics.

calico Ancient fabric first made in Calicut in southwest Madras, India. Calico is a durable coarse cotton cloth which is usually dyed. Often used as household cloth, it has been made up into casual summer attire since the 1940s.

Callot Soeurs Couture house founded in Paris in 1895 by the four daughters of a Parisian antique dealer, who specialized in the sale of lace. The sisters began by selling ribbons and lingerie. They then used old velvet and lace to construct elaborate day dresses which were often adorned with tiers of beads and more lace. For eveningwear Callot Soeurs designed heavy satin gowns and were among the first designers to promote lamé dresses. Their designs were popular with actresses and international hostesses. Callot Soeurs closed in 1937.

Calman Links Company founded in London in 1893 by Hungarian-born Calman Links (1868–1925). The company specialized in producing high quality *FUR garments. Father was succeeded by son, Joseph G. Links (b. 1904), who in the 1930s developed production methods aimed at reducing the cost of high grade furs without sacrificing style. The company's attempts to produce fur garments designed with young people in mind were halted by World War II. After the war, Calman Links worked with BALMAIN, DIOR, AMIES, CAVANAGH and LACHASSE. In 1955 the company was appointed Furriers to the Queen.

cambric Closely woven white cotton fabric first made in Cambrai, France, which is finished

venture was soon abandoned and Cacharel started a company designing for women. In the early 1960s he introduced a highly successful *chemisier crêpon* based on a man's shirt and made up in a fabric usually associated with nightwear. During the 1960s he became famous for his fitted blouses and shirts – often made in LIBERTY print/floral cottons – as well as for his CULOTTE skirts and gabardine MINI SKIRTS with three pleats at each side. His skirts were worn with short, tight, brightly coloured Shetland sweaters over delicately printed shirts, and blouses with embroidered collars. This style of dressing was widely copied. During the 1970s, Cacharel introduced to his ready-to-wear designs bolder, more colourful patterns, many of which were inspired by the prints and weaves of Africa and the Far East. Emanuelle KHANH worked with him from 1962 until 1967. Cacharel employed photographer Sarah MOON to create the company's romantic marketing image.

caftan Believed to have originated in Ancient Mesopotamia. Loosely cut, ankle-length garment, open at the front, with long, wide

with a slight gloss on one side. It was used in the 9th century for making simple blouses and SHIFTS.

camel hair Used in the 19th century to make outer garments for men and women, camel hair, also known as camel hair wool, is the short, soft undercoat of the camel. In its natural colour it was a popular fibre for coats. During the 19th century a cloth known as camel hair – a blend of cashmere and wool – became popular. It was dyed the same colour as natural camel hair. Camel hair coats, both real and imitation, continue to maintain their popularity. *See also* JAEGER *and* POLO COAT.

cameo Hard stone, usually agate, onyx or sardonyx, into which a design is cut in relief. Cameos were popular in Greece during the Hellenistic period. During the 1st century BC, cameo cutting was centred in Rome. Throughout the 18th and 19th centuries, copies of ancient cameos were the most fashionable form of jewelry, pinned to blouses and dresses or worn on a band around the neck.

camiknickers Item of underwear combining CAMISOLE and a pair of knickers that often buttoned between the legs. At the turn of the 20th century there were many varieties of camiknickers. Some fastened with buttons at the side or in the front; some voluminous versions did not have fastenings but were drawn about the waist by ribbons or elastic. The camisole top usually had thin straps, often made of ribbon, and was trimmed with lace or embroidery. The knicker length varied from the knee to the top of the thigh. Over the years, camiknickers have been adapted according to the prevailing styles in clothes. During the 1920s and 1930s slim-line garments required lightweight, unobtrusive underwear. At this time, camiknickers were called 'step-ins' – a reference to the method of putting them on. Originally made of cotton, lawn, satin or silk, camiknickers have since the 1970s been made mostly of easycare synthetic fabrics. They have become short and very brief and are less popular since the introduction of the more androgynous underwear of cotton briefs which follow the outline of the body and are better suited to active lifestyles.

Cameo brooch, dating from the 1850s.

camisole Item of underwear introduced during the early 19th century which is based on a loose, sleeveless BODICE or CHEMISE. It was originally worn between the CORSET and dress as a protective layer. It covers the body from the bust to the waist and has fine shoulder straps. In the early part of the 20th century, when many women discarded their corsets, the camisole was worn next to the skin. Early versions were made of cotton or lawn, with more elegant designs trimmed with lace. Satin and silk were popular fabrics for camisoles during the 1930s. The gradual introduction of synthetic, easycare fibres has increased the appeal of the camisole. *See* NAINSOOK.

camp shirt US term for a generously cut blouse with breast pockets and wide sleeves that reach almost to the elbow. The camp shirt buttons down the front and is made up in both inexpensive and luxurious fabrics.

canvas Strong, plain-woven cloth, used in both its heavy and light weights for footwear and sportswear. It featured strongly in post-World War II summer fashions. *See* CASHIN.

cap Brimless covering for the head, with a stiff peak over the forehead, originally worn by workmen. During the 1960s, large, brightly coloured versions, often made of leather or PVC, were popular. *See* BUTCHER'S BOY CAP.

cap sleeve Small, triangular sleeve which sits on the shoulders, either forming a stiff cap or falling onto the arms to provide minimal coverage. It has been used on dresses and blouses and is especially popular for summer wear.

cape Full outer garment, traditionally a shorter version of the CLOAK but without slits for the arms. Capes were fashionable during the late 19th century and from the 1950s to the mid-1970s, in varying lengths and fabrics. *See* BAL-MAIN *and* TRIGERE.

Capezio US company founded in 1887 to make ballet shoes. In 1944 Claire MCCARDELL persuaded Capezio to make PUMPS based on ballet shoes. These became widely popular.

capri pants During the 1950s fairly loose pants, tapered to the mid-calf, became fashionable for summer wear. They were named after the Italian island of Capri – a popular holiday resort at the time.

Capucci, Roberto 1929–. Designer. Born in Rome, Italy. Capucci studied at the Accademia delle Belle Arti in Rome. He worked for designer Emilio Schuberth before opening his

The classic **cardigan**, shown here in 1918.

In 1957 Roberto **Capucci** created this unusual evening dress with two large panniers attached to the bodice above the belted waist.

own house at the age of twenty-one. Acclaimed in Italy, Capucci went to Paris in 1962, only to return to Rome seven years later. He cuts and drapes fabric into extraordinary, extravagant and daring clothes that give the impression of being created for a woman whose own presence is rarely felt; she is there only to display Capucci's mastery of line and cut.

car coat Woollen outdoor garment which originated in the USA in the 1950s. Styled to be convenient for driving, it is a hip-length semi-fitted jacket, often double-breasted.

caracul *See* KARACUL.

cardigan Long-sleeved military jacket of knitted worsted, trimmed with fur or braid and buttoned down the front. It was worn by British Army officers during the Crimean War and named after the 7th Earl of Cardigan, James Thomas Brudenell (1797–1868), who led the Charge of the Light Brigade. In the 20th century the style, minus the collar, was adapted for daywear. The cardigan became a popular garment with home knitters, and knitwear manufacturers produced a variety of styles and designs based on a woollen (or wool mix) garment which buttons down the front and has long sleeves. CHANEL helped to popularize the cardigan during the 1920s and 1930s as part of a two-piece outfit of cardigan-jacket and skirt or a three-piece outfit of cardigan-jacket, sweater and skirt. During the 1950s there was a brief vogue for wearing cardigans back to front. *See* PRINGLE *and* TWINSET.

Cardin, Pierre 1922–. Designer. Born in San Biagio di Callalta, near Venice, to French parents. Cardin was brought up in St Etienne in the Loire region of France. He left home at seventeen to work for a tailor in Vichy, where he began making suits for women. In 1944, after the Liberation of France, Cardin went to Paris where, one year later, he found work with PAQUIN and SCHIAPARELLI. He met Christian BERARD and Jean COCTEAU and made the costumes for Cocteau's film *Beauty and the Beast* (1947). Cardin also worked for DIOR. In 1949 he began producing theatrical costumes. Over the following seven years Cardin gained a reputation as both a maker of men's suits and a designer of extravagant and fantastic costumes. During this period he took over a small shop for his own menswear and womenswear. In 1957 he produced his first women's collection, followed six years later by a ready-to-wear line. During the 1950s he designed coats with draped hemlines and loose back panels, BUBBLE skirts and unstructured CHEMISES. In the 1960s he introduced coloured wigs made by the Carita sisters. His CUT-OUT DRESSES; coats that flared from curved, stitched collars; and large, APPLIQUE pockets were widely influential. Cardin's 1964 *SPACE AGE collection comprised knitted CATSUITS, tight leather trousers, close-fitting HELMETS and BATWING JUMPSUITS. In the same decade he raised skirts to four inches above the knee and plunged necklines, back and front, to the navel. Cardin is associated with the use of supple, knitted fabrics made up into BODYSTOCKINGS, catsuits, tubular dresses, TABARD tops over LEGGINGS and tights. He has frequently used the BIAS CUT to produce spiral dresses and is fond of COWL draping. During the 1960s and 1970s Cardin's creations revealed a strong, forceful designer, in whose work the shape of the body sometimes took second place to the line of his clothes. His designs were unfussy and bold, often with

irregular outlines. Cardin is a conceptual designer, able to carry an idea through a complete collection. The clear, coherent aspects of his work have been copied and translated into styling details by numerous other designers and manufacturers.

Carnaby Street Street in the West End of London which became famous in the 1960s for its many BOUTIQUES selling fashionable, inexpensive clothes, such as T-SHIRTS, MINI SKIRTS, BELL BOTTOMS and HIPSTERS, as well as trendy accessories. The name is now synonymous with the youth cult of the 'swinging sixties'. *See also* KING'S ROAD *and* *BOUTIQUE.

Carnegie, Hattie 1889–1956. Designer, manufacturer. Born Henrietta Kanengeiser in Vienna, Austria. The family moved to the USA and changed their name to Carnegie. At fifteen, Carnegie began work in Macy's New York department store, dressing hats. In 1909 she opened a hat shop with a partner who made dresses. Carnegie bought out her partner four years later and took over the clothing design. Although she was unable to sew or draw, she had a talent for communicating her ideas to others, who carried them out. She launched her first collection in 1918, followed by a ready-to-wear collection ten years later. Between the two World Wars she imported many designs from French couturiers and much of her success lay in her ability to translate French fashion sense into American taste. She was widely influential among other designers and employed at various times Claire MCCARDELL, Pauline TRIGERE, James GALANOS, Gustave TASSELL and Travis BANTON. During the 1930s and 1940s Carnegie's name was synonymous with smart, conventional suits and dresses. Her tailored suits in grey worsted with straight skirts, tidy collars and jewelled buttons, and her neat black dresses became status symbols for American women. Inspired by haute couture, Carnegie avoided any theatricality or extravagance in her designs. She was famous for a shade of blue, 'Carnegie blue', and favoured black. At her salon in New York, a woman could purchase a complete outfit, including accessories such as COSTUME JEWELRY, hats, gloves and lingerie. She became a highly visible designer during World War II, when the unavailability of French clothing

Carrickmacross lace of the 19th century, worked in floral patterns.

thrust her own designs into the spotlight, along with the American textile companies she patronized. She died in 1956. The custom salon continued until 1965 and the wholesale business until the 1970s.

Carosa Italian firm founded in Rome in 1947 by Princess Giovanna Caracciolo. The house produced high quality fashions in good fabrics. It closed in 1974.

Carrickmacross lace Muslin lace with APPLIQUE motifs, originating in the town of Carrickmacross in County Monaghan, Ireland. This fine, gauzy lace was first made in 1820 and its popularity endured for one hundred years.

Cartier Company manufacturing jewels and bijouterie founded in Paris in 1847 by Louis-François Cartier (1819–1904). Alfred Cartier (1841–1925), son of the founder, moved the company to its luxurious premises on Paris's Rue de la Paix in 1898. In the same year, Alfred Cartier's son Louis-Joseph (1875–1942) entered the business. By the turn of the century, Cartier was a well-established jewelry company, suppliers to royal houses around the world. In 1902, Alfred Cartier's second son, Pierre (1878–1964), opened a branch in London. In 1909 a branch was opened in New York. Cartier is famous both for its jewelry and for its

development of the wristwatch, including in 1907 a design for the Brazilian aviator, Alberto Santos-Dumont, and in 1931 the production of a luxury waterproof watch.

cartwheel hat Hat with a very large, often straight but occasionally downward curving brim of even width. It has a shallow crown and

Cartier snake necklace – diamonds and emeralds in a setting of platinum and grey gold, 1968.

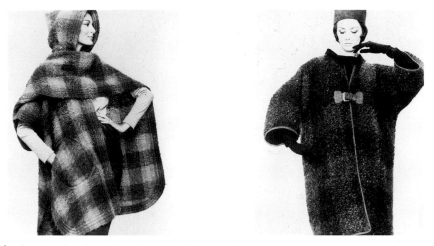

From the pioneering American designer Bonnie **Cashin,** two of her typically comfortable, loose-fitting designs: *above left:* Cashin's 1961 poncho in mohair and wool; *right:* her 1962 'Noh' classic coat in mohair edged with suede.

is usually made of straw. The cartwheel hat was popular before and after World War II until the late 1950s. See BEATON.

Carven House founded in 1945 in Paris by Carven de Tommaso (born *c.*1909), a dressmaker who specialized in designing for the petite woman and who adjusted the proportions of accessories accordingly. In 1956, the house introduced two sweater collections which became the first in a long line of licensed products marketed worldwide. Known for her ultra-feminine detailing on clothing, such as white on white and lace and embroidery trim, Carven produced delicately scaled clothing, along with her famous perfume, Ma Griffe. In 1993, Maguy Muzy took over as designer of the haute couture collection.

Casely-Hayford, Joe 1956–. Designer. Born in Kent, England. Casely-Hayford worked in London's Savile Row before beginning his formal training at the Tailor and Cutter Academy in 1974. The following year he enrolled at St Martin's School of Art, graduating in 1979 to attend a one-year History of Art course. Working in the music industry, Casely-Hayford became well-known as a designer of clothing for rock groups. Demand for his clothes off-stage resulted in freelance contracts

as well as commissions for costumes for both theatre and film. Casely-Hayford understands the impact of STREET STYLE and is able to interpret it into the mainstream of fashion in a sophisticated feminine style which combines masterly cut and high-tech fabrics.

Cashin, Bonnie 1915–. Designer. Born in Oakland, California, USA. Cashin was the daughter of a dressmaker. In the early 1930s she travelled with a ballet company to New York, where she attended the Art Students League and designed costumes for the Roxy Music Hall dance chorus. In 1937 she produced a collection for the SPORTSWEAR firm Adler & Adler, for whom she subsequently worked full time. In 1943 she moved to 20th Century-Fox in Hollywood and over the next six years created costumes for more than thirty major films. Returning to New York in 1949, Cashin opened her own business four years later. One of the great American designers of the 20th century, Cashin believed in clean, uncomplicated designs; her clothes were loose-fitting and functional, and were often worn with layers which could be discarded according to climate or temperature. Many of her designs are still relevant today. She was skilled at mixing fabrics and worked frequently with canvas, leather, poplin, suede and tweed. During the 1950s and

Jacqueline Kennedy, on President Kennedy's 1961 state visit to Paris, wearing one of her most famous outfits: the pillbox hat, the Chanel-like beads at the neck, the short, slightly tailored two-piece with three-quarter-length sleeves, and the long gloves.

Jacqueline Kennedy's outfit was widely copied throughout the USA. It was created for her by the American designer Oleg **Cassini**, whose sketch for it is shown above left. Also shown is the same designer's sketch for a dinner dress, again for Mrs Kennedy. Based on the empire line, its focus was the eye-catching decoration pinned to the front.

1960s – her most creative years – she produced, among numerous other garments, Chinese-style jackets over dresses, canvas and poplin raincoats, fringed suede dresses, wool TABARDS, KIMONO coats piped with leather, and long dinner jackets made of upholstery fabric. She is most often associated with the popularization of the PONCHO as a fashion garment; with long, fringed at-home skirts made from plaid mohair; and with her signature funnel-necked PULLOVER sweater featuring a neck doubling as a hood. Many contemporary designs can be traced to the intense practicality and purposeful, direct lines of Cashin's clothing. She retired in 1977.

cashmere Rare natural fibre combed from the fleece of the kashmir goat, which is found in Inner Mongolia, the People's Republic of China, Iran, Iraq, Turkey and Afghanistan. Known since the 14th century, cashmere has been used extensively in Europe since the 19th century, when it was often made up into children's dresses and blended with other fibres to make women's outer garments. In the 20th century, cashmere was used for coats, dresses, scarves and sweaters. It is expensive to produce,

and is often mixed with other fibres, such as wool. A garment made of cashmere alone is considered a luxury item. *See also* PRINGLE *and* TWINSET.

Cassini, Oleg 1913–. Designer. Born Oleg Loiewski in Paris, France, of Russian parents. Cassini was educated in Florence at the English Catholic School and graduated from the Accademia delle Belle Arti in 1934. His mother ran a dress shop in Florence and after working with her for a brief period Cassini opened a small salon making one-off designs. In 1936 he went to New York, where he was employed by various manufacturers on SEVENTH AVENUE until 1940, when he joined 20th Century-Fox in Hollywood. After World War II, Cassini became head of the wardrobe department at Eagle-Lion Studios. By 1950 he was back on Seventh Avenue. During the 1950s the name Cassini was associated with glamorous, ready-to-wear SHEATH dresses, knitted suits, jackets and COCKTAIL DRESSES. He also designed extensively for musicals and television. In 1961 Jacqueline Kennedy (ONASSIS) appointed him official designer for her wardrobe. He worked closely with her in the evolution of her personal clothing style, creating many widely copied garments. These included a high-necked, silk ottoman evening gown and a fawn-coloured, semi-fitted wool coat with a removable circular collar of Russian sable, which was worn over a matching wool dress.

Castelbajac, Jean-Charles de 1950–. Designer. Born in Casablanca, Morocco. Castelbajac moved to France with his family in the mid-1950s. In 1968 he began designing for his mother, who had her own clothing business. Shortly afterwards he created several lines for Paris manufacturer Pierre d'Alby before opening his own business in 1975. Castelbajac achieved fame in the mid-1970s with his functional, modernist, high-tech clothing. As a foil to the clearly defined structure of his designs, he uses natural fabrics and fibres. In 1974 he lengthened the ski jacket to make a quilted coat which became widely copied, and the following year he joined the Italian firm of Max Mara to create Sportmax. Always mixing his personal life and his interest in movies, music, art and the environment with his clothing design, Castelbajac has created many clothes featuring printed logos, messages or images. He is famous for his chic yet rugged daywear and also for his hand-painted fabrics which did much to influence the 'wearable art' garments popular during the 1980s. Castelbajac began designing for André COURREGES in the mid-1990s.

Castillo, Antonio 1908–84. Designer. Born Antonio Canovas del Castillo del Rey in Madrid, Spain. Castillo studied at the Colegio del Pilar in Madrid, at the University of Madrid and at El Sacro Monte in Granada. He designed dresses, jewelry and hats for the houses of PAQUIN and PIGUET from 1936 until 1944, when Elizabeth Arden persuaded him to join her salon in New York. Castillo worked with Arden from 1945 to 1950 and produced collections based on natural shoulder lines and slim silhouettes topped with small hats. He was also in demand as a costume designer for the New

York Metropolitan Opera and Broadway. In 1950 he returned to Paris and joined LANVIN. In one of his first collections for this house, in 1951, he showed white satin evening gowns trimmed with mink. Castillo continued to produce designs based on Lanvin's original ROBES DE STYLE, with close fitting BODICES and long, flowing skirts. He employed soft fabrics for his coats and dresses, which were often draped at the hip or panelled at the side. Between 1956 and 1960, capes featured often in his collections, fringed and triple-tiered in 1956, hip or floor length by 1960. In 1962 Castillo left Lanvin and two years later opened his own business. He continued to create elegant clothes and elaborate costumes for private clients, the theatre and the movies, notably for the film *Nicholas and Alexandra* (1971). He closed his house in 1970.

Castle, Irene 1893–1969. Dancer. Born Irene Foote in New Rochelle, New York, USA. In the 1910s, Irene Castle and her husband, Vernon Blythe Castle, became a popular dance team, working first at the Café de Paris in Paris,

The dancer Irene **Castle** epitomized the modern woman. She created a vogue for short haircuts and for clothes that did not restrict movement.

but travelling often to other parts of Europe and to the USA. Irene Castle adapted her clothes for dancing by shortening them, using soft, flowing fabrics, and either slitting her skirts or adding extra fullness. Her buckled shoes, narrow velvet HEADBAND trimmed with pearls, and her habit of wearing men's coats and CAPS were widely copied. She also bobbed her hair and helped to popularize the boyish silhouette of the post-World War I years.

catsuit All-in-one garment, usually with long sleeves, which is either zipped or buttoned at the front from the navel to the neck. The catsuit was popular in the 1960s and owed its name to the fact that it was made from slinky, clinging fabrics. Catsuits were often worn with boots. *See* CARDIN.

Caumont, Jean-Baptiste 1932–. Designer. Born in Béarn, France. Caumont studied art in Paris. He worked briefly for BALMAIN and illustrated fashion for *VOGUE* and *Marie-Claire*. Towards the end of the 1950s he began to work for the Italian department store La Rinascente in Milan and in 1965 he established his own ready-to-wear label in that city. He is well known for his knitwear designs. His menswear range, 'Caumont Monsieur', dates from 1970.

Nino **Cerruti**'s 1980–81 collection included these classic examples of suits for both sexes.

Cavanagh, John 1914–. Designer. Born in Ireland. Cavanagh trained at MOLYNEUX in London and Paris in the 1930s. After World War II, he studied fashion in the USA and in 1947 joined BALMAIN in Paris. Four years later he returned to London where, in 1952, he opened his own house. Successful from the start, Cavanagh approached his work as a couturier with a keen eye for cut and line. He promoted full-skirted, round-shouldered looks as effectively as lean, long lines. His 1950s designs anticipated the SACK or CHEMISE DRESS. His success continued throughout the 1960s with the production of wholesale and ready-to-wear lines. He retired in 1974. *See* ★KLEIN, BERNAT.

Cerruti, Nino 1930–. Designer. Born Antonio Cerruti in Biella, Italy. The Cerruti family textile business was established in 1881 by three brothers. Centred around an old mill, the company specialized in producing high quality woollen fabrics. At the age of twenty, Nino Cerruti, eldest grandson of one of the three brothers, left university and took over the firm. During the 1950s, as a means of promotion, he commissioned four plays for which he designed the costumes. In 1963 he launched a knitwear line. His first men's ready-to-wear venture was established in 1967, the same year in which he set up his studio in Paris. Nine years later Cerruti launched a womenswear line. His clothes for men and women, usually daywear, are classically tailored, elegant and made of high quality fabrics. In the field of menswear, he is an acknowledged leader in suits.

Chalayan, Hussein 1970–. Designer. Born in Nicosia, Cyprus. Chalayan graduated in fashion from Central St Martin's School of Art in London in 1993. His final-year collection was featured by Browns, London's leading designer store, and in 1994 he presented his first solo collection. He is known for fine tailoring in soft fluid luxurious fabrics. In 1997 he showed a collection of eveningwear in the form of column dresses in fine matt jersey decorated with jet beads, gold embroidery or gold chains.

challis Lightweight plain-woven fabric originally made from silk and wool and printed with a delicate floral pattern. The word is believed to derive from the Anglo-Indian word *shale*

veningwear design for Autumn/Winter 1997–98 from ⌐ussein **Chalayan**.

oft'. Since the beginning of the 20th-century, ⌐hallis has been made from wool mixed with ⌐otton and rayon and has been mostly used as a ⌐ress fabric.

Chambre Syndicale de la Couture ⌐ee HAUTE COUTURE.

Chambre Syndicale de la Couture Parisi-nne See HAUTE COUTURE.

Chambre Syndicale de la Haute Couture ⌐ee HAUTE COUTURE.

Chanel, Coco 1883–1971. Designer. Born ⌐abrielle Bonheur Chanel in Saumur, France. ⌐lthough many questions surround Chanel's ⌐rly life, it is generally believed that she had ⌐quired some experience in dressmaking and ⌐illinery before she opened a hat shop in Paris ⌐ 1910. This was followed three years later by

the opening of a boutique in Deauville and another in Biarritz in 1915. Chanel made and sold hats, simple loose blouses, and CHEMISES. Chanel's clothes were designed to be worn without CORSETS and were constructed with fewer linings to make them lighter and less rigid. As early as 1914 she was showing a simple chemise dress. In 1916 she began to make garments from jersey, a cheap fabric previously used only for underwear. Later, demand for this fabric and for a specially woven knit called kasha persuaded Chanel to manufacture them. In 1918 Chanel was producing CARDIGANS and TWINSETS. She adapted men's sweaters and showed them worn over plain, straight skirts. In 1920 she introduced wide-legged trousers for women, based on sailor's BELL BOTTOMS, which she called 'yachting pants'. These were followed two years later by wide, generously cut beach PYJAMAS. Chanel's personal life brought her into the public eye and increased her influence on fashion during the post-World War I years. She herself wore the clothes she had adapted from traditional menswear: belted raincoats, plain open-neck shirts, BLAZERS, cardigans, trousers and soft BERETS. Grey and

Coco **Chanel**, sporting her famous knitted three-piece cardigan suit, ropes of pearls and two-tone shoes.

Chanel evening dress in black mousseline de soie, accessorized with pearls, 1925.

The unmistakable flat-chested, slender figure of Coco **Chanel**, sketched here by her friend and colleague Jean Cocteau. In 1937, when this sketch was made, Chanel was still at the height of her career. Her own design for evening features many of the fashion touches that made her famous: the collarless, elegant dress, the obvious jewelry trimmings and the large bow in her hair.

navy-blue were her favourite colours but she also created a vogue for beige. She became a celebrated figure, the archetypal GARCONNE – flat-chested, slender, wearing loose, comfortable clothes and sporting a short, boyish haircut. Throughout the 1920s Chanel introduced one fashion idea after another. She teamed tweed skirts with sweaters and strings of pearls, transformed PEA JACKETS and raincoats into fashionable attire, and popularized the LITTLE BLACK DRESS. Her collarless cardigan-jacket was braid-trimmed, accessorized with PATCH POCKETS, and worn with knee-length tweed skirts. Her simple chemise dresses had round, straight or BATEAU NECKLINES, hung loosely to the mid- or lower calf and were worn with waist- or hip-length belts. Her other innovations of the period included oversized flat black bows, gilt buttons on blazers, SLING-BACK SANDALS and handbags with gilt chains. She had a

particularly strong influence on jewelry, showing smart tweed suits worn with rows of artificial pearls or gilt chains. During the 1930s she commissioned Fulco ★DI VERDURA to design elaborate COSTUME JEWELRY using fake and semi-precious stones in ostentatious settings. In 1929 Chanel opened a boutique in her Paris salon to sell accessories: bags, belts, scarves and jewelry. The following year she went to

British designer Caroline **Charles**'s cotton voile top and skirt reflect the gypsy vogue of the 1970s.

Hollywood to design clothes for several United Artists films, including those for Gloria Swanson in *Tonight or Never*. Back in France in the mid-1930s, Chanel focused much of her attention on manufacturing. She closed her salon in 1939, at the outbreak of World War II. In 1954, at the age of seventy-one, she made her comeback, reopening her house and showing once again the neat suits that had been her hallmark before World War II. The fashion world was shocked to see revamped prewar fashions but more women than ever took to wearing the Chanel suit, and by the 1960s it had become a symbol of traditional elegance, worn (as in the 1920s) with a gilt chain bag and a string of pearls. The look endures today, particularly in the USA.

Chantilly lace Bobbin lace woven in many European towns, including Grammont in Bel-gium, and Chantilly and Bayeux in France. It is usually black with swags of flowers and scattered dots on a fine background. The Chantilly SHAWL, in black or white, was popular during the late 19th century. *See* ★LACE.

Charles, Caroline 1942–. Designer. Born in Cairo, Egypt, of English parents. Charles attended Swindon School of Art, Wiltshire, until 1960, when she became an apprentice to Michael SHERARD. She spent almost two years working with Mary QUANT before setting up on her own in late 1963. During the 1960s Charles proved to be a popular designer of young, fashionable clothing. She created MINI DRESSES and skirts in pure cotton and flannel. From the TUNICS and trousers of the late 1960s Charles moved with ease to the long, flowing fashion lines that predominated in the early 1970s. Using beautiful, often luxurious, prints and patterns, she established herself as a designer of more sophisticated clothes. Her collections are essentially practical, and are based on the idea of a cohesive working wardrobe.

charleston An American dance of the 1920s. Its energetic side-kicks from the knees made shorter dresses for women desirable. The hems of these mostly simple, tubular dresses were often fringed to give the appearance of length without impeding movement.

charmeuse Trade name of a lustrous, light-weight cotton, rayon or silk fabric of satin weave, developed in the 20th century.

Chase, Edna Woolman 1887–1957. Editor. Born Edna Alloway in New Jersey, USA. Chase started her career in the circulation department at *VOGUE* in the late 1890s. She became a reporter, then managing editor, and in 1914 was appointed editor. In that year, she persuaded a US manufacturer to put on a fashion show using live models in the Parisian manner. Rather than attempt to depend on Paris during the World War I years, Chase encouraged US manufacturers to provide fashion for the many rather than the few, and championed a 'more taste than money theme' in *Vogue*. As *Vogue*'s editor-in-chief, she fashioned the American woman's taste for nearly forty years. In 1933 she went to London, where her efforts prevented the closure of British *Vogue*. Chase returned to New York to retire nineteen years later, in 1952.

chatelaine Created in the 17th century to carry watches and seals, a chatelaine was a set of chains, usually of silver, which wound round the waist and hung down over the skirt. Chatelaines were revived in the 1830s. From 1849 chatelaines made of steel were used to hold an increasing number of practical objects – scissors, thimble, keys, etc. They were rarely seen after the 1880s.

check Checks were developed by landowners in Scotland during the 19th century as an alternative to TARTAN, which was considered unsuitable for everyday wear or workwear. They were adapted from local weaves, based on tartan patterns and colours. It was also

The **chemise**, a 19th-century undergarment from which most 20th-century dress styles evolved.

common to issue checks as commemorative patterns. During the 20th century checks were first used for men's suits and coats but quickly became popular for women, made up into suits, coats, dresses, skirts and, in the 1960s, trousers.

cheesecloth Thin, loosely woven, plain-weave cotton which originated in India. Cheesecloth has mainly been used as a house-hold fabric and for interlining garments. During the late 1960s and 1970s it was developed as a fashion fabric, dyed in bright colours and embroidered. Many of the cheesecloth dresses and skirts and the PEASANT-style blouses popular at the time were imported from India.

Chelsea Area of London which has been synonymous with fashion since the 19th century, when it became a popular habitat for artists. In the 20th century the 'Chelsea look' has taken many forms, too various to itemize. The last distinctive style is associated with the 1960s, when BOUTIQUES and shops sprang up in Chelsea's main street, the KING'S ROAD, which attracted customers of all ages. The shops specialized in inexpensive, ready-to-wear clothes, many directly from designers. The 1960s 'Chelsea look' consisted of MINI SKIRTS, thigh-high leather boots and tight SKINNY-RIB sweaters. *See* JOHN, AUGUSTUS; *and* QUANT.

chemise One of the simplest of garments, the chemise has existed in one form or another for thousands of years. Usually constructed from two rectangular pieces of fabric sewn at the shoulders and sides, it can be collarless and sleeveless. Chemises are made of cotton, linen, lawn or silk, and the more luxurious of these fabrics are often decorated. Before the 19th century the chemise was also known as a SMOCK and was worn as an undergarment, either on its own or between the body and a CORSET or STAYS. Most chemises were drawn on over the head and had back-fastening buttons or ties. During the 19th century, the chemise became a shirt-like blouse. *See also* CHEMISE DRESS.

chemise dress In the early 20th century the CHEMISE shape was adapted by many designers. CHANEL was one of the first to create chemise dresses; simple, loose garments with long sleeves and a belt that tied under the bust, around the waist or at the hips. LANVIN, PAQUIN and WORTH also designed chemise dresses. In the 1950s a loose dress, based on the chemise, appeared in BALENCIAGA's collections. *See also* DIOR and SACK.

chenille Fabric with a fur-like texture created by weaving the warp threads in groups, originating in France during the late 17th century. Chenille can be made from cotton, silk, rayon or wool. It was used in the late 19th century domestically as an upholstery fabric as well as for evening gowns. During the late 20th century it was extensively revived and employed for both clothes and upholstery.

cheongsam Close-fitting SHIFT dress, originating in the Far East. It usually has a MANDARIN COLLAR, long sleeves and a slit at both sides of the skirt. It was briefly popular in the late 1950s and 1960s as eveningwear.

Cheruit, Madeleine dates unknown. Designer. Born in France. Cheruit trained with the couture house of Raudnitz in Paris. Around 1906 she opened her own house and became well known in 1914 for her walking suits and afternoon dresses. After World War I she designed cinema capes and full evening skirts. In 1925 she created handpainted Cubist-

The turn-of-the-century **chesterfield**, with velvet collar and cuffs.

inspired dresses. Many of Cheruit's gowns were heavily ornamented and embroidered; they started to lose their appeal in the mid-1920s when less complicated attire became fashionable. The house closed in 1935.

chesterfield The chesterfield was named in the 1830s after Philip Dormer Stanhope, 4th Earl of Chesterfield. The 19th-century chesterfield was a man's grey wool overcoat with a fitted waist and velvet collar. (In the previous century black velvet strips had been sewn on to coat collars of the French nobility as a sign of mourning after the death, in 1793, of Louis XVI.) After World War I the long-line chesterfield with black velvet collar was copied for young women. Variations of the style – double-breasted with pockets – appeared throughout the 19th and 20th centuries.

chiffon Light, gossamer-sheer fabric created by tightly twisted yarns. Chiffon is made of silk, wool or synthetics. It has been used almost exclusively for eveningwear. Chiffon scarves have been in and out of fashion since the beginning of the 20th century.

chignon Hairstyle created by coiling long hair into a loose, but carefully pinned, bun-shape at the back of the neck. It was a common style from the 19th century until the 1920s, often decorated. The chignon was popular during the late 1960s and early 1970s as part of the revival of EDWARDIAN-STYLE fashions.

chinchilla Long, dense, soft fur of a rodent which originates in the Andes mountain range of South America. The fur is usually pale grey, with a black streak running the length of the tail. It was fashionable at the turn of the century for trimming coats and cloaks. Since around 1900, most chinchilla has been ranched.

chintz From the Hindu, *chint*, 'a printed cloth', chintz is a cotton cloth that is glazed by starch. It usually features designs of flowers, fruits and birds and has been popular as a furnishing fabric since the 1600s. Most chintz was originally imported from India but as production in the UK increased, the British began to export chintz to Europe. It has been employed to make jackets and waistcoats during the 20th century, notably during the 1960s and in the early 1980s, and it invariably appears in collections whenever the current vogue is for floral decorative patterns.

chiton Garment originating from ancient Greece. Although various versions are recorded, the chiton was generally made from a large, rectangular piece of cloth which was wrapped around the body, secured at one shoulder, and belted under or over the waist. Alternatively, it was constructed by fastening the top edges of two pieces with a series of clasps along both arms, which created sleeves, and tying the garment under the bust. The chiton has been adapted to numerous cuts and styles throughout the ages. FORTUNY used the chiton shape for his 'Delphos gowns'.

Chloé Ready-to-wear company founded in France in 1952 by Jacques Lenoir and Gaby Aghion. Karl LAGERFELD designed for Chloé from 1965 to 1983; Martine SITBON between 1987 and 1991. In 1992 Lagerfeld headed up the design team once more. Chloé specializes in high quality ready-to-wear comprising simple, elegant, uncluttered and fluid garments made of luxurious fabric and distinctively coloured. Thanks to Lagerfeld, the house remains at the forefront of fashion. In 1997 Stella McCartney was brought in as head designer.

choker Collar of pearls, or a band of fabric, often velvet, worn closely around the throat and decorated with jewels. Used in the 19th century for evening wear, the choker came back into vogue in the late 1960s and early 1970s. Also known as a dog collar.

Chong, Monica 1957–. Designer. Born in Hong Kong. Chong was educated in Hong Kong and Australia. In the early 1970s she moved to England, where she studied fashion design at Chelsea College of Art in London from 1974 to 1977. She then worked for the London store Browns before producing in 1978 a first collection composed of twelve pieces for a young market. Since then she has produced numerous day and eveningwear lines.

Cierach, Lindka 1952–. Designer. Born in Lesotho, Africa, of Polish-English parents. During the mid-1970s Cierach worked for British VOGUE, studied at the London College of Fashion and became an apprentice to YUKI. In 1978 she launched her own couture business, producing precisely tailored, classic clothing. The 1986 commission to design the wedding dress for the Duchess of York brought her international attention, and a year later saw her first ready-to-wear collection. She specializes in fine embroidery and beading which she incorporates in her feminine but formal clothes for day and evening.

cigarette pants Narrow trousers cut to taper towards the ankle which first became popular in the 1950s.

circular skirt Cut from one or two pieces of fabric, the circular skirt was all the rage during the 1950s when it was often worn with layers of petticoats. It is closely associated with the rock 'n' roll era.

Circular skirts for fashionable teenagers in 1953, advertised by the American mail order firm of Sears, Roebuck. The shape was achieved with the aid of layers of stiff petticoats.

ciré French for 'waxed'. Process whereby wax, heat and pressure are applied to fabrics such as satin, producing a smooth, polished, lustrous effect. Ciré fabrics were especially popular during the 1920s, 1930s and 1960s.

Claiborne, Liz 1929–. Designer. Born in Brussels, Belgium. Claiborne studied at the Fine Arts School and Painter's Studio in Belgium, and also in France and the USA. In 1949 she won a HARPER'S BAZAAR Jacques HEIM design contest which entitled her to travel and sketch in Europe. Upon her return to New York she joined Tina LESER and then, shortly after, Omar KIAM. In 1960 she began to design for the Youth Guild Inc. In the following year she was one of many designers who helped promote the idea of removing the strict classifications of clothes for specific occasions by designing complete wardrobes of mix-and-match separates. In 1976, Claiborne opened her own company. She continues to produce predominantly youthful, fashion-conscious clothes.

Clark, Ossie 1942–96. Designer. Born Raymond Clark in Liverpool, England. Clark attended Manchester College of Art from 1957 to 1961 and then spent three years at the Royal College of Art in London. While at the RCA, he began designing for Quorum, a company dating from the early 1960s which became one of the most popular BOUTIQUES in CHELSEA. Clark joined it full-time in 1966. During the late 1960s and early 1970s Clark was one of the most important designers of his time, responsible for introducing and popularizing a variety of trends. His work has continued to be influential and is now recognized as being at the forefront of the avant-garde 'swinging sixties'. Clark's large-collared, leather motorcycle jacket, cut very short and zipped on one side at the front, became a widely copied high-fashion garment. He produced HOT PANTS, MAXI COATS, and GYPSY dresses with HANDKERCHIEF POINTS. In the late 1960s Clark used metallic leather and snakeskin as fabrics, but his skill is mainly associated with the use of crepe, satin, jersey and chiffon. These fabrics he ruched and draped into dresses and blouses whose plunging necklines, tiny waists and full sleeves emphasized the shape of the body. In the early 1970s his crepe, ankle-length, large-sleeved WRAPAROUND

Cleaver, Allan

Blouse from the Edwardian revival of 1970, designed by Ossie **Clark**.

dresses, which fitted at the back leaving a triangle of bare skin, attracted enormous attention and were in great demand. Many of his dress fabrics were designed by his wife, Celia Birtwell. In 1975 Clark worked for the London dress manufacturer Radley, where his crepe and chiffon ready-to-wear evening dresses were produced. He left after a few years and but for a brief comeback in 1983 continued to design solely for individual clients.

Cleaver, Allan *See* BYBLOS.

Clements Ribeiro Design team. Suzanne Clements (b. 1968, Surrey, England) and Inacio Ribeiro (b. 1963, Itapecerica, Brazil). Clements and Ribeiro both studied at St Martin's School of Art, London. They graduated in 1991 and married in 1992. After working as design consultants for various fashion companies, they started their own house in London in 1993. Clements Ribeiro combine simple uncluttered shapes with an eccentric and exuberant use of colours, prints and materials. They invert established values by using couture fabrics for basic daywear: a T-shirt in pure cashmere, for example. In 1996 they produced a collection comprising multicoloured stripes and diagonal checks as well as a knitted cashmere range in rainbow stripes.

Clergerie, Robert 1934–. Shoe designer. Born in Paris, France. In 1895 Joseph Fenestrier purchased a small shoe manufacturing firm in Romans, France, and turned the company into an award-winning enterprise. He died in 1910 and in 1922 the firm was taken over by his son, Joseph Emile Jean Fenestrier. Fenestrier died in 1966. Twelve years later Robert Clergerie, after a management career and seven years at Charles JOURDAN, obtained a controlling interest in the company Unic Fenestrier. The clean architectural lines of Clergerie's shoes have ensured him worldwide success. While his footwear is

The design team of **Clements Ribeiro** became known for their use of multicoloured stripes and diagonal checks. This sweater is from their Autumn/Winter 1997 collection.

signed not to distract from the clothes, this
nderstated style has in itself become widely
popular.

oak Generic term for a loose outer garment,
ith or without sleeves, which covers the body
om the shoulders to the hips, knees or ankles.
can be collarless, but is often made with
ther a high, stiff collar or a flat collar that sits
the shoulders. Cloaks were popular in the
e 19th century and during the 20th century,
rticularly in the 1960s. *See* BALMAIN, CAPE *and*
IGERE.

oche Woman's hat worn from *c.*1915 until
e mid-1930s, achieving greatest popularity
ring the 1920s. The cloche is tight-fitting,
vering the head from the back of the neck
d worn pulled down low over the forehead.
can be brimmed or brimless. In the 1920s
ches were often decorated with grosgrain
bon.

utch bag (US: clutch purse) Known in the
20s and 1930s as a *pochette*, a clutch bag is a
NDBAG without straps. It has been popular
ice the early 20th century in various shapes
d sizes, from the small beaded evening bag to
e large ENVELOPE BAG.

The **cloche** hat of the 1920s was worn pulled down
low onto the forehead. Note the elaborate bow.

coat dress *See* COAT FROCK.

coat frock A fashion innovation dating from
World War I, the coat frock is a one-piece,
long-sleeved garment tailored along the lines of
a coat but trimmed in the manner of a dress.
During the second half of the 20th century, it
became known as a coat dress.

llection of **cloaks** from Maison Gagelin, where Charles Frederick Worth worked when he arrived in Paris. He
rried one of the shop assistants, who inspired him to become the founder of haute couture. Cloaks were ideal
terwear over crinolines. This illustration is from an 1850s issue of the *Petit Courier des Dames*.

An evening gown from Sybil **Connolly**, the *grande dame* of Irish dress design. Connolly produced both evening and day wear. This dress dates from the early 1960s.

cocktail dress Cocktails – a US invention – became popular in the early 1920s. The cocktail dress, worn for both the cocktail hour and for dinner, banished the TEA GOWN or afternoon dress once and for all. It was short (to the knee or below), usually made of lightweight wool, satin, silk, velvet and other luxurious fabrics, embroidered or decoratively trimmed, and often cut to reveal the shoulders and arms. One form of the dress, based on the simple lines of the CHEMISE, has become a staple of the cocktail hour and, in black, known as a LITTLE BLACK DRESS, has been an essential item in many women's wardrobes. Originally heavily promoted by CHANEL and MOLYNEUX in the 1920s and 1930s, the cocktail dress remains popular. *See* ★GIVENCHY, ★LELONG *and* ★OLDFIELD.

Cocteau, Jean 1889–1963. Artist, stage designer, illustrator, poet, playwright. Born in Maisons-Lafitte, France. Cocteau was closely associated with the world of fashion through both the theatre and his friendship with Elsa ★SCHIAPARELLI. He designed for DIAGHILEV's ballets and worked closely with Schiaparelli, who encouraged his nonconformist attitudes and applied his surreal themes to her fashion accessories. Cocteau also designed covers for a number of magazines, notably *HARPER'S BAZAAR*. *See* ★CHANEL.

Comme des Garçons *See* KAWAKUBO.

Connolly, Sybil 1921–. Designer. Born in Dublin, Ireland. Connolly was educated in Waterford, Ireland. In 1938 she went to London to study dress design at Bradley's dressmaking establishment but returned to Dublin at the outbreak of World War II. Connolly joined the Irish fashion house of Richard Alan and was

corsage

made a director at the age of twenty-two. From 1953, she designed a couture line under her own name for Richard Alan, becoming extremely successful and well-known in Ireland, the USA and later Australia, and promoting the use of Irish linen, wool, tweed and lace. In 1957 she parted with Richard Alan and established her own fashion house. During the early 1950s Connolly attracted a great deal of attention with her method of hand-pleating fine handkerchief linen, which she made up into delicate blouses and dresses. She specialized in adapting traditional textiles – such as Irish crochet and linens, Carrickmacross lace and Donegal tweeds – to fashion garments. Throughout the 1950s and 1960s Connolly helped popularize handwoven woollens, tweeds and mohairs as fashion fabrics. She also developed an international reputation as an interior designer.

Conran, Jasper 1959–. Designer. Born in London, England. Son of Sir Terence Conran, who has influenced British and European home furnishing design since the 1960s. Conran attended Parsons School of Design in New York from 1975 to 1977. He spent a brief period as a designer at FIORUCCI before returning to London where he created a womenswear collection for the New York department store Henri Bendel. In 1977 he joined the British firm of Wallis as a consultant. His first collection under his own name was shown one year later. Conran rarely strays from the style set by this early collection. He retains a simplicity of approach which produces an easy, soft fit that suits many women. He uses quality fabrics, cut into comfortable garments which do not impose on the wearer.

Conway, Gordon 1894–1956. Illustrator, costume designer. Born in Clairborne, Texas, USA. Conway was educated in the USA and Italy. Around 1915 she began working for *VOGUE*, *VANITY FAIR* and *HARPER'S BAZAAR*. Her soft, colourist style was strongly influenced by BARBIER, ERTE and LEPAPE. In 1920 she arrived in London where she worked for French and British publications. In 1930 she began to design costumes for British films and theatre. She retired to Virginia in 1936.

coolie hat Southeast Asian hat made of bamboo leaves or straw, traditionally worn by labourers to provide protection from sun and rain. Generally made in one piece, the coolie hat is cone shaped and slopes downwards on a steep, straight slant which completely covers the head. Popular during the 1930s and 1950s.

corduroy Perhaps from the French *corde du roi*, 'cloth of the king'. Corduroy is a durable cotton or rayon velvet cut-pile fabric which has wide or narrow wales, cords or ribs. Up to the 19th century, it was associated with livery and was also used for the work clothes of agricultural labourers. During the 19th century it was made into breeches, coats and hunting attire. In the 20th century it became popular for casual dress, mainly jackets, skirts and trousers.

co-respondent shoe (US: spectator shoe) Two-tone shoe (usually black and white or brown and white) worn initially for casual attire. It was popular in the 1920s and 1930s and again in the 1960s.

Corfam Trade name for a chemically made leather substitute, developed by DU PONT in the USA, which was soft, supple and porous, allowing the feet to breathe. Introduced during the 1960s, Corfam was used by the British shoe manufacturers RAYNE to make women's COURT SHOES. Mary QUANT used it for ankle boots.

Corolle line *See* NEW LOOK.

corsage Small floral arrangement worn at the waist or bosom of evening gowns during the 19th century and in the early 20th century.

Man's **co-respondent** shoe in tan Russian calf and white buckskin, *c.* 1935.

February 2nd, 1901   *THE LADIES' FIELD*

THE "SPÉCIALITÉ CORSET"

IS A DREAM OF COMFORT.

Regd. Design No. 2517.

THE "SPÉCIALITÉ CORSET" is manufactured under scientific supervision, the cut and make being perfect. Each bone is placed in the position requiring support, without impeding or checking the proper exercise of the muscles, allowing perfect freedom of action to the whole frame; all these advantages are obtained, with an additional elegance of form, as the Illustration will show.

The "Spécialité Corset" is made of the best materials, and fitted throughout with REAL WHALEBONE (busks and side-steels excepted), best sewing and perfect finish. The quality of the "Spécialité Corset" will be found 25 per cent. better, at the price, than any other Corset offered to the public.

THE NEW STRAIGHT-FRONTED "SPÉCIALITÉ CORSET" (*as illustration*), in White Coutille and real Whalebone, price 27/6 ; in Black Coutille, unlined, 29/6.
THE "SPÉCIALITÉ CORSET."—TYPE 1A.—Long waist, in Black Italian Cloth and Real Whalebone, 19/6 complete ; in Black Satin, 27/6.
TYPE 1B.—Extra long waist, in Black Italian Cloth and Real Whalebone, 21/- complete ; in Black Satin, 29/6.
TYPE 1C.—Long waist, cut longer below the waist, and extra fully boned to give greater support to stout figures, in Black or White, 25/- complete.
TYPE 2D.—Long waist, in White Coutille and Real Whalebone, 18/6.
TYPE 2E.—Extra long waist, 21/- complete.

The S-bend silhouette was still fashionable at the turn of the century. In 1901 *The Ladies' Field* introduced its readers to the 'Spécialité **Corset**', made of 'real whalebone', and promising 'an additional elegance of form'.

corset The 19th-century corset, used to achieve the fashionable small waist of the period, was a descendant of the 15th-century BODICE, which was stiffened by two pieces of linen pasted together. Worn under a dress but often over a thin cotton or muslin SHIFT, corsets were usually constructed of WHALE-BONE pieces inserted as panelling into a fabric shape. They laced tightly at the front or back of the waist and were the subject of great controversy from around 1850, when reform groups on both sides of the Atlantic protested at the physical damage caused by tight lacing. Despite these protests, the late 19th century produced the most elaborate shapes achieved by corsetry. The S-BEND SILHOUETTE became popular, created by corsets which reached down over the hips and thrust the bust forward. In the early 1900s POIRET claimed to have freed women from corsets, as did LUCILE and VIONNET. At this time the boned corset was replaced by woven elastic material which flattened the waist rather than drawing it in. Undergarments in the 1920s heralded the approach of the ROLL ON and GIRDLE of the 1930s. In 1947 the WASPIE emerged to create the tiny waists of the NEW LOOK. Corsets have always been made in different colours, the most popular of which are

From *La Vie Parisienne* of June 1924, a cartoon of a woman being laced into her **corset** – now made from woven elastic, rather than whalebone.

black, white, grey and pink. In 1987 Vivienne WESTWOOD included push-up corsets, based on 18th-century models, in her collection. In the 1990s many designers included corsetry in their designs for both underwear and outerwear, such as short evening dresses with flared skirts attached to corset bodices, bras built into business suit jackets, metallic and leather corsets worn over dresses as vests. These corsets are made of foam and Lycra, with plastic stays. *See also* BUSTIER *and* STAYS.

Cossack Word describing the inhabitants of southeastern Russia. In the early 20th century the term Cossack was associated with Russian soldiers, who wore dark-coloured overcoats with flared sleeves and full skirts, leather boots and astrakhan hats. In the late 1960s Yves SAINT LAURENT was just one designer who delved into RUSSIAN costume history to produce a 'Cossack' collection composed of baggy trousers tucked into tall boots, full flowing skirts, dresses and coats which were often tied with bold SASHES, and large fur hats.

costume jewelry Jewelry made either from gemstones which resemble precious stones or from imitation stones which meet periodic fashion trends. Costume jewelry was developed in the 18th century, mainly for the emerging middle classes and the wealthy who, for reasons of security, wore valueless jewelry while travelling. It continued to be popular throughout the 19th century. In the 1920s costume jewelry developed into an accessory in its own right rather than mere imitation. In the hands of CHANEL and SCHIAPARELLI it became witty and ostentatious. Following this period, new design approaches to costume jewelry produced fashionable pieces which were no longer thought of as second-rate. Various materials are employed, often painted imitations of silver and gold, as well as resins and other plastics, which imitated precious stones. As clothing changes, so does the demand for non-traditional jewelry. Bracelets, earrings and pins, as well as rings, have all been reinvented, many in structured or sculptural forms. Costume jewelry is now an integral part of the fashion scene. It is very collectible and high prices are commanded for exceptional designs. *See* LANE *and* RABANNE.

cotton The cotton plant, which grows to a height of between three and five feet, produces a fibre-covered seed pod. The cotton is picked by hand or machine and the fibres are removed by a gin, invented in 1792 in the American South by Eli Whitney. Cotton has been used for every kind of fashion garment, though it is particularly suited to underwear and lightweight summer clothing.

Various designers produced versions of the **Cossack** look in the 1970s, but perhaps none so·successfully as Yves Saint Laurent, who created these Russian-inspired clothes for his 'Ballets Russes–Opéra' collection of 1976.

Courrèges, André

This 1965 outfit from André **Courrèges**, the 'Space Age' designer, is typically stark and futuristic. Note the famous Courrèges boots.

Courrèges, André 1923–. Designer. Born in Pau, France. Courrèges studied to be a civil engineer but after a brief period he abandoned this career and went to Paris to work in a small fashion house. In 1949 he joined BALENCIAGA, where he remained until he opened his own house in 1961. During the early 1960s Courrèges introduced very short skirts; MINI dresses with trousers and TROUSER SUITS in white and silver; tube-shaped trousers and trousers cut on the BIAS; white dresses trimmed with beige and vice-versa; mid-calf white BOOTS; and goggles. His clothes were sharp, angular and subject to a highly disciplined design. Simple, stark, TRAPEZE-shaped dresses and coats were boldly piped in contrasting colours. During the late 1960s Courrèges produced ready-to-wear lines. He softened the austerity of his clothes – which by this time had begun to give the impression of a uniform – by using curves, and showed cosmonaut suits, knitted CATSUITS, coats with welt seams around the armholes and over the ribs, and SEE-THROUGH and CUT-OUT DRESSES. His all-white collections were trimmed with bright orange, navy, pink and blue. He became known as the 'SPACE AGE' designer because of his functional, uncluttered, futuristic designs. Considered by many to be an 'architect' of fashion design because of his devotion to construction, Courrèges took inspiration from the male wardrobe, finding its practicality suitable for modern women. His styles were widely copied, in greatly diluted form. In 1965 he sold his business to L'Oréal. He returned to the design world two years later and has remained active, producing clearly defined, sporty clothes, many in pastel shades. A revival of 1960s-style clothing in the 1990s brought about a renewed interest in his work.

Courrèges boot Introduced in the 1960s by André COURRÈGES to conform to the silhouette of his clothing, and in response to the teetering heels of the STILETTO, the boot was made of white kid, calf or patent leather. It was designed to reach the mid-calf with open slots at the top and a bow or tassel in front.

court shoe Introduced in the mid-19th century, the court shoe is an enclosed shoe with a low or medium heel and a line which narrows toward the toe. It has been popular since its introduction, though fashion dictates the heel type and height in every decade. In the USA it is known as a pump.

Courtauld In 1809 George Courtauld set up a silk mill in Essex, England. His son, Samuel Courtauld III (1793–1881), extended the family business from 1816. By 1850 Samuel Courtauld & Company was the largest manufacturer of silk mourning crape in England. Considerable quantities were exported abroad until the vogue for MOURNING DRESS declined in the mid-1880s. In 1904 the company bought the exclusive British rights to the viscose process of making artificial silk, which was later known as RAYON. By 1914 Courtauld's had established a monopoly of viscose yarn production in Great Britain and the USA. Throughout the 20th century, Courtauld's was a giant of the synthetic fibre manufacturing industry, producing Britain's first acrylic fibre, Courtelle, in the 1950s.

couture Abbreviation of HAUTE COUTURE. The term couture refers to individually created, rather than mass-produced clothes. It also covers limited editions of clothing.

Coveri, Enrico 1952–90. Designer. Born in Florence, Italy. Coveri studied at the Accademia delle Belle Arti in Florence. In 1973 he began working freelance for several companies, creating knitwear and daywear lines under the name Touche, among others. He moved to Paris in 1978 to work at the Espace Cardin. Shortly after, he returned to Italy and established his own company. Coveri was a bold designer of young, fun-loving fashions. He blended strong colours into striking, clever designs of knitted tops and trousers that had a broad appeal. He was also known for including comic characters and pop art designs in his clothes.

cowboy Fashion based on the working clothes of American cowboys and early American pioneers, which included check cotton shirts, BANDANNAS, JEANS or GAUCHOS, and thick-heeled BOOTS decorated with tooled leather. PONCHOS and fringed leather jackets were also worn. Cowboy fashions were popular in the late 1960s and 1970s.

The **cowboy** boot has always been an indispensable component of the cowboy look. This traditional brown lizard-skin boot is by Paul Smith, 1989.

Patrick **Cox** is famous for his shoes for both men and women. This high-heeled boot is from his Autumn/Winter 1997–98 collection.

cowl Piece of material attached to a garment at the neck, which can be used as a hood or left draped at the back or front. In the 20th century cowl-neck sweaters and dresses became popular, cut so that the drape fell in soft folds around the neck and onto the chest.

Cox, Patrick 1963–. Shoe designer. Born in Edmonton, Canada. An early interest in British fashion brought Cox to Cordwainer's College, London. While a student he designed a line of footwear for Vivienne WESTWOOD, notably gold PLATFORM shoes with large knots, and was subsequently invited to design for young British designers BODYMAP and John GALLIANO. Cox quickly became known for wittily incorporating materials such as chain mesh, silk fringes and crucifixes into classic women's shoe silhouettes. Gradually refining his style into one of increased classicism, in 1991 he opened a London store which showcased his footwear designs alongside antique furniture. Two years later he introduced his 'Wannabe' LOAFERS: flat and stacked-heeled shoes of bulky, exaggerated proportions that appealed to both sexes.

Crahay, Jules-François 1917–88. Designer. Born in Liège, Belgium. Crahay worked in his mother's dressmaking shop in Liège and as a salesman for the house of Jane Regny in Paris. In 1952 he joined Nina RICCI in Paris, where he became chief designer. Crahay's 1959 collection, which featured low, plunging necklines, anticipated the GYPSY style popular in the early 1960s. Throughout his career at Ricci, Crahay achieved a reputation as an accomplished eveningwear designer. In 1963 he moved to LANVIN, succeeding Antonio del CASTILLO. He retired in 1984.

crape 1. Crepe. 2. Thin worsted fabric used for clerical gowns and MOURNING attire in the 19th century.

Creed, Charles 1909–66. Designer. Born in Paris, France, of English parents. Creed was educated in England before being sent to Vienna, Austria, to study tailoring and art. On his return to England he joined LINTON TWEED Ltd in Carlisle to learn about weaving. This was followed by a spell with New York department store Bergdorf Goodman. In the 1930s Creed joined his family's tailoring firm in Paris. During the World War II years he managed to design while on leave from the army and became involved in the UTILITY SCHEME. After the war he opened his own house in London which was noted for its classically tailored and refined suits. He worked in London and New York during the remainder of the 1940s, creating lines for US SPORTSWEAR manufacturers. He was not a fashion innovator but, like his father and grandfather, he produced woollen and tweed suits of careful and cautious distinction. *See* CREED, HENRY (THE ELDER); *and* CREED, HENRY (THE YOUNGER).

Creed, Henry (the elder) dates unknown. Born in England. The first Creed firm of tailors was established in London at the beginning of the 18th century. Henry Creed opened a branch in Paris during the 1850s. *See* CREED, CHARLES; *and* CREED, HENRY (THE YOUNGER).

Creed, Henry (the younger) 1863–? Designer. Born in Paris, France, of English parents. The son of a tailor who had established a business in Paris, Creed made riding habits for the British royal family. He became famous for his tailored suits (TAILLEURS), which he produced for women in the early 1900s and which became immensely popular. The suits were cut with a BASQUE jacket and full skirt flaring over

the hips. Creed promoted the use of tweed in his suits. *See* CREED, CHARLES; *and* CREED, HENRY (THE ELDER).

crepe Word describing a variety of fabrics, natural and synthetic, which have been given a crinkled texture by the use of heat and a crepe weave.

crepe de chine Crepe made from raw silk. Popular since the 19th century for lightweight garments, such as lingerie and blouses.

crepe georgette Sheer, highly creped fabric, usually made of silk, silk and cotton, silk and rayon, or other mixtures. Since the early 20th century it has been used for lightweight blouses and eveningwear.

crepon Generic term for a crinkle-weave fabric which resembles crepe. In the second half of the 20th century it was used for dresses, blouses, underwear and nightwear. In the early 1960s CACHAREL designed a crepon shirt for women.

crewneck sweater SWEATER with a high, flat neckline that sits close to the neck.

crinoline In the 1840s, the crinoline was a small BUSTLE made of horsehair (from the French *crin*, 'horsehair'). During the 1850s the cage-frame crinoline, made of steel hoops, was introduced. This produced skirts of extraordinary width. The style was promoted in Paris by the Empress EUGENIE, and women in Europe followed her lead. In *c.*1865 the shape altered to flatten the skirts in front, while producing a fullness at the back. *See also* WINTERHALTER.

crochet Decorative craftwork created by looping yarn or thread with a specially hooked needle. Often used for shawls and blankets. In the 1960s, as part of the PEASANT and HIPPIE styles, crocheted clothes became popular as dresses, WAISTCOATS and jackets. Crochet enjoyed a revival in the 1990s in the form of machine-made crochet-knit stockings, waistcoats and bags.

crop Short, boyish hairstyle worn by young women from the mid-1950s and 1960s, with a revival in the 1990s.

In the days of the **crinoline** it was impossible to get dressed alone; many pairs of hands were needed for this complicated and time-consuming process.

ross During the late 1980s the cross or crucifix began to appear on runways as a jewelry accessory. By the 1990s it was a popular motif, in different forms and sizes, worn as a necklace, pin or brooch, and also as a shoe buckle.

Cruz, Miguel 1944–. Designer. Born in Cuba. Cruz trained at the Ecole de la Chambre Syndicale de la Haute Couture (*See* HAUTE COUTURE) in Paris and then worked for CASTILLO and BALENCIAGA. In 1963 he moved to Italy where he designed freelance before opening his own ready-to-wear business in Rome. Cruz is noted for his leather, suede and knitwear designs. He produces his own lines in addition to designing for other companies.

Cuban heels The gauchos of South America wore BOOTS with short, straight, rather thick heels which supported their feet in stirrups. These were known as 'Cuban heels' and they became popular on boots and shoes for men in the 1950s and 1960s. There was a also vogue in the 1970s for women to wear cuban-heeled boots with trousers tucked into them, or to team them with long, flared, denim skirts.

Cubism Abstract art movement dating from the early 20th century, spearheaded by Georges BRAQUE and Pablo PICASSO. The artists superimposed several viewpoints of the subject, broken down and recomposed in geometric components. Artists such as Sonia DELAUNAY and designers such as Jean PATOU took inspiration from Cubism to create bold geometric shapes and patterns in textile design. The influence of Cubism was widespread, affecting not only clothes, but also accessories, particularly handbags, compact cases, jewelry and shoes.

culottes (divided skirt) Originally French workmen's trousers, culottes are very wide trousers that give the appearance of a skirt. In the 19th century, they were worn for cycling. They can be of varying lengths. In the 1930s they were very full, making the division less obvious. Since that time they have been popular for casual wear in both summer and winter. In the 1960s and 1970s, calf-length versions of culottes, called GAUCHOS, were popular.

cummerbund From the Hindi and Persian *kamarband*, 'loincloth'. Wide cloth band worn as a waist SASH, part of traditional male dress in India, Iran and South America. In the late 19th century the cummerbund was adopted by European men, in silk, satin or faille, and worn as eveningwear in place of a WAISTCOAT. Women adopted it for day and evening in a variety of fabrics during the 20th century.

cut-out dress Dress with large circles cut out at each side and/or in the centre back and front. André COURREGES was one of the first designers to introduce cut-out dresses and TUNICS in the early 1960s.

cycling pants (US: bike shorts) Tight-fitting, stretch above-the-knee SHORTS, as worn by professional cyclists, became popular during the 1980s as part of the 'exercisewear-as-everyday-wear' movement. They were worn by themselves with an oversize TUNIC top or under a short dress.

D

Daché, Lilly c.1904–89. Milliner. Born in Bègles, France. While still a teenager, Daché was apprenticed to a Bordeaux milliner. Several years later she moved to Paris and worked for Caroline REBOUX. In 1924, after emigrating to the USA, she became a millinery saleswoman for Macy's department store in New York. That same year, after a short period of employment at The Bonnet Shop, she bought out the owner and expanded the business. Towards the end of America's Depression years, in an era when hats were *de rigueur*, she erected the Lilly Daché Building on East 56th Street. Working with Travis BANTON in Hollywood, she also designed hats for movies, such as towering, fruit-bedecked Carmen Miranda TURBANS, and attracted a movie-star clientele. Shortly after World War II she added dresses, accessories and perfumes to her millinery line. Known for her sometimes outrageously flamboyant style, Daché was famous for draped turbans, close-fitting brimmed CLOCHE hats, SNOODS and CAPS. For almost three decades, she was one of the foremost milliners in the USA. See *PARNIS.

Dacron Tradename for a man-made fibre manufactured by DU PONT in the USA during the early 1950s. It was a popular choice for ruffled blouses of the mid-1950s. See POLYESTER.

Dagworthy, Wendy 1950–. Designer. Born in Gravesend, Kent, England. Dagworthy attended Medway College of Art from 1966 to 1968 and studied art and design at Middlesex Polytechnic from 1968 to 1971. She then joined wholesale manufacturer Radley, before opening her own business in London in 1973. Dagworthy specialized in loose, easy, ready-to-wear shapes in natural fibres, employing resourceful features such as double pockets and detachable hoods. Her clothes for both men and women were practical and flexible, embracing all occasions and seasons. She enjoyed mixing patterns, textures and colours in a spirited youthful style. She closed her business in 1988 and from 1989 was director of the BA fashion course at Central St. Martin's. In 1998 she was appointed Professor of Fashion at the Royal College of Art.

Dahl-Wolfe, Louise 1895–1989. Photographer. Born in San Francisco, California, USA. In 1914 Dahl-Wolfe attended the San Francisco Institute of Art. For the next twenty years she studied, worked as an interior decorator, and travelled. It was not until the mid-1930s that she turned her attention seriously to a lifelong interest – photography. Her first job as a fashion photographer was with Saks Fifth Avenue store in New York. In 1936 she joined HARPER'S BAZAAR, to which she contributed regularly until she retired. Dahl-Wolfe was noted for her painterly use of colour.

Wendy **Dagworthy**'s skill in mixing patterns and textures was revealed in her 1985 collection.

Dali, Salvador 1904–89. Painter. Born in Figueras, Spain. Originally a Cubist, Dali became a Surrealist in 1929. His wild, fantastic imagery was meticulously carried out in the detail of his work. He designed fabrics for *SCHIAPARELLI and contributed many ideas to jewelry and fashion design. *See* SURREALISM.

damask Originally a richly decorated silk fabric brought to the West in the 12th century via Damascus in Syria, where it was also produced. Damask has a figured pattern which is part of the weave and is self-coloured. It was a popular dress fabric during the 19th century but in the 20th century it became associated with home furnishings.

Danskin In 1882 Joel and Benson Goodman established a dry goods business in Manhattan, New York, selling hosiery, leatherware and women's and children's clothes. In 1923 the Goodman sons took over and created Triumph Hosiery Mills in Philadelphia, Pennsylvania. During the 1930s the company specialized in producing theatrical stockings and cotton and silk hosiery in hard-to-fit sizes. The name Danskin was created in the 1950s, at the same time that the firm produced its first leotards, as well as the first dance tights to make a serious attempt to counteract bagginess at knee and ankle. In the following decade Danskin introduced a fashionable range of children's nylon sportswear, sweaters, seamless exercise and dance tights, and fashion tights. A snap-crotch bodysuit was introduced in 1970. Throughout the 1970s, in response to the upsurge of international interest in gymnastics and dance, Danskin created numerous leotard and swimsuit designs in shiny nylon and Spandex blends. The company's up-to-date attitude to dance and exercise clothes helped to move dancewear from the exercise studio onto the streets. The leotard became popular wear at DISCOS and often replaced the swimsuit on the beach. In turn,

The US designer Oscar **de la Renta** used dramatic frills and an oversize bow for part of his eveningwear collection of 1984.

leotards helped to regenerate interest in one-piece swimsuits. Danskin uses cotton and wool blends and Antron and Spandex fibres.

dart Pointed tuck sewn on the reverse of a garment to shape it to the lines of the body. *See* BODICE.

David, Jules 1808–92. Illustrator. Prolific and accomplished illustrator, working in Paris, who contributed to many French, English and German magazines and other publications. He had a precise, clear style and used colour in a more adventurous manner than did his contemporaries. David's models were also more animated than the traditional, stiff fashion-plate models of the mid- to late 19th century. *See* PRINCESS LINE.

de la Renta, Oscar 1932–. Designer. Born in Santo Domingo, Dominican Republic. De la Renta studied at the University of Santo Domingo and the Açademia de San Fernando

in Madrid, Spain. Although he intended to become an abstract painter, he took the first step towards a career in fashion when he designed a gown for the debutante daughter of the US ambassador to Spain which was featured on the cover of *Life*. Shortly after, de la Renta joined BALENCIAGA's couture house in Madrid. In 1961 he went to Paris as an assistant to Antonio del CASTILLO at the house of Lanvin-Castillo. Two years later he moved to Elizabeth Arden's couture and ready-to-wear salon in New York. In 1965, de la Renta moved to Jane Derby and on her retirement that same year he established his own business. During the 1960s he swiftly developed a reputation as a designer of extravagant, opulent, yet tasteful clothes. He created a variety of theme collections based on fashions of the *belle époque*, abstract art prints, orientally inspired evening clothes, and exotic flamenco dresses. His 1967 GYPSY collection attracted a great deal of attention. Over the following years de la Renta established himself as a couture and ready-to-wear designer of positive, vibrant dresses, coats, suits and daywear, created with a bold yet controlled use of colour. He is famous for his eveningwear: COCKTAIL DRESSES and formal gowns, many of which are elaborately trimmed with embroidery, frills and ruffles.

de Luca, Jean-Claude 1948–. Designer. Born in Paris, France. De Luca studied law in Switzerland and Italy. He worked for GIVENCHY for one year before leaving to join DOROTHEE BIS in 1972. Shortly after, he turned to freelance designing. De Luca has designed under his own name since 1976. He produces glamorous, sophisticated and traditional clothing along fluid lines.

de Meyer, Baron Adolphe 1868–1949. Photographer. Born in Paris, France. De Meyer was brought up in Saxony, studied in Paris, and moved to London in 1895. In 1901, after his marriage, he became Baron de Meyer, ennobled by the King of Saxony. In 1913 he moved to New York and began working for Condé NAST at *VOGUE*. He produced romantic, soft-focus pictures, which relied heavily on backlighting, of society women in fashionable clothes. He was not a portraitist – his subjects were only one part of the picture – but a pictorialist. His work concentrated on the sparkle of white and silver, on shiny surfaces, and on the suggestion of ethereal beauty and nonchalance. In 1918 De Meyer returned to Paris on a contract from *HARPER'S BAZAAR* and he remained with the magazine until 1932. During his reign at *Vogue* and the early years at *Harper's Bazaar*, his work was widely imitated but by the early 1930s his style had gone out of fashion and his influence had waned.

de Rauch, Madeleine 1896–1985. Designer. Born in Ville-d'Avray, France. De Rauch designed her own clothes before opening a couture house with her two sisters in 1928. The house was well known for its sporty day clothes. It closed in 1973.

décolleté Low-necklined BODICE of a blouse or dress. The Victorian version was cut low on the shoulders. The décolleté neckline is a traditional component of evening dresses and ball gowns.

deconstructionists Term used in the 1990s to describe a group of designers whose elemental, raw-edged designs in drab colours were widely influential and were perceived by some to be an intellectual form of GRUNGE. By breaking down the component parts of fashion and reassembling them – usually in non-traditional forms – these designers have forced a revaluation of clothes and how they are worn. The deconstructionist designers have strong artistic leanings, treating their clothes as surfaces for experimental dyeing processes. They appear to be making cultural statements with their inside-out seams and hospital gowns. Their clothes have been described as raw and deliberately unattractive but the long-term influences of this pared-down style and its subsequent reconstruction cannot be disputed. *See* DEMEULE-MEESTER, LANG *and* MARGIELA.

deerstalker Man's traditional tweed hunting cap. The deerstalker has back and front peaks, and some versions have earflaps. In the 20th century it was also worn by women.

Delaunay, Sonia 1884–1979. Artist. Born Sonia Terk in Odessa, Russia. Delaunay was brought up in St Petersburg, where she studied

Charles Frederick Worth's tasteful **décolleté** line for the Comtesse de Greffuhle's evening dress of 1896. Photograph by Nadar.

painting. In 1905 she moved to Paris to further her studies and married the artist Robert Delaunay in 1910. She painted bold, abstract canvases dominated by curves, triangles and squares. In 1925 she worked with the textile company BIANCHINI-FERIER and created printed geometric designs in contrasting colours. In the same year she produced PATCHWORK designs which were made into coats by Jacques HEIM. Her influence can be noted in the work of PATOU, SCHIAPARELLI and other designers of the 1920s and 1930s.

Delineator, The In New York in the early 1870s, Ebenezer BUTTERICK produced a magazine, *The Ladies' Quarterly Review of Broadway Fashions*, to promote the sale of his paper patterns. In 1877 he merged the magazine with *Metropolitan*, which subsequently, as *The Delineator*, became one of the top-selling women's journals. Until 1894, when the base of the magazine was broadened to include general features on the home, *The Delineator* was devoted entirely to fashion. Later, it also included fiction. By 1920 it had achieved a circulation of one million and had several overseas editions. In 1928 the Butterick Publishing Company merged another magazine, *The Designer*, with *The Delineator*. In turn, *The Delineator* was absorbed by *The Pictorial Review* in 1937.

Dell'Olio, Louis 1948–. Designer. Born in New York, USA. Dell'Olio graduated from Parsons School of Design in 1969. He worked with Teal Traina and other wholesale companies until 1974, when he joined Anne KLEIN. With Donna KARAN, Dell'Olio interpreted the original SPORTSWEAR styles of the company into relevant, contemporary clothes cut on clean lines. Karan left the company in 1984 but Dell'Olio continued to produce consistently tailored designs for Anne Klein until 1993.

Delman, Herman B. 1895–1955. Shoe manufacturer. Born in Portersville, California, USA. Delman was educated in Portland, Oregon, where his family owned a small shoe shop. After service in the US Marine Corps during World War I, he opened a shoe store in Hollywood, followed by a branch on New York's Madison Avenue. He promoted young shoe designers, whom he hired to make shoes in the windows of his shops. In 1938 Delman signed up Roger VIVIER, and though this association was interrupted by World War II, it was renewed in 1945 and Delman manufactured Vivier's shoes and represented Vivier worldwide for several years. *See also* RAYNE.

Demeulemeester, Ann 1959–. Designer. Born in Kortrijk, Belgium. After graduating from art school in Brugge, Demeulemeester studied fashion design at the Royal Academy of Fine Arts, Antwerp. In 1981, she began six years of freelance designing for international ready-to-wear collections before launching her own line in 1985. A member of a group of experimentally minded designers which emerged from Belgium in the mid-1980s, Demeulemeester is a DECONSTRUCTIONIST who eschews ornament and colour in favour of close attention to detail, and unusual pairing of fabrics. Her styles often incorporate contradictions: an austerity of outline is marked with gently

A design for eveningwear from the Belgian designer Ann **Demeulemeester**, Spring/Summer 1996–97.

draped fabrics or antique-like fabrics; nostalgic HIPPIE style materials with frayed edges are mixed with stark coats. Her long coats and dresses have become her signature classic style, along with HALTER VESTS, blouses disguised as neckties, and trousers and skirts which expose the hip bone.

denim Cotton twill weave fabric of white and blue threads which originates from the French town of Nîmes, hence the origin of the word – *serge de Nîmes*. In the 20th century denim was used for workwear, being strong, durable and washable. By the 1940s, it was being made into fashion dresses, skirts, jackets and trousers. Denim reached the height of its popularity in the 1970s with the mass manufacture of JEANS, often with designer labels. *See also* STRAUSS.

department stores Until the early 19th century, clothes and accessories were sold in stores alongside other utilities. In 1838 the Englishman Emerson Muschamp Bainbridge opened a store in Newcastle upon Tyne with a draper, William Dunn, and by 1849 they had divided the store into thirty-two departments. Monsieur and Madame Boucicauts started the Paris department store Au Bon Marché in 1852. Department stores increased in popularity during the second half of the 19th century and during the 20th century they played an important part in the promotion of fashion. The New York store Bloomingdale's was one of the first to organize small fashion departments that enabled designers to show a restricted selection of clothes in a BOUTIQUE environment to a large number of people.

derby *See* BOWLER.

derby Shoe style similar to an OXFORD which ties with eyelets and laces. It has quarters and facings stitched onto the vamp.

Dessès, Jean 1904–70. Designer. Born Jean Dimitre Verginie in Alexandria, Egypt, of Greek parents. In 1925 Dessès abandoned his legal studies and began working for Maison Jane, a Parisian couture house. He opened his own establishment in 1937. After World War II he returned to Egypt and Greece. His designs in the 1940s and 1950s reflected the influences of his travels. He specialized in creating draped evening gowns in chiffon and mousseline based on early Greek and EGYPTIAN robes; embroidered dresses; and SHEATH dresses with tight jackets and flowing skirts. He was a popular designer with European royalty and movie stars. In 1949 he began producing ready-to-wear lines for the US market.

di Camarino, Roberta 1920–. Designer. Born Giuliana Coen Camerino in Venice, Italy. Finding refuge in Switzerland during World War II, di Camarino began making handbags. In 1945 she returned to Venice where she started a firm, 'Roberta di Camarino'. From striped velvet satchels and carved leather bags, di Camarino progressed to scarves, umbrellas, belts, shoes and gloves. She has also designed and produced fabrics and garments which are sold throughout the world under the 'Roberta di Camarino' label. Her innovative design ideas

Top: **Di Verdura** design for Chanel, c. 1930.
Above: Stylized bee brooch with coral body, 1960s.

put the spotlight on fashion accessories in the post-World War II years.

di Verdura, Fulco 1898–1978. Jeweler. Born Fulco Santostefano della Cerda, duke of Verdura, in Palermo, Sicily. Di Verdura went to Paris in 1927 and worked as a textile and jewelry designer for CHANEL. In 1937 he moved to New York, where he was employed by the jeweler Paul Flato, who soon put him in charge of his Californian branch. In 1939 Di Verdura opened his own shop in New York. He became associated with the revival of gold mounts, rather than platinum, and the promotion of baked enamel jewelry. He often worked in gold and produced a collection of small boxes. His great skill lay in mixing semiprecious and precious pieces in the same setting, the ideas for which he took from nature: shells, feathers, wings leaves, etc. Di Verdura also used classical motifs, such as tassels from coats of arms

Christian **Dior**'s famous 'Bar' suit, the keynote model of his controversial 'Corolle' collection of 1947, known always as the New Look. Photograph by Willy Maywald, 1947.

and mariners' knots. His twisted baroque pearls and his gold chains were highly prized. He is an influential jeweler, whose timeless designs have been a source of inspiration to others. He sold his business in 1973.

Diaghilev, Sergei 1872–1929. Ballet impresario. Born in Novgorod, Russia. After completing his studies in St Petersburg, Diaghilev founded a magazine entitled *Mir Iskusstra* ('The World of Art'). The preparation and organization of an exhibition of Russian art at the Salon d'Automne took him to Paris in 1906. In 1909 Diaghilev returned to Paris with the BALLETS RUSSES. Over the following years he intro-

duced to Europe the dancers Nijinsky, Pavlova and Rubinstein; the music of Stravinsky, Ravel and Prokofiev; the stage sets, designs and costumes of PICASSO, Derain, de Chirico, Matisse and BAKST; and the choreography of Balanchine.

diamanté Decoration on clothes, accessories and textiles consisting of diamond-like, glittering stones. Throughout the 20th century diamanté has been popular for evening wear.

Diana, Princess of Wales 1961–97. Born Lady Diana Frances Spencer in Northamptonshire, England. Before her engagement to the

The positioning of the buttons, and the trimming on collar and pockets add further crispness to the classic, streamlined look of this perfectly proportioned suit from **Dior**'s 1949 collection. Photograph by Willy Maywald, 1949.

Knife-pleated skirt in **Dior**'s 1951–52 collection. Note the controlled collar shape and the long darts that emphasize the bust and narrow waist. A large hat balances the width of the skirt. Photograph by Willy Maywald, 1951.

Prince of Wales, Lady Diana Spencer favoured ruffled blouses and simple dresses and skirts in plain or small floral prints. After her marriage in 1981 her style of dress was widely copied. The Princess of Wales was responsible for promoting low-heeled PUMPS, SAILOR COLLARS, ruffled collars, strapless evening gowns and hats. In the late 1980s and throughout the 1990s her style became increasingly elegant and sophisticated. In 1997 a collection of her dresses, both evening and cocktail wear, by various designers, was auctioned at Christie's, New York, raising more than 3 million dollars for charity. *See* ★EMANUEL.

Dior, Christian 1905–57. Designer. Born in Granville, Normandy, France. Dior abandoned his political science studies to take up music but instead spent his time running an art gallery and travelling, until 1935, when he began earning a living in Paris selling fashion sketches to newspapers. In 1938 he joined Robert PIGUET. He moved in 1942 to LELONG, where he worked alongside Pierre BALMAIN until cotton magnate Marcel Boussac offered him the opportunity to open his own couture house. Dior's first collec-

tion, in 1947, originally called the Corolle line, was nicknamed the NEW LOOK. New Look dresses had huge skirts which blossomed out from tiny waists, and stiffened, boned BODICES. Skirts were longer than in previous years, pleated, gathered, draped and panelled, often lined with tulle to create fullness. Hats were worn on the side of the head and often accompanied by a CHOKER necklace. In Dior's 1948 collection, ENVOL, skirts were scooped up at the back, worn with jackets that were cut with loose, fly-away backs and stand-up collars. The following year Dior showed slim skirts with a pleat at the back, strapless evening dresses, and bloused bodices and jackets. In 1950 skirts were shorter and jackets were large and box-shaped, some with HORSESHOE COLLARS. Over the following seven years Dior introduced his version of the COOLIE HAT, which was worn low over the eyes and trimmed with bows; and a popular PRINCESS LINE which gave the illusion of a high waist by employing curved shoulder lines on short jackets and by placing belts on the back of coats and jackets. His three-piece of 1952 – cardigan-jacket, simple top worn outside, and soft skirt made of crepe in pastel shades – influenced fashions for many years. Many of his collections featured three-quarter-length sleeves and stoles which remained popular throughout the 1950s. In 1953 he raised skirts again to a couple of inches below the knee and showed them with top-heavy BARREL-shaped coats and jackets. Dior spearheaded a revival of men's suiting in 1954, naming his collection that year the H-LINE. Hats were either closely cropped or huge CARTWHEELS. He made a white handkerchief-lawn jacket, softly pleated and bloused, the neckline filled in with white beads. The H-line was particularly suited to eveningwear. The *A-LINE and the Y-LINE, featuring large, V-shaped collars and giant stoles, followed in 1955. Many orientally inspired clothes became fashionable that year, including Dior's version of the CAFTAN and CHEONGSAM. He also achieved considerable success with a high-waisted, spaghetti-strapped chiffon dress and a long-length SHEATH. Dior's last collection, in 1957, was based on the VAREUSE, a garment with a stand-away collar, cut to hang loosely on

to the hips. He also showed khaki bush jackets with button-down flap pockets, a belted vareuse, Oriental TUNIC dresses, and a beltless CHEMISE DRESS with standaway collar and PATCH POCKETS. Dior favoured black, navy blue and white. He accessorized his clothes by pinning brooches to the neck, shoulder and waist. Ropes of pearls wound around the neck have been an extensively copied fashion since Dior introduced them in the 1950s. His undisputed elegance of line and sculptured structures have influenced decades of women and designers.

directoire Popular term for a high-waisted line. The *style directoire* is associated with the French directory period (1795–99), when French designers revived early Greek and Roman dress. The *directoire* dress has a long straight skirt, an exaggeratedly high waistline, low DECOLLETE, and small, tight PUFF SLEEVES. It was popular in the 1880s and 1900s and again in the 1960s. See EMPIRE LINE.

dirndl Full skirt loosely gathered into the waistband to create soft pleats. Originally part of PEASANT costume, dirndl skirts are thought to have originated in the Austrian Tyrol. The style has been popular since the 1940s. See also TYROLEAN COSTUME.

disco The emergence of discotheques in the 1960s prompted many extremes of style, but by the 1970s disco fashions had become acceptable for day as well as eveningwear. US designers, such as Stephen BURROWS, Betsey JOHNSON and Norma KAMALI, produced clothes which adapted to, or were designed for, disco dancing. These included leotards, T-shirts, shorts and stretch jeans, all of which allowed ease of movement. The US firm of DANSKIN sold numerous leotards with matching tights and contrast-colour WRAPAROUND skirts as disco-wear. Fabrics for dance clothes ranged from cotton, corduroy and denim, to suede and velvet. The addition of Spandex fibre to many fabrics increased their stretch capabilities. Eye-catching metallic accessories, RHINE-STONES and SEQUINS were popular, as were tropical print patterns, imitation snakeskin, football sweaters and bright silk shirts. The discos of the 1970s were showcases for extravagant, exotic fashions.

A **disco** hat from 1976, created by the British hat designer David Shilling.

Domenico Dolce and Stefano Gabbana have been powerful forces in Italian fashion since they showed their first collection, as **Dolce & Gabbana**, in 1985. Taking inspiration from Italian cinema, they create voluptuous, often body-hugging daywear and eveningwear. Both designs shown here are from their Spring/Summer 1990 collection.

divided skirt *See* CULOTTES *and* GAUCHOS.

djellabah Hooded CLOAK of Moroccan origin with long, wide sleeves, worn open at the neck and reaching to the knee or longer. It was originally made of cotton or wool and often trimmed with braid. During the 1960s and 1970s the djellabah shape was used by many designers as inspiration for coat and dress styles.

Doc Martens *See* BOOTS.

Doeuillet Couture house founded in Paris in 1900 by Georges Doeuillet who had trained with CALLOT SOEURS. After the death of Jacques DOUCET in 1929 the houses merged and Doeuillet continued to produce highly detailed dresses of elaborate design. The house closed in 1937.

dog collar *See* CHOKER.

dogstooth Cloth with even, broken checks woven into it. Popular since the late 19th century for outerwear, jackets, skirts and trousers.

Dolce & Gabbana Design firm. Domenico Dolce (b. 1958, near Palermo, Sicily) and Stefano Gabbana (b. 1962, Milan, Italy) formed a fashion consulting studio in 1982. Three years later, the pair showed their first major womenswear collection in Milan. Their earliest designs consisted of unstructured clothing with complicated systems for fastenings. By 1987, inspired by classic southern Italian cinema, they created a collection marked by romanticism and voluptuousness; the full skirts, ruffled blouses and lace shawls met with immediate success. Later collections included signature ideas such as CORSET dresses, gangster pinstripe TROUSER SUITS, floral embroidered coats, sexy black suits, EMPIRE LINE jackets and LEGGINGS. In 1991 MADONNA popularized their RHINESTONE-covered BODICE.

The **dolman**-style woman's coat of the 19th century. Usually three-quarter length with wide sleeves, it fitted over the bustle at the back.

Many of their designs are adapted from traditional women's clothing from a pre-feminist era, which they glamourize and modernize. During the 1990s they became one of Italy's most important and successful ready-to-wear companies.

Dolly Varden Style of dress popular from c.1870, named after the heroine of Charles Dickens's novel *Barnaby Rudge* (1841). The costume consisted of a flower-sprigged dress with a tight BODICE, panniered overskirt and BUSTLE, worn over a differently coloured underskirt. A large, drooping, flower-trimmed hat completed the outfit. *See also* WATTEAU.

dolman *1*. Man's long, coat-like garment originating in Turkey. The dolman was first adapted to a male fashion garment in the 18th century as a loose-sleeved robe. In the 19th century it was introduced in various forms for women. Worn as an outer garment, the dolman was often three-quarter-length, loose-sleeved, and fastened at the neck. It was straight in the front and fitted over the BUSTLE at the back. *2*. From the 20th century the word dolman describes any ankle-length wrap with long, generous sleeves, which is trimmed with lace, fringed and ruched. The dolman shape has been imitated as a coat, often made of cashmere, velvet, wool and PAISLEY-patterned fabrics.

dolman sleeve Cut as an extension of the BODICE of a dress, blouse or jacket, the dolman sleeve is designed without a socket for the shoulder, thus creating a deep, wide armhole that reaches from the waist to a narrowed wrist. This type of sleeve was popular during the 1930s. Also known as a batwing sleeve.

Donegal tweed Handspun tweed that originated from County Donegal in Ireland. In the 20th century the name applied to a variety of machine-made tweeds which have coloured slubs woven into the fabric.

donkey jacket Originally a workman's jacket, the donkey jacket is hip-length and cut with wide shoulders and long sleeves. Made of melton, serge or wool, it was first adapted to casual wear during the 1920s and became popular again in the 1950s. Some versions have leather patches sewn over the elbows and across the shoulders.

Donovan, Terence 1936–96. Photographer. Born in London, England. After a photographic apprenticeship and a stint as a military photographer, Donovan worked for John FRENCH. In 1957 he opened his own studio and over the following years his name became a familiar byline on the fashion pages and covers of many magazines in France and Britain. See QUANT.

Dorothée Bis Chain of stores opened in 1962 by Elie and Jacqueline Jacobson in Paris, and later in the USA. The stores sold adult versions of young girls' clothing: knee socks, peaked CAPS, CUT-OUT DRESSES and TROUSER SUITS. Jacqueline Jacobson also designed knitwear and the store became known for ribbed POOR-BOYS, crochet sweaters, and dresses that looked like very long hand-knitted sweaters. Most of the knitwear was teamed with woollen tights, crochet scarves and CLOCHE hats. See also KHANH.

dorothy bag HANDBAG named after a character of the same name in A. J. Munby's play, *Dorothy*, which was popular in England during the 1880s. A dorothy bag is a rectangular piece of fabric with a drawstring ribbon or chain at the neck which, when pulled, closes the bag, making a small frill. A popular style between the 1880s and the 1920s.

Doucet, Jacques 1853–1929. Designer. Born in Paris, France. Doucet inherited a lingerie shop from his grandparents before he was twenty. In 1875 he opened a couture house where he created extravagant gowns made of lace, mousseline, satin and silk. His TEA GOWNS, tailored suits and fur-lined coats were extremely popular. He was one of the best known and most highly respected couturiers of the late 19th and early 20th centuries. Actresses, socialites and royalty chose Doucet's salon both for his taste in fabrics and for the quality and workmanship of his clothes. He became famous for his delicate treatment of pastel colours and fabrics – particularly iridescent silks – and for his way of using fur as if it were a lighter, softer fabric. He took 17th- and 18th-century paintings, of which he was an avid collector, as inspiration for dresses and ball gowns. In the early part of the 20th century, Doucet embraced the movement to oust the rigid CORSET, but retained the quality and classical treatment of fabric in many of the models he produced. After his death the house merged with DOEUILLET.

drainpipe trousers Tight, narrow trousers which were first popular for men in the UK in the 1950s. Similar trousers were worn by women in the 1960s.

drawers Long, baggy knickers, originally on view below skirts, which by the early 19th century had become general items of underwear. Many styles opened at the back, others fastened at both front and back as almost separate sections. In most cases, the legs were loose fitting. Drawers were usually made of cotton and linen. As slimmer silhouettes became fashionable in the early 1900s, drawers were replaced by less voluminous garments, such as CAMIKNICKERS.

Drécoll Couture house founded in Vienna in 1902 by Christoff von Drécoll. Drécoll dressed the ladies of the Imperial Viennese court. He opened a branch in Paris which was run by Monsieur and Madame Besançon de Wagner. In 1929, the Besançon daughter, Maggy, took over with her husband, Pierre. In the same year, Drécoll merged with the house of BEER. In 1931, a further merger took place, with the house of Agnès, which had been established around 1906. Agnès-Drécoll closed its doors in 1963.

LA MARSEILLAISE

'La Marseillaise', an elegant illustration by the French artist Etienne **Drian**. This appeared in the *Gazette du bon ton* in 1915 and the colours used in the clothing reflect the patriotism of the period.

dress clip Fashion item which first appeared around 1930. It consisted of two jeweled clips attached to each side of a dress or blouse, just below the shoulders. Often made of DIA-MANTE, the dress clip remained an important accessory in the 1930s and 1940s, worn mostly on evening and COCKTAIL DRESSES.

dressing gown Garment which evolved from the PEIGNOIR in the early 19th century. The dressing gown – literally, a robe to put on between changes of dress or before dressing – was a loose, long-sleeved, coat-like gown, usually made of lightweight, luxurious fabric. In the course of the 20th century, dressing gowns were designed to be suitable for wear around the house, rather than just in the bedroom, and were made of heavier fabrics. Each decade produced designs in sympathy with prevailing trends, though the basic shape – ankle-length and long-sleeved – has rarely altered. A dressing gown wraps or ties at the waist or is buttoned

from the neck to the knee or ankle. *See also* HOUSECOAT, KIMONO *and* TEA GOWN.

Drian, Etienne 1890–1965. Illustrator. Born in Bulgneville, France. Drian worked in Paris between 1910 and the mid-1920s. His highly distinctive style illustrated the exclusive pages of the *GAZETTE DU BON TON*, *FEMINA* and other magazines. His figures are easily recognized by their extreme fluidity of movement.

drill Strong cotton fabric, similar to denim. Traditionally used in the USA as a fabric for workwear, it has been utilized since the 1940s as a fashion fabric for summer attire.

dry cleaning Process invented in 1849 by a French tailor, Monsieur Jolly-Bollin, who discovered the stain-removing qualities of turpentine. By the late 19th century, it was possible to clean complete garments rather than unpick and later resew stained sections, a method used by early cleaners.

Dryden, Helen 1887–1934. Illustrator. Born in Baltimore, Maryland, USA. Dryden studied at the Pennsylvania Academy of Fine Arts. She became well known in the early 1920s as a designer of magazine covers and articles, especially for *VOGUE*.

Du Pont Firm founded in 1802 by Eleuthère Irénée du Pont de Nemours (1771–1834) in Wilmington, Delaware, USA, to manufacture gunpowder. Du Pont's sons added a woollen mill and so began a textile business that was to pass through generations of the same family until the 1970s. In the 1920s the company acquired from France the licence to produce cellophane. This was followed by the acquisition of a further French invention, rayon. The American-based company has been extensively involved in the production of synthetic fibres since the early 20th century. *See also* CORFAM *and* NYLON.

duffle bag Sturdy, cylindrical canvas bag originally used by servicemen for carrying kit. Stout cord is threaded through metal eyelets and drawn together to seal the top. The duffle bag shape has been used in SHOULDER BAGS, made of various fabrics, from the 1970s.

'Tortoises', detail of a Raoul **Dufy** textile design for the textile company Bianchini-Férier, 1912–20.

duffle coat Short coat, with or without a hood, worn during World War II by men of the British Royal Navy. Cut to hip or knee length, the coat was made of a heavy woollen material and fastened with rod-shaped wooden TOGGLES that passed through rope or leather loops. Surplus duffle coats were sold to the public after World War II and became popular winter garments for both men and women. Restyled, they are also seen on fashion runways.

Dufy, Raoul 1877–1953. Artist. Born in Le Havre, France. Dufy left school at fourteen to work in a coffee importing company. In 1895 he started evening classes in drawing and painting at the Ecole Municipale des Beaux-Arts in Le Havre. In 1900, after a year's military service, he moved to the Beaux-Arts in Paris. Somewhat later Dufy came into contact with the Fauves, a group of artists who were devel-

oping a new painting style characterized by bold handling of strong colours. He held his first one-man show in 1906. During the following years Dufy's tone and use of colour became more subdued. Dufy worked closely with the decorative arts throughout his life. In 1911, with Paul POIRET, he became involved in the development of dye techniques and colour printing. Shortly after, he joined the French textile company BIANCHINI-FERIER as artistic director. Dufy designed silks and brocades in bold, often crude lines and strong colours. Many women who took no interest in his paintings wore clothes made from fabrics of his design or decorated their homes with his furnishing textiles. Dufy also designed sets for the theatre, opera and ballet. *See* FAUVISM.

Duncan, Isadora 1878–1927. Dancer, choreographer. Born in San Francisco, California,

The **duster** protected clothes from the ill-effects of motoring in the early 20th century.

USA. Duncan was interested in music, poetry and dance from an early age. In San Francisco, New York and Chicago, she scandalized audiences with her loose, flowing and often revealing Grecian-style robes and her improvised ballet pieces which she danced barefoot. In the early 1900s she left the USA for Europe and was eventually acclaimed in London, Paris and other European cities. Duncan established a school of dance near Berlin in 1904 and another in Moscow in 1921. Her constant travels throughout Europe helped popularize a general trend towards less restrictive clothing.

dungarees From the Hindi *dungri*, a coarse calico material. Dungarees were used by workmen in the early 20th century and adopted by women during both world wars. In the late 1940s and early 1950s denim dungarees became fashionable. Dungarees consist of trousers and a bib panel with shoulder straps. Various pockets and flaps have been added at different times, notably during the 1960s.

duster Long, lightweight coat, made of gabardine or wool, introduced during the late 19th century for motoring. The duster had long sleeves and a high collar and enveloped the body from the neck to the ankles.

Dynasty American television soap opera about the private lives of members of wealthy US oil families first seen in 1983. The actresses wore costly silk and satin tailored clothing, often styled in the manner of Hollywood costumes of the 1930s, though in keeping with 1980s fashion trends.

Edward VIII, shown in Sir William Orpen's portrait wearing a Fair Isle sweater, plus-fours, brogues and cap – all items of dress which he helped to popularize.

Women at an art gallery in 1902, dressed in typically elegant **Edwardian** style.

E

Edward VIII 1894–1972. Born Albert Christian George Andrew Patrick David in Richmond, Surrey, England. Edward was Prince of Wales from 1910 until 1936, when he became King Edward VIII. He abdicated the same year to marry in 1937 Mrs Wallis Simpson, and was given the title of Duke of Windsor. As a young man, the Prince of Wales was responsible for many male fashions. During the 1920s he promoted the wearing of suede shoes, PLUS FOURS, PANAMA HATS and Fair Isle sweaters. Trips he made to Paris in the 1930s inspired French designers to use the Prince's suiting material, known as Prince of Wales check, for womenswear. *See also* ★SAILOR SUIT.

Edwardian style The so-called Edwardian style of dress is associated with the period between the 1890s and 1910. Its silhouette is high-collared and long sleeved, with an ample bosom and a tightly fitted and boned waistline curving onto full hips. The bulk of the skirts are gathered onto the buttocks and flow behind and in front to reach the ankles. Skirts were enlarged with GODETS, and BUSTLES were worn to increase fullness. Some dresses, especially evening gowns, were worn off the shoulder. Hats were either small, floral affairs or enormous plumed versions. A PARASOL or small handbag was carried. The well-to-do Edwardian woman of the period was required to make many changes of dress during the day. Most of her clothes were made of sumptuous fabrics and heavily trimmed with lace and ribbons. Elaborate hatpins and jewelry, often PARURES, were also worn. In the 1970s a major revival of Edwardian fashion took place. Lacy blouses with high, frilly necklines were worn with long, full skirts and laced boots. CHOKERS and PASTE jewelry of the period were also popular, particularly the brooch pinned at the base of the throat. Laura ASHLEY was an exponent of this style of dressing. *See also* ALEXANDRA, QUEEN; BLOOMERS; *CLARK; GIBSON GIRL; MERRY WIDOW; *and* S-BEND.

Egyptian fashions Excavations in Egypt during the 1890s prompted a fashion for imitations of Egyptian dress, particularly headdresses and jewelry. The discovery of Tutankhamun's tomb in 1922 caused an escalation in fashions for draped, flowing dresses, fringes (bangs), HEADBANDS, and pyramid and scarab motifs.

Eisen, Mark 1960–. Designer. Born in Cape Town, South Africa. The son of a clothing manufacturer, Eisen studied business in the USA. While a student at the University of Southern California he designed a football helmet for the school which sold in its thousands. In 1988 he showed his first collection, consisting of carefully detailed denim suits bleached white and recoloured with special dyes. His trademark suit of a slim dress and tailored jacket was widely adopted. Eisen's silhouettes are narrow and abbreviated, often made from stretch fabrics which drape well. He uses electric, light-reflecting colours.

Eisenhower jacket Garment introduced during World War II and named after American Dwight Eisenhower who in 1943 became

The American sportswear designer Perry **Ellis** was initially known for his menswear. Here he adapts the man's suit to the female figure in a typically relaxed but stylish design for the 1980s.

Supreme Allied Commander in Western Europe and organized the D-Day invasion of France and the Allied landing in Normandy. The Eisenhower jacket was waist-length, belted, with a turn-down collar and sleeves that buttoned at the cuffs. The style has been popular for casual attire for both sexes since the 1940s. *See also* BATTLE JACKET *and* BOMBER JACKET.

elastic Fabric made from interwoven threads of indiarubber. By 1830 elastic panels had replaced the spiral metal bands which had earlier been used for CORSETS and underwear. Because of its flexibility, elastic has been used extensively since the 19th century in the manufacture of underwear, swimwear and exercise garments.

Ellis, Perry 1940–86. Designer. Born in Portsmouth, Virginia, USA. Ellis gained a BA in business studies at the College of William and Mary and then took an MA course in retailing at New York University. From 1963 to 1967 he worked as a buyer for the Miller Rhodes department store in Richmond, Virginia. In 1968 he joined John Meyer of Norwich, New York, as design director. Six years later he became SPORTSWEAR designer for the Vera companies, where, in 1978, he was given his own label. Ellis started his own company in 1980. His contemporary, classic menswear designs were already widely acclaimed in the USA, and he swiftly gained a reputation for crisply stylish women's coats, trousers and knitwear. Ellis's designs for women were spirited and graceful and he will be remembered as a quintessential American sportswear designer. Many of his clothes were cut on mannish lines but skilfully adapted for the female figure. He frequently used textured wools and tweeds.

Emanuel, David and **Elizabeth** Designers. David Emanuel 1953–. Born in Bridgend, Glamorgan, Wales. Elizabeth Weiner 1953–. Born in London, England. Emanuel and Weiner met at Harrow School of Art. In 1975, after their marriage, they entered the Royal College of Art and in 1977 showed their final-year collection. Demand for their designs was sufficient for them to open a salon in London immediately on leaving college. The Emanuels specialized in off-the-shoulder, bouffant-style eveningwear for the wholesale market. In 1979 they began designing couture clothes for women worldwide plus a ready-to-wear line. They became famous for their very feminine dresses and for their luxurious evening attire, particularly their ball gowns, which were generally full-skirted and made of lace, silk, taffeta, tulle and velvet. In 1981 DIANA, Princess of Wales (then Lady Diana Spencer), commissioned the Emanuels to design her wedding dress. In 1990 the Emanuels dissolved their partnership. *See* ★SAILOR COLLAR.

embroidery Ornamental needlework of coloured designs worked onto fabric. Embroidery has been used for centuries to decorate many items of womenswear. It was created by hand until the 20th century. *See also* FOLKLORIC *and* ★LESAGE.

empire line Low-cut dress gathered underneath the bust, popularized by Empress Josephine during the French Napoleonic

Sketch of the wedding dress for Lady Diana Spencer, for her marriage to the Prince of Wales, designed by David and Elizabeth **Emanuel** in 1981.

Embroidery has always been used to add luxury or colour to fabric. Here white embroidery enriches a court mantle of white velvet at the coronation of Nicholas II, Paris, 1896.

Empire (1804–14). The style is also known as the DIRECTOIRE or the *RECAMIER.

engageantes Washable half-sleeves that could be tied to the arm inside a bell-shaped or a PAGODA sleeve. They ended at the wrist in closed cuffs or open frills. Engageantes were worn from the mid- to the late 19th century.

envelope bag Rectangular HANDBAG of various sizes with a fastening panel shaped like an envelope flap. Like the CLUTCH BAG, it is strapless. A fashionable handbag shape during the 20th century.

Envol Name, meaning 'flight' or 'winged', given by Christian DIOR to his 1948 collection. Skirts were scooped at the back like a BUSTLE, or to one side, and worn with short jackets which had deep cuffs and standaway collars. Other jackets were flared into full shapes at the back and worn with straight, tubular skirts.

epaulet *1.* Shoulder strap on a military jacket or coat used as a means of keeping military accoutrements in place. It was also employed as decoration. Popular in the late 19th century, the epaulet also appeared on military-style jackets and coats throughout the 20th century, notably in the 1930s and 1960s.

éponge From the French for 'sponge', the term éponge refers to a group of fabrics that are spongy, porous and soft. Fabrics in this group, many of which are made of cotton, have been popular for beachwear and summerwear since the 1930s.

Eric 1891–1958. Illustrator. Born Carl Oscar August Erickson in Joliet, Illinois, USA, of Swedish parents. Eric attended Chicago's Academy of Arts for two years. He left around 1909 and worked for several years as a commercial artist and sign painter before moving to New York in 1914. In 1916 his first illustrations appeared in *VOGUE* and by 1925 he was a regular artist on the magazine, specializing in drawings of people in fashionable settings. During the 1920s Eric married and moved to Paris. His illustrations were lively, fluid and confident, in contrast with the flat, linear styles of the 1920s. In his fashion sketches, he stressed the

importance of detail. He continued working for *Vogue* until the 1950s.

Erté 1892–1990. Illustrator, designer. Born Romain de Tirtoff in St Petersburg, Russia. Erté (adapted from the French pronunciation of his initials, R. T.) studied painting in Russia before leaving for Paris in 1911. He was employed by Paul POIRET from 1913 to 1914 and also worked briefly with DIAGHILEV on theatre and ballet decor. From 1916 to 1926 he produced numerous covers for American *HARPER'S BAZAAR* and in the 1920s he worked in Paris and New York designing sets for the Folies-Bergère and the Ziegfeld Follies. He also created many costumes for Josephine BAKER. On a visit to Hollywood in 1925, he worked as a designer on several films. Erté's style was strongly influenced by 16th-century Persian and Indian miniatures. His drawings of the female form were curvilinear, expressive and highly stylized: elegant, often decadent, women, trailing furs, jewels and accessories, were subject to idiosyncratic motifs and precise detail. After World War II Erté continued to design costumes and decor for the opera, theatre and ballet.

espadrille Braided, corded or rope-soled shoe with a canvas upper which originates in Mediterranean countries, where it was mainly worn by fishermen. It became a popular summer shoe for women during the second half of the 20th century.

Esprit Design firm. Founded by American husband and wife team Susie Russell and Doug Tompkins (both b. 1943). Esprit de Corps was launched in 1968 out of the Plain Jane Dress Company which manufactured simply cut 1940s-style dresses. The firm took the name Esprit in 1972. The company's skilful marketing since the 1970s of its colourful, all-American sporty clothes, designed for a young age group, has made it a household name.

Estevez, Luis 1930–. Designer. Born in Havana, Cuba. Estevez was educated in the USA and then studied architecture in Havana. He attended the Traphagen School of Fashion in New York before leaving for Paris to work for two years for PATOU. In 1955 Estevez opened his own business in New York. He moved to California in 1968 and established himself as a designer of glamorous eveningwear, especially for the Eva Gabor collection. A line was produced under Estevez's own name in 1974. Since 1977 he has, once again, run his own company, specializing in an elegant, smooth, restrained style that epitomizes the West Coast of the USA.

ethnic Term used by fashion designers, stylists and writers to describe garments inspired by clothes indigenous to any non-Westernized peoples, particularly those of South America, Africa, the Middle and Far East, the Orient, the Pacific and countries with large peasant communities. Ethnic clothes can be simple and practical as well as skilfully made and elaborately decorated. Designers have found inspiration in both types. Since the 1960s, when people began to experiment with alternative lifestyles, fashion design has incorporated many images of other cultures into cut, pattern and decoration. The multicultural message is now firmly established in contemporary fashion.

Eton crop Short, straight hairstyle for women, with the hair cut well above the ears. It takes its name from the haircut of the boys of Eton College, the English public school. A popular style in the 1920s and 1930s. In later years a curl was extended onto the cheek.

Eton jacket Short, square BLAZER worn by boys at Eton College in England from the mid-19th until the early 20th century.

Eugénie, Empress 1826–1920. Born Eugenia Maria del Montijo in Granada, Spain. On her marriage to Napoleon III in 1853, Eugénie became Empress of France. In 1870 she was exiled to England. A fashion leader throughout her reign, she is generally associated with the popularization of the CRINOLINE in the 1850s. From 1860 WORTH created many of her gowns and these were eagerly copied by ladies of her own court and others throughout Europe. ADRIAN designed a hat, the 'Eugénie', named after the versions worn by the Empress. See *WINTERHALTER.

Eugénie hat See ADRIAN and EUGENIE.

In 1977 the US company Sears, Roebuck advertised the 4-piece vested suit, ideal for the **executive** woman.

executive During the 1970s, as more women took on highly paid jobs traditionally held by men, 'executive' dress for women became part of the general fashion picture, not restricted to working women. It consisted of tailored suits – skirts and jackets – often in pinstriped fabric, worn either with a man's shirt and tie or with a blouse and BOW TIE or knotted silk scarf at the neck. BLAZERS became popular for both day and eveningwear, worn not only as part of a tailored silhouette but also with full skirts or casual trousers.

F

Fabiani, Alberto dates unknown. Designer. Born in Tivoli, Italy. Fabiani went to Paris as an apprentice tailor at the age of eighteen, returning to Rome three years later to work in his family's retail clothing business. After five years he took over the business. During the 1950s Fabiani achieved international acclaim for his uncompromising but imaginative tailored suits and dresses. In 1953 he married rival designer SIMONETTA and during the 1960s they opened a house together in Paris – Simonetta e Fabiani. Fabiani returned after several years to Rome, where he resumed his career as a leading couturier and accessory designer until his retirement in the early 1970s.

Fabrice, Simon 1951–. Designer. Born in Haiti. Fabrice moved to New York with his family at the age of fourteen. After studying at the Fashion Institute of Technology, he became a fabric designer and in 1975 opened his own business. He quickly gained a reputation as a competent designer of luxurious and sexy eveningwear. His signature dresses are handpainted and frequently beaded.

faconné Faconné, the French word for figured, describes certain fabrics that have scattered motifs or patterns woven into the cloth.

faggoting Criss-crossed stitch used to make an open, decorative join between two edges of fabric, often the seam of a garment.

faille Light, soft, glossy silk or rayon cloth fabric with a cross-wise rib effect. Similar to grosgrain, but much softer, faille has been used since the mid-19th century for many women's garments, especially coats and dresses.

Fair Isle Multicoloured geometric design, named after Fair Isle, one of the Scottish Shetland Isles where it originated. On a sweater, the Fair Isle design is frequently confined to a band across the upper chest which often drapes around the neck from shoulder to shoulder. During the 1920s the Prince of Wales helped to popularize the Fair Isle sweater, which he wore to play golf. *See* ★EDWARD VIII *and* ★RONAY.

Fairchild, John 1927–. Publisher. Born in Newark, New Jersey, USA. After graduating from Princeton in 1949, Fairchild worked for two years in a research company before joining Fairchild Publications, founded by his grandfather Edmund Fairchild. He became a reporter for the clothing trade newspaper, WOMEN'S WEAR DAILY, in New York. In 1954 he was sent to Paris as head of the newspaper's French

Knitwear in the traditional **Fair Isle** design which originated in one of the Shetland Isles, Scotland.

bureau. Once there, Fairchild broke with traditional fashion journalism by filing gossip pieces along with fashion news, ignoring embargoes set by couture houses on publishing sketches ahead of the preset deadlines, and presenting his articles in a lively, informal and irreverent style. In 1960, Fairchild returned to New York and took over as publisher of *Women's Wear Daily*. He immediately gave space to first-rate fashion illustrators and continued to report both useful, factual trade stories and society news of charity events and parties. In 1965 he became chief executive of Fairchild Publications, resuming the role of publisher of *WWD* in 1971. In 1970 he launched a new paper, *W*, and later *M*, for the men and women he had named 'The Beautiful People'.

fan The folding fan came to Europe through Eastern trade in the late 15th or early 16th centuries. It reached the height of its popularity and elegance in the 18th century, when many fans were handpainted and depicted mythological and biblical figures as well as birds, animals and flowers in pastoral scenes. Printing superseded painting in the 19th century and many

In the 19th century many commemorative **fans** were issued. This fan is a souvenir of the Exposition Universelle, held in Paris in 1855.

commemorative fans were issued. Fans waned in popularity after the turn of the 20th century. They have been made from sandalwood, ivory, mother-of-pearl and TORTOISE-SHELL, and their sticks have been covered with FEATH-ERS, animal skins, silk, paper and lace. In the 18th century fans were used both during the day and in the evening, but by the second half of the 19th century their use was usually restricted to the evening.

Fath, Jacques 1912–54. Designer. Born in Maison-Lafitte, France. Fath worked as a book-keeper and broker at the Paris Bourse (Stock Exchange). In the early 1930s, after a year's mil-itary service, he spent several years in private study of costume and fashion design. In 1937 he opened a salon and swiftly gained a reputation as a leader of French fashion, though it was not until after World War II that his name became known worldwide. Fath was famous for his HOURGLASS shapes, plunging necklines, tiny waists and full skirts. To some extent an unsung hero of fashion, he anticipated in 1939 the style of dress which in 1947 became known in DIOR's hands as the NEW LOOK. In 1948 he visited the USA and designed a ready-to-wear line. Throughout his career, Fath was a popular designer in America, where his lighthearted and witty clothes were welcomed. His

garments were almost without exception creat-ed on soft lines with curving, simple, structured shapes. Credit is also given to Fath for intro-ducing stockings with Chantilly lace tops.

Fauvism Art movement of the early 1900s, generally associated with the 1905 Salon d'Au-tomne in Paris and the work of a group of artists including Henri Matisse and André Derain. Their brightly coloured distorted shapes in flat, two-dimensional patterns prompted a critic to name them *Les Fauves* (the wild beasts). Fauvist use of colour had a considerable impact on both fashion and textile design.

feathers The widespread use of feathers in late-19th-century fashion created a worldwide demand. Many species became extinct as plumage hunters plundered sources in the USA, Burma, Malaya, Indonesia, China, Australia and Europe. The American Ornithologists' Union, founded in 1883, estimated that 5 million birds were killed each year to supply feathers for fash-ion items such as fans, hats and muffs. The most popular feathers came from the egret. These were used extensively for AIGRETTES and in millinery.

fedora Soft, felt hat from the Austrian Tyrol which has a tapered crown with a centre crease,

Coats in chartreuse Mongolian lamb from **Fendi**'s haute-couture collection of Autumn/Winter 1984–85.

a pinched front and a snap brim. It was named after *Fédora*, a play by the French dramatist Victorien Sardou shown in Paris in 1882. Women began to wear fedoras towards the end of the 19th century, especially for sporting activities. Fedoras were popular for men from the same period until the 1950s. *See also* HOMBURG.

felt Nonwoven fabric made by matting or bonding fibres such as cotton, fur, rayon and wool. Traditionally used to make hats and serving during the 19th century as a lining, felt became popular in the 1950s made up into coats and CIRCULAR SKIRTS, which were often decorated with APPLIQUE motifs.

Fémina Fashion review first published in 1901. It was published intermittently and also as *Femina et vie heureuse réunis* until 1956. Some of the most celebrated artists, illustrators and, in the years following World War II, photographers, contributed to the magazine.

Fendi Company founded in 1918 by Adele Fendi (1897–1978) which has been run since 1954 by her five daughters, their husbands and their children. The sisters are Paola (born 1931), Anna (born 1933), Franca (born 1935), Carla (born 1937) and Alda (born 1940). The company produced soft leather handbags and summer bags made of woven strips of binding canvas. In 1962 Karl LAGERFELD was employed to design furs and four years later Fendi began showing fur collections to international buyers. The company's major contributions to fashion lie in its pioneering techniques of fur cutting, it use of dyed furs and its high quality workmanship. Lagerfeld is responsible for attracting international attention to the company with his innovative designs such as a denim coat lined with fur, and a double 'F' logo. The company also produces a successful line of accessories which capitalize on its name.

Feraud, Louis 1921–. Designer. Born in Arles, France. Feraud was active in the French Resistance. In 1949 he established a house in Cannes which was patronized by many movie stars visiting the festival. He subsequently became a costume designer before moving in 1960 to Paris, where he opened a ready-to-wear business. A practising painter, Feraud has been inspired by the art of other cultures, notably those of South America. There is a sensitive use of colour in his designs which, since the 1960s have become increasingly classical.

Ferragamo, Salvatore 1898–1960. Shoe designer. Born in Bonito, near Naples, Italy. Ferragamo was apprenticed as a shoemaker from the ages of nine to fourteen. When he was sixteen he joined his brothers in California, where he made shoes by hand for the American Film Company. This led to private commissions from actors and actresses. During the 1920s he designed roman SANDALS with laces which tied around the ankles. In 1923 he went to Hollywood to work for the film studios of Warner Bros, Universal and Metro-Goldwyn-Mayer. He returned to Italy in 1927 and set up a workshop in Florence with approximately sixty workers – the first large-scale production of hand-made shoes. Clients from all over the world came to Ferragamo. He claimed to have originated the wedge heel (in 1938), PLATFORM SOLES and metal support in high heels. The shortage of leather during the war led Ferragamo to experiment with unconventional alternatives, including cork, cellophane, raffia and manila hemp. He also made shoes from lace, needlework, snailshells, raw silk, webbing, taffeta and nylon. In 1947 he invented the 'invisible shoe', made with uppers of clear nylon and a black suede heel. Though he was no slave to fashion, Ferragamo was responsible for innovations and designs that were well in advance of contemporary styles. By 1957 he had created more than 20,000 styles and registered 350 patents.

Four shoes from the master shoe designer **Ferragamo**.

Below: Ferragamo's famous 'invisible' shoe of 1947 created with nylon threads set a vogue which has been observed in almost every decade since, particularly in the 1970s. The kid-covered heel is known as the 'F' shape.

Top right: Shoe with patchwork upper in square suede pieces with oval toe and wedge heel covered with strips of various coloured suedes, 1942–44.

Right: 'Calipso' black satin sling-back sandal with suede reinforcement, metal buckle and brass 'cage' high stiletto heel, 1955–56.

Bottom right: Sandal with upper of padded gold kid straps and platform sole and heel in cork layers covered with various coloured suedes, 1938.

Ferre, Gianfranco 1944–. Designer. Born in Legnano, Italy. Ferre qualified as an architect in Milan in 1967, but turned instead to designing jewelry for Walter ALBINI. Established as a freelance designer since 1970, Ferre completed jewelry commissions for LAGERFELD and FIORUCCI. By the mid-1970s he was designing SPORTSWEAR and outerwear. Since the establishment of his own house in 1978, he has emerged as one of the most talented Italian designers of ready-to-wear clothes. His garments are usually graphically created in strong shapes and bright colours. Highly sensitive to form and outline, Ferre shows collections that bear the hallmarks of one whose early training was in the careful study of detail, in analysis and in planning. His intellectual approach to design produces powerful and controlled clothes which are often folded and layered to create his precise statements. Dubbed the 'Frank Lloyd Wright of Italian fashion', Ferre became noted for his expert use of stark colours, especially red, black, white and gold, and his extravagant use of luxurious fabrics such as fur, leather and taffeta. Between 1986 and 1988 he launched a couture collection and in 1989 was appointed artistic director of DIOR. He left Dior in 1996 to head up his own house.

Feuillets d'art, Les Luxurious arts review published from 1919 to 1922. Although planned as a twice-monthly publication, its appearance was irregular. It consisted of a wallet containing plates covering fashion and the arts. Contributors included BARBIER, Robert Bonfils, DRIAN, MARTY and LEPAPE.

fichu 1. Small scarf or SHAWL worn draped around the shoulders and fastened with a brooch at the breast. 2. Ruffle or piece of fabric, often lace, which is sewn across the bosom of a blouse or dress.

Figueroa, Bernard 1961–. Shoe designer. Born in Montpellier, France. Figueroa studied at the Studio Berçot, an avant-garde fashion school in Paris. For a student show he created sculpted metal-heeled shoes detailed by abstract musical notes, fish and foliage. These brought him to the attention of Thierry MUGLER, who commissioned shoes for his own collections. Figueroa worked for Christian DIOR and Claude

Fichu in tulle and cream-coloured lace, fastened with a flower brooch. From *La Mode universelle*, 16 June 1876.

MONTANA before moving to Boston, Massachusetts, to work for the American company Rockport, a manufacturer of upscale walking shoes. Two years later Figueroa moved to New York and, in 1992, launched his own made-to-order couture shoe line which included hand-sculpted heels, often architecturally formed in shapes reminiscent of tree branches, or plated in 22-carat gold or mother of pearl. His pale suede GHILLIES have cutouts in the instep and his MULES are made with wire mesh that moulds to the foot.

Fiorucci, Elio 1935–. Designer. Born in Milan, Italy. Fiorucci inherited a shoe store from his father in 1962. In the mid-1960s he began travelling to London to bring MINI SKIRTS and other fashionable garments back to his shop in Milan. In 1967 he opened a larger store, selling clothes from London's youth-oriented designers. Fiorucci became world famous in the mid-1970s. A constant traveller, he collected ideas and items which he passed on to a team of designers. Fiorucci stores opened throughout the world, each cleverly designed so that merchandising, packaging and display all reflected the company's image. The garments in the stores were fresh, new and often amusing: plastic galoshes in bright colours, JELLIES, electronic accessories, computer graffiti

T-shirts, *platforms, fluorescent socks and scarves. Fiorucci captured the spirit of the moment for a mainly young market, recycling old ideas in new ways. His tightly cut, streamlined jeans of the 1970s were in great demand.

Fisher, Harrison 1875–1934. Illustrator. Born in New York, USA. Fisher was taught by his father, landscape painter Hugh Antoine Fisher. At the age of sixteen, after studying at the Mark Hopkins Institute of Art in San Francisco, Fisher began selling his illustrations. He became well-known for his graceful drawings of mobile and animated young women, notably on the covers of the fashion magazine *Cosmopolitan*.

fishnet Large, open-weave knit associated in the 20th century with STOCKINGS and TIGHTS. It became popular in the 1960s and was revived as part of PUNK dress in the late 1970s and early 1980s.

flannel Generic term which covers many woollen fabrics woven in different weights of worsted. The term includes man-made fibres. Flannel is usually soft and made of a plain or twilled weave slightly napped on one side. In the 19th century it was often used to make petticoats. During the 20th century various weights of flannel were used for underwear, outerwear, jackets, dresses, skirts and trousers.

flannelette Soft cotton fabric that is slightly napped on one side. It has been used since the late 19th century for underwear, nightwear and children's clothes.

flapper Term used in the early 1900s to describe a young girl who had yet to become a debutante. By the 1920s it meant any young woman who cut her hair short, wore CLOCHE hats and later BERETS, a short skirt and blouse, stockings rolled at the knees, and heeled – usually T-BAR – shoes. She was commonly thought of then, as now, as a rather dizzy young thing who spent her time dancing the CHARLESTON.

flea market clothes Clothes bought at flea markets are invariably old and usually inexpensive compared to new ready-to-wear garments, though the late-20th-century vogue for antique items increased prices. Shopping at flea markets

for clothes of the 1900s to 1940s and, more recently, of the 1950s, became popular in Europe and the USA during the early 1970s when prevailing fashions included an EDWARDIAN revival and many styles based on ETHNIC and FOLKLORIC costumes.

flounce Strip of material that is gathered and sewn onto the hem of a garment, usually a skirt. The flounce can be of the same fabric as the garment or of a different material. Flounces have adorned dresses and skirts, particularly eveningwear, throughout the 19th and 20th centuries.

flying suit See JUMPSUIT.

Fogarty, Anne 1919–80. Designer. Born Anne Whitney in Pittsburgh, Pennsylvania, USA. Fogarty became interested in costume design while studying drama at the Carnegie Institute of Technology in Pittsburgh. She transferred to East Hartman School of Design in 1939 and shortly afterwards moved to New York to work as a copywriter and fitting model. In 1948 she joined the Youth Guild, where she adapted the postwar NEW LOOK of narrow waist, full skirt and fitted bodice to the American teenage market. In 1950 she moved to Margot Dresses where she designed junior-size coats, hats, shoes, jewelry and lingerie, while continuing to employ her 'paper doll' silhouette of fitted bodice and waist over a full skirt for day and evening. Fogarty's ballet-length cotton dresses featured skirts held away from the body by layers of stiffened petticoats made of nylon net. In 1957, Fogarty began designing for Saks Fifth Avenue and five years later opened her own business. She added new silhouettes to her line: a tea-cosy dress in which a full skirt fell from a dropped waist, a narrow EMPIRE silhouette with a full skirt, and many blouses and skirts with ruffles. She was one of the first American designers to produce BIKINIS. In 1970 she closed her business but continued to design on a freelance basis.

folkloric Style of dress associated with PEASANT costume. The influence of Russian costume on fashion started at the end of World War I, by which time large numbers of Russian émigrés had settled in Paris. Russian and

An exhibition in London in 1985 stimulated a great deal of renewed interest in the clothes of **Fortuny**, worn here in a contemporary, off-the-shoulder style.

Bulgarian embroidery patterns were used to decorate garments. In the 1930s DIRNDL skirts became popular and East European embroidery – usually simple, bright shapes of flowers, plants and leaves – enjoyed a revival. During the 1960s and 1970s peasant-inspired fashions became fashionable once more, as part of the ETHNIC vogue of that period. *See* RUSSIAN, SAINT LAURENT *and* TYROLEAN COSTUME.

Fontana Italian fashion house founded in Rome in 1943 by three sisters, Zoe (1911–78), Micol (1913–) and Giovanna (1915–). In the 1950s the house of Fontana became known for its glamorous and theatrical clothing, particularly eveningwear and lace wedding dresses. The house continues with a strong accessory line but it is always associated with its successful curvaceous styles of the 1950s and 1960s.

Gold pendant designed in 1899 by Georges **Fouquet**, who worked mainly in the Art Nouveau style. Fouquet's jewelry often included coloured gemstones, such as these cabochon rubies and pendant cabochon sapphires.

Fortuny, Mariano 1871–1949. Textile and dress designer. Born Mariano Fortuny y Madrazo in Granada, Spain. Fortuny studied painting and drawing in Spain before spending periods in France and also in Germany, where he learned about chemistry and dyes. In 1889 he settled in Venice, taking photographs, painting, sculpting, and making etchings and drawings. Fascinated by the effects of diffused light, he created stage sets for the theatre and opera. In the late 1890s, Fortuny began to print textiles. Taking inspiration from the velvets and brocades of the Italian 15th and 16th centuries, tapestries from the East, and Grecian robes, he created pleated gowns and cloaks which he dyed with vegetable dyes. Although made of silk, they resembled rich velvets. Between 1901 and 1934 he registered more than twenty inventions in Paris for stage lighting systems and textile printing processes. His 'Knossos' scarf of 1906 was inspired by Cycladic art. It was a rectangular silk VEIL which could be used in a number of ways, tied around the body or worn as a decoration with the 'Delphos' gown, a cylindrically shaped, loose-fitting silk satin garment which undulated with rich colour, created by a special pleating process which Fortuny patented in 1909. The Delphos gown was sleeveless or had DOLMAN SLEEVES, and could be tied about the waist with a silk cord. All Fortuny's dresses emphasized the female form in movement. Isadora DUNCAN was one of his most famous clients. Fortuny adapted most forms of ETHNIC dress into lavish, exotic garments: the Japanese KIMONO, North African BURNOUS and DJELLABAH, Indian SARI and Turkish DOLMAN. He was famous for his printed patterns and often took vegetables as motifs. Many of Fortuny's gowns and veils were weighted with delicate Murano beads, which also served as trimming. After his death, the Fortuny process was bought by Countess Gozzi, who, as Elsie McNeill, had earlier helped Fortuny to market his furnishing fabric in the USA. A mixture of artist and couturier, Fortuny had an enlightened view of dress design, combining colour and texture with cut in a manner so unique that it has earned him one of the crowns of fashion.

Fouquet, Georges 1862–1957. Jeweler. Born in Paris, France. Son of a French jeweler, Alphonse Fouquet (1828–1911). Fouquet joined his father's firm in 1891. He specialized in ART NOUVEAU jewelry, particularly pieces designed by Alphonse MUCHA. Fouquet also created some neoclassical pieces.

fourreau style *See* PRINCESS LINE.

fox Soft, glossy, luxuriant, long fur of an animal found in most of the world's cool climates, particularly Scandinavia and Canada. Since the early 20th century, most fox fur has been ranched. Fox is distinguished by its long underfur. It can be beige, blue, brown, red, silver or white. Different colours have been popular at different times, but the fur itself is seldom out of fashion.

Fox, Frederick 1931–. Milliner. Born in New South Wales, Australia. Fox trained as a milliner for nine years in Sydney before leaving in 1958 for London. He worked with the milliners Longee in Brook Street until he opened his own business in the mid-1960s. Fox became the favourite milliner of a number of designers, including Hardy AMIES and John BATES. He has an international clientele and

A floating, frilly bridal design from Gina **Fratini** for Spring/Summer 1978.

has created hats for Queen Elizabeth and other members of the British royal family.

Fratini, Gina 1934–. Designer. Born Georgina Butler in Kobe, Japan, of English parents. Fratini enrolled at the Royal College of Art Fashion School in London in 1950. After graduation she spent two years travelling with the Katherine Dunham Dance Company of California, designing scenery and costumes. Back in England, she established her own business and produced her first collection in 1966. A widely influential designer at the start of her career, she set her own style and remained faithful to it. Some of her first garments were SMOCKS and long, velvet PINAFORES. She followed these with gauze and chiffon dresses, all totally in keeping with the 1970s. Her signature garment is the floating, frilly tulle, silk and lace dress. She designs romantic evening gowns and lighthearted, easy daywear.

Frederics, John See MR JOHN.

French, John 1907–66. Photographer. Born in London, England. French attended Hornsey School of Art from 1926 to 1927 and then spent a brief period with a block-making firm and in a commercial art studio before leaving London in 1930 to study painting in Italy. He returned after six years and found employment as a freelance illustrator for the English newspaper, the *Daily Express*. In the same year he began work as an art director for a photographic studio, Carlton Artists. After World War II French returned to Carlton Artists, only to establish his own company and photographic studio in London two years later. He worked for major newspapers, magazines, designers and advertising agencies throughout the 1950s. French became famous for his clear, stylish, uncluttered black and white photographs taken against clean backgrounds. He strongly influenced many younger photographers who worked with him.

frill Narrow ruffle gathered to the edge of a neckline, armhole, cuff or hem.

Frissell, Toni 1907–88. Photographer. Born Antoinette Frissell in New York, USA. Working as a caption writer on American *VOGUE* in 1930, Frissell was encouraged by Editor Carmel SNOW to experiment with photography. A year later Frissell's fashion pictures began to appear in magazines such as *Vogue* and *Town and Country*, and she was soon placed under contract at *Vogue* to cover the fashion pages and take on general assignments. In 1947 she moved to *HARPER'S BAZAAR*. Frissell's casual, lively pictures reflected her own active, sporty life. She shot fashion outdoors in natural settings – an avant-garde approach at a time when models were usually carefully posed in a studio. Frissell was also an avid traveller, a war correspondent and a portrait photographer specializing in children. See PUCCI.

Frizon, Maud 1941–. Shoe designer. Born in Paris, France. Frizon worked for many years as a model in Paris and was a particular favourite of COURRÈGES. In 1970 she launched her first shoe collection, in which each pair of shoes was hand-cut and finished. She was an overnight success. Frizon designs elegant, highly sophisticated and often witty shoes in unusual combinations: lizard and snake, suede and satin, canvas and crocodile. Her name is associated

Models disembarking, prior to a **fur** fashion show by the British furrier Calman Links, 1966.

with the promotion of the cone heel. She has designed shoes for ALAIA, MISSONI, MONTANA, MUGLER and RYKIEL.

frock coat The 19th-century frock coat was adapted from a military coat, and became formal dress for men. It appeared in various forms but was basically a long-sleeved, knee-length garment with pleats, collar, REVERS, buttoning and back VENTS. It was full-skirted for brief periods during the 19th century. The basic coat was used as a foundation for many styles of women's coats during the 20th century.

frogging Decorative braid fastening which loops over buttons or a braid TOGGLE. Originally used on military uniforms, frogging fastenings have adorned women's coats and jackets since the 19th century. See ANNA KARENINA.

fun fur Since the 1960s, imitation fur coats have become the fashionable alternative to the real thing. They are made from a variety of fibres that often include mixtures of acrylic, modacrylic and polyester. Imitation fur has two advantages over real fur: it can be dyed bold, brilliant 'fun' colours, and it is relatively cheap.

fur Fur became fashionable in the 19th century, reaching the peak of its popularity in the 1890s and early 1900s. Sealskin was the first popular fur and was used for capes and fitted jackets and later for coats. Many other furs have been used over the years, depending on availability and fashion trends. Fur has been used for coats, jackets, hats, muffs, stoles and TIPPETS as well as for trimming on dresses and evening gowns. The animal rights movements of the late 20th century made fur much less popular, particularly in Europe. See also ASTRAKHAN, CHINCHILLA, *FENDI, FOX, KARACUL, MINK, RACCOON, SABLE, SEAL and SQUIRREL.

furbelow Term dating from the 19th century which describes a trimming, originally of fur, usually at the hem of a skirt.

G

gabardine *1.* Clear-surfaced, twill weave fabric with a fine diagonal rib effect. Gabardine can be made in a variety of weights from natural and synthetic fibres. It has been used since the 19th century for suits, coats, dresses, skirts and trousers. *2.* A registered tradename. *See* BURBERRY.

Gabbana, Stefano *See* DOLCE & GABBANA.

Galanos, James 1924–. Designer. Born in Philadelphia, Pennsylvania, USA. After graduating from the Traphagen School of Fashion in New York, Galanos sold fashion sketches to several New York designers. In 1944 he moved to Columbia Studios in California as an assistant to Jean LOUIS. In 1947 he took up a one-year apprenticeship in Paris with PIGUET, returning to New York as a ready-to-wear designer. In 1951 he was back in California and three years later showed his first collection in Los Angeles. He swiftly gained a reputation among US women for his precisely executed and clever clothes. Galanos was acclaimed for the cut of his dresses, suits and coats, made up in European fabrics, but he was patronized mostly for his eveningwear and COCKTAIL DRESSES. In the 1950s he was one of the first designers to show the HORSESHOE NECKLINE on suits and to pioneer bold prints for after-six garments. During the 1960s and 1970s he created slimline, classically draped evening dresses with billowing sleeves. Galanos frequently works with chiffon, printed silks, velvets, brocades and hand-painted silks and laces. He has used wool for eveningwear and is known for low-backed, black wool crepe dresses.

Galitzine, Princess Irene *c.*1916–. Designer. Born in Tiflis, Russia. The Princess's family fled to Rome during the Russian Revolution. After studying languages and art, she joined the FONTANA sisters, for whom she worked for three years. Towards the end of the 1940s she opened her own house. Her first collection was shown in 1959 but it was not until the following year that she achieved her greatest success with the launch of her 'Palazzo PYJAMAS' –

The 1964 version of Princess **Galitzine**'s famous palazzo pyjamas.

wide-legged evening pyjamas made of soft silk. Evening pyjamas became a firm fixture of the fashion scene during the 1960s. Princess Galitzine was also noted for her eveningwear, especially dinner suits and open-sided gowns. The house closed in 1968.

Galliano, John 1960–. Designer. Born in Gibraltar. Galliano graduated from St Martin's School of Art, London. While still a student he devised a way of making a sleeve by spiral cutting. His final year show, in 1984, called 'Les Incroyables', was influenced by the exaggerated clothing of 18th-century France. The collection was purchased by a London store, subsequently sold out, and earned Galliano his first investor. One of the most highly inventive and original designers of the late 20th century, Galliano prefers his designs to be historically based. His thematic collections, with titles such as 'Afghanistan Repudiates Western Ideals', 'Fallen Angels', 'Forgotten Innocents', 'Olivia the Filibuster' and 'Princess Lucretia', have a tremendous sense of romance and whimsical

Above: **Galliano**, Autumn/Winter 1985–86.

Above: Galliano, Summer 1994.

Below: Galliano for Dior 'C', Summer 1997.

Below: Galliano for Dior 'C', Autumn/Winter 1997–98.

charm coupled with precision tailoring and bias-cutting. His clothes are often shocking. Who would expect, in the late 20th century, 19th century CRINOLINES to appear on the catwalk? – but the way they are constructed, the fabrics, textures and colours, are up to date and often visionary in context. Galliano knows no boundaries. From the Highlands of Scotland to the Russian steppes, from thirties-style sleek evening gowns, to KILTS, tulle ball gowns, farthingales, FROCK COATS, HOURGLASS SILHOUETTES and 1940s gangster garb, he raids history for ideas. His interpretation is unique, with a highly defined sense of the theatrical, derivative but not copyist, and his technical skills are thoroughly modern. In 1986 he created a scissor dress cut to cross in front of the body to form a BASQUE at the hip. In 1988 he created a disappearing lapel on a jacket, followed by an L-shaped skirt and a 'winking' seam which opens at intervals to expose flesh. Many of his designs are seen in diluted form in the collections of other designers. In 1995 Galliano was appointed as head designer for GIVENCHY's couture and ready-to-wear collections but left in 1996 to take over the house of DIOR.

gamine French for tomboy or street urchin. In a fashion context the word gamine has two meanings. The gamine 'look' is exemplified by Audrey HEPBURN and Zizi JEANMAIRE. Both had short haircuts that framed their elfin faces. The gamine style of dress is understood to mean an outfit comprising a sleeveless PULLOVER, cardigan, KNICKERBOCKERS, tweed CAP and long muffler or scarf. François Truffaut's film *Jules et Jim* (1962) created a vogue for this style.

Gap, The Clothing manufacturer and retailer, established in California, USA, in 1969. Founded by a real estate dealer and named after 'the generation gap', the first Gap store opened in San Francisco and sold denim jeans, jackets and shirts. By the mid-1990s The Gap had evolved into one of the most successful retailers in the history of fashion, with stores worldwide. Its key elements are casual, relaxed, reasonably priced, colour-coordinated clothing that appeals to both men and women between the ages of twenty and fifty. Wardrobe basics such as jeans, trousers, sweaters, T-SHIRTS and jackets continue to be offered in popular colours.

Before the introduction of suspenders, stockings were held up by **garters**. These were often ornate in design and were sometimes trimmed with lace or ribbon. This 1930s example was made of metal.

Garbo, Greta 1905–1990. Actress. Born Greta Gustafsson in Stockholm, Sweden. Garbo attended the Royal Dramatic Theatre training school in Stockholm. She made several films in 1923 and 1924 before moving in the following year to the USA, where she was engaged by Louis B. Mayer for the Metro-Goldwyn-Mayer studios. Between then and 1941, when she renounced the cinema, Garbo starred in many films, including *Queen Christina* (1933), *Anna Karenina* (1935), *Camille* (1937) and *Ninotchka* (1939).Her shoulder-length hairstyle was widely copied and she created a fashion for SLOUCH HATS and TRENCHCOATS. *See* ADRIAN.

garçonne *La Garçonne* was the title of a novel by Victor Margueritte, published in 1922. It was considered at the time to be extremely risqué, describing as it did the relaxed sexual mores of a Sorbonne student who had an illegitimate child. The heroine, who cuts her hair short and wears a shirt, TIE, jacket and other mannish clothes, became a symbol of the liberated, active modern women. The garçonne style came to be identified with a boyish silhouette, short hair and little make-up.

garibaldi Shirt/blouse worn by women in the early 1860s, named after the Italian soldier and patriot Giuseppe Garibaldi. The garibaldi was a scarlet blouse made of merino or muslin and worn with a black silk skirt. Black braid was sewn onto the narrow collar. Some versions had full sleeves that were gathered at the wrist; other 'red shirts', as they were known, were worn beneath the dress BODICE, revealing only the sleeves. It was fashionable to complete the look by banding the hem of a skirt with scarlet fabric. *See also* ZOUAVE JACKET.

garter Band of decorated elastic worn around the thigh to hold STOCKINGS in position. The introduction in the 1880s of the SUSPENDER BELT (US: garter belt) signalled the decline of the garter, though it continued to be worn until the 1930s.

gather Fabric drawn together by threads to create fullness.

gaucho pants Trousers adapted from the wide-bottomed, mid-calf divided skirts worn by the South American cowboy. SAINT LAURENT popularized gauchos in the 1960s, when they were worn with BOOTS, shirts and wide belts with large silver buckles. *See also* CULOTTES.

Gaultier, Jean-Paul 1952–. Designer. Born in Paris, France. Gaultier first sketched ideas for collections at the age of fourteen. When he was seventeen he dispatched his sketches to several major designers and was invited by Pierre CARDIN to join his company for one year. Gaultier then worked for Jacques Esterel, Jean PATOU and, in 1974, for Cardin's manufacturing operation in the Philippines before starting his own firm in 1977. Since that time he has become one of the most influential young French ready-to-wear designers. His clothes are humorous, showy and extremely clever – a mixture of tomboy zest and film star glamour. Gaultier successfully mixes old and new in fabrics and cuts. He has produced SWEATSHIRTS trimmed with lace and satin, upside-down Eiffel Towers as heels for shoes, and bracelets which resemble tin cans. Fun-loving and witty, Gaultier's designs challenge many ideas of dress without offending. In the early 1980s he had several strong seasons, showing various plaids

Above: Sketch by Jean-Paul **Gaultier** for a 'boneless' dress. Women, Spring/Summer 1993.

Below: Jean-Paul **Gaultier**, Women, Autumn/Winter 1984–85.

Three sketches by Jean-Paul **Gaultier** from his 1990s collections.
Above: Men and Women, Spring/Summer 1991;
above left: Men, Autumn/Winter 1996–97;
below left: Women, Spring/Summer 1994.

worn together and cut-away T-SHIRTS, worn loosely over each other, leaving parts of the arms and shoulders exposed. Both these and other Gaultier looks have their origins in the London STREET STYLES of the late 1970s, in PUNK style and FLEA-MARKET dressing. One of his most significant contributions to fashion is the focus he placed on the bustline in the 1980s. Gaultier liberated the outmoded CORSET as an undergarment and recreated it as outerwear. His designs, reminiscent of the sweater girls of the 1950s, were interpreted as power dressing eveningwear, especially when worn by pop star MADONNA on her world tours during the late 1980s and early 1990s. Gaultier's seemingly kitsch designs are always underlined by his technical knowledge and skills.

gauntlets GLOVES with close-fitting hands and long, wide arms reaching almost to the elbow.

Medieval-style gauntlets, made in soft suede and leather that fell in folds over the wrists, were popular during the 1920s and 1930s.

gauze Thin, open-weave, transparent fabric which has been used for trimming since the 19th century.

Gazette du bon ton Witty, sophisticated arts and fashion magazine founded in 1912 by Lucien VOGEL. It contained fashion illustrations printed by the *pochoir* method, a very time-consuming and expensive process in which the images were created by building up hand-painted gouaches with metal stencils. This method produced plates in brilliant colours. The magazine was published monthly until 1915, and then irregularly until 1925, when it was bought by Condé NAST and merged with VOGUE. The *Gazette du bon ton* attracted some of the best artists of the time: BARBIER, BAKST, BENITO, BOUTET DE MONVEL, *DRIAN, IRIBE, *LEPAPE, MARTY and MARTIN, all of whom illustrated articles and produced clear, stylish fashion plates of garments in anecdotal settings.

Genny Italian ready-to-wear company founded in 1961 by Arnoldo and Donatella Girombelli. Since the 1970s the company has consistently produced quality tailored clothing of high fashion status under the lines of Genny, Genny Due, BYBLOS and Complice, the latter line being designed by DOLCE & GABBANA. In the past, designers such as Guy PAULIN, Gianni VERSACE and Claude MONTANA have worked for one or the other of these internationally known lines.

georgette Silk or rayon fabric, similar to chiffon, which is used for eveningwear. A crepe version has a dull-textured surface.

Gernreich, Rudi 1922–85. Designer. Born Rudolph Gernreich in Vienna, Austria. Gernreich's father was a hosiery manufacturer and his aunt kept a dress shop in which Gernreich worked as a teenager. In 1938, with numerous other refugees, Gernreich fled to California. He attended the Los Angeles City College from 1938 to 1941 and then spent a year at the Los Angeles Art Centre School. For the next six years he worked with a dance troupe as a dancer

The arts and fashion magazine *Gazette du bon ton* was a showcase for some of the most talented illustrators of the early 20th century. This 1913 illustration of a Redfern outfit, entitled 'De la Pomme aux lèvres' (From Apple to Lips), is by Charles Martin.

Bathing suit designed by Rudi **Gernreich** in 1965, worn with a visor and thigh-high ciré boots.

Evening dress from the British design house **Ghost**, Autumn/Winter 1994.

Bill **Gibb** favoured exotic, floating fabrics, as shown by this ultra-feminine dress for 1977.

and costume designer. In 1948 he became a freelance fashion designer until, in 1951, he formed a partnership with manufacturer Walter Bass to supply clothes to Jax, a Los Angeles BOUTIQUE. Some years later he opened his own company, G. R. Designs Inc., which became Rudi Gernreich Inc. in 1964. In the 1960s Gernreich proved to be a competent and innovative designer of SPORTSWEAR for a predominantly young market. He made SHIRT-WAIST dresses in luxurious fabrics, reversible cape coats, and swimsuits without inner foundations. His best known fashion contributions are the TOPLESS BATHING SUIT, with straps from a high waistband at the front to the back, which was introduced in 1964 to a scandalized world; the 'no-bra bra', made of moulded nylon cups attached to shoulder straps and a narrow elastic band encircling the rib cage; the 'no-sides bra', which was cut low in front with deep armholes to be worn with deep DECOLLETE evening dresses; the 'no-front

bra', with a sculptured front for dresses which were slit to the waist; and the 'no-back bra', which was anchored about the waist instead of the rib cage. In 1964 CORSET manufacturers WARNER BROS CO commissioned Gernreich to design a BODYSTOCKING, made up in flesh-coloured stretch nylon.

ghillie Originally a Scottish heeled dancing shoe popularized by EDWARD VIII when he was Prince of Wales. It had laces which criss-crossed through loops of leather on the vamp. During the 1950s, the name was given to flat SANDALS with criss-cross laces.

Ghost British company founded in 1985 by Tanya Sarne. The Ghost label produces loose, flowing separates that can be added to each season. Made from woven viscose yarns, the clothes are designed before dyeing and are cut larger to allow for the shrinkage process. The result is a vintage crepe-type fabric. Many of the clothes have elasticated waists. Long waistcoats, trousers with wide and narrow legs, TUNICS and A-LINE skirts are all popular Ghost pieces.

Gibb, Bill 1943–88. Designer. Born in Fraserburgh, Scotland. Gibb studied at St Martin's School of Art and the Royal College of Art in London. He sold an early collection to Henri Bendel's New York store and left the RCA in 1968 before completing his course. After three years with Baccarat he struck out on his own in 1972 and opened a retail business three years later. Gibb was highly acclaimed in the 1970s, famous particularly for his eveningwear: floating chiffon dresses and supple jersey dresses adorned with APPLIQUE and embroidery. In 1974 he produced a knitwear collection which became highly successful. Despite his considerable design talents and his skill in handling lavish and exotic fabrics, Gibb was forced for financial reasons to close his firm in the late 1970s. *See* ★KILT.

Gibson, Charles Dana 1867–1944. Illustrator. Born in Roxbury, Massachusetts, USA. Gibson studied at the Art Students League in New York from 1884 to 1885. He worked first with silhouettes before turning to pen and ink drawings which he sold in 1886 to the humorous weekly *Life*. Five years later Gibson's drawings were the paper's star attraction. From 1886 to 1889 he worked for the weekly *Tid-Bits* (which became *Time*), *Collier's Weekly*, *Harper's Monthly*, HARPER'S BAZAAR, *Scribner's* and many other publications. From 1890, Gibson chronicled the lives of his fellow Americans through his patriotic, romantic, and often satirical, drawings. He was most famous for his ★GIBSON GIRL.

Gibson Girl Character created by Charles Dana GIBSON, who appeared in his pen and ink drawings from 1890 until 1910. The 'Gibson Girl' was tall, slender and poised, her hair piled into a CHIGNON or tucked under a plumed hat. She wore a starched blouse and long, flowing skirts over a small BUSTLE. She represented the modern, active woman and was shown in some illustrations wearing shorter skirts, especially when she was cycling or engaged in other sporting activities. The Gibson Girl image was appropriated by manufacturers of CORSETS, skirts, shoes and household items. She inspired the song 'Why Do They Call Me a Gibson Girl?', from the musical *The Belle of Mayfair* (1906), and the revue *The Gibson Bathing Girl*,

The famous **Gibson Girl,** representing the modern woman, created by Charles Dana Gibson in 1890.

which was performed by the Ziegfeld Follies (1907). In Britain she was personified by the American actress Camille Clifford, who first appeared on the London stage in 1904, and in the USA by Irene Langhorne, who married Gibson in 1895.

Gigli, Romeo 1951–. Designer. Born in Bologna, Italy. Gigli studied architecture for a short period. From his first collection in 1984, he brought a new look to Italian fashion, replacing its tailored, colourful traditions with a subtle colour range and fluid garments which would be widely influential. Often made of stretch fabrics, his clothes gently drape the body in a classical sense, but are thoroughly modern in treatment: in the manner and angles at which they fasten or attach, or in their unexpected, exaggerated shapes. Gigli's womenswear designs are essentially romantic. His velvet and embroidered capes and boleros, and his wrapped tops and skirts, were highly successful during the mid-1980s. His palette is subdued but deeply vibrant and ultimately highly sophisticated.

gigot sleeve *See* LEG-OF-MUTTON SLEEVE.

gilet Sleeveless garment with a blouse, shirt or BODICE front, worn over blouses and dresses since the 19th century. *See* WAISTCOAT.

gingham From the Malayan *ginggang*, 'striped'. A light- or medium-weight fabric originally made of linen and later of cotton. Gingham is woven from predyed yarns into checks of various sizes. It was a popular fabric for summer dresses during the 19th century and became fashionable in the 1940s and 1950s for dresses, blouses, skirts, PLAYSUITS and BIKINIS. *See* BARDOT.

Girbaud, François and **Marithé** Design team. François Girbaud (b. 1945 in Mazamet, France). Marithé Bachellerie (b. 1942 in Lyon, France). The couple met in Paris in the mid-1960s and in 1969 opened a BOUTIQUE selling American-style jeans of their own design. In 1970 they sold BELL BOTTOMS made of denim, and in the 1970s set a style for both stone-washed jeans and baggy jeans. Many of their ideas found their way into the hands of other designers.

girdle Boneless, lightweight, elastic CORSET introduced during the 1920s. It encased the hips and stomach, often with elastic side panels, supporting STOCKINGS with a SUSPENDER BELT (US: garter belt). The girdle became progressively lighter in weight, especially during the 1930s. During the second half of the 20th century, the girdle was largely replaced by the ROLL-ON, as women rejected rigid corsetry which could not be worn under trousers. Since the late 1960s women have favoured a more natural look, which has in its turn made the roll-on unfashionable. *See* CORSET, GAULTIER *and* MADONNA.

Givenchy, Hubert de 1927–. Designer. Born in Beauvais, France. Givenchy attended the Ecole des Beaux-Arts in Paris and briefly studied law. He worked for FATH from 1945 to 1949. He was then employed by SCHIAPARELLI until he opened his own business in 1952. Givenchy's collection contained many garments made of men's shirting and included the *BETTINA BLOUSE. He is thought by many to have taken over BALENCIAGA's mantle in producing elegant, often formal, clothes and high-style ball gowns and evening dresses. The two designers met in 1953 and Balenciaga shared with Givenchy the sketches and drawings of his atelier. Each designer had a desire to express a

purity of line rather than decoration and a consistent perfection. Many of Givenchy's ideas were ahead of his time. He designed an evening dress with a BODICE that could be removed and worn with a straight skirt or trousers. During the 1950s he exaggerated the CHEMISE (SACK) shape into a kite outline, wide at the top and tapered toward the hem. The clothes he created for actress Audrey HEPBURN were enormously influential and are still used as a source of inspiration for many designers, in particular the outfits she wore in the 1954 movie *Sabrina*. The short, sculpted tops showed off Hepburn's shoulders, and the BATEAU neckline and cropped sleeves are still copied today. Hepburn wore Givenchy's clothes for years off and on screen. Givenchy was favoured by many other internationally prominent women. In 1988 he sold his firm but continued to head up the company until 1996, when he retired from couture. *See* GALLIANO.

Glamour Originally *Glamour of Hollywood*, a monthly magazine that offered patterns to its readers when it was first published in 1939 by Condé NAST. It became *Glamour* during the 1940s and the patterns were dropped. *Glamour* caters to the twenty-five to forty-five age group and covers fashion, beauty, the home, travel and general features of interest to women.

gloves Since early times gloves have been made from pliable fabrics to follow the contour of the hand. During the 19th century they were worn for both day and evening and were an essential part of dress. Numerous styles were popular, including fingerless MITTENS, short and long leather and kid gloves, and gloves with leather hands and lace arms. Gloves were also made from embroidered silk, cotton, net and knitted silk, and were fastened by tiny buttons at the wrist. In the 20th century, with the exception of long evening gloves, gloves became utilitarian items. By the end of the 1950s they were rarely seen, except in cold weather or as high fashion accessories, and had ceased to be a symbol of status and wealth. Fingerless mittens became fashionable in the late 1970s and early 1980s.

godet Piece of fabric of triangular shape, wider at the bottom than at the top, which is sewn

Like his mentor, Cristobal Balenciaga, the French designer Hubert de **Givenchy** created clothes of supreme elegance and simplicity. He shunned decoration, preferring to concentrate on purity of line. These cocktail dresses are from his collections of 1957 *(above and top)* and 1958 *(top right)*.

into a skirt, dress or coat to increase fullness. Godets have been used in dressmaking since the 19th century.

Goma, Michel 1932–. Designer. Born in Montpellier, France. Goma studied dressmaking and art. At the age of nineteen he moved to Paris where he sold his fashion sketches. From 1950 to 1958 he worked for Lafaurie and eventually bought the company, renaming it Michel Goma. He closed down in 1963 and joined PATOU, where he worked for ten years before becoming a freelance designer.

Gordon, Lady Duff *See* LUCILE.

gore Flared panel sewn into skirts to increase their width. Gored skirts were popular during the 19th century. Exaggerated gores, with pointed ends near the waist and fullness at the hem, became fashionable during the 1930s.

Goût du jour, Le Fashion and arts review published in Paris from 1920 to 1922. It contained the work of notable illustrators of the period, including BENITO and MARTY.

granny style Style of dress popular during the late 1960s and early 1970s. 'Granny clothes' included collarless 'grandfather' shirts; *SHAWLS; long, full skirts; small round-rimmed spectacles; and either thick-heeled, round-toed shoes or high, laced *BOOTS.

Greco, Juliette 1927–. Singer. Born in Montpellier, France. Greco has been involved with the French theatre as both singer and dramatist since 1942. She became known to the fashion world in the 1940s when she created a vogue for long, straight hair, black clothes, and a loosely tied raincoat worn with the collar turned up.

Greenaway, Kate 1846–1901. Book illustrator, painter. Born in London, England. Greenaway illustrated children's books from the 1870s to the 1890s, notably *Under the Window* (1879). The clothes in her illustrations were reminiscent of 18th-century costume. The picturesque manner in which Greenaway detailed garments such as BONNETS, SMOCKS and EMPIRE-LINE dresses with frilled necks and sleeves inspired many designers, dressmakers and fashion trends in the late 19th century.

Greer, Howard 1886–1974. Costume designer. Born in Nebraska, USA. Greer left the University of Nebraska in 1916 and joined the fashion house of LUCILE in New York. After World War I he worked in Paris for Lucile,

MOLYNEUX and POIRET. He returned to New York in 1921 and designed costumes for the Greenwich Village Follies. In 1923 he joined Paramount Pictures in Hollywood. Over the next five years Greer created costumes for many films. In 1927 he opened a couture shop but continued to work freelance for movie companies. He was known for his glamorous, sophisticated evening gowns and dresses. He retired in 1962.

Grès, Madame 1903–93. Designer. Born Germaine Emilie Krebs in Paris, France. Frustrated in her ambition to become a sculptor, Grès began her design career by making TOILES, which she sold to major Paris fashion houses. She also worked for the Edwardian house of PREMET. In 1934 she opened her own establishment as Alix Barton. She reopened her house in Paris in 1942, during the German occupation of France, under the name Grès. Grès' designs were individual and uncompromising and brought her an international reputation as a classicist. She draped and moulded jersey, silk and wool – her favourite fabrics – until the dresses resembled Greek sculptures. Many of her loose coats and simple dresses were constructed with deceptive detail. Her famous evening gowns were often the result of hours of work, with fabric pleated into precise configurations to achieve an elegant simplicity. Although she influenced many designers, no one equalled her particular mastery of draping

Kate **Greenaway**'s illustrations in the late 19th century influenced fashions both of her own time and since.

fabric in this manner. Grès often used asymmetric shapes, BIAS CUTS and DOLMAN SLEEVES. Her clothes excelled in independence and quality. She sold her business in 1986 and retired in 1987. The house of Grès continues under the designer Frédéric Molenac.

gretchen neckline Low-cut, round, gathered neckline based on a PEASANT blouse, introduced during the 1920s. It was a popular style on both dresses and blouses.

Griffe, Jacques 1917–. Designer. Born in Carcassonne, France. Griffe trained with a tailor for several years in his home town and while still a teenager went to Toulouse to extend his apprenticeship with a couturier. In 1936, after completing his military service, he joined VIONNET in Paris. Here he learned to drape and cut material on small wooden dummies in the Vionnet tradition. After World War II Griffe worked briefly for MOLYNEUX before opening his own couture and ready-to-wear business in 1946. He was a craftsman at cutting and draping, and his clothes were fluid and soft. He retired in the 1960s.

Grima, Andrew 1921–. Jewelry designer. Born in Rome, Italy. In 1946 Grima established a company in London to manufacture traditional pieces of jewelry. During the 1960s he began to design contemporary jewelry and in 1966 opened a shop in Jermyn Street, London, where he specialized in creating gold pieces adorned with quartz, tourmaline and citrine stones. He received a Royal Warrant in 1970.

Grimm, Gerd 1911–. Illustrator. Born in Baden, Germany. Grimm was educated at the arts school in Karlsruhe and at an industrial arts school in Nüremberg. In the 1920s he published his first advertising work and shortly after was asked to join the staff of the magazine *Die Dame*. Throughout the Nazi regime, Grimm lived in France and Italy. In 1950 he emigrated to the USA, but a decade later returned to Baden. Grimm's work as a prominent advertising and editorial illustrator spans many years. His unusual perspectives, set in eye-catching colour and arrangement, reflect a joyous sensitivity to fashion.

A large, square-cut citrine is surrounded by gold and diamonds in one of Andrew **Grima**'s designs.

Andrew **Grima**'s tourmaline and diamond clip of yellow gold.

grosgrain Closely woven, heavily ribbed fabric, usually made of silk, which originated in the Middle Ages. It has been used since the 1920s for millinery.

Gruau, René 1909–. Illustrator. Born Renato de Zavagli in Rimini, Italy. While still a teenager, Gruau made fashion sketches which were accepted by German, French and Italian magazines. Professional by the age of eighteen, he moved in 1924 to Paris where he worked for more than twenty years. From 1947 Gruau illustrated advertisements for DIOR perfumes. His bold, rhythmic, colourful drawings of, among others, modish women are still relevant today. His style ranges from open-faced, friendly women who look as if they enjoy wearing fashionable clothes to elegant, seductive creatures who wear their garments with an air of mystery. Gruau is one of the few artists whose design career successfully spanned five decades. See *BALMAIN.

grunge Style of dress which evolved from the 'street' culture of thriftstore clothing and vagabond living in the early 1990s. 'Grunge' spread quickly from teenagers and rock bands to the fashion runways. Its mismatched clothing – often of torn, and over- or obviously undersized items – inspired many designers who adapted the scale and odd pairings to their own lines. Although short-lived, grunge had plenty of shock-value. It has been linked to the DECONSTRUCTIONISTS, but whereas these designers dismantled clothing to explore it and reassemble it in a different way, grunge was more concerned with making a political, anti-consumerist, anti-fashion statement.

G-string *1.* Single strip of cloth worn between the legs which is kept on by means of a cord around the waist or hips. *2.* The scantiest version of the BIKINI, first seen in Europe during the 1950s.

Gucci When the family millinery business failed in 1906, Guccio Gucci started a saddlery shop in Florence, Italy. He was succeeded by his sons and grandsons. Taking traditional leather accessories, the company redesigned them using equestrian motifs. A successful DUFFLE BAG was launched in 1925. In 1932 the famous MOCCASIN shoe with the tongue caught in a gilt bit became popular. In the 1950s the Gucci double-G intertwined trademark was firmly established as a status favourite. From the mid-1960s Gucci became increasingly involved in the sale of handbags, belts and shoes, many bearing stirrup or bit designs. By the 1970s the house of Gucci was no longer at the accessory fashion front and the company restructured and eventually sold out. It was purchased by an investment firm in 1993 and one year later the American designer Tom Ford was hired as design director.

guêpière *See* WASPIE.

The ultimate in status symbols: crocodile oxford (left) and crocodile loafer by the house of **Gucci**, 1988.

guernsey Probably derived from 'gansey', a worsted yarn used to make a shirt-like garment worn by fishermen in the Channel Islands. In the late 19th century the word guernsey came to be identified with a CREWNECK SWEATER worn by fishermen on Guernsey and Jersey. Usually made of dark blue wool, the guernsey became associated with casual wear during the second half of the 20th century.

Guirlande, La Fashion, art and literary review published monthly in Paris from 1919 to 1920 which contained illustrations by artists such as George BARBIER and Umberto BRUNELLESCHI.

gusset Small triangular or diamond-shaped piece of fabric which is inserted in the seams of a garment to increase strength and facilitate movement.

gypsy Style of dress comprising full, flounced skirts and blouses with low-cut, often elasticated, necklines, usually made of lightweight and brightly coloured fabrics. Scarves wound around the neck or waist are a dominant feature of gypsy-style dress. In 1959 Jules-François

CRAHAY produced a gypsy collection and in the early 1970s Thea *PORTER and Caroline *CHARLES created dresses and two-piece outfits based on gypsy costume.

H

hacking jacket Fitted, single-breasted jacket which is flared from the waist and has a single back VENT. It has been worn since the 19th century for riding and was adapted as a fashion garment during the latter half of the 20th century.

Halston 1932–90. Designer. Born Roy Halston Frowick in Des Moines, Iowa, USA. Halston attended the University of Indiana and the Chicago Institute. In 1953 he opened a millinery salon in a Chicago hotel, where his clients included Gloria Swanson and Deborah Kerr. In 1958, he joined Lilly DACHÉ in New York, moving shortly after to the millinery salon of Bergdorf Goodman's New York department store. Halston designed many hats for Jacqueline Kennedy (ONASSIS), including a beige felt PILLBOX that was widely copied. In 1966 he began designing ready-to-wear garments, leaving Bergdorf Goodman to open his own business. During the late 1960s and 1970s Halston established a reputation as a designer of knitwear, sweaters and wide-legged jersey trousers, TURTLENECKS, long slinky HALTER-NECK dresses, cashmere dresses for day and evening, sweater sets, and boxy, square jackets and coats. He also TIE-DYED chiffon and used matte jersey in many of his collections. In 1972 he made a SHIRTWAISTER of Ultrasuede, which inspired many imitations. American socialites patronized him as an eveningwear designer. *See* ONASSIS.

halter neck High panel on the front of a dress or blouse which is tied around the nape of the neck, leaving the back and shoulders exposed. The halter neck was popular during the 1930s for evening and beach attire. *See* HALSTON.

Hamnett, Katharine 1948–. Designer. Born in Gravesend, Kent, England. Hamnett attended St Martin's School of Art in London. She graduated in 1970 and increased her freelance

A quintessential **Halston** design from 1972 : silk jersey halter-neck jumpsuit and suede coat.

design commissions working for British, French, Italian and Hong Kong firms. In 1979 she established her own business. Many of her garments were based on the workwear of different countries which she adapted to fashionable clothing. A supporter of the peace movement, she produced in 1984 oversize T-SHIRTS printed with anti-war slogans. These will always be remembered as her major contribution to fashion. She also uses her clothing designs to create public awareness of both environmental and political issues.

handbag (US: purse) Bag which is carried in the hand, of any shape, size or fabric, according to fashion trends, with flat or rounded sides, zip or clasp fastenings on top, GUSSETs inside, and pockets outside and in. The first handbags were the RETICULES of the 18th and 19th centuries. By the mid-1850s travel created a demand for bags which could be carried by hand and which were roomy and strong enough to hold personal effects. Towards the end of the century, small, flat POCKETBOOKS, designed to fit into a coat pocket, became fashionable, followed by oversize bags which were the subject of much derision. The flowing fashions of the early 20th century left little or no room for bulky items to be carried about the person and since that time handbags have been an important fashion accessory. Every decade has seen recurring fashions in shape and style, and the design of handbags, in common with that of other accessories, has been influenced by art movements such as CUBISM and SURREALISM. Shoulder bags became popular after World War II, and from the 1960s photographer's bags, airline bags and tote bags came into use as handbags. The 1970s and 1980s saw fashions for satchels, DUFFLE BAGS and imitations of the classic, doctor's Gladstone bag. In the 1990s the BACKPACK was introduced as a fashion bag.

handkerchief A highly fashionable accessory during the 19th century, the handkerchief was an embroidered, lace-edged square of cambric, linen, muslin or silk. Subsequently, its purpose has generally been a functional one, though there are vogues in almost every decade for a decorative handkerchief tucked into the breast pocket of a coat or jacket.

handkerchief points Zigzag hem of a skirt or dress composed of deep V points similar to one of the corners of a HANDKERCHIEF. A periodically popular style during the 20th century, notably in the late 1960s and early 1970s.

Handley-Seymour, Mrs Dressmaker who founded a business in London shortly before World War I. She received a Royal Warrant and was extremely popular during the 1920s and 1930s. Queen Mary was her most famous client.

haori Loose, knee-length, long-sleeved coat originating in Japan. The shape has been adapted to various fashion trends during the 20th century.

Hardwick, Cathy 1933–. Designer. Born Cathaline Kaesuk Sur in Seoul, Korea. Hardwick studied music in Korea and Japan before emigrating to the USA in the early 1950s. She opened a BOUTIQUE in San Francisco and worked as a freelance designer before moving to New York in 1972 and opening her own business. Hardwick designs adventurous, middle-range, ready-to-wear clothing which often fuses elements of East and West. Traditional Korean clothing has inspired many of her simple shapes. She is especially noted for her creative handling of silk.

Perfect for the tango, deep bordered **handkerchief dresses** of *c*. 1910 like this one allowed women to move freely without showing too much leg.

Harem pants were all the rage in the 1930s. This version has a cuffed and buttoned ankle

harem pants/skirt Full, ankle-length divided skirt or trousers, pleated or gathered into a band at the ankle. Based on the trousers worn by Turkish women, harem pants first became popular when the BALLETS RUSSES performed in Europe in the early 1900s. They were worn as eveningwear in the early 20th century, reaching the height of their popularity in the 1930s.

Haring, Keith 1962–90. Artist. Born in Kutztown, Pennsylvania. Haring spent two years at Manhattan's School of Visual Arts. In December 1980 he started to draw groups of small white figures on billboards in Manhattan subway stations. The figures, which resembled the outlines of cookie-cutters, attracted so much attention that in the early 1980s Haring began to use them on T-SHIRTS, buttons and garments. Clothes painted with Haring's figures soon became collectors' items.

Harp, Holly 1939–95. Designer. Born in Buffalo, New York, USA. Harp studied art and costume design at North Texas State University and after graduating opened a BOUTIQUE in Los Angeles in 1968. Her collections were sold at the New York department store Henri Bendel in 1972. The following year she began manufacturing her own clothes. Harp was known for her theatrical, nostalgic creations of handprinted silk and matte jersey, and her ultra-soft fabrics. Many of her flowing designs had a romantic appeal.

Harper's Bazaar In 1867 Fletcher Harper of the US publishers Harper Brothers launched *Harper's Bazar*, a women's magazine covering the home and fashion. It was published weekly until 1901, when it became monthly. In 1913 *Harper's Bazar* was bought by the Hearst publishing empire and in 1929 the second 'a' was added to 'Bazar'. A widely influential magazine, never more so than when under the editorship of Carmel SNOW, *Harper's Bazaar* promoted fashion design, photography and illustration. It was in direct competition with American *VOGUE* for most of the 20th century.

Harris tweed Soft, thick tweed originally handloomed from woollen yarns dyed with vegetable dye by the inhabitants of the Scottish Outer Hebrides Islands of Barra, Harris, Lewis

Norman **Hartnell**'s historic coronation dress for Queen Elizabeth II, embroidered with the emblems of Great Britain and the Commonwealth.

and Uist. The tweed was exported to the mainland during the 1840s and since that time has been used to make coats, jackets and suits for both men and women.

Hartnell, Norman 1901–79. Designer. Born in London, England. After leaving Cambridge University without a degree, Hartnell began designing clothes. In 1923 he worked briefly with LUCILE before opening his own premises in London. He showed his first collection in Paris in 1927, followed by a second, highly acclaimed, collection in 1930. He was appointed dressmaker to the British royal family in 1938 and designed gowns for their overseas visits. Hartnell made clothes for the Queen Mother as well as Queen Elizabeth II's wedding and going-away dress and, in 1953, her Coronation gown. He also created dresses for many actresses. Hartnell gained a reputation for his imaginative use of satin, tulle, embroidery and trimmings on evening gowns, ball gowns and wedding dresses. He was also known for his tailored suits, coats and woollen tweed garments. From 1942, Hartnell produced ready-to-wear lines and he designed for Berketex from the late 1940s. Between 1990 and 1992, Marc BOHAN directed the firm.

haute couture The French word 'couture' means sewing or needlework. 'Haute couture' is high quality fashion design and construction. The designer or couturier creates models from a TOILE, made in fine linen or muslin, which bears his or her name. Garments based on the *toile* are then made to measure for clients. A union of dress designers, the Chambre Syndicale de la Confection et de la Couture pour Dames et Fillettes, was founded in Paris in 1868 to prevent designs being plagiarized. In 1910 the Chambre Syndicale de la Couture Parisienne – couturiers separate from the original guilds that comprised the earlier organization – showed their collections together to promote French fashion overseas. After World War II, in 1945, the Chambre created a travelling exhibition of clothes, the Théâtre de la Mode, in an attempt to reestablish Paris as the fashion capital of the world. Fifty-three houses participated in this exhibition. The Chambre, which is part of the Fédération Française de la Couture du Prêt-à-Porter des Couturiers et des Créateurs de Mode, is also known as the Chambre Syndicale de la Couture, and the Chambre Syndicale de la Haute Couture. The organization dictates that couture houses must employ at least twenty people in their workshops and present at least fifty original designs to the Press in Paris during the Spring/Summer season collections (shown in January) and the Autumn/Winter season collections (shown in July). The designs presented are either made up for clients by the respective houses or sold as paper or linen patterns to authorized buyers. Haute couture relies heavily on a group of specialists, who make buttons, gloves, costume jewelry, millinery and trimmings to a high level of workmanship. It is labour-intensive and costly. In 1946 there were 106 couture houses. By 1997 this number had fallen to eighteen couture houses, with five associated houses. Couture houses grant manufacturers the right to use their name on clothing and accessory items. *See* READY-TO-WEAR.

Hawaiian shirt Man's oversized shirt printed with brightly coloured designs of fruit, flowers, exotic birds and dancing girls. Hawaiian shirts were made popular by US tourists returning from Hawaii in the 1950s. Also known as an aloha shirt.

Hawes, Elizabeth 1903–71. Designer. Born in New Jersey, USA. Hawes studied at Vassar College and at Parsons School of Design in New York. In 1925 she went to Paris where she worked for several years as a sketcher at fashion shows. Macy's and Lord & Taylor, the New York department stores, appointed her their Paris based stylist. In 1928 she returned to New York and opened her own business. Hawes's clothes were simple and soft, and followed natural proportions. She became well known with the publication of her first book, *Fashion Is Spinach* (1938).

Head, Edith 1899–1981. Costume designer. Born in Los Angeles, California, USA. Head graduated from Stanford University and the University of California, and then continued her studies at the Otis Institute and Chouinard Art School in Los Angeles. In 1923 she worked for Howard GREER at Paramount Pictures in Hollywood. After a spell as Travis BANTON's assistant in 1927, she was made head designer of the studio in 1938, a position she held until 1967. In the late 1960s she worked for Universal Films. During her time at Paramount, Head also designed for films made by Metro-Goldwyn-Mayer, Columbia, 20th Century-Fox and Warner Bros. She has more than one thousand screen credits to her name. Mae West, Marlene Dietrich, Elizabeth Taylor and Grace Kelly are among the actresses for whom she designed. In 1936 Head's SARONG for Dorothy LAMOUR in *The Jungle Princess* was widely copied. In 1951 she created a strapless evening dress with a fitted BODICE covered with white violets and a skirt made of white tulle over green satin. This dress, which Elizabeth Taylor wore in *A Place in the Sun*, was copied throughout the USA. Head helped to popularize South American clothes, in particular the Spanish *camisa* (shirt), *rebozo* (scarf) and PONCHO.

headband *See* BANDEAU.

headscarf Square piece of fabric, folded into a triangle, which is worn over the head and tied under the chin. Traditionally a rural garment, it became briefly fashionable as part of the FOLK-LORIC and PEASANT trends of the 1970s. From the 1920s to the 1970s headscarves, often made of silk, were often worn by women for sporting activities. Since that time they have faded from fashion. In the 1950s and 1960s there was a vogue for crossing a headscarf under the chin and tying it at the back of the neck. *See* HERMES.

Hechter, Daniel 1938–. Designer. Born in Paris, France. Hechter's father owned a ready-to-wear clothing company. Hechter worked for Pierre d'Alby from 1958 until he opened his own house in 1962. His first designs were ready-to-wear separates for young girls. He produced raincoats, sweaters and military-style MAXI coats. In 1964 he showed TROUSER SUITS and SMOKING JACKETS; in 1966 gabardine khaki raincoats; in 1967 boot-top-length divided skirts and fur coats with leather strips; in 1968 ribbed DUFFLE COATS; and in the 1970s jersey wool greatcoats. Hechter's skill lies in his outerwear – sporty yet sophisticated jackets, BLAZERS and coats, for both men and women.

heel-less shoes First introduced in the late 1950s and early 1960s, the heel-less shoe was a sculptured wedge with a cutaway heel and extended sole. *See also* WEDGIE.

Heim, Jacques 1899–1967. Designer. Born in Paris, France. In 1923 Heim took over the furrier business started by his parents in 1898. He designed women's clothing for the firm until 1930, when he established his own couture house. In 1936 he introduced his Heim Jeunes Filles collection, aimed at a young audience. Heim is one of the designers who has been credited with the introduction and promotion of the BIKINI. He produced several beachwear collections, one featuring a draped bathing suit. Heim popularized cotton for beachwear when he used the fabric for a couture collection. He was an original, inventive designer whose efforts are largely ignored today. Between 1946 and 1966 he opened a chain of BOUTIQUES selling SPORTSWEAR.

Headscarf from Hermès, 'Le Débuché', 1969.

helmet Close-fitting cap with sides that cover the ears. Popularized by Pierre CARDIN in the 1960s. *See also* SPACE AGE.

Hepburn, Audrey 1929–93. Actress. Born Edda Hepburn van Heemstra in Brussels, Belgium. Hepburn trained as a dancer in London in 1951 but achieved fame in the 1950s as an actress. Her GAMINE looks – small, slight figure and elfin haircut and face – were accentuated by her clothes: black TURTLENECK PULLOVER, PEDAL PUSHERS or CAPRI PANTS, and flat CAPEZIO PUMPS. She also popularized a mode of wearing a shirt (often over a sweater) with the ends unbuttoned and tied in the front at waist level. Her best-known films are *Sabrina* (1954), *Funny Face* (1957), *Breakfast at Tiffany's* (1961) and *My Fair Lady* (1964).

Hepburn, Katharine 1907–. Actress. Born in Hartford, Connecticut, USA. After graduating from Bryn Mawr in 1928, Hepburn began her acting career playing on Broadway. In the 1930s she moved to Hollywood. Hepburn is a highly respected actress of both stage and screen. To many Americans she represents the ideal free-spirited woman, almost always wearing trousers and with little or no make up. Her casual, sporty elegance has been widely influential.

Diagonal stripes of silver and gold wrap around the sleek evening silhouette in a 1982 silk crepe gown by Carolina **Herrera**.

The fashionable **hippie**, complete with bed roll, returns from a pop concert in 1970.

Hermès The Hermès company dates from 1837, when a saddler, Thierry Hermès, opened a shop in Paris selling moneybelts, GAUNTLETS, gloves and boots. In the 1920s his grandson, Emile, began designing garments made from deerskin. The company's main concern lies with the production of handcrafted leather goods, though it has become famous for two items: equestrian motif headscarves and the Kelly bag. The latter, based on a saddle bag, was first launched in 1935. In 1955, it was named after the actress Grace Kelly, who was frequently seen carrying one. *See* ★HEADSCARF.

Herrera, Carolina 1939–. Designer. Born Maria Carolina Josefina Pacanins y Nino in Caracas, Venezuela. After years on the US list of Best-Dressed Women, Herrera created her first ready-to-wear collection in 1981. A New York based designer, she produced a collection of layered clothes which used a variety of fabrics in different lengths. Working with an increasingly slimmer silhouette, she has become known for elegant daywear and eveningwear.

herringbone Pattern which resembles the skeletal structure of a herring, its zigzag effect produced by a broken twill weave. Herringbone has been popular since the 19th century for outer garments, suits, coats and skirts.

hippie Nineteen-sixties successor to the beatnik. Hippies often grew their hair long, walked barefoot, and wore colourful (often old) clothes and accessories. In the 1970s many designers copied hippie fashions, such as PATCHWORK skirts and coats; long, flowing, flounced skirts; and PSYCHEDELIC patterns and prints. The seemingly short-lived hippie style continues to influence fashion, especially in the form of

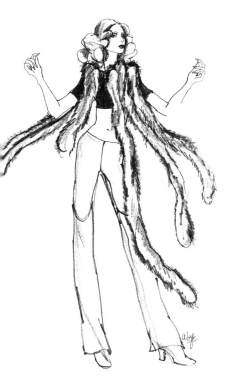

Hipster pants created by the British designer
Thea Porter in 1971 were worn with a suede top
decorated with red fox strips.

Léon Bakst drawing of his own design for a hobble
skirt made by Paquin and published in a 1913 edition of
the *Gazette du bon ton*.

relaxed, loose clothing with ETHNIC overtones
and in the use of exotic fabrics.

hipster Style of skirt or trousers first introduced in the 1960s. Hipsters were cut to fit
snugly around the hips rather than the waist and
were often held in place by a large, wide belt.

H-line Introduced by Christian DIOR in 1954,
this dress style pushed the bust up as high as
possible and dropped the waist to hip-level,
creating the cross-bar of the letter H. It was
most evident in Dior's designs for eveningwear.

hobble skirt Skirt style introduced by Paul
POIRET in the pre-World War I years. The
material was cut and draped to narrow severely
at some point between the knee and the ankle.
At its narrow section, it was often encircled by a
band which stretched downwards from the

knee. The skirt allowed only the briefest of
steps to be taken and was denounced by the
Pope, satirized by cartoonists, and made the
subject of fierce public debate.

Holah, David *See* BODY MAP.

homburg Man's felt hat with a rolled edge
and centre dent, first worn in Prussia. Also
known as a TRILBY.

Honiton lace Lace made in Honiton, Devon,
England. The lace-making industry was established in Honiton in the late 16th century. In
1839 Honiton lace was used for Queen VICTO-
RIA's wedding dress and subsequently became
fashionable for the remainder of the 19th century. It is adorned with motifs from nature,
particularly flowers, and is made on a net background that is often spotted. *See* ★LACE.

horseshoe collar Deep, U-shaped collar which featured on blouses and suit jackets from the early 1950s. *See* DIOR *and* GALANOS.

Horst P. Horst 1906–. Photographer. Born in Weissenfels, Germany. Horst studied architecture at the Kunstgewerbeschule in Hamburg from 1926 to 1928 and briefly with Le Corbusier in Paris in 1930. He posed for photographer George HOYNINGEN-HUENE and subsequently became his pupil. French *VOGUE* employed Horst as a photographer in 1932. Three years later, he emigrated to the USA. He served in the US Army in World War II and returned to a career in photography in 1946. Fashion pictures and portraits of society people are Horst's speciality. He uses elaborate settings and props, often utilizing blown-up backgrounds to create crowded but dramatic photographs. He is famous for the technical excellence of his lighting.

hot-pants Very brief SHORTS, often made of velvet, which were sometimes trimmed with embroidery or beads. The name 'hot-pants' was coined by *WOMEN'S WEAR DAILY* in 1970.

hound's-tooth *See* DOG'S TOOTH.

hourglass Shape associated with late 19th- and early 20th-century women, who wore constricting CORSETS which pulled in the waist and pushed out the hips and bust. The silhouette was revived in DIOR's NEW LOOK of 1947. *See also* S-BEND SILHOUETTE.

housecoat Loose, long-sleeved coat made of luxurious fabrics and worn around the house. It usually buttons or zips to a high neckline. The housecoat was popular between 1930 and the end of the 1960s.

Howell, Margaret 1946–. Designer. Born in Tadworth, Surrey, England. Howell attended Goldsmith's College, London, from 1966 to 1970. In 1971 she created a range of accessories followed in 1972 by a range of clothes. Two years later she established her own company and at the same time began working with Joseph. Shortly afterwards she opened a retail outlet. Howell specializes in classic ready-to-wear garments created by adapting traditional styles and fabrics into fashion shapes. She favours pinstripes and suiting materials – wool, tweed and melton – which she makes into up-to-the-minute riding jackets, TUXEDO suits and tailored blouses. Her silhouettes are usually elongated and soft.

Hoyningen-Huene, George 1900–68. Photographer. Born in St Petersburg, Russia. Hoyningen-Huene was educated in St Petersburg and Yalta before attending an art course at the Académie de la Grande Chaumière, Paris, from 1919 to 1920. He studied with Cubist painter André Lhote from 1922 to 1924. In the early 1920s he worked in Paris as a sketcher for many magazines, including *HARPER'S BAZAAR, JARDIN DES MODES* and *VOGUE*. In 1926 he became chief photographer of French *Vogue* but he worked for other Condé NAST publications in Europe and New York before emigrating to the USA in 1935. For the next ten years he was a staff fashion photographer at *Harper's Bazaar*, under editor Carmel SNOW and art director Alexey BRODOVITCH. In 1946 he moved to Hollywood to work in the film industry as a colour coordinator. Hoyningen-Huene was influenced by Classical Greek art, posing statuesque models in sophisticated settings to resemble a tableau or frieze. He created rich, tonal effects, was famous for his clear, ethereal lighting, and was one of the first photographers to take pictures of models from above, arranging their skirts around them like an open fan. Hoyningen-Huene was among the 20th-century's most prolific chroniclers of fashion and society.

Hulanicki, Barbara 1936–. Designer. Born in Palestine of Polish parents. Hulanicki moved to England in 1948, and attended Brighton Art College, Sussex. In 1955 she won a beachwear design competition in the London *Evening Standard*. She left college during her second year and joined a London company of commercial artists. She illustrated fashions for major newspapers and for women's magazines, including *VOGUE* and *Tatler*, and also worked for the London office of *WOMEN'S WEAR DAILY*. In 1961 she married Stephen Fitz-Simon. Two years later the couple started a mail-order company with an offer for a skirt in the *Daily Express*. A more successful offer

Barbara **Hulanicki** opened her famous Biba boutique in 1964. These designs – a droopy coat with matching skirt and a 1930s trousers with scarf – are from a Biba catalogue of the early 1970s.

of a pink gingham dress in the *Daily Mirror* one year later, in 1964, prompted the opening of Biba, a BOUTIQUE in London's Kensington. Here Hulanicki sold her own designs – brown SMOCKS with kerchiefs, MINI SKIRTS and dresses – high-fashion, inexpensive clothes that were attractive to a wide, predominantly young, market. So successful was the venture that two more shops were opened. The name Biba became synonymous with floppy, felt cut-out hats, vamp dresses, TROUSER SUITS, T-shirts with SWEETHEART NECKLINES,

billowing crepe dresses, MOB CAPS and ankle-length smocks, JERKIN suits in ribbed rayon, and cotton BIKINIS with matching jackets. The most famous Biba shop, in Kensington High Street, was decorated in nostalgic 1930s style. As part of the London youth trend of the 1960s, it attracted visitors from all over the world who bought and copied the clothes and accessories. In 1973 Biba took over an entire department store in Kensington, but the Biba style failed to make a successful transition into the 1970s. *See also* BOUTIQUE.

I

ikat Silk fabrics made in Java and Sumatra, Indonesia. Often used in ETHNIC fashions.

intarsia Design fitted into certain parts of a sweater, such as the neckline or cuffs. *See* FAIR ISLE.

Irene 1907–62. Costume designer. Born Irene Lentz in Brookings, South Dakota, USA. Irene studied at the Wolfe School of Design in Los Angeles, California, and then opened a dress shop which was patronized by Hollywood stars. In 1933 she became head of the Bullocks Wiltshire Costume Design Salon in Hollywood, where she created on- and off-screen clothes for actresses. Irene designed freelance from 1938 to 1942, when she was appointed head designer for Metro-Goldwyn-Mayer. Throughout her career she produced costumes for more than 260 films made by Metro-Goldwyn-Mayer, Paramount, RKO, United Artists and Columbia Pictures. Her clients included Judy Garland, Greer Garson, Hedy Lamarr and Lana Turner. She was particularly noted for her softly tailored suits.

Iribe, Paul 1883–1935. Illustrator. Born Paul Iribarnegaray in Angoulême, France. Iribe was educated in Paris where, in his early twenties, he became an apprentice printer at *Le Temps* newspaper. From 1900 he submitted illustrations to such French satirical papers as *Rire*, *Sourire* and *L'Assiette au beurre*. He became famous in 1908 as an illustrator of fashion, when Paul POIRET, who was looking for an artist to present his clothes in an original manner, asked him to compile a promotional publication. The resulting brochure, *Les Robes de Paul Poiret*, was widely influential both in terms of fashion and of illustrative style. Iribe's illustrations were clean, crisp and balanced. He kept background objects to a minimum and concentrated on the stylish outline and witty detail of the garments. A contributor to *VOGUE* and *FEMINA*, Iribe also designed advertisements for PAQUIN and the house of CALLOT, perfume bottles, fabrics for BIANCHINI-FERIER, and furniture and interiors. He spent six years in Hollywood working on film costumes and theatrical interiors for Paramount. Returning to Paris in 1928, he divided his time between contributing satirical illustrations to the weekly political paper *Le Témoin* and designing jewelry for CHANEL.

Ivy League Style of dress worn by students and graduates of US East Coast colleges. For men, the outfit usually comprises a grey flannel suit with a narrow-shouldered, loose-waisted jacket, a white shirt with a button-down collar, a narrow striped TIE, a camel-hair coat or a CHESTERFIELD, and heavy-soled OXFORD shoes. Women wear a cashmere TWINSET with a KILT or tweed skirt, a BLAZER, Shetland sweater, pearl necklace and BROGUES. In summer, woollens are replaced by LIBERTY print or madras blouses (often with PETER PAN COLLARS), BERMUDA SHORTS or a flannel skirt, and PUMPS. *See also* BROOKS BROTHERS, LAUREN *and* PREPPIE.

J

jabot Decorative frill of lace or other delicate fabric pinned at the chest or base of the neck. Originally a 16th-century item of male dress, the jabot was popular with women from the mid-19th century until the 1920s and 1930s.

Doucet's patron, the actress Réjane, wearing an astrakhan and sequin jacket and lace **jabot**.

Jackson, Betty 1940–. Designer. Born in Backup, Lancashire, England. Jackson attended Birmingham College of Art from 1968 to 1971. She then worked in London as a freelance illustrator until 1973, when she joined Wendy DAGWORTHY. From 1975 to 1981 Jackson worked first for Quorum and then for Cooper's, both clothing manufacturers. Since 1981 she has produced collections under her own name and has swiftly achieved an international reputation as a designer of young, up-to-the-minute clothes. She rescales separates into different, often larger, proportions and makes them up in boldly coloured and patterned fabrics. Her clothes are sporty, and texture plays an important part in her work. She explores and exploits the possibilities of different materials, designs and colours.

Jacobs, Marc 1960–. Designer. Born in New York, USA. In 1984, in his final year at Parsons School of Design, Jacobs created a collection of handknit sweaters which won him the Perry Ellis Golden Thimble award. After graduating he designed his own label for two years, creating irreverent take-offs of 1960s HIPPIE-style clothing and offbeat versions of PATCHWORK and gingham. In 1988 he joined Perry ELLIS where he became known for a youthful, witty style which showed confident use of colour and spare silhouettes. He created a red and white tablecloth check ensemble embroidered with black ants, and a Freudian 'slip' imprinted with Freud's face. He was designing under his own name by 1994. Jacobs favours sensuous fabrics such as angora, cashmere and mohair and will occasionally surprise with neon rubber separates and laminated sequined jeans.

jacquard Decorative weave created by a jacquard loom and used for brocades and damasks since the mid-19th century. *See* JACQUARD, JOSEPH-MARIE.

Jacquard, Joseph-Marie 1752–1834. French mechanical engineer who developed an

Two outfits from the designer Betty **Jackson**.
Left: Autumn/Winter 1983–84; *right:* Autumn/Winter 1992.

attachment for machine powered looms which created elaborate weaves in fabric. *See* JACQUARD.

Jaeger In the 1880s Dr Gustav Jaeger, Professor of Zoology and Physiology at Stuttgart University, campaigned for what he believed to be the benefits to health of wearing wool next to the skin. Inspired by Jaeger's studies and experiments, Lewis Tomalin, the London manager of a wholesale grocery firm, secured the rights, patents and Jaeger name. In 1884 Tomalin began manufacturing 100 percent wool sanitary underwear: CHEMISES, combinations, DRAWERS and petticoats in undyed sheep's wool or camel-hair wool. In the 1900s Jaeger expanded its operations to include the manufacture of cardigans, dressing gowns, gymnastic sweaters, knitted jumper suits and laceknit shawls. During the 1920s, fashion demanded lighter, more practical undergarments and Jaeger's lines were no longer popular. The company produced instead its own fashionable clothing line, including coats, skirts, ★JUMPERS, SLACKS and TWINSETS. Many of the garments were made of wool. In the second half of the 20th century Jaeger was recognized as a fashion company selling good quality dresses, coats, suits and knitwear to an international market.

James, Charles 1906–78. Designer. Born in Sandhurst, England. James briefly attended the University of Bordeaux before being sent to Chicago by his family to work for a utilities magnate. He resigned almost immediately and in 1926 opened a hat shop, 'Charles Boucheron'. Two years later he moved to New York and took up dress designing, showing his first collection in 1928. The following year James began commuting between London and New York. His designs are so timeless that his 1932 CULOTTES for the New York department store Lord & Taylor were still being sold in the 1950s. In 1934 and 1935 James worked in Paris under the patronage of Paul POIRET, designing fabrics for French textile manufacturers Colcombet. New York became James's base from 1940 until 1947 and during part of that period he designed clothes for Elizabeth Arden's salon. He showed one of his most successful collections in Paris in 1947. In the 1950s he spent most of his time in New York. James looked

In 1884, the **Jaeger** company was best known for its 'sanitary' woollen clothing.

upon his dresses as works of art, as did many of his customers. Year after year he reworked original designs, ignoring the sacrosanct schedule of seasons. The components of the precisely constructed designs were interchangeable so that James had a never-ending fund of ideas on which to draw. He is most famous for his sculpted ball gowns made in lavish fabrics and to exacting tailoring standards, but is also remembered for his capes and coats, often trimmed with fur and embroidery, his spiral zipped dresses, and his white satin quilted jackets. James retired in 1958. *See* ANTONIO.

Japanese Since Japan opened its doors to the Western world in the 19th century, it has been a source of inspiration for many designers. The first major Japanese garment to be exported and widely copied was the KIMONO, though much is lost in the West of the symbolism and structure of the original. Japanese dress is concerned with ritual and tradition, with concealing rather than revealing the body, and with the dimensions between the body and the robe. By the early 1970s, several Japanese designers had established themselves in Paris. Hanae MORI used the traditional kimono as a basis for elegant eveningwear. Issey MIYAKE and KENZO concentrated on textiles and experimented with the relationship between Eastern and Western dress, mixing Japanese traditions with European ideas. In the late 1970s a different breed of designer came from Japan to Europe. Kansai YAMAMOTO, Yohji YAMAMOTO, and Rei KAWAKUBO of Comme des Garçons settled in Paris and proceeded to turn the fashion world upside down. Through their clothes they reflected an attitude toward dressing – almost an anti-fashion style – which was less concerned with dressing for occasion and season and more involved with constant adaptation of traditional Japanese dress. For the most part they ignored the Western stress on a sleek, proportioned body shape and focused on the creation of alternative dimensions and texture. Garments were cut away and slashed in strategic places to emphasize proportions and colour; either drab, dark colours or boldly patterned mixtures dominated over the structure. Japanese influences on fashion, through these and other designers, have contributed to a greater flexibility in dressing. Western designers have begun to create more relaxed garments which, in Japanese style, concentrate on the flow and drape of the fabric.

Jardin des modes, Le Monthly magazine, with many supplements, first published in 1922 by Lucien VOGEL. It is one of the most prominent fashion journals in France.

Jeanmaire, Zizi 1924–. Dancer. Born in Paris, France. Jeanmaire became famous with the Ballets de Paris company in 1949 in its production of *Carmen*. She starred in the film *Hans Christian Andersen* (1952) and in the Broadway musical *The Girl in Pink Tights* (1953). In the 1950s she epitomized the GAMINE style, with her short, boyish haircut and slender figure.

jeans From *Gênes*, the French for Genoa, Italy, a port where sailors wore sturdy work trousers. Jeans is a strong cotton cloth originally loomed in Nîmes, France, and is also the name for trousers made from that cloth. During the 1850s, Levi STRAUSS introduced denim jeans in San Francisco, California, as workwear for goldminers. They became fashionable in the 1950s in the USA. Since then jeans have been made in a variety of styles: narrow or baggy; HIPSTERS and BELL BOTTOMS; stitched with flowers or patched; tailored and stretch. Whatever the style or cut, the indigo blue fabric is still associated with casual wear. *See* DENIM.

jellies Brightly coloured plastic sandals introduced in the 1970s for both adults and children.

Jenny House opened in Paris in 1909 by Jeanne Adele Bernard (1872–1962). Specializing in elegant, aristocratic evening clothes and day dresses, throughout the 1920s Jenny successfully attracted a clientele of American and European women. The house merged with Lucile Paray in 1938 and closed in 1940.

jerkin Hip-length garment, with or without sleeves, which fastens at the side or on the shoulders. It is often cut with slits at the sides. A popular garment in the mid-20th century. *See also* TABARD.

Spring 1922 design by **Jenny**, featuring the low waist typical of the period.

jersey *1.* Soft, stretchable knitted fabric first used on the Channel Island of Jersey in the late 19th century for sportswear and outer garments. In the 1920s, pioneered by CHANEL, it was made up into dresses and two-piece suits and became the most fashionable fabric of the period. It can be made of cotton, nylon, rayon, wool or synthetic fibres. *2.* Type of thick, knitted SWEATER originally worn by fishermen. *See* JERSEY COSTUME.

jersey costume In the 1870s, Lillie LANGTRY, the Edwardian actress, popularized a finely knitted silk or wool garment that clung to the figure down to the mid-thigh, where it was swathed around the knees and worn over a flannel or serge skirt. Known as a jersey costume, it fastened at the back and was worn for sporting activities.

jet Dense form of black lignite coal obtained from decomposed driftwood found at Whitby on the Yorkshire coast of England. Although it has been known since Roman times, jet did not become popular until the 19th century, when it was associated with mourning jewelry. It was most fashionable in the 1870s and 1880s, when it was made into lockets, pendants, brooches and bracelets, elaborately cut into fruit, flower and animal designs.

jodhpurs Riding breeches, taking their name from a former state in northwest India. Jodhpurs are very full from the hip to the knee, billowing out at the sides in a semicircle, and skintight from knee to ankle. They are finished either with a cuff or with a piece of fabric that goes under the foot. Jodhpurs enjoy periodic revivals as a fashion style.

jogging suit *See* TRACKSUIT.

John, Augustus 1878–1961. Painter. Born in Tenby, Wales. Portrait painter who inspired a Bohemian clothing style worn in London's CHELSEA during the 1920s. John's long cloaks, wide black hats and homespun garments were imitated by many young men. Women copied the SANDALS, GYPSY-like HEADSCARVES, and ankle-length flowing skirts of his wife, Dorelia, a look that became popular through his portrait of Dorelia, *The Smiling Woman*.

The UK did not have a monopoly on 'swinging' designs in the 1960s. The American designer Betsey **Johnson** became well known in the same decade for her young, radical creations, including her 'Body-color flippy minis!' of 1965 *(top)* and her silver motorcycle jacket and mini skirt, 'Motor-Madness', of 1966 *(above)*.

Johnson, Betsey 1942–. Designer. Born in Hartford, Connecticut, USA. Johnson spent a year at the Pratt Institute in Brooklyn, New York, before graduating from Syracuse University in 1964. In that year she was guest editor on the summer college issue of *Mademoiselle* and was hired by the magazine for one year after graduation. During that period she made and sold clothing designs in her spare time and later became a freelance designer, retailing through Paraphernalia, a New York BOUTIQUE. In the 1960s Johnson gained a reputation as a radical young designer, producing chalk-striped 'gangster' TROUSER SUITS, a clear vinyl dress sold with paste-your-own star motifs, a 'noise' dress made of jersey with loose grommets attached to the hem, silvery motorcycle suits, clinging T-SHIRT dresses, and a wrapped cowhide MINI DRESS which was worn with thigh-high leather boots. In 1969 she opened a New York boutique called 'Betsey, Bunkey, and Nini'. In the 1970s Johnson turned to DISCO wear and showed extravagant, body-conscious clothes, many made up in stretch jersey. She opened her own SPORTSWEAR business in 1978.

Jones, Stephen 1957–. Milliner. Born in West Kirby, Liverpool, England. Jones graduated in 1979 from St Martin's School of Art in London. In the same year he designed a hat collection for FIORUCCI. He then joined LACHASSE briefly before opening his own business in 1980. Jones's often asymmetric and outrageous hats quickly became popular with designers such as Jean-Paul GAULTIER, Claude MONTANA, Thierry MUGLER and Zandra RHODES. He also designed for various pop groups and for singers such as MADONNA, Boy George and George Michael. In 1984 Jones became the first British milliner to work in Paris. Since that time he has designed for the collections of Antonio BERARDI, John GALLIANO, Katharine HAMNETT, Emanuel UNGARO and Vivienne WESTWOOD, among others. He is credited with helping to revive millinery arts during the latter part of the 20th century.

Jourdan, Charles 1883–1976. Shoemaker. In 1921 Jourdan began a shoe workshop at Romans, in the Drôme region of France. The business prospered, particularly in sales of

A 1980s hat from the milliner Stephen **Jones**.

Top: Charles **Jourdan**'s 'Madly' design, 1972.
Above: 'Maxime', a 1958 design which became one of Jourdan's most popular shoes.

The adventurous **jumpsuit** of 1979.

A **jumper**, from the Jaeger catalogue of 1926.

women's shoes. After World War II Jourdan was joined by his three sons and in 1957 they opened a BOUTIQUE in Paris. In 1959 the House of DIOR granted the company a licence to design and manufacture Dior shoes. Jourdan's designs are up-to-the-minute. In the late 1960s and early 1970s the company created an avant-garde image for itself by using the surrealist photographer Guy BOURDIN for its advertising campaign. During this period the company sold vast quantities of two notable styles: 'Maxime', a low-heeled, square-toed COURT SHOE with a satin bow, and 'Madly', a thick-heeled PLATFORM SOLE shoe with a high vamp in red or black patent leather. The firm also makes Pierre CARDIN and Xavier Danaud shoes, among others. During the 1980s and 1990s Charles Jourdan was associated with a more conservative look.

Journal des dames et des modes, Le Trimonthly journal published in Paris from 1912 to 1914, which contained copperplate fashion illustrations and articles on literature, the theatre, fash-

ion and the arts. It was based on a journal of the same name which appeared from 1798 to 1839. Contributing artists included BAKST, BARBIER, Pierre Brissaud, BRUNELLESCHI, DRIAN, IRIBE and MARTIN.

Juliet cap Small, round cap which fits snugly on top of the head, made of an open-weave fabric that is usually decorated with pearls or semi-precious stones. The cap was popularized by actress Norma Shearer in the film *Romeo and Juliet* (1930).

jumper *1.* A short, sack-like coat with a narrow turn-down collar which buttoned to the neck, worn by men in the 19th century. 2. US name for a PINAFORE. 3. (Chiefly UK) A long-sleeved woollen SWEATER. *See* JAEGER.

jumpsuit One-piece suit with long sleeves and legs, which zips from the waist or below to the collar. It has been worn by women since the early 20th century. Also known as a flying suit or boilersuit.

jute Glossy lustrous fibre obtained from the jute plant of East India. Since the 19th century it has been mixed with silk and wool to create fabrics for both indoor and outdoor garments.

K

kaftan *See* CAFTAN.

Kamali, Norma 1945–. Designer. Born Norma Arraez in New York, Kamali studied fashion illustration at the Fashion Institute of Technology in New York. She graduated in 1964 and worked in clerical jobs before opening a BOUTIQUE with her husband in 1967. Kamali's highly original clothes were popular among people from show business, the theatre and the music world. Gold lamé MAILLOTS and garments made of leopard print chamois were just some of her high fashion designs. After her divorce she started another business, OMO (On My Own), in 1978. Her weightless, fibre-filled nylon fabric coats made from the down of sleeping bags and her JUMPSUITS of parachute nylon received international attention. In the late 1970s she began working with SWEAT-SHIRTING, a fabric previously used only for athletics and SPORTSWEAR. She made jackets, skirts, and narrow and baggy trousers. Her RAH-RAH SKIRTS were the first short skirts to sell in any volume since the MINI SKIRT of the early 1960s. She made frequent use of jersey for broad-shouldered dresses and tops. Kamali's clothes are witty and dramatic enough to make accessories unnecessary. One of the most innovative designers of the 1970s and 1980s, she showed boldness in her choice of fabric, making up skirts from Mexican tablecloths or remnants from the cutting-room floor. In the 1980s she produced several successful collections of sportswear and one-piece bathing suits which were remarkable for their cut-out sections and strong use of colour. The 1990s saw her revive many 1970s fashions, such as BELL BOTTOMS. She is an innovative designer who blends RETRO style with up-to-date, even futuristic, fabrics for a highly individual look.

Kangol Company established in 1938 by Frenchman Jacques Spreiregen at Cleator, Cumbria, England, to produce traditional BERETS. Kangol provided British and overseas armed forces with military berets during World War II. Its berets and soft angora hats were

A fashion perennial, the beret has been worn by everyone from gangster's molls to English schoolgirls. This one, the traditional 'Modelaine', is by the British firm **Kangol**, whose name has been synonymous with berets since World War II.

Norma **Kamali**'s 'sweats' collection of 1981, showing her broad, padded shoulders, teamed in this design with a basque-style waist and knickerbocker legs.

particularly popular during the 1950s. *See also*
SMITH, GRAHAM.

Kaplan, Jacques 1924–. Fur designer. Born in
Paris, France. In 1941 Kaplan joined the New
York branch of the furrier business established
by his father in Paris in 1889. He became
famous for his stencilled and coloured FURS, FUN
FURS, and fur dresses, boots and hats. He retired
in 1971.

karacul Tightly curled, glossy black fur of the
young broadtail sheep found in Southern
Russia. Karacul was a popular fur for coats and
hats in the late 19th and early 20th centuries. It
is also the name given to a fabric which imitates
the fur. *See also* ASTRAKHAN.

Karan, Donna 1948–. Designer. Born Donna
Faske in Forest Hills, New York, USA. Karan's
father was a haberdasher and her mother a
model and saleswoman. Karan attended Parsons
School of Design in New York and during her
second year was employed in the summer as a
sketcher at Anne KLEIN. This temporary position was extended to a full-time job and she
remained at Anne Klein and was appointed
Klein's successor in 1969. After Klein's death in
1974, Karan and Louis DELL'OLIO became co-
designers for the company. Karan produced
highly wearable, moderately priced SPORTS-
WEAR for the Anne Klein label until 1984,
when she left to design under her own name.
Her first collection was launched in 1985 and
since that time she has been at the international
forefront of women's fashion. In sympathy with
women whose body shapes were difficult to
dress, Karan used fabrics that draped and flat-
tered. She created WRAPAROUND skirts and
well-cut BLAZERS, as well as BODYSUITS of Lycra
that could be worn as easily under a suit as with
a pair of jeans. Her bodywrap styles of cashmere
and stretch fabrics disguised less than perfect
bodies, yet for all their casual approach Karan's
clothes made the transition from office to home
and thus spoke of practicality to millions of
women. Using a sophisticated palette, often of
black or dark blue, Karan provided women

Donna **Karan** is known not only for her casual
bodywrap styles but also for glamorous eveningwear.
Top: Spring 1997; *bottom:* Autumn 1987.

with chic clothes that were rarely fussy or trendy, and whose ease of cut and manner reflected an up-to-date attitude that was widely successful.

kasha Soft, silky fabric made of a wool mixed with goat's hair. Kasha first became popular during the 1920s.

Kasper, Herbert 1926–. Designer. Born in New York, USA. Kasper studied English and advertising at New York University but left college prematurely to serve with the US Army in Europe. After demobilization he returned to New York where he studied at Parsons School of Design. In the following years he went to Paris, attended classes at the Ecole de la Chambre Syndicale de la Haute Couture (*See* HAUTE COUTURE), and worked for Jacques FATH, Marcel ROCHAS and *Elle* magazine. On his return to the USA in the early 1960s, he joined MR JOHN as a millinery designer. In 1965 he moved to Joan Leslie, where he remains as vice president. Kasper's clothes have always been associated with couture garments at SPORTSWEAR prices. He is a master at translating an expensive, tailored cut to a mass-market price tag and excels in knitwear, suedes and silks.

Kawakubo, Rei 1942–. Designer. Born in Tokyo, Japan. Kawakubo studied literature at Tokyo's Keio University. After graduating in 1964 she joined the Japanese textile company Asahi Kasei. Two years later she became a freelance fashion designer and in 1969 formed the Comme des Garçons company. Her menswear line, Homme, was introduced in 1978. Kawakubo achieved her greatest attention in Paris during the late 1970s and early 1980s with her non-traditional clothing, which attempted to redefine accepted ideas of womenswear in both the East and the West. Her torn, crumpled garments, draped around the body with seemingly no acknowledgement of body shape, were initially viewed as ugly and ridiculous. Nonetheless, her sombre shades and flat, sexless image had a considerable impact on dress styles of the 1980s. Many of her garments have randomly placed buttons and sleeves and her knitwear is often tattered and ripped.

kelly bag *See* HERMES.

Kelly, Patrick 1954–90. Designer. Born in Vicksburg, Mississippi, USA. Kelly attended Jackson State University where he studied art history. He worked with a tailor in Atlanta, Georgia, before moving to New York to study at Parsons School of Design. He arrived in Paris in 1979 and began his career in the fashion business by designing and selling, on Parisian sidewalks, cut-out cotton tube dresses. He soon had a large following for his whimsical clothes. Kelly's promising career was cut short by an early death.

Kennedy, Jacqueline *See* ONASSIS.

Kenzo 1940–. Designer. Born Kenzo Takada in Kyoto, Japan. Kenzo studied art in Japan and after graduating he designed patterns for a Tokyo magazine. In 1964 he moved to Paris and for the remainder of the 1960s created freelance collections and sold designs to Louis FERAUD. In 1970 he opened his own shop,

Kenzo's use of vivid colour and his mastery of draping are combined in this eye-catching evening dress from a 1979 collection.

Kenzo's lively and youthful Spring/Summer collection of 1981 featured both short and long skirts.

Jungle Jap. Success followed almost immediately. Kenzo's early clothes in cotton were very popular. By 1972 he was established, known initially for his audacious designs in either raucous Kabuki colours or austere shades. A master at mixing prints and layering, Kenzo produced oriental-style blouses, TUNICS, SMOCKS, wide-legged trousers and printed velvet garments. He also focused fashion attention on knitwear. His trendsetting approach to knitted fabrics ensured his position as a leading ready-to-wear knitwear designer, injecting colour and new proportions into classic designs.

kersey Thick, heavy, cotton and wool twill fabric which has a closely sheared surface and resembles melton. It was popular for coats during the 19th century.

kerseymere Closely woven twilled cloth similar to KERSEY, popular during the 19th century.

Khanh, Emanuelle 1937–. Designer. Born in Paris, France. Khanh worked as a model for BALENCIAGA in the mid-1950s and later for GIVENCHY. She began sketching, made up several garments, and in 1961 some of her clothes were featured in *Elle*. She joined DOROTHEE BIS for a brief period and then worked for CACHAREL from 1962 to 1967. In 1970 Khanh established her own business. She has continued to work freelance while pursuing her own lines.

In the 1960s she became famous for her long, droopy collars on jackets, dresses and blouses; highly cut armholes; low-slung skirts; tiny, round collars on blouses; short, frilly skirts; linen outfits with lace trimming; and embroidered blouses. Her name is associated with the YEYE fashions of the 1960s.

Kiam, Omar 1894–1954. Costume designer. Born Alexander Kiam in Monterey, Mexico. Kiam attended the Poughkeepsie Military Academy in New York. By 1912 he was working for a department store in Houston, Texas, where he became head designer of the millinery section. He moved to New York to design clothes, furs and theatrical costumes on a freelance basis. Kiam also spent some years working in Paris. By the 1930s he had returned to New York to create costumes for Broadway. In 1935 he was hired as head designer for Samuel Goldwyn's production company in Hollywood, designing specifically for actresses Merle Oberon and Loretta Young. In 1941 Kiam started producing a ready-to-wear line for a New York manufacturer.

kick pleat Short, inverted pleat which is inserted at the centre back or side hem of a tightly fitting skirt to provide greater mobility. It was often used by designers in the 1940s and 1950s when a strictly tailored silhouette was fashionable.

The **kilt** has featured in many designers' collections. Bill Gibb's version is for the mini-skirt years of the 1960s.

kilt In early times the kilt was a long, toga-like garment, woven of vegetable-dyed yarns, which was gathered at the shoulders. It served as both clothing and a blanket. From the Middle Ages it was made from a plaid – a piece of fabric, usually 16 foot by 5 foot, which was wrapped around the lower torso to make a calf-length skirt, with the other end draped across the chest and over the shoulder. By the 17th century the kilt had become identified with Scotland. It consisted of a skirt of seven and a half yards of TARTAN cloth, most of which was pleated, except for the last half yard at each end which was left unpleated. The unpleated ends were crossed over each other in the front and held in place by buckles or a large pin. By this time the plaid was a separate piece, worn over the shoulder. In Europe interest in kilts was promoted by Queen VICTORIA and her consort, Prince Albert, who, in the mid-19th century, spent a good deal of time at Balmoral,

their Scottish estate. As fashion garments for women, kilts (usually the skirt without the plaid) have been popular since the 1940s. Modern versions are made from two yards of woollen material and do not conform to Scottish traditions. Fashion kilts were notably popular during the 1970s and formed part of IVY LEAGUE and PREPPIE dress for women.

kimono Loose, wide-sleeved JAPANESE robe which has a broad SASH that fastens around the waist. The kimono was introduced to Europe in the late 19th century. The shape, design, styling and overall symbolism of the kimono inspired painters such as Toulouse Lautrec, MUCHA and KLIMT. Toulouse Lautrec took to wearing the garment; others were satisfied to paint kimono-clad women. The kimono became the symbol of a general preoccupation with Japanese ideas, designs and spatial concepts. In fashion terms, the kimono became popular in the late 19th and early 20th centuries, worn as an alternative to the TEA GOWN, and its long, flowing lines were frequently imitated in Hollywood film costumes of the 1930s. Throughout the 20th century, the kimono shape was used for DRESSING GOWNS.

kimono sleeve Extra-large sleeve panel which is set into a deep armhole that reaches from shoulder to waist. The kimono sleeve has been used by designers since the late 19th century for coats, dresses, jackets and sweaters.

King's Road Street in London's CHELSEA which has been the scene of many new trends in fashion since the proliferation of BOUTIQUES in the 1960s. The King's Road became the focus of fashion in the late 1970s when it was the favourite promenade of PUNKS.

Klein, Anne 1921–74. Designer. Born Hannah Golofski in New York, USA. In 1938 Golofski was working as a sketcher on New York's SEVENTH AVENUE. The following year she married Ben Klein and joined Varden Petites, where she was responsible for the junior lines. Shortly after, she formed Junior Sophisticates and made even more inroads on the fashion scene for young women. In 1968 Anne Klein & Co. was formed. Klein made young fashions sophisticated. She was one of the most

The textile designer **Bernat Klein** produced this brown, sand and white wool fabric which was designed into a coat by John Cavanagh in 1963.

An example of **Calvin Klein**'s sleek, smooth lines for Autumn 1983. Here elements of a man's wardrobe are tailored for women: double-breasted plaid coat, double-breasted plaid blazer, and grey flannel trousers. The whole effect is one of understated sophistication.

popular SPORTSWEAR designers in the USA, famous for matching dresses and jackets, wasp-waisted dresses, BLAZERS and BATTLE JACKETS, hooded BLOUSON tops and slinky jersey dresses. Her clothes were smart, practical and fashionable. After her death Donna KARAN and Louis DELL'OLIO took over the design side of Anne Klein & Co.

Klein, Bernat 1922–. Textile designer and painter. Born in Senta, Yugoslavia. Klein attended the Bezalel Academy of Arts and Design in Jerusalem. After World War II he went to England where he studied textile technology at Leeds University. Klein then worked briefly for a large cotton mill in Lancashire and a woollen mill in Edinburgh before setting up on his own in Galashiels, Scotland, in 1951. Klein's work is based on continuous development and innovation in textile design. His personal contribution is associated with his approach to colour.

Klein, Calvin 1942–. Designer. Born in New York, USA. Klein graduated from the Fashion Institute of Technology in 1962 and then spent two years with Dan Millstein, New York, as assistant designer. From 1964 to 1968 he worked for various coat and suit manufacturers before starting his own business. For many years he specialized in designing coats and suits but during the mid-1970s he gained recognition for the softly tailored, clean lines of his SPORTS-WEAR collections. PEA JACKETS, fur-collared melton overcoats, TURTLENECK sweaters and long-line SLACKS in muted shades were as much Klein hallmarks as silk crepe-de-chine shirt-style jackets, striped silk blouses and velvet daytime separates. In the late 1970s Klein's designs became increasingly sophisticated. His collections featured long, slim lines on coats, loose unfussy jackets that hung straight from broadened shoulders, and carefully proportioned BLAZERS and blouses. Klein favours linen, silks and woollen fabrics. In the mid-1970s his 'designer' jeans were widely copied yet managed to remain one of the most respected brands. Klein's clothes are immediately identifiable by their smooth, understated look. His clothing is perfectly in keeping with the MINIMALIST attitudes of the late 20th century. Although he often uses luxurious fabrics, there is a notable absence of superficial detail and whimsy in his designs. Instead, his garments have a pared-down ease and sober colour palette that appeals to men and women alike. It is this androgynous, UNISEX approach that Klein has marketed with phenomenal success, particularly in the field of underwear – his underpants for men and women were an international success in the early 1990s.

Klein, Roland 1938–. Designer. Born in Rouen, France. Klein studied in Paris at the Ecole de la Chambre Syndicale de la Haute Couture (*See* HAUTE COUTURE) from 1955 to 1957. After two years with DIOR, he moved in 1962 to PATOU, where he worked as Karl LAGERFELD's assistant. Klein travelled to London in 1965 to join the firm of Marcel Fenez. In 1973 he became managing director and in 1979 he opened his own shop, Roland Klein. Klein creates well-proportioned clothes along restrained lines.

Klimt, Gustav 1862–1918. Painter. Born in Vienna, Austria. Artist who became closely associated with ART NOUVEAU. Klimt's female figures of the early 1880s wore soft, flowing gowns. He designed dresses for a Viennese couture house and also worked on theatre and poster design.

Knapp, Sonia *See* UNGARO.

knickerbockers Loose, full breeches which are gathered below the knee and fastened by a button or buckle. Worn by men since the 18th century, they became an integral part of sporting attire for women in the 1890s, teamed with a NORFOLK JACKET. In the late 1960s and early 1970s knickerbockers became fashionable once again, promoted by Yves *SAINT LAURENT.

knife pleats Narrow pleats pressed to form regular, sharp edges on a skirt or dress. Popular during both the late 19th and the 20th centuries, particularly from the 1920s to the 1950s.

knitting A craft that can be traced back to the Ancient Egyptians, knitting is the interlocking of one loop of thread or yarn through another, using two needles. In the past, hand-knitting was popular for both functional and decorative garments in country areas where wool was readily available. By the 19th century knitting machines had come into use but it was not until the wool-related health cult of the late 19th century that woollen garments achieved wide popularity. Sport also helped to promote wool.

Roland **Klein** evening dress, Spring/Summer 1997.

Knitting reached new heights in the 1980s. This design is from a Patricia Roberts pattern published in 1983.

141

By the turn of the century fashionable outdoor knitted garments were being made up for women by both hand and machine. SWEATERS, previously worn only as sporting wear, became the vogue in the 1920s and continued to be popular through the 1930s. During both world wars women knitted garments for soldiers, some of which (the BALACLAVA, for example) became fashion items. In the 1950s knitwear became more fashion conscious: new and more flexible fibres were blended with wool to create a far wider range in design, colour, texture and wearability. The 1960s saw knitwear firmly established as a fashion force and in the late 1960s and early 1970s a revival took place of homeknitting, due in large part to the availability of brightly coloured yarns and up-to-date patterns. This revival, particularly in the 1970s, was associated with ETHNIC fashions. *See also* ARAN, FAIR ISLE, ROBERTS, SWEATER, TROMPE L'OEIL *and* TWINSET.

Kors, Michael 1959–. Designer. Born in Long Island, New York, USA. After studying at the Fashion Institute of Technology, Kors established his own SPORTSWEAR label in 1981. His clinging, scaled-down JUMPSUITS called attention to the body which he then layered with jackets. Working frequently with natural fabrics and neutral colours, Kors creates garments that are noted for their MINIMALIST approach, yet the cut is curvaceous and designed to flatter. His separates are often practical – the body-hugging dress is worn with a more tailored jacket, other jackets double as shirts. Many of his designs are inspired by the great American sportswear designer Claire MCCARDELL.

Koshino, Hiroko 1938–. Designer. Born in Tokyo, Japan. One of many JAPANESE designers who went to Paris in the early 1980s, Koshino formed her own company and shows separates in designs which draw on the basic KIMONO shape. Her confidently scaled garments have earned her a wide reputation.

Koshino, Michiko 1950–. Designer. Born in Osaka, Japan. Michiko graduated from Bunka Fukuso Gakuin, the Japanese college of design, in 1974. The following year she went to London and soon established herself as a confident, successful designer, able to merge oriental and occidental ideas in a modern manner. Michiko's attention to detail can be observed particularly in her seaming and in the positioning of pockets on her clothes.

Krizia Company – Kriziamaglia – founded in Milan, Italy, in 1954 by Mariuccia Mandelli (b. 1933). Mandelli, who had trained as a teacher, began by selling skirts and dresses. In 1967 she branched out into knitwear design and later into complete ranges of ready-to-wear clothes. Krizia's designs are always distinctive. Clever, lighthearted and often witty, they manage nonetheless to retain considerable grace and glamour. In the 1970s Mandelli's signature animal motif began to feature each season on many garments. Krizia has become a giant of the Milanese fashion scene, charting its own course with panache.

Kumagai, Tokio 1947–87. Shoe designer. Born in Sendai, Japan. After graduating in 1970 from the Bunka Fukuso Gakuin, the Japanese college of design, Kumagai went to Paris. Throughout the 1970s he designed for a number of companies, notably CASTELBAJAC, Rodier and Pierre d'Alby in France and FIORUCCI in Italy. In 1979 he began hand-painting shoes. He opened his first BOUTIQUE in 1980. Inspired by SURREALISM, abstract and expressionist styles, and artists such as Kandinsky, Pollock and MONDRIAN, Kumagai handpainted his shoes in a manner reminiscent of a particular artist's style. He often altered the structure of the shoe to accommodate his painting.

L

lace A textile patterned with holes and designs created by hand or machine. The two most common kinds of lace are bobbin lace and needlepoint lace. Bobbin lace is created by the manipulation of numerous threads, each attached to a bobbin, and is usually worked on a pillow. Needlepoint lace is made by looping yarn – one end of it threaded through a needle, the other fixed to a base – in simple or elaborate stitches to create a preset pattern or design. Bobbin lace is believed to have originated in Flanders and needlepoint lace in Italy. In the

Parasol cover executed in Chantilly **lace**, 1850s.

An example of 19th-century English Honiton **lace**.

18th and 19th centuries the centres for bobbin lace were Chantilly and Valenciennes. Alençon, Argentan and Venice are associated with needlepoint. Early use of lace was restricted to ecclesiastics and royalty, but by the 17th and 18th centuries lace was in general use for headdresses, FLOUNCES, aprons and dress trimmings. In the early part of the 19th century lace was used extensively, for dresses, VEILS, TEA GOWNS, jackets, gloves, and trimmings on PARASOLS and muffs. BERTHAS, FICHUS, handkerchiefs and shawls have also been made of lace. Before the 19th century lace was commonly made from linen thread but cotton became more usual during the 1800s. Machine-made lace came into use during the late 18th century. The popularity of lace decreased during the latter part of the 19th century and it is now rarely used, except on lingerie and bridalwear. *See* ALENCON LACE, ARGENTAN LACE, ★CARRICKMACROSS LACE, CHANTILLY LACE *and* VALENCIENNES LACE.

Lachasse Fashion house founded in London in 1928, which sold sports and country clothes. Digby MORTON was the first designer to be hired and he remained with the firm until 1933. Morton was followed by Hardy AMIES and then, in 1939, by MICHAEL Donellan who left in 1953. During this time Clive was employed as a blouse designer. Peter Lewis-Crown became chief designer in 1974. The house of Lachasse

was best known for impeccably tailored suits and dresses, many designed in tweed, and for its quintessentially 'English' style. The house also designed for British royalty and the stage.

Lacoste In 1934 tennis star René Lacoste (1904–96), nicknamed 'Le Crocodile', launched a white, short-sleeved knitted tennis shirt with a small crocodile emblem on the chest. The shirt was longer at the back than at the front so that it would remain tucked in during a game. Lacoste founded La Société Chemise Lacoste of Paris, which continues to make POLO SHIRTS in many different colours. *See* POLO SHIRT.

The **Lacoste** crocodile, named after René Lacoste, the celebrated tennis player of the 1920s. Nicknamed 'The Crocodile', he invented the short-sleeved polo shirt.

Three haute couture designs by Christian **Lacroix**.
Above left: Bridal gown, model no. 65 ('Qui a le droit'),
Autumn/Winter 1992–93. *Above right:* Raw linen jacket
and shot taffeta skirt, model no. 16 ('Volute'),
Spring/Summer 1988. *Right:* Sketch by Christian
Lacroix, model no. 46, Autumn/Winter 1997–98.

Lacroix, Christian 1951–. Designer. Born in
Arles, France. Lacroix studied art history at
Montpellier University and museum studies at
the Sorbonne, Paris. He then worked at HERMES
as assistant to Guy PAULIN from 1978 before
joining PATOU as head of haute couture in
1981. In 1987 he opened his own couture
house in Paris and sent reverberations through
the fashion world. Although Lacroix's clothes
had shock value, he proved to be a sure-handed
designer, confidently mixing offbeat combinations of overpowering colours and prints with
high waists, asymmetrical draping and baby-doll
shapes, particularly the 'POUF', a full, puffed
skirt which was sometimes tucked up at the
back. He stimulated ready-to-wear interest in
couture and his designs were widely copied.
His colours are often luminous, his textures
elaborate and ornate. Many retrospective elements are evident in Lacroix's collections, as

These three examples of Karl **Lagerfeld**'s designs reveal his impeccable craftsmanship. The sketch above shows his flirtation with the hourglass shape in a design for 1986–87. Note the fan trademark.

Above and below: These eminently stylish and feminine designs are from **Lagerfeld**'s ready-to-wear collection of Spring/Summer 1991.

well as influences as varied as the theatre, the FLEA MARKET and Provençal costume.

Lagerfeld, Karl 1938–. Designer. Born in Hamburg, Germany. At the age of fourteen Lagerfeld was sent to Paris to further his studies. Three years later, in 1955, after winning first prize in a coat design competition sponsored by the International Wool Secretariat, he was hired by BALMAIN, who put the coat into production. Lagerfeld stayed with Balmain for three years before joining PATOU as art director at the age of twenty. In 1964, disillusioned with the world of haute couture, Lagerfeld left Paris to study art history in Italy. But the lure of fashion was such that the following year he was back, working as a freelance designer for CHLOE, KRIZIA, VALENTINO and shoe manufacturer Charles JOURDAN. In 1967 he joined FENDI as a consultant designer. For Fendi, Lagerfeld created some truly innovative work in fur jackets and coats. He took mole,

rabbit and squirrel – furs previously considered unfashionable or unsuitable for coats – and dyed them in vibrant colours. He launched a reversible fur-lined coat and a KIMONO-style coat and also mixed fur with leather and various fabrics. His name is equally associated with the firm of CHLOE, where he became famous for his top-quality ready-to-wear garments. Every collection was expressed in positive, unhesitating terms, whether Lagerfeld showed shepherdess dresses with scarves tied as BODICES, shawls or about the waist (1975); MINI SKIRTS (1980), or layered skirts over trousers (1981). An exacting, confident stylist, Lagerfeld accessorizes his clothes in an imaginative manner. His ideas are sophisticated, often impudent but always stylishly executed. In 1983 he became design director of CHANEL. The following year he launched his first collection under his own name. From the mid-1970s Lagerfeld has been a major force in fashion, a designer who is not only able to move with the times but to move the times. He is a proven expert at elevating elements of STREET STYLE to haute couture, blending classic looks with current quirks that subsequently seep into mainstream fashion. His influence as designer and stylist in this field is considerable.

Lalique, René 1860–1945. Jeweler, glass designer. Born in Ay, Marne, France. Lalique studied drawing in Paris from 1876 to 1881. He worked as a goldsmith and spent several years in London before returning to Paris. After a period as a freelance designer specializing in jewelry, textiles and fans, Lalique opened his own company in 1885, designing and manufacturing jewelry which he sold to Boucheron, CARTIER and other French jewelry companies. In 1891 he created stage jewelry for actress Sarah Bernhardt. At the Paris Exhibition of 1900 he achieved considerable success with his ART NOUVEAU jewelry designs. From about 1895 Lalique's distinctive, sinuous style usually incorporated human forms with natural and symbolic motifs. Famous for both his glass and jewelry, Lalique was a prolific worker, crafting lavish designs onto rich materials. He was widely influential.

lambswool Wool from young sheep, used in the 20th century to make cardigans and sweaters.

Brooch/pendant of black patinated silver with a glass face covered with a layer of opalescent enamel surrounded by poppies, by the Art Nouveau jeweler René **Lalique,** c. 1898–1900.

lamé From the French word for trimmings of gold or silver, lamé is the name given to fabrics woven with flat, metallic threads. It has been popular for eveningwear since the 1930s.

Lamour, Dorothy 1914–96. Actress. Born Mary Leta Dorothy Kaumeyer in New Orleans, Louisiana, USA. Lamour's major contribution to fashion was her popularization of the SARONG, which she wore in her first film, *The Jungle Princess* (1936), and in many subsequent films. *See* HEAD.

Lancetti, Pino 1932–. Designer. Born in Perugia, Italy. Lancetti studied at the Art Institute of Perugia. In the 1950s he moved to

Model Paulene Stone decked out in Kenneth J. **Lane**'s opulent costume jewelry for 1967.

Rome where he sold sketches to designers such as SIMONETTA and FONTANA and worked freelance for several companies, including CAROSA, before establishing his own business in 1961. Lancetti is a well known Roman designer who concentrates on cut and colour, producing many sophisticated garments in silk and chiffon.

Lane, Kenneth Jay 1932–. Jewelry designer. Born in Detroit, Michigan, USA. Lane studied at the University of Michigan and Rhode Island School of Design. Graduating with a degree in advertising design, he joined the art department of *VOGUE* in New York in 1954. Two years later, he left to become VIVIER's assistant, designing shoes for DELMAN. From 1956 to 1963 Lane also worked with Vivier in Paris, producing shoes for DIOR. In 1963, as an experiment, he started making jewelry from the RHINESTONES used to decorate evening shoes. One year later his part-time jewelry business had become a successful full-time operation. Lane's talent lay in his unashamed copying of valuable pieces and his inventive manner of mixing plastics or semi-precious stones. His strange and original creations have influenced many young jewelry designers.

Lang, Helmut 1956–. Born in Vienna, Austria. Lang opened his own fashion studio in Vienna in 1977 and specialized in stylized

From the Autumn/Winter 1988 ready-to-wear collection of the Austrian designer Helmut **Lang,** who employs a sober palette in his inventive designs.

avant-garde clothing which disregarded convention. A 'deconstructionist', Lang works in an essentially urban style; he blends cheap and expensive fabrics, and blurs the lines between traditional menswear and womenswear. He has a stark, sober palette, often slashed with bright colour, which reflects a modern, even futuristic perspective. His cleverly thought out clothes are cleanly and precisely tailored, but in an exploratory, quirky manner. His fabric combinations reveal a forward-looking approach.

Langtry, Lillie 1852–1929. Born Emilie Charlotte le Breton on the Channel Island of Jersey. After her marriage to Edward Langtry in 1874, Lillie Langtry achieved notoriety as the mistress of the Prince of Wales (later Edward VII) and in 1881 went on the stage. Known as the 'Jersey Lily', she was famous for her beauty. She popularized the JERSEY COSTUME and gave her name to a BUSTLE and a shoe style.

Lanvin, Jeanne

Jeanne **Lanvin**'s active fashion career spanned fifty years, beginning in the 1890s. *Left:* The sleek lines of a 1931 Lanvin evening gown. *Centre:* Lanvin design for 1947, which retains some of the 'picture dress' style for which the designer was famous. *Right:* Lanvin version of the New Look, 1947.

Lanvin, Jeanne 1867–1946. Designer. Born in Brittany, France. Lanvin trained first as a dressmaker and then as a milliner. In 1890 she opened a millinery shop in Paris. During the early years of the 20th century the clothes she made for her younger sister and later for her small daughter attracted so much attention from customers that Lanvin created copies and introduced new lines to sell in her store. Over the following years demand by young women persuaded Lanvin to open a couture house selling matching mother-and-daughter garments. Shortly before World War I she created her famous 'robes de style', based on 18th-century

Lanvin began her career as a milliner: these designs are from 1927–28 *(left)* and 1924 *(right)*.

148

designs. These waisted, full-skirted dresses remained popular until the early 1920s with only slight adjustments. She also designed romantic 'picture' dresses based on softened Victorian shapes and lavishly trimmed with embroidery. Influenced by orientalism from around 1910, Lanvin turned to exotic evening-wear in Eastern-style velvets and satins. At the beginning of World War I she made a simple CHEMISE DRESS which later became the basic outline for the 1920s. Lanvin's postwar clothes were in the spirit of the age. In 1921 a Riviera collection introduced Aztec embroideries. The following year the Lanvin Breton suit appeared, comprising a gently gathered skirt, a short, braided jacket with lots of small buttons, and a big white organdy collar turning down over a red satin bow. A sailor hat or round straw hat topped the outfit. Lanvin also sold beaded dance dresses, a wool jersey sportsdress patterned in check of gold and silver thread, dinner PYJAMAS, and capes. Her work was easily recognizable by her skilful use of embroidery and her fine craftsmanship. She used a particular shade of blue so often that it came to be called 'Lanvin blue'. In 1997 Claude MONTANA began designing for the house of Lanvin. *See also* CASTILLO *and* CRAHAY.

GUY LAROCHE HAUTE COUTURE
AUTOMNE-HIVER 85-86

Guy **Laroche** haute couture design, Autumn/Winter, 1985–86.

lapel Part of the front neckline of a blouse, coat, dress or jacket which turns back or folds over.

Lapidus, Ted 1929–. Designer. Born Edmond Lapidus in Paris, France. Lapidus is the son of a tailor. After studying technical engineering in Tokyo, Japan, Lapidus opened a BOUTIQUE in Paris in the early 1950s. He designed his clothes as a technician, concerned as much with cut as with design, and his precise garments soon earned him recognition. During the 1960s he produced a SAFARI JACKET which became widely popular. Lapidus's ideas were perfectly in tune with the UNISEX styles of that decade and he made his name in both mens-wear and womenswear. Since the mid-1970s his clothes have become far more classic in style.

Laroche, Guy 1923–89. Designer. Born in La Rochelle, near Bordeaux, France. Laroche went to Paris at an early age and worked with a milliner. After World War II he spent two years in New York as a milliner on SEVENTH AVENUE. On his return to Paris he was given a job with Jean DESSES. He worked with Dessès for eight years before establishing his own business in 1957. At first Laroche produced couture lines but in 1960 he launched his ready-to-wear collection. He was known for his skilful cutting and tailoring. In 1996 Michel Klein began designing the line.

Lars, Byron 1965–. Designer. Born in Oakland, California, USA. After studying in New York and Paris, Lars first became known in 1992 with a collection of aviator jackets inspired by Amelia Earhart. Lars's modern sensibility focuses on menswear which he adapts to a women's wardrobe, close-fitting jackets (for example, bull-fighter jackets) and capes. Ever conscious of the female shape, he focuses many of his designs on the waist. Lars often uses flamboyant, luxurious fabrics. His less extravagant garments are hallmarked by clever stitching and attention to detail.

Lastex

The man who created the 'prairie look' and 'frontier fashions' in the USA, Ralph **Lauren** also tailored Englishwomen in 1982 with a Norfolk jacket, lace jabot blouse and dogstooth Cambridge skirt.

Lastex US Rubber Company's trade name for an elastic yarn made of rubber combined with silk, cotton or rayon. Lastex was used in foundation garments and underwear, particularly CORSETS and GIRDLES, during the early part of the 20th century.

Lauren, Ralph 1939–. Designer. Born Ralph Lipschitz in New York, USA. Lauren worked in New York at BROOKS BROTHERS, Allied stores, and as a glove salesman while attending nightschool in business studies at City College. In 1967 he joined Beau Brummell Neckwear, where he created the Polo division to produce wide, handmade, expensive neckties. The following year Lauren established the Polo range of men's clothing, featuring the natural shoulder line of the IVY LEAGUE style. In 1971 he turned his attention to womenswear and produced a collection of tailored shirts. The 'Ralph Lauren' label was launched the following year

with a complete range of garments for women in cashmere, cotton and tweed. HACKING JACKETS, Fair Isle sweaters, pleated skirts, CREWNECK shirts, lace-collared velvet dresses, flannel trousers and flannel skirts all featured in Lauren's subsequent collections. In 1978 he introduced the casual/sophisticated 'prairie look': denim skirts worn over layers of white cotton petticoats, fringed buckskin jackets, leather belts, and full-sleeved, soft blouses. In 1980 he showed hooded capes, linen ruffled blouses, madras shirts and full skirts as part of his American frontier fashions. Lauren continues to uphold tradition with his choice of quality fabrics. He is successful in expressing a purely American style of casual gentrification.

lawn Named after the French town of Laon, lawn is a fine, lightweight sheer cotton or linen fabric which is plain woven and given a crisp finish. It was used for underwear and delicate blouses in the 19th and early 20th centuries.

leather Hide or skin of an animal which is tanned or chemically preserved. Used for accessories until the 20th century, when it was made up, notably during the 1960s, into dresses, suits, TROUSER SUITS, jackets and coats. *See* BATES, MONTANA *and* VERSACE.

Léger, Hervé 1957–. Designer. Born in Bapaume, France. After working as a hairdresser, hatmaker and knitwear designer, Léger moved in 1980 to Rome to assist Karl LAGERFELD at FENDI, and subsequently moved with Lagerfeld to CHANEL in Paris. In 1985 he opened his own company but continued to design freelance for LANVIN, CHLOE and Charles JOURDAN, among others. His famous 'bandage' dresses, first introduced in 1989, are made of elasticized wool, silk or Lycra which is woven horizontally around the body, emphasizing its natural shape and curves in a manner more usually associated with foundation garments. Léger's work is glamorous in the modern sense: he uses a neutral palette of black, navy and white which gives stark emphasis to the curvaceous, highly enhanced silhouettes of his dresses.

leggings Fitted leg covering which extends from the foot to the waist, thigh or knee and is often fastened under the instep. Leggings or leg

Stylish **leg-of-mutton** sleeves incorporated into riding habits of 1896.

The French designer Hervé **Léger** created these typically glamorous and body-hugging designs for his ready-to-wear collection of Spring/Summer 1997.

bindings have been used since the Middle Ages as protection against the cold. They were worn by children and young girls from the mid-19th century until the early 20th century. In the 1980s they emerged as fashion items, chiefly in black, but also in bright colours and patterns, and were swiftly adopted as leisure items.

leg-of-mutton sleeve Sleeve that is tight-fitting from wrist to elbow, then balloons out from elbow to shoulder, where it is gathered or pleated into the BODICE of a dress or blouse. A popular sleeve-style in the late 19th century and during the EDWARDIAN-STYLE revivals of the late 1960s and early 1970s.

Legroux Soeurs House founded by two sisters, Germaine and Héloise Legroux, who opened a millinery store in 1913 in Roubaix, near the French border with Belgium. In 1917 they moved to Paris, achieving much success in the 1920s. In the following decade they began

to export their hats to the USA. In the 1950s one of their nieces, Madame Serge Robert, took over the business.

legwarmers Traditionally worn by ballet dancers, legwarmers are long, woollen, footless socks worn around the calves and ankles to maintain body heat before, during and after exercising. During the health cult of the 1970s, they became fashionable worn over trousers and tucked into boots, or under long skirts. They were made up in a spectrum of shades.

Leiber, Judith 1921–. Handbag designer. Born Judith Peto in Budapest, Hungary. Leiber apprenticed with the Handbag Guild in Hungary, which would appoint her its first woman Meister. Emigrating to New York in 1947, she began a long association with Nettie ROSENSTEIN as an accessories designer. Leiber became known for her exquisite craftsmanship and artistry and in 1963 she opened her own firm. Almost always small in scale, her daytime bags are made of exotic skins such as python, shark, ostrich and horn alligator, often worked

Glamorous cocktail dress, created by the French couturier Lucien **Lelong**, c. 1936.

into supple pleats and adorned with braid, unusual trimmings and closings. Her evening bags incorporate soft, supple materials such as Japanese OBIS, fine silks and gorgeous embroideries. But it is her whimsical, RHINESTONE-studded evening bags, often crafted in the form of *minaudières*, which have brought her lasting fame. Brightly coloured, small-scale and delicate yet sturdily engineered, they are covered with handset Austrian crystal and semi-precious stones, duplicating flora and fauna.

Lelong, Lucien 1889–1958. Designer. Born in Paris, France. Lelong's father founded a textile house three years before Lelong's birth. Lelong trained for a business career at the Hautes Etudes des Commerciales, Paris, from 1911 to 1913. His first collection was prepared for 1914 but was postponed because of his mobilization. After the war Lelong established his own business. Noted more for the skill and workmanship of beautiful fabrics than for innovative design, he was one of the earliest designers to diversify into lingerie and stockings. He introduced a line of ready-to-wear in

1934 which he labelled 'editions'. In 1939, just before the outbreak of World War II, Lelong showed tightly waisted, full skirts – a style which became the NEW LOOK in DIOR's hands in 1947. President of the Chambre Syndicale de la Couture (*See* HAUTE COUTURE) from 1937 until 1947, Lelong was instrumental in persuading the occupying Germans to permit French couture houses to remain in Paris rather than transferring to Berlin. It was largely due to his efforts that ninety-two houses stayed open during the war. Lelong's own house reopened in 1941. After the war, in 1947, Lelong showed pencil-slim dresses; pleated, tiered, harem hemlines; and suits with wasp waists, cutaway fronts and square shoulders. His second wife, Princess Natalie Paley, daughter of Grand Duke Paul of Russia, was a noted beauty who wore her husband's designs.

Lenglen, Suzanne 1899–1938. Tennis player. Born in Compiègne, France. Lenglen won the Wimbledon women's final from 1919 to 1926. Her impact as a tennis player was almost matched by her impact on the fashion world. She dispensed with the traditional tennis outfit – blouse, tie and long skirt – and wore instead a thin, one-piece, loose-fitting dress or a sweater and skirt. She replaced her SUSPENDER BELT with knee GARTERS and discarded her CORSET and petticoat. Jean PATOU designed many of Lenglen's clothes: a pleated silk skirt reaching just to the knee and a straight, white, sleeveless cardigan teamed with a bright orange HEAD-BAND. This outfit was widely copied off the tennis court.

leotard One-piece long-sleeved garment first worn by the 19th-century French trapeze artist, Jules Léotard. The leotard is cut low at the neck and fitted between the legs. It was adopted by dancers and gymnasts and until the 1950s it was invariably black. In 1965 André COURREGES and Jacques HEIM were just two French designers who experimented with the shape of the leotard. Leotards of strong, flexible, man-made fabrics became fashionable during the 1970s, in association with DISCO fashions and the general interest in exercise and dance. They have been made in various fabrics, many of which contain Spandex, and in many different styles of sleeve, neckline and general

WORTH and DOUCET. In 1924 Albert Lesage purchased the business. He married a milliner employed by VIONNET and received an exclusive contract with Vionnet as a wedding gift. Lesage also worked for SCHIAPARELLI, embroidering astral symbols in gold and silver lamé onto coats. After Lesage died in 1949, the business was taken over by his son François, who continued to supply Paris-based designers such as DIOR, BALMAIN, FATH and BALENCIAGA. Since 1969 he has collaborated with Yves SAINT LAURENT and since 1987 with Christian LACROIX, among others. Due to the high cost of production, Lesage is one of the few embroidery houses remaining in Paris in the 1990s.

Leser, Tina 1910–86. Designer. Born Christine Wetherill Shillard-Smith in Philadelphia, Pennsylvania, USA. Leser studied at the Philadelphia Academy of fine Arts and the Sorbonne in Paris. In 1953, she opened a small dress store in Honolulu, Hawaii, in which she

'Serais-je en avance?' (Am I Going to Be Early?). A design for a theatre coat by Paul Poiret. Illustration by Georges **Lepape** from the *Gazette du bon ton*, 1912. Lepape was strongly influenced by the Ballets Russes.

body cut. *See also* CAPEZIO, DANSKIN, JOHNSON *and* KAMALI.

Lepape, Georges 1887–1971. Illustrator. Born in Paris, France. Lepape studied at the Ecole des Beaux-Arts in Paris. In 1909 he began working for Paul POIRET and two years later illustrated Poiret's famous brochure, *Les Choses de Paul Poiret...vue par Georges Lepape*. Lepape moved to Jean PATOU in 1912, to illustrate Patou's collections. He also worked freelance for many magazines, among them the *GAZETTE DU BON TON*, *FEMINA*, *VOGUE*, *HARPER'S BAZAAR* and *LES FEUILLETS D'ART*. Lepape was strongly influenced by orientalism and the BALLETS RUSSES. His work showed a distinctive, curvilinear style. He was better known than many other illustrators of the period, chiefly through his designs of posters and books and his work as a printmaker.

Lesage Embroidery house, originally called Michonet, founded in Paris in 1868. The house's earliest patrons were European royalty and aristocracy as well as designers such as

Detail of contemporary lace design from **Lesage**, the world's most famous embroidery house, supplier to many of Paris's couturiers.

sold Chinese brocade items as well as garments made of cotton, sailcloth and silk, onto which she had hand-blocked prints. Specializing in SPORTSWEAR and PLAYSUITS, Leser gained a reputation as an innovative designer. In 1940 she visited New York, where her playsuits were shown to fashion editors. Leser was subsequently introduced to the Saks Fifth Avenue department store which ordered five hundred playsuits. Two years later Leser moved to the city and designed for a clothing manufacturer until 1953, when she opened her own business. She produced RESORTWEAR during the 1950s: Lastex bathing suits, SARONG-style skirts, TOREADOR PANTS and Lurex PYJAMAS. Many garments featured bold ETHNIC prints and patterns. Leser was also noted for cashmere dresses, plaid blanket dresses, sweaters cut like jackets and at-home clothes.

levi's See *STRAUSS.

Leyendecker, Joseph 1874–1951. Painter, illustrator. Born in Montabour, Germany. Leyendecker moved to Chicago, USA, at the age of seven. He studied at the Art Institute of Chicago and later at the Académie Julian in Paris. It was in Paris at the 1897 Salon Champ de Mars that his first major exhibition of paintings was held. Leyendecker then worked as a commercial artist in Chicago and Philadelphia, before finally moving to New York in 1900. Throughout the early 1900s he illustrated covers for the *Saturday Evening Post, Collier's Weekly* and other magazines. After achieving fame through his Chesterfield cigarette advertisements, he was hired by the *ARROW collar and shirt company to illustrate their publicity material. Leyendecker's work was so true to life that women were convinced that his characters (clean-cut, upstanding young American men) were portraits of real people.

Liberman, Alexander 1912–. Magazine editorial director. Born in Kiev, Russia. Liberman studied mathematics, architecture and philosophy in Moscow and England. He emigrated to France and was hired at the age of twenty by Lucien VOGEL to work on *Vu*, a photojournalism magazine published in Paris. Within one year Liberman became art director and eventually managing editor. He then spent sev-

eral years painting in the South of France before moving in 1941 to New York, where he became art director of *VOGUE* in 1943. In 1962 he was appointed editorial director of Condé NAST publications. His influence on the world of fashion is considerable. An internationally recognized artist, he has promoted all forms of art through the Condé Nast publications.

Liberty, Arthur Lasenby 1843–1917. Storeowner. Born in Chesham, Buckinghamshire, England. Liberty's father was a draper. At the age of fifteen Liberty worked in the lace warehouse of his uncle's Nottingham-based company. In 1861 he moved to London and soon joined Farmer and Rogers's Great Shawl and Cloak Emporiums where he was eventually put in charge of the oriental warehouse. Liberty set up on his own in 1875 selling Eastern silks and orientally inspired household goods and costumes. He specialized in the importation of handwoven silks from Mysore and Nagpur in India, cashmere from Persia, shantung and Shanghai silks from China, and crepes and satins from Japan. Silk was promoted by a series of exhibitions in the Regent Street store. At the turn of the century Liberty was selling hand-blocked PAISLEY designs and machine-made lawns, linens and wools. He commissioned designers to produce Grecian- and medieval-style gowns, metalwork and furnishing fabrics. The Liberty store was patronized by supporters of the *AESTHETIC DRESS movement and also by admirers of ART NOUVEAU. See *SHAWL.

liberty bodice Undergarment introduced in the early 20th century by a British CORSET manufacturing company. It is a front-buttoning BODICE constructed of taped bands and made of a soft, knitted fabric. Lightweight versions were produced during the 1920s and 1930s. The bodice was manufactured until the 1950s.

linen Name given to any fabric made from flax fibre, obtained from the flax plant. Strong and smooth-surfaced, linen varies in weight and texture. Depending on the weave, it is possible to manufacture linen to be as fine as cambric or as coarse as canvas. It was used throughout the 19th century for underwear and became popular during the 20th century for blouses, jackets, skirts and outerwear.

Linton tweed Distinctive tweed used for summer and winter coating produced by Linton Tweed Ltd of Carlisle, England. The company was founded in 1919 by William Linton. Until the outbreak of World War II it supplied international designers such as CHANEL, HARTNELL, MOLYNEUX, SCHIAPARELLI and STIEBEL. After the war the company also supplied BALENCIAGA, BALMAIN, AMIES, COURREGES, DIOR and SAINT LAURENT.

lisle Handspun two-ply cotton yarn twisted to compact the fibres. Named after the French town of Lille, where it originated, it was chiefly used until the mid-1940s for STOCKINGS.

little black dress Emerging in the 1920s, the little black dress was based on the simple lines of the CHEMISE. It became a staple of the cocktail hour and an essential ingredient of every woman's wardrobe. Heavily promoted by CHANEL and MOLYNEUX in the 1920s and 1930s, it has been popular at some point in most decades. *See* COCKTAIL DRESS *and* *OLDFIELD.

Little Lord Fauntleroy Hero of a children's book of the same name by Frances Hodgson Burnett, published in New York and London in 1886. The book's illustrations by Reginald Birch showed Little Lord Fauntleroy dressed in a black or dark blue velvet suit (jacket and KNICKERBOCKERS), a white blouse with a VANDYKE collar, a coloured SASH, silk stockings, buckled PUMPS and an oversize BERET. This outfit resembled male AESTHETIC DRESS of the period. Little Lord Fauntleroy clothes for women became fashionable in the 1970s.

loafer Low-heeled shoe, resembling a leather MOCCASIN, which originated in Norway. It was introduced in the USA in the 1940s. Like the moccasin, the loafer is a slip-on shoe with a laced front panel. Traditionally worn by men, it is also used as casual footwear by women. *See also* BASS WEEJUNS.

loden *1.* Sturdy fabric originating in the Tyrol region of Austria. Loden was once made of sheep's wool but in the 20th century alpaca, camel hair and mohair came into use. At the turn of the century, the traditional colours – red, black or white – were succeeded by a shade of green which came to be permanently associated with the fabric. *2.* Dark green, coarse woollen jacket trimmed with braid and with a PRUSSIAN COLLAR, which was popular for casual wear during the mid-20th century.

louis heel The louis heel was first named in the reign of the French King Louis XIV (1643–1715), when it described the method of making the sole and heel in one section. In the second half of the 19th century the term louis heel referred to a thick, often covered heel, which is tapered at the mid-section before flaring outward, first worn in the reign of Louis XV of France (1715–74).

Louis, Jean 1907–97. Costume designer. Born Jean Louis Berthault in Paris, France. After studying at the Arts Décoratifs in Paris, Louis worked for Agnès DRECOLL. In 1935 he went to New York, where he showed his sketches to Hattie CARNEGIE, who subsequently employed him for seven years. In 1944 he was appointed head designer at Columbia Pictures in Hollywood. For Rita Hayworth in the film *Gilda* (1946), Louis created a black satin strapless evening dress, designed to give the actress sufficient mobility for an energetic dance scene. The dress was widely copied. In 1958 Louis moved to Universal Studios. From 1961 to 1988 he operated a ready-to-wear business, specializing in eveningwear, while continuing to create for the screen on a freelance basis.

Louiseboulanger 1878–c.1950. Designer. Born Louise Melenot in Paris, France. At thirteen Boulanger became an apprentice at a dressmaking establishment. Later she worked with Madeleine CHERUIT until in 1927 she opened her own establishment with her husband, Louis Boulanger. For the next twenty years Louiseboulanger was a successful designer of graceful, elegant clothes often cut on the BIAS. She showed evening skirts which were knee-length in front but fell to the ankles at the back. Bold colours and heavy fabrics such as taffeta were her trademarks.

Lucas, Otto 1903–71. Milliner. Born in Germany. Lucas opened a London salon in 1932 after studying in Paris and Berlin. He became a highly successful milliner, popular on both sides

Lucile was best known for her romantic turn-of-the-century gowns in predominantly pastel shades.

of the Atlantic. Lucas supplied hats to stores and dress designers in addition to creating styles for his private clientele and for the cinema.

Lucile 1863–1935. Designer. Born Lucy Sutherland in London, England. After a divorce in 1890, Lucile started dressmaking for her friends and in 1891 she opened her own house. She married Sir Cosmo Duff Gordon in 1900. For the first twenty years of the 20th century Lucile was a well known designer with branches in London, New York (1909), Chicago (1911) and Paris (1911). She was most famous for her TEA GOWNS, made in flimsy gauzes, taffetas, poplins and silks. Her clients included Irene CASTLE, Sarah Bernhardt, film stars and royalty. Lucile claimed to have revolutionized women's underwear by refining the CORSET to make it less restrictive. In 1907 she created the costumes for Lily Elsie, star of *The Merry Widow*, a London stage production. Copies of these clothes were briefly fashionable in Britain. Lucile is also associated with the promotion of coloured underwear; the use of models, whom she took with her to the USA; subtle, soft colour schemes of predominantly pastel shades; and orientally inspired, romantic dresses which were particularly well-suited for eveningwear. She was also a noted designer of formal ball gowns covered in lace and beads. During World War I Lucile designed costumes for the Ziegfeld Follies. She sold her business in 1918. *See* ★MERRY WIDOW HAT.

Lurex Trademark of the Dow Badische Company for its metallic fibre yarn which was introduced during the 1940s. Woven or knitted with cotton, nylon, rayon, silk or wool fibres, Lurex is made into dresses, cardigans and sweaters. It is particularly suitable for eveningwear and was popular until the 1970s.

Lycra Man-made fibre introduced in 1958 by DU PONT of Delaware, USA. Lycra is elastic, abrasion resistant and has stretch and recovery powers. Since its introduction, it has been an essential component of underwear, particularly GIRDLES and ROLL-ONS. During the 1970s it was incorporated into tights, swimwear and exercise clothes.

M

Macintosh, Charles 1766–1843. Scottish chemist who, in 1823, took out a patent to waterproof fabrics by cementing together two layers of woollen material with indiarubber dissolved in naptha. In 1830 Thomas Hancock, who had been in competition with Macintosh vulcanizing rubber to develop waterproof clothing, joined Charles Macintosh and Co. *See* MACKINTOSH.

Mackie, Bob 1940–. Designer. Born in Los Angeles, California, USA. Mackie studied at Chouinard Art Institute in Los Angeles before beginning his design career as a sketch artist for Jean LOUIS. He also worked for Edith HEAD at Paramount. While continuing his work in films, Mackie gained further design experience by creating costumes for the Judy Garland television show (1963) and later for the Carol Burnett show. He is best known for his glamorous evening clothes, swimwear and fur lines.

mackintosh Waterproof coat developed in stages during the 19th century. In 1823 the Scottish chemist Charles MACINTOSH patented a waterproof woollen fabric. Sixteen years later Charles Goodyear of the USA introduced vulcanized rubber. Joseph Mandleburg of Lancashire, England, tackled the problem of the rubber smell in woollen waterproof garments and in 1851 launched the first odour-free waterproof coat. The first 'macs' of the late 19th century were voluminous, neck-to-ankle garments, designed to keep the wearer completely dry. In the 20th century, fashion adapted the

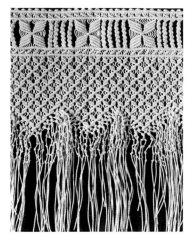

Late-19th-century cotton **macramé** border. Macramé enjoyed a revival in the 1960s as part of that decade's vogue for ethnic fashions.

mackintosh into a number of styles, including the civilian TRENCHCOAT and the raincoat. Cotton blends and, later in the century, synthetic blends were used to make waterproof coats. *See also* AQUASCUTUM *and* BURBERRY.

macramé Decorative knotting originating in Arabia. Macramé was used for fringes in home furnishings during the 19th century but did not become associated with clothing until the 1960s when a revival of macramé included its use in the construction of dresses and tops. The 1990s saw another revival of macramé in sweaters and handbags.

Mad Carpentier Composite name for two of Madeleine VIONNET's protégées, Mad Maltezos and Suzie Carpentier, who continued to direct Vionnet's business after her retirement in 1939.

Madonna 1960–. Rock singer. Born Madonna Louise Ciccone in Bay City, Michigan, USA. Madonna spent one year at the University of Michigan and then left for New York, where she earned money working as a model and became a singer with a band. In 1983 she began to launch her own records and to appear on MTV. Madonna had an enormous impact on fashion, especially among teenagers. She popularized the wearing of lingerie (particularly bras) as outerwear; tube skirts that rolled down onto the hips, exposing the navel; black elbow-length gloves; tight skirts and spiked heels; lace TANK TOPS, and strings of beads and pearls. Her first film, *Desperately Seeking Susan* (1984), further increased her influence. On her world tours of the late 1980s and early 1990s, she wore BUSTIERS designed by Jean-Paul GAULTIER which became widely influential in the trend towards underwear as outerwear. *See* BUSTIER *and* GAULTIER.

madras Fabric of vegetable dyed cotton yarns handwoven in large bold checks which originated in India in the late 19th century. Machine-made madras is produced in a variety of weaves. It is used for daywear and summer attire.

Magyar dress Derived from traditional Hungarian costume, Magyar dress consists of brightly coloured clothes: flounced skirts and blouses with fitted BODICES and very full sleeves that are gathered at the wrist. Variations on Magyar dress have entered the fashion picture in the late 19th century, the 1930s, the late 1960s and the early 1970s.

Magyar sleeve *See* MAGYAR DRESS.

maillot 1. Dancer's or gymnast's TIGHTS which take their name from a Monsieur Maillot, a French costume and hosiery maker for the Paris Opéra, who, during the 1800s, designed knitted tights and matching LEOTARD which were known as 'fleshings'. 2. Modern word for a one-piece, tight-fitting BATHING SUIT.

Mainbocher 1891–1976. Designer. Born Main Rousseau Bocher in Chicago, USA. Mainbocher attended the University of Chicago, the Chicago Academy of Fine Arts and the Art Students League in New York. From 1911 to 1917 he studied and worked in Munich, Paris and London. In 1917 he served with the American hospital unit en route to France and at the end of the war he stayed on in Paris, intending to study singing. The loss of his voice forced him to seek an alternative career and in 1922 he joined *HARPER'S BAZAAR* as a fashion artist. The following year he was invited by Condé NAST to become fashion editor, and

later editor-in-chief of French *VOGUE*, a position he held until 1929. In 1930 Mainbocher became the first American to open a successful couture salon in Paris. His success continued throughout the 1930s. He was famous for his eveningwear: decorated evening sweaters, embroidered apron-style evening dresses, BIAS-CUT dresses, and theatre dinner suits that were worn with blouses. His wedding gown for Mrs Wallis Simpson on her marriage to the Duke of Windsor created a vogue for 'Wallis blue'. Mainbocher's dresses were often described as 'well-bred', elegant and refined. Several times he revamped the LITTLE BLACK DRESS. A memorable collection, in 1939, previewed the NEW LOOK of 1947, with small waists and tightly laced CORSET-like garments. In 1940 Mainbocher returned to New York and opened a salon. He closed in 1971.

Man Ray *See* RAY, MAN.

mandarin collar Stand-up collar on jackets, dresses and blouses. Adapted from a close-fitting Asian collar. *See* MANDARIN JACKET.

mandarin jacket Straight, loose jacket or coat traditionally worn by Chinese officials. Often richly embroidered, the jacket has a small, standing collar and fastens in front or across the shoulder. *See also* MANDARIN COLLAR.

Mandelli, Mariuccia *See* KRIZIA.

mantle Hooded CLOAK with silk tassels worn by women as an outer garment in the mid- and late 19th century. It was usually waist- or hip-length and made of light woollen materials. *See* BURNOUS.

Mao suit Simple suit named after Mao Zedong (1893–1976), founder of the People's Republic of China. Made in black crepe and designed along straight lines, the suit consists of a pair of trousers and a jacket with long sleeves, a high-standing collar and front buttons. It appeared in London in the mid-1960s as a man's suit but Paris soon adapted it to womenswear. Its popularity in the 1960s was associated both with UNISEX experimentation in dress and with the support of young people of the period for left-wing politics.

Marcel Grateau, creator of the **Marcel wave**, 1922.

marabou Feathers from a species of stork, used in the 19th and early 20th centuries to decorate hats and to trim evening gowns.

Marcel wave Wavy hairstyle created in 1872 by a French hairdresser, Marcel Grateau, who reversed curling tongs to produce a curl rather than a crimp. Marcelling was popular until the 1930s, when the PERMANENT WAVE was introduced.

Margiela, Martin 1957–. Designer. Born in Louvain, Belgium. After completing his studies at the Royal Academy of Fine Art in Antwerp, Margiela became a freelance fashion stylist. In 1982, he moved to Paris to work for Jean-Paul GAULTIER. In 1989 he showed his first collection and gained widespread attention. His clothes were slashed and faded, with exposed linings and frayed edges. Many looked destroyed, and Margiela quickly earned a DECONSTRUCTIONIST label. He is, however, a highly skilled tailor who pays great attention to detail. His raw-edged seams are well-finished. His jackets, from which the sleeves have been ripped off, are beautifully made. Margiela likes juxtapositions – fragility with hardness, structured shapes with softness – and this is reflected in the wide range of fabrics he uses, such as recycled FLEA MARKET finds of antique tulle mixed with floral PATCH-WORK. He has also made dresses from plastic bags and sellotape. Margiela's shredding of existing clothes enables him to create new ones. He often uses a palette of red, black and white.

Marimekko Company founded in 1951 by Armi Ratia (1912–79), specializing in bright and cheerful prints for dresses and home furnishings. The Jokapoika, a plain Finnish farmer's shirt, was first introduced in the late 1950s. It has been produced in 450 colourways. Marimekko was particularly successful in the USA. Its brightly coloured, simply designed SHIFT dresses featured huge checks and nonfigurative prints. The firm extended its cotton lines and introduced jersey dresses in the 1960s. Today the company produces mainly household furnishings.

Martin, Charles 1848–1934. Born in Montpellier, France. Artist who illustrated fashion for many magazines, including LE JOURNAL DES DAMES ET DES MODES, MODES ET MANIERES D'AUJOURD'HUI and the ★GAZETTE DU BON TON.

Marty, André 1882–1974. Born in Paris, France. Artist who illustrated fashion for many magazines, including the GAZETTE DU BON TON, LE GOUT DU JOUR, FEMINA, VOGUE, LES FEUILLETS D'ART, HARPER'S BAZAAR and MODES ET MANIERES D'AUJOURD'HUI.

mary janes Ankle-strap, button shoes, either flat or with small heels, which were originally designed for children. During the 1920s they became a popular style for women.

matinée hat Large-brimmed picture hat worn in the early 20th century for teas and afternoon excursions.

Matsuda, Mitsuhiro 1934–. Designer. Born in Tokyo, Japan. Matsuda attended the Japanese college of fashion, Bunka Fukuso Gakuin, from which he graduated in 1962. In 1965 he spent six months in Paris. He opened his own company, Nicole, in Tokyo in 1967. Throughout the 1970s Matsuda started both menswear and womenswear BOUTIQUES in Japan and in 1982 he expanded to the USA and Hong Kong. His collections are planned with an international clientele in mind. He pays special attention to fabric and is sometimes whimsical in design.

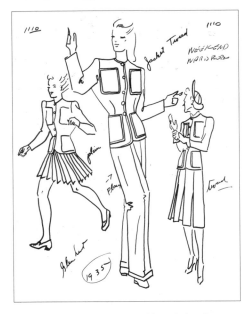

Vera **Maxwell**'s practical weekend wardrobe of 1935.

Mattli, Giuseppe 1907–82. Designer. Born in Locarno, Switzerland. After a period in London, learning English, Mattli moved to Paris and worked for the couture house of PREMET. Returning to London in 1934, he opened his own house, producing both couture and ready-to-wear lines. Mattli was known to the fashion world on both sides of the Channel. In 1955 he dropped his couture line, though he continued with other lines until the early 1970s. He was famous during the 1960s for his COCKTAIL DRESSES and theatre coats, which he designed to be worn over low-cut dresses.

Maxfield Parrish Company established in London in 1974 by Nigel Preston (b. 1946), who made clothes for pop stars. Maxfield Parrish is known for suede and leather garments, classically styled along fluid, sensitive lines.

maxi skirt Ankle- or floor-length, often full skirt which became popular during the late 1960s. The maxi skirt was often worn with boots. See EDWARDIAN STYLE and MINI SKIRT.

Maxwell, Vera 1901–95. Designer. Born Vera Huppé in New York, USA. Maxwell's parents were Viennese. She trained as a ballet dancer, joining the Metropolitan Opera Ballet in 1919. In 1924, after her marriage, she worked as a model for a wholesale company, and, in 1929, started to sketch, design and model her own clothes. Influenced by numerous European childhood tours and a brief period in London studying tailoring, Maxwell produced classic styles made of the finest fabrics: silks, tweeds and wools. By the mid-1930s her freelance collections received attention in New York. She designed a 'weekend wardrobe' in 1935 and a collarless tweed 'Einstein' jacket in 1936 – two of many innovative dressing ideas. In 1947 Maxwell opened her own business. She became known for classic separates and suits, dresses teamed with jackets, print dresses with matching print-lined coats, riding jacket suits, PRINCESS-LINE COAT DRESSES, CHESTERFIELD coats and *WRAPAROUND jersey dresses. She closed her business in 1985.

McCardell, Claire 1905–58. Designer. Born in Frederick, Maryland, USA. McCardell studied for two years at Hood College in Frederick before transferring in 1927 to Parsons School of Design in New York and later to Parsons' Paris branch. Back in New York at the end of the 1920s she worked as a sketcher for a dress shop. In 1929 she joined designer Richard Turk, moving with him in 1931 to manufacturers Townley Frocks. Turk died shortly afterwards and McCardell took over his job as designer. In 1938 she introduced her 'monastic dress', a highly successful, free-flowing garment, waistless and cut on the BIAS. Shortly after, McCardell moved to Hattie CARNEGIE, where she stayed for two years. In 1940 she returned to Townley Frocks to design under her own label. Over the following years McCardell drew up the blueprint for American SPORTSWEAR. She designed practical clothing for women with practical lives. Taking simple fabrics – cotton, denim, mattress ticking, gingham and jersey – she created clean, purposeful shapes, often using detail as a fashion focus. McCardell hallmarked her clothes with large PATCH POCKETS, metal rivets, top stitching, visible hooks, deep armholes, SHIRTWAIST sleeves and shoestring ties over the shoulder. She launched many fashions throughout the 1940s and 1950s, notably the 'popover' (1942), an unstructured

WRAPAROUND dress which would become an American classic; and a diaper-style one-piece bathing suit (1943). In 1944 she persuaded CAPEZIO to produce PUMPS based on ballet shoes. Other innovations were soft, EMPIRE-LINE dresses; bloomer-like PLAYSUITS; DIRNDL skirts; elasticated, strapless TUBE tops; and bare-back summer dresses. Many of McCardell's ideas have proved to be lasting and she is considered to have been one of the USA's most influential designers.

McFadden, Mary 1938–. Designer. Born in New York, USA. McFadden went to Paris to study at the Ecole Lubec and the Sorbonne. In 1957 she attended New York's Traphagen School of Design before taking a sociology degree at Columbia University. Her first job was in public relations for DIOR, followed by a position as South African *VOGUE*'s merchandising editor. In 1970 she returned to the USA and worked as a special projects editor for *Vogue*. Her first designs, in 1973, for which she used African and oriental fabrics, attracted a great deal of attention. She formed her own company in 1976 and gained a reputation as a designer of individual, original jackets, coats and dresses based on PEASANT designs of the Middle East and Asia. She uses lavish fabrics, especially hand-printed silks, and has experimented with pleating fabrics which, when made into dresses, resemble FORTUNY gowns. McFadden has been acclaimed for her evening gowns and intricately quilted and decorated jackets.

McQueen, Alexander 1969–. Designer. Born in London, England. At age sixteen McQueen began work as a pattern cutter for a Savile Row tailor. He then worked for Koji Tatsuno and Romeo GIGLI in Milan before returning to London to enroll at St Martin's School of Art. In 1993 he opened his own business and promptly became the *enfant terrible* of the London fashion world. McQueen introduced a rebellious, hard-edged style which included low-riding 'bum-ter' trousers, slashed clothing and garments designed to emphasize and at the same time

The British designer Alexander **McQueen** produced some of the most creative, original styles of the late 1990s. *Top:* Autumn/Winter 1996–97; *right:* Spring/Summer 1996.

deride the body's erogenous zones. Despite the shock value of McQueen's clothes, he is a highly creative designer with a fine technique. He has shown laminated lace dresses, a rivetted vinyl PRINCESS LINE dress with a red tartan PVC FROCK COAT, alongside more practical items. In 1996 he was appointed head designer at GIVENCHY.

medici collar Collar used on gowns worn by the women of the Medici family, rulers of Florence in the 15th century. Made of stiffened lace, the collar was raised across the shoulders away from the neck. It was popular during the late 19th century on ball gowns.

Meisel, Steven 1954–. Photographer. Born in New York, USA. While attending Parsons School of Design in New York, Meisel met Anna SUI, with whom he would eventually collaborate, and Stephen SPROUSE, whose career he would help launch. Leaving school before graduation, he soon obtained assignments from fashion magazines, along with designers and manufacturers such as Calvin KLEIN, PRADA and GAP. Meisel produces distinctive, highly art-directed photographs which frequently have a stark, androgynous quality.

melton Thick, wool fabric in twill or satin weave which has a smooth surface. A popular choice of cloth for men's, and later women's, coats in the 19th century.

mercerization Process developed in 1884 by a calico dyer, John Mercer of Lancashire, England, whereby cotton is treated with caustic soda to give a silky, lustrous finish which helps to increase the strength of the fabric.

merino Thin, woollen, twilled cloth developed during the 19th century from the wool of the Merino sheep, for outdoor garments.

Merry Widow hat In 1907 actress Lily Elsie starred in the operetta *The Merry Widow* on the London stage. Her high-waisted chiffon and crepe-de-chine dresses were designed by LUCILE, who was also responsible for her extremely large, plume-laden hat. Merry Widow hats were fashionable for several years. They were usually made of straw, with a deep

crown swathed in black tulle and ostrich FEATHERS.

metal dress *See* RABANNE.

Michael 1915–85. Designer. Born Michael Donnellan in Ballinlough, County Roscommon, Ireland. Donellan studied medicine before serving in World War II. After the war he became a student at the British Fashion Institute and then moved to LACHASSE as a suit designer. In 1953 he opened his own company, Michael of Carlos Place, London. He was known for his perfectly executed suits and dresses, and was successful until the demise of couture in the 1960s. He retired in 1971.

micro skirt Very short skirt, just covering the behind, which was briefly popular in the 1960s.

midi skirt A calf-length skirt, introduced in the late 1960s. Between MINI and MAXI length, it was often worn with knee-high boots. The style was not widely popular at the time, but ten years later it evolved, untitled, as an acceptable fashion length for skirts and dresses.

military Style based on garments worn by servicemen. Military-style jackets and coats are

The elaborately trimmed **Merry Widow** hat, created by Lucile – a highly fashionable style in the early 20th century.

By the end of the 1960s it was possible to see **minis**, midis and maxis on the street as women continued to experiment with skirt lengths before settling down to the more uniform lengths of the 1970s.

severely cut and usually have EPAULETS, stiff collars, brass buttons and belts. This style was popular during the late 1930s and also in the 1960s, when ARMY SURPLUS gear was worn.

mini skirt Skirt that ended well above the knee, popular from 1965 to 1970. Considered daring at its introduction, the mini skirt was later generally adopted by younger women. *See* BATES, COURREGES *and* QUANT.

minimalism Term first used in a fashion context in the mid-1980s when it described the trend for spare, pared-down clothing in neutral tones, inspired by the clean, sculptural shapes of JAPANESE designers working in Europe. Minimalism became increasingly popular in the 1990s. Minimalist garments are refined, simply cut, but of quality fabrics; the colours are often solid neutrals in dark and light shades and there is a noted absence of detailing and accessories. *See* KLEIN, CALVIN; SANDER *and* ZORAN.

One of Simone **Mirman**'s youthful hat styles during the swinging sixties.

mink Either of two species of semi-aquatic weasel found originally in Eurasia and North America. Mink was not trapped in any quantity until the 19th century and did not become fashionable for coats until the mid-20th century. It is a short-napped, thick, glossy and hardwearing fur. There are two types of mink: wild and ranched. Wild mink is naturally dark in colour whereas ranched mink is dyed various shades. Mink was first ranched in c.1940 and careful genetic development has produced different strains. Mink is an expensive fur. Most of it comes from North America.

Mirman, Simone c. 1920–. Milliner. Born Simone Parmentier in Paris, France. Mirman was the daughter of a dressmaker. As a girl, she worked with milliner Rose Valois and for SCHIAPARELLI. After eloping to London in 1937, Mirman found work at Schiaparelli's London salon. In 1947 she set up her own millinery establishment. Five years later Princess Margaret ordered several models and introduced the milliner to the rest of the British royal family. Mirman's hats were in great demand in the 1950s and 1960s. She designed collections for the London house of DIOR and SAINT LAURENT and for Norman HARTNELL.

Miroir des modes, Le Magazine published monthly by the BUTTERICK Publishing Company from 1897 to 1934.

Mischka, James *See* BADGLEY MISCHKA.

Top: Illustration by Antonio Lopez of two Autumn/Winter 1983 designs by the Italian knitwear company **Missoni**.
Bottom left: Missoni, Spring/Summer 1994; *bottom right:* Missoni, Spring/Summer 1989.

Missoni Husband-and-wife design team. Ottavio Missoni (b. 1921, Dalmatia, Italy) and Rosita Jelmini (b. 1932, Varese, Italy) founded the Missoni company in 1953. Ottavio had previously owned a firm that made TRACKSUITS and Rosita had worked for her family's bedding company. With just a few knitting machines, the couple began to produce knitwear which they sold to other designers. By the 1970s they were manufacturing under their own label highly individual knitwear in bold patterns and designs and cleverly blended colours. They made sweaters, suits, jackets, coats and dresses. Missoni did much to alter the fashion world's attitude to knitwear. It is most famous for its long cardigan-jackets and sweaters, but all its garments have become status symbols.

mitten In 1850 a mitten was a GLOVE of net or lace with the thumb and fingers cut off from the first row of knuckles. The word has come to mean a glove that covers the fingers in one part and the thumb in another. It is worn as casual attire, especially for sporting wear, and is usually made of wool or sheepskin. *See* SCHIAPARELLI.

Miyake, Issey 1935–. Designer. Born in Hiroshima, Japan. Miyake graduated in graphic design from Tama University, Tokyo, in 1964 and went to Paris the following year to study fashion. He joined LAROCHE in 1966, leaving in 1968 to work for GIVENCHY. In 1969 he travelled to New York and spent two years with Geoffrey BEENE. In 1970 he founded the Miyake Design Studio (MDS) in Tokyo. Miyake held his first show in New York in 1971 and a second in Paris two years later. At this time he developed the layered and wrapped look that was to become his hallmark. His fascination with texture expresses itself in his attitude toward design; he creates his linear and geometric shapes from the drape and flow of fabric. He works on a bold scale, often with his own fabrics, to produce inspired clothes, a balance of the influences of East and West. In 1988 he embarked on his groundbreaking and later highly successful 'Pleats Please Issey Miyake' designs. He is an uncompromising and innovative creator.

Mizrahi, Isaac 1961–. Designer. Born in New York, USA. After graduating from Parsons School of Design in 1982, Mizrahi worked for Perry ELLIS. He then designed for Jeff BANKS and Calvin KLEIN, before forming his own company in 1987. His earliest design influences

Issey **Miyake** is considered to be Japan's most visionary designer. Shown here is a sculptured bodice from his 1984 Bodyworks exhibition at the Victoria and Albert Museum in London.

stemmed from his mother's all-American wardrobe, which included clothing from HAL-STON, Geoffrey BEENE, Claire MCCARDELL and Norman NORELL. Mizrahi has integrated these influences with his own facility for colour and luxurious materials. He has designed everything from BABY-DOLL dresses and evening JUMPSUITS to PLAYSUITS and flounced TUBE dresses. Many of his designs are carried out in fresh colours and inventive patterns.

mob cap Larger, fuller and less decorated than a BOUDOIR CAP, the mob cap was worn indoors during the 19th century to protect the hair. It was briefly popular in the 1960s.

moccasin Traditionally a piece of leather which wrapped the foot from underneath. Surplus material was gathered and seamed along the uppers. The moccasin is believed to have originated with Native Americans. Moccasins were adapted to casual footwear for men and women during the 20th century.

Mod UK term (from Modernist) applied in the late 1950s and early 1960s to a style adopted by certain teenage boys. Mods favoured a neat appearance, with short haircuts. They wore Italian-style suits, long PARKAS with zips and hoods, and rode about on motor scooters.

Modes et manières d'aujourd'hui Fashion review published irregularly in France between 1912 and 1920 by Pierre Corrard and printed by the *pochoir* method – a time-consuming and laborious process in which the image was built up with numerous hand-coloured metal stencils. The journal featured the work of many notable artists, including BARBIER, LEPAPE, MARTIN and MARTY.

mohair Fabric made from the long, lustrous hair of the angora goat which is loose-woven with cotton, silk or wool to produce a fuzzy texture. Popular for jackets, coats, skirts and sweaters since the 1950s. *See also* CASHIN.

moiré Watered effect on fabric, usually silk, achieved by applying heated and engraved copper rollers. Watered silk was a popular fabric during the late 19th century. During the 20th century it was frequently used for eveningwear.

The pleated neckline is complemented by the sleek lines of the skirt in this 1933 evening outfit by **Molyneux**.

Molyneux, Edward 1891–1974. Designer. Born in London, England, of Irish parentage. Molyneux studied art and began to earn his living sketching for advertisements and magazines. In 1911 his sketch for an evening dress won him first prize in a competition set by LUCILE, who subsequently engaged him as a sketcher in her London salon. Over the following years Molyneux travelled with Lucile to her salons in Paris, New York and Chicago. After serving as a captain in the army during World War I, he opened a dressmaking salon in Paris in 1919. Between 1925 and 1932 he established branches in Monte Carlo, Cannes, Biarritz and London. He was based in London from the mid-1930s until the end of World War II, when he returned to Paris. In 1950 Molyneux closed all but one of his houses and retired to Jamaica, handing over to Jacques GRIFFE. Fifteen years later, in an attempt at a comeback, Molyneux reopened and took a ready-to-wear collection to the USA. Unfortunately for him, his particular design skills were not attractive to the

1960s public and he retired once again, this time handing over to a South African designer, John Tullis. Molyneux's reputation was based on the purity of line and cut of his tailored suits, pleated skirts and discreet matching ensembles. The aristocratic elegance of his clothes made him a fashionable designer for film stars and society women. Gertrude Lawrence wore many of his garments on stage. During the 1930s he promoted the LITTLE BLACK DRESS, orientally inspired clothes with bamboo motifs, DIRNDL skirts and BIAS-CUT dresses. He was a well-respected designer throughout his career.

Mondrian, Piet 1872–1944. Artist. Born in Holland. In 1911 Mondrian went to Paris where he abandoned his realistic landscape painting to take up CUBISM. His work from 1917 on – coloured shapes divided by a grid of black bands – was to inspire Yves SAINT LAURENT to produce in 1965 a line of dresses based on Mondrian's paintings.

monkey Long, silky, black hair and skin of the Ethiopian monkey, which was highly fashionable as a trimming during the early 20th century.

Montana, Claude 1949–. Designer. Born in Paris, France. After taking his baccalaureate, Montana went to London. At the end of the 1960s he began designing Mexican papier-mâché jewelry which he decorated with RHINESTONES and sold in London street markets. He returned to Paris in 1972 and two years later started to work for MacDouglas, a large leather manufacturer. He launched his first clothing collection under his own name in 1977. Montana is a forceful, influential designer with an international reputation. He works best in leather, creating strong silhouettes with hard, fairly masculine, lines. His broad-shouldered jackets and coats of the late 1970s gave the appearance of being tough and aggressive. Montana makes his fashion statements through a mix of detail and bold colour: brilliant hues of leather adorned with chains and buckles, for example. His day wear collections are authoritatively designed and well executed.

Moon, Sarah 1940–. Photographer. Born Marielle Hadengue in England of French parents. Moon studied drawing and taught herself photography. In the 1960s she worked as a fashion model in Paris before becoming a freelance photographer hired by CACHAREL for the company's advertising campaigns. Moon also took pictures for magazines such as *Elle, Marie-Claire, Nova, VOGUE* and *HARPER'S BAZAAR*. Biba employed her to photograph advertisements for its cosmetics range. Moon's models are soft, dreamy and mysterious, promoting a completely feminine, soft-focus, close-range image. Her colour photography is muted, subtly blended and verges on the surreal.

Moreni, Popy 1949–. Designer. Born in Turin, Italy. The daughter of a painter and a sculptor, Moreni studied costume design in Turin. At the age of seventeen she went to Paris. She joined the Promostyl company in 1967 and worked for them and the Italian firm Timmi until 1973, when she opened her own business. Moreni is an inventive daywear designer who combines a predominantly French style with a colour sense that is rooted in strong Italian traditions. She opened her own BOUTIQUE in 1976. Moreni's clothes are often witty and lighthearted. She was one of the first designers to dye plastic shoes bright colours.

Mori, Hanae 1926–. Designer. Born in Tokyo, Japan. Mori studied at Tokyo Christian University. She returned to college some years later to study fashion design and then began dressmaking for the Japanese film industry. She opened her first shop in Shinjuku and in 1955 moved to the Ginza, the smart shopping area of Tokyo. Her appeal to an international audience began in the early 1970s, when she opened a salon in New York, and was extended by her first couture showing in Paris in 1977. Many of Mori's designs are based on the KIMONO. She adapts the style to eveningwear, in soft silky fabrics, belting her garments with the traditional OBI. Her ready-to-wear and couture lines, especially her COCKTAIL DRESSES and evening dresses, are popular worldwide.

morocain Heavy, crepe fabric made of silk, rayon or wool mixtures and used in the 19th and 20th centuries for dresses and outerwear.

Morris, Robert Lee 1947–. Jewelry designer. Born in Nuremburg, Germany. In 1972, several years after graduating from college in the USA, where he studied anthropology, Morris showed his first jewelry collection. Initially exhibited by a New York gallery, Morris's early work was strongly influenced by ancient suits of armour made of flexible chainmail. From the beginning his style was one of contemporary classicism with a clear emphasis on bold, clean forms and shapes. He experimented with metallic finishes and created two trademark looks: a muted golden finish of 24-carat gold over brass, and a rough green patina that mimicked stone. He has included Celtic crosses, heart-shaped pins and disc belts in his work. Morris collaborates with many prominent designers.

Morton, Digby 1906–83. Designer. Born in Dublin, Ireland. Morton studied art and architecture in Ireland before moving to London where, in 1928, he joined the house of LACHASSE. Five years later he opened his own business. Morton was largely responsible for transforming the severe, tailor-made suit into a fashionable garment. Using delicately shaded tweeds, which he teamed with silk blouses, he added grace and flow to the classic outfit. He also favoured Aran knits and Donegal tweeds. In 1939 he designed uniforms for the Women's Voluntary Service in the UK. After the war, Morton created several collections for US manufacturers. He closed his house in 1957.

Mosca, Bianca ?–1949. Italian designer who moved to London after fifteen years with SCHIAPARELLI. In 1946 she opened her own house, specializing in soft, romantic dresses.

Moschino, Franco 1950–94. Designer. Born in Abbiategrasso, Italy. While studying life drawing at the Accademia di Belle Arti in Milan, Moschino undertook design and illustration commissions for fashion houses and magazines. After graduating in 1971 he worked for VERSACE before moving to Cadette, where he spent five years as a designer. In 1983 he opened his own business and quickly became known for his highly provocative and irreverent style. An expert tailor, Moschino liked to make visual puns. He created a dinner suit with a knife and fork appliquéd on the bodice; his blazers had windmills for buttons and many of his clothes parodied the women who purchased them.

A typically witty creation from Franco **Moschino**, fashion's arch parodist, Spring/Summer 1988. Note the *trompe-l'oeil* design on the skirt.

Moschino's clothing, while sometimes gimmicky, was usually flattering. His brightly printed waistcoats and black satin evening dresses, as well as POLKA DOT 'Minnie Mouse' dresses, were very popular.

mourning dress Queen VICTORIA's strict observance of mourning after the death of Prince Albert in 1861 helped promote a huge vogue for black garments, particularly of crape. Caps, hats, coats, dresses, stockings, VEILS, MANTLES, gloves and blouses were available in black crape muslin, gauze, cotton and wool. Jet jewelry was worn. Mourning wear was discarded gradually: black changed to purple, then to lavender and white for summer. The fashion for mourning clothes had almost disappeared by the end of the 19th century. *See also* JET.

mousseline Fine, lightweight, plain-woven fabric, usually cotton, silk or wool, which has a slight stiffness. *Mousseline de soie* is the most popular version, used particularly during the 19th century for dresses, blouses and skirts.

Mr John 1906–93. Milliner. Born Hansi Harberger in Vienna, Austria. Mr John's mother opened a millinery shop on New York's Madison Avenue when the family emigrated to the USA after World War I. Sent to study medicine at the University of Lucerne, Mr John transferred to the Sorbonne in Paris to study art. He eventually returned to New York and started a millinery business which later, with partner Frederic Hirst, became the company John Frederics. In 1948 the business partnership dissolved and Mr John continued on his own. For over thirty years he was famous for his glamorous confections of chiffon, georgette and tulle. He also created hats made of crochet and permanently pleated collapsible straw. He trimmed felt hats with pearls and JET and dressed tailored hats with tulle.

MTV Abbreviated form of Music Television, a company started in the USA in 1981 by Warner Amex Satellite Entertainment Company, through the national cable television network. MTV is a hugely popular twenty-four-hour television station featuring rock videos and contemporary music. It has had an impact on fashion both through the highly stylized dress of its rock video performers and through the publicity it has given to singers such as MADONNA. The station became a venue for STREET STYLE worn by urban black rappers.

Mucha, Alphonse 1860–1939. Decorative artist. Born in Moravia, the Czech Republic. Mucha was a prominent and prolific designer of furniture, wallpaper panels and posters. He also designed jewelry for Georges FOUQUET. His flowing, curvilinear designs are the epitome of ART NOUVEAU.

muff Accessory, usually cylindrical, into which the hands can be slipped for warmth. Muffs were popular in the late 19th century and were also used to carry personal items and as a form of decoration. They varied in size and shape; by the early 1900s many resembled a small pillow. Muffs were made of silk, satin, taffeta and feathers as well as of sturdier materials such as wool, gabardine and fur. Many were elaborately lined with satin and trimmed with tulle and artificial flowers. The HANDBAG began to replace the muff in the early 20th century.

Thierry **Mugler**'s confidently stylish clothes are often body-hugging, with exaggerated shoulders and nipped-in waist. Shown here is a design from 1988.

Mugler, Thierry 1948–. Designer. Born in Strasbourg, France. Mugler spent one year as a dancer with the Opéra de Rhin in Strasbourg before studying for a year at the city's School of Fine Arts. He made clothing as a teenager and later worked as a window dresser in a Parisian store. In 1968 he visited London and Amsterdam, returning to Paris in 1971 to design a collection under the name Café de Paris. By 1973 he was designing under his own name. Mugler is a confident stylist, aware that his garments, as well as being both shocking and amusing, are well thought out and engineered, and greatly admired. He is strongly influenced by 1940s and 1950s fashions and produces consistently figure-hugging and body-conscious garments. He exaggerates shoulders, waists, hips and heads in oder to explore and express the female shape. His designs are theatrical and sexy and can evoke anything from science fiction to industrial design to Hollywood glamour.

Actress Joanna Lumley wears Jean **Muir**'s fluid jersey tunic and culottes, from the designer's Autumn/Winter 1975 collection. Hat by Graham Smith.

Muir, Jean 1933–95. Designer. Born in London, England. Muir joined LIBERTY in 1950, first working in the stockroom, then selling in the made-to-measure department, and finally sketching at the London store. She was employed by JAEGER from 1956 until 1961, when she began to produce her own clothing line under the name Jane & Jane. In 1966 Muir went on to found her own company, Jean Muir. Working with fabrics that she knew well – jersey and suede – Muir manipulated the material by cutting, stitching and seaming to create garments that carried her distinctive hallmark: fluidity achieved by discipline. Highly conscious of weight and balance, she tailored matte and rayon jersey into restrained and mannered dresses, skirts and tops which were always subtle and never stiff. She punched, printed, and stitched suede into equally fluid shapes. In the 1960s she designed SMOCKS, PEASANT dresses, shawls, draw-string-waist dresses and two-piece suits. Muir was a craftswoman of the highest calibre who gained an international reputation. Though rarely in the forefront of fashion, her clothes had a nonchalant, easy elegance and a timeless, classic appeal.

mule Heeled or heel-less backless slipper. Popular since the 1940s. See ★VIVIER.

Munkacsi, Martin 1896–1963. Photographer. Born Martin Marmorstein in Kolozsvar, in the Munkacsi district of Hungary. In 1902 the family name was changed to Munkacsi. Munkacsi was educated in Hungary and after serving in the army he rapidly became one of that country's top photojournalists. Periods in Berlin and New York working for various magazines were followed in 1934 by his emigration to the USA, where he was placed under contract to Hearst Newspapers Inc., taking fashion photographs for HARPER'S BAZAAR and *Town and Country*, among others. Munkacsi's first pictures for Carmel SNOW of *Harper's Bazaar* show the influence of his early work as a sports photographer and they broke new ground in fashion magazine photography. His work concentrated on movement and spontaneity – a new feature at the time. He shot action pictures in the open air from previously inconceivable angles and was an inspiration to many later photographers. Munkacsi's work set the photographic fashion climate for the following thirty years.

muslin Fabric originally made in the city of Mosul (now in Iraq) and imported to Europe in the 17th century. By the 18th century, muslin was manufactured in both England and France. A plain-woven fabric made in a wide range of weights, it was used extensively in the 19th century for undergarments, blouses and summer dresses. In the 20th century its popularity was at its greatest in the 1960s, when there was a vogue for printed muslins imported from India.

N

nainsook Fine, soft, plain-woven cotton made in various weights. Heavier than lawn, nainsook often resembles cambric. Nainsook was popular during the 19th century for lingerie and undergarments.

nankeen Yellow or buff-coloured cottoncloth, originally handwoven in Nanking, China, which was popular in the mid-19th century for summer wear.

Nast, Condé 1873–1942. Publisher. Born William Condé Nast in New York, USA. Nast was brought up in St Louis, Missouri, and attended Georgetown University in Washington, DC. In 1897 he joined *Collier's Weekly* and was appointed advertising manager three years later. In 1904, as a personal venture, Nast became vice-president of the Home Pattern Company, a firm which manufactured and distributed women's dress patterns. When, a year later, he was promoted to business manager of *Collier's Weekly*, he divided the USA into different marketing areas to increase sales and also promoted the use of double-page spreads. It was Nast who encouraged Charles Dana GIBSON's work in the magazine. Nast left *Collier's Weekly* in 1907 and two years later bought *VOGUE* – a society periodical at that time. Several years later he acquired *Vanity Fair* and *House and Garden*. Nast raised magazine publishing to new heights. He sought out the best talents in photography, art, fashion, illustration, typography and writing. He mixed society with business, art, the theatre and show business. Each of his magazines adopted a strong editorial voice. In 1914 Nast established *Vogue Patterns* and later introduced foreign editions of the magazine.

needlepoint lace *See* LACE.

negligée Light, loose robe trimmed with lace and ruffles worn as informal attire at home during the 19th century. The negligée allowed women to loosen or remove their CORSETS between changes of dress. Its nearest relative is the PEIGNOIR. At the turn of the 20th century the negligée was replaced by the TEA GOWN. Subsequently, it has usually been a luxurious, lightweight DRESSING GOWN, often made of a sheer fabric.

Nehru jacket Straight, slim, hip-length jacket, buttoned in front to a straight, standing collar, worn by Jawaharlal Nehru (1889–1964), Prime Minister of India from 1947 to 1964. American *VOGUE* promoted the Nehru jacket, which was often white, in the late 1960s.

New Look Style of dress generally attributed to Christian *DIOR. In 1947, Dior introduced the Corolle line, so called because of its huge skirts which spread like corollas from fitted bodices and tiny waists. The line was nick-named the New Look by US fashion editor Carmel SNOW. Skirts often used fifteen or even twenty-five yards of material, which was then lined with tulle to increase the swollen shape. Dress bodices were tightly constructed to emphasize the bust and minimize the waist. Although other designers – BALENCIAGA, BALMAIN and FATH – had already been working toward this shape by 1939, their efforts had been interrupted by the outbreak of World War II. Two years after the war Dior's show created an international sensation. The New Look was the exact opposite of the pared-down, economical garments demanded by rationing and the style caused controversy throughout the Western world. Although many women adopted it, others reacted against it, deploring what they saw as its extravagance and artificiality. The House of Dior was picketed by indignant women and the resulting publicity made Dior a household name overnight. The New Look continued in various forms until the mid-1950s.

Newton, Helmut 1920–. Photographer. Born in Berlin, Germany. Newton worked as an apprentice to Eva, a Berlin fashion photographer, before emigrating to Australia, where he served in the army during World War II. After the war he worked in Sydney as a freelance photographer, also spending some time in Paris taking fashion pictures for *Elle, Marie-Claire, JARDIN DES MODES* and *VOGUE*. In the 1960s he moved to Paris and became a regular contributor to the German magazine *Stern* and to French and American *Vogue*. His fine fashion photographs are often shocking, hinting at a decadence in society. Carefully posed models are tense, often aggressive; they seem to be playing out a secret drama hidden just beyond the range of the lens. Newton's work also contains elements of voyeurism and fantasy.

Norell, Norman 1900–72. Designer. Born Norman Levinson in Noblesville, Indiana, USA. During World War I Norell spent a brief period at military school. In 1918 he attended Parsons School of Design in New York but returned home after one year to open a small dress fabric shop. Back in New York in 1920, Norell studied design at the Pratt Institute in Brooklyn. In 1922 he joined the New York studio of Paramount Pictures where he

The **Norfolk jacket**, illustrated in the April 1905 issue of the *Tailor and Cutter (above)* and, some 20 years later, worn by the centre figure in the photograph *(right)*.

designed clothes for Gloria Swanson and other stars of silent movies. He then worked as a costume designer on Broadway, for the Brooks Costume Company, and for wholesale dress manufacturer Charles Armour. In 1928, he was hired by Hattie CARNEGIE and remained with her until 1941. Anthony Traina then invited him to form Traina-Norell, with Traina as businessman and Norell as designer. By 1944 Norell had launched CHEMISE DRESSES, evening shirt dresses, fur TRENCHCOATS, sequined evening SHEATHS, fur SLACKS and EMPIRE-LINE dresses. In 1960 he opened his own company. His first collection featured CULOTTES for day and eveningwear, HAREM PANTS and DECOLLETE evening dresses. In the 1960s Norell was acclaimed for his well-proportioned suits and clean, precisely tailored silhouettes. He used fabric flamboyantly, trimming garments in fur and feathers. Considered to be one of the foremost US designers, on a par with

the French couturiers, Norell is best remembered for his sequin-covered sheath dresses.

Norfolk jacket Originally worn by men in the second half of the 19th century, the Norfolk jacket, named after the Duke of Norfolk, was a hip-length garment made of wool tweed, with large PATCH POCKETS, BOX PLEATS front and back, and a self-fabric belt. It was adopted by women in the 1890s for sporting activities, worn with KNICKERBOCKERS. *See* ★LAUREN.

nylon Generic term for a manufactured fibre in which the fibre-forming substance is any long chain synthetic polyamide with recurring amide groups. Nylon was the result of research started in 1927 by Dr Wallace H. Carothers at the DU PONT Company of Delaware, USA. The company first introduced nylon in 1938 and it was tested in knitted hosiery in 1939. Nylon STOCKINGS were launched in 1940. Since then nylon has been used extensively in underwear and dress manufacture.

nylons *See* STOCKINGS.

O

obi Wide, stiffened Japanese SASH made of brocaded silk and lined with a contrasting colour. The obi usually measures fifteen inches wide by four to six feet long. It is tied around the waist into a large bow at the back. In the 1980s it was adapted to fashion by Japanese designers working in Paris. *See* JAPANESE.

Oldfield, Bruce 1950–. Designer. Born in London, England. Oldfield taught art before studying fashion at Ravensbourne College of Art in Kent from 1968 to 1971. He furthered his studies at St Martin's School of Art in London from 1972 to 1973 and then became a freelance designer. Oldfield created a line for the Henri Bendel department store in New York and sold sketches to Yves SAINT LAURENT. In 1975 he showed his first collection. Oldfield later produced ready-to-wear lines. He is most famous for his eveningwear, which is glamorous and often theatrical. He is a popular designer among film stars and socialites and created many outfits for DIANA, PRINCESS OF WALES.

Oldham, Todd 1961–. Designer. Born in Corpus Christi, Texas, USA. Drawn to fashion, though without any formal training, Oldham showed his first collection, which was bought by the department store Neiman Marcus, in 1981. In 1988 he moved to New York and launched the 'Times 7' line which featured unusual buttons and accessories. The following year a womenswear line was produced. Oldham is a maverick designer with a great sense of fun. His combinations of clothes and colours show a wild, childlike sensibility designed to amuse. Fond of ornament, he often shows beaded and sequined gowns and jackets along with brightly patterned sweaters and waistcoats frequently done in PATCHWORK.

Onassis, Jacqueline (Kennedy) 1929–94. US First Lady 1961–63. Born Jacqueline Lee Bouvier in East Hampton, New York. In 1953, Bouvier married John Fitzgerald Kennedy, who was elected President of the USA in 1961. While she was First Lady, Mrs Kennedy's clothes were widely copied. From 1960

The little black dress of 1986, made in silk crepe and chiffon by Bruce **Oldfield**.

onwards, she often wore clothes of her own design, made up for her by Oleg CASSINI. Her famous PILLBOXES were created by HALSTON. Mrs Kennedy frequently wore a two-piece outfit: a dress and waistlength, semi-fitted jacket. She favoured round, oval or BATEAU NECKLINES. Her sleeves reached just to the elbow, while her slim-line, A-shaped skirts grazed the knee. She was often seen wearing COURT SHOES and fur-trimmed garments. She carried a gilt chain handbag – a style which became very popular. Her bouffant hairstyle was also imitated. *See* BATTELLE *and* ★CASSINI.

Ong, Benny 1949–. Designer. Born in Singapore, of Chinese parentage. Ong moved to London in 1968 and studied at St Martin's School of Art. After graduating he worked freelance for various companies before establishing his own business in 1974. He designs clothes that are pretty, graceful, and quite often loosely cut.

Op Art

Op Art Art form which emerged in the 1920s but became fashionable, printed onto fabrics, in the 1960s. The American dress manufacturer Larry Aldrich commissioned textile designer Julian Tomchin to create fabric based on paintings by Bridget RILEY. The resulting spirals, circles and squares are arranged so as to give an illusion of movement.

opossum Marsupial species found in the USA, Australia and New Zealand. The opossum has dense, long hair in various shades of brown, grey and black. The fur was used extensively at the turn of the 20th century for lining coats and as a trimming.

organdy A very lightweight, fine, sheer, transparent cotton fabric which is stiffened by chemical treatment. It was popular in the late 19th and early 20th centuries for dress trimmings, particularly eveningwear. Since World War II, organdy has been made from rayon, silk and other fibres.

Orlon Acrylic fibre produced by the US firm of DU PONT during World War II. Full-scale production for consumer use began in 1950. Orlon is a regular component of knitwear fabrics, where it acts as a substitute for wool.

Fashions for feathers prompted the London store of Debenham & Freebody to put out this 1906 advertisement announcing sales of **ostrich feather** stoles in assorted colours.

The craze for **Oxford bags** originated among students in England in 1925. The style was a boon to cartoonists.

Orry-Kelly 1897–1964. Costume designer. Born John Kelly in Sydney, Australia. Orry-Kelly joined Warner Brothers in Hollywood in 1932 as a costume designer. He also worked on Bette Davis movies for Fox, and as a freelance for Universal, RKO and Metro-Goldwyn-Mayer. Orry-Kelly designed costumes for hundreds of films from 1932 to 1964, notably for *An American in Paris* (1951) and for Marilyn Monroe in *Some Like It Hot* (1959).

ostrich feather Plume-like feather from the wing or tail of the African ostrich. The white feathers were used extensively in the late 19th and early 20th centuries for millinery, feather BOAS and exotic trimmings. *See* FEATHERS.

overalls Complete cover garment with long sleeves and legs, worn by women in the munitions factories and for agricultural labour during World War II. Overalls have also featured as part of American workwear. They were particularly popular for womenswear during the 1960s, made of cotton and trimmed with pockets, flaps and buckles. *See also* SIREN SUIT.

oxford Originally a half-boot worn in England during the 17th century. By the 20th century, the oxford had become a man's, woman's or child's low-cut shoe, laced over the instep. *See* BROGUE *and* ★GUCCI.

Oxford bags Baggy trousers worn by undergraduates at Oxford University, England, in the 1920s. The hem measured approximately 20 inches (50 cm) wide and was cuffed. Oxford bags were a popular trouser style for women during the 1930s and 1970s.

Ozbek, Rifat 1953–. Designer. Born in Istanbul, Turkey. Ozbek moved to England at the age of eighteen to study architecture at Liverpool University, but transferred in 1974 to St Martin's School of Art in London to study fashion design. After serving in the military in Turkey, he worked for Walter ALBINI in Milan but in 1980 returned to London. He designed for Monsoon between 1980 and 1984 and then showed his own first collection. Ozbek quickly became known for exotic, sophisticated clothes, such as brocade jackets, made up in beautiful, luxurious fabrics and brilliant colours

influenced by the Far East and the Ottoman Empire. He was also successful with his embroidered black cocktail suits. In the 1990s he shifted emphasis and created a line of separates – mostly in white – which proclaimed the New Age with slogans such as 'Nirvana', but returned after several seasons to more sophisticated interpretations of ETHNIC clothing, often in complex and powerful colours.

P

page boy Hairstyle in which hair of shoulder length or longer is rolled under at each side, from the top of the ears to the nape of the neck. It was popular during World War II and in the 1960s and 1970s.

pagoda sleeve Three-quarter- or half-length sleeve style which was frilled to the elbow where it widened into either several tiers of FLOUNCES or one large flounce seamed to curve in a shape resembling a pagoda. It was a popular style in the mid-19th century. The flounces were often trimmed with ribbons and bows.

Paisley Scottish town, famous for the production of a worsted fabric during the 19th century. As cashmere SHAWLS from India

In its report on Paris Fashions for April, the *Illustrated London News* of March 1856 shows a dress (*left*) with sleeves of 'four flounces of similar pattern only smaller'. This was to be known as the **pagoda sleeve**.

became popular, Paisley firms adapted the Kashmiri cone motif, weaving it onto large, square shawls in shades of red and brown. This particular pattern became known as Paisley and featured mainly on shawls and DRESSING GOWNS in the 19th and early 20th centuries. In the 1980s Paisley enjoyed a revival, made into tights, skirts, dresses, shawls and handbags.

paletot The word paletot has been used for many different garments since the 19th century.

In the early 19th century it was a single-breasted man's FROCK COAT with the skirt sections sewn on, and in early versions it was similar to a riding coat. By the mid-19th century it had become a heavy, slightly waisted three-quarter-length overcoat. The paletot in the second half of the 19th century was a woman's partially or completely fitted three-quarter- or waist-length coat, often made of cashmere or wool cloth and decoratively embroidered. By the early 20th century the word described an outdoor jacket.

Norman **Parkinson** photographed this Zandra Rhodes dress in Florida, USA, in 1971. The dress is in 'Indian Feather Sunspray' print on silk chiffon, cut to the shape of the print, with handrolled edges.

panama hat Light-coloured hat of various shapes, made from tightly woven straw of the plant *Carloduvica palmata*, found in Ecuador and neighbouring countries. It is called a panama because US President Theodore Roosevelt wore one during a tour of the Panama Canal in 1906. Panama hats remained popular summer wear, mainly for men, until World War II.

panne Velvet-like fabric with the pile pressed flat in one direction.

pantiehose *See* TIGHTS.

pants *See* TROUSERS.

pants stockings *See* POP SOCKS.

pants suit *See* TROUSER SUIT.

paper clothes Paper clothing enjoyed a brief vogue in the 1960s. Paper suits and underwear for men and women were cheap and disposable.

Paquin, Mme The House of Paquin was founded in 1891 in Paris by Jeanne Beckers (b. Saint Denis; 1869–1936) and her husband Isidore Jacobs. The couple became known as Monsieur and Madame Paquin. Mme Paquin trained at Maison ROUFF. In 1900 she was appointed president of the Fashion Section of the Paris Exposition and in 1902 she opened branches in London, Buenos Aires and Madrid. She was noted for her rich, glamorous, romantic clothes and fine workmanship. Her gowns, described as 'from fairyland', were popular with actresses and socialites. A woman of considerable elegance, Mme Paquin was a skilful publicist and paraded her models at race meetings. She accepted dress designs by Paul IRIBE and Léon BAKST which she made up into garments. In 1913 she created day dresses that could also be worn into the evening. Many of her gowns were a blend of drapery and tailoring, suitable for the more active woman of the early 20th century, and her tailored suits were cut to facilitate walking. She was also famous for her TANGO DRESSES, lingerie and an extensive fur department. She retired in 1920, though her house remained open. In 1953 the House of Paquin merged with the House of WORTH. Paquin-Worth closed in 1956.

parasol Parasols were used from the mid-16th century as functional and fashionable accessories. In the 18th century, they were heavily decorated and sometimes trimmed with gold lace. In the 18th and 19th centuries, many parasols had elaborately carved ivory handles and silk linings, and were deeply fringed and ruffled. They were rarely carried after World War I. *See* UMBRELLA.

pardessus From the French for 'passed over'. In the 19th century the word pardessus described various fitted overcoats for men and women.

pareo Polynesian skirt or loincloth printed with bold flower patterns. Pareos have been used since the 1960s as beachwear.

Paris élégant Bimonthly fashion magazine published in France from 1836 to 1881. A monthly magazine of the same name was brought out by a different publisher between 1909 and 1936.

parka Hooded garment similar to an ANORAK but usually longer and more loosely cut. It was a popular casual jacket in the 1950s and 1960s. *See also* MOD *and* WINDCHEATER.

Parkinson, Norman 1913–90. Photographer. Born Roland William Parkinson Smith in Roehampton, Surrey, England. In 1931 Parkinson became an apprentice at Speaight Ltd, a London photographic company which specialized in portraits of debutantes. He remained there until 1933. The following year he opened his own studio and embarked on a photographic career working for magazines such as *Life*, *Look* and *VOGUE*, while pursuing interests in farming. During World War II he worked as both a military photographer and a farmer. After the war Parkinson achieved great success as a fashion photographer for *Vogue* and other fashion magazines and advertising agencies in London, New York and Paris. In the 1950s he became a royal portrait photographer. Parkinson's work was usually vigorous and vivacious in style, often humorous in content. He managed successfully to merge the rustic with the sophisticated. His clean-cut images were overlaid with gentle wit.

Parnis, Mollie

Parnis, Mollie 1905–92. Designer. Born Sara Rosen Parnis in New York, USA. Parnis started her fashion career as an assistant saleswoman in the showroom of a blouse manufacturer, but soon turned to designing. She worked briefly for another dress manufacturing company, David Westheim, before her marriage to a textile specialist in 1930. Three years later, she opened her own business with her textile-designer husband, making smart, mannered, ready-to-wear suits and dresses. A popular American designer from the 1930s to the 1960s, Parnis turned out reliably fashion-conscious garments which were often understated, always well-tailored, and which reached a wide, appreciative audience. She was noted as a designer for several American First Ladies.

Partos, Emeric 1905–75. Fur designer. Born in Budapest, Hungary. Partos studied in Budapest and Paris. In the 1930s he took French citizenship and after World War II, in 1947, he joined DIOR. He later moved to New York and in 1955 became head fur designer for the New York store Bergdorf Goodman. Partos tailored furs, working vertically and horizontally with skins, to create fine coats, jackets, cardigans and even dresses. He was well-known for his patterns: bold stripes and flowers were two of his hallmarks. *See also* FUR.

parure Matching set of jewelry, consisting of a necklace, earrings, bracelet, brooch, rings and sometimes a head ornament, worn on formal evening occasions during the 19th century.

Pasquali, Guido 1946–. Shoe designer. Born in Verona, Italy. The Pasquali company was founded in 1918 by Guido Pasquali's grandfather. After studying mechanics and engineering at Bocconi University in Milan, Pasquali took over the company in 1967. During the 1970s he supplied shoes to Italian designers such as ALBINI, ARMANI and MISSONI.

paste Compound of potash, glass and white oxide of lead used to make artificial gemstones. Developed in the 15th century in Italy, paste became popular in jewelry design and manufacture in the 18th century in France and England. Demand for inexpensive but genuine-looking jewelry resulted in innumerable items made of

Mollie **Parnis**'s navy wool dress and jacket for Spring 1961, teamed with a hat by Lilly Daché.

colourless glass compounds often backed with a piece of coloured foil. Paste continued to be popular until the 1950s. It was revived in the 1980s, made into elaborate settings. *See* COSTUME JEWELRY.

patch pocket A large, square pocket, in use since the early 20th century, which is sewn onto the exterior of coats, jackets and dresses.

patchwork The sewing together of small pieces of different materials has flourished since ancient times as a thrifty form of needlework for the household. In the 1960s patchwork coats, trousers, dresses and jackets made of square, round or hexagonal pieces became fashionable.

patent leather High-gloss waterproof material used for many shoe styles since the 1930s, when it was developed by leather varnishers or japanners.

Patou, Jean 1880–1936. Designer. Born in Normandy, France. Patou's father was a leading tanner and his uncle owned a fur business which Patou joined in 1907. Five years later

Jean **Patou** in 1924, with the six American models he brought over to Paris to show his new collections.

Patou opened Maison Parry, a small dress-making establishment in Paris, and sold his entire 1914 collection to an American buyer. His career was then interrupted by the war, which he spent as a captain in the Zouaves. In 1919 Patou reopened his salon, this time under his own name. His collections were successful from the start. He showed bell-skirted, high-waisted shepherdess-style dresses, many embroidered in the RUSSIAN style. He designed for actresses such as Constance Bennett and Louise Brooks, but his finest achievements were in the field of sporting wear, which always occupied an important position in his collection. In the early 1920s his inspired work in this field gave fashion another dimension. He dressed tennis star Suzanne LENGLEN in styles that she wore on and off the court. These garments – calf-length pleated skirts and sleeveless CARDIGANS – endure today. Like CHANEL, Patou created clothes for modern women, those who were active and those who wanted to look as if they were active. His branches in

Louise Brooks was one of many actresses to wear **Patou**'s gowns in the 1920s.

Patou, Jean

Monte Carlo, Biarritz, Deauville and Venice sold to the international café society. The key to his design philosophy was simplicity. He promoted the natural waistline and an uncluttered silhouette. Sweaters were always heavily featured and in the early 1920s he showed Cubistic sweaters which were highly successful. He was also famous for his bathing suits. In 1924 he put his monogram on his clothing and in the same year brought six tall American models to Paris to show his new collections. Patou worked with the French textile companies BIANCHINI-FERIER and Rodier, constantly searching for fabrics that would adapt to his sporting garments and bathing suits. In 1929 he showed a PRINCESS LINE dress which was moulded from a high waist, giving the impression that the hips were level with the waistline. From 1919 until his death Patou was a giant of the fashion world, dominating both couture and ready-to-wear. The house continued after his death, run by family members, with BOHAN, GOMA, LAGERFELD, PIPART and LACROIX as designers.

Patou created clothes for the modern, active woman: he specialized in sportswear. He was also one of the first designers to sign his outfits with his monogram.

Patou tea gown in white silk with drawn threadwork, c. 1922.

Patou evening ensemble in velvet and satin, c. 1922.

Paulette, Mme dates unknown. Milliner. Born Pauline Adam in Normandy, France. The name Paulette was adopted when Adam opened her second millinery shop in 1929. She became famous in 1942 for her draped wool TURBANS. She created styles for many actresses, including Rita Hayworth and Gloria Swanson, and had branches in both London and Paris. Scarves and draped fabrics were predominant features of her hats, which were also noted for their lightness. During the 1960s she produced various fur hats. In the 1970s and 1980s she provided millinery for Emanuel ★UNGARO, among other designers. Mme Paulette is one of the most famous names in French millinery.

Paulin, Guy 1945–90. Designer. Born in Lorraine, France. While working as a lift boy at the Parisian department store Printemps, Paulin sold the company some sketches. He moved briefly to rival store Prisunic, and later to manufacturer Jimper, DOROTHEE BIS and the US firm of Paraphernalia. Paulin's extensive freelance experience took him to Italy and France, working for Georges Edelman, Mic Mac, BYBLOS and others. He opened his own business at the end of the 1970s, only to close it in 1984 when he joined CHLOE, stepping into Karl LAGERFELD's shoes. Paulin was essentially a knitwear designer.

pea jacket The term 'pea jacket' comes from the Dutch word *pij*, which describes a rough, warm, woollen fabric. In the 19th century the pea jacket was a heavy, double-breasted, hip-length jacket worn by sailors, fishermen and workmen. In the 1920s the shape was popularized by CHANEL.

pearls Pearls were used throughout antiquity as decorative items sewn onto robes. They are created in the salt or freshwater mollusc – abalone, mussel or oyster – when an irritant gets into (or is placed in) the shell and causes the mollusc to secrete nacre, a calcium carbonate crystalline substance. In the 18th century, the discovery of diamonds in Brazil resulted in a decrease in the interest in pearls. Interest revived in the late 19th century with the commercial production of cultured pearls, developed mainly by Kokichi Mikimoto of Japan. Cultured pearls are created when a tiny bead

made from the shell of a mussel and a piece of mother-of-pearl, or other substance, are placed into the pearl oyster. The oyster is returned to salt or fresh water for several years until nacre is secreted. Nacre accounts for 10 percent of a cultured pearl. Pearls are often dyed. In the early 1920s pearl SAUTOIRS became popular. Since the 1950s, a short necklace of pearls has symbolized conservative dressing and taste. *See also* ALEXANDRA.

peasant Style of dress that refers to rural costumes of many countries, usually interpreted into fashionable attire with calf-length full skirts; full, PUFF-SLEEVED blouses, smocked or embroidered across the chest; and HEADSCARVES. An unsophisticated style of dress, it was nonetheless fashionable in many periods during the 20th century, notably in the 1930s, 1960s and 1970s. *See* FOLKLORIC.

pedal pushers Loose, calf-length trousers, often made with cuffs, which became popular during the 1950s.

The ever popular **pea jacket**. This version, with gold buttons, was designed by Yves Saint Laurent in 1962.

Nylon printed tricot nightdress by the American designer Sylvia **Pedlar** for Iris in 1964.

Black Spanish lace **pelerine** of 1881, the neck edged with jet, and with jet sprays terminating in a fringe.

Pedlar, Sylvia 1901–72. Designer. Born Sylvia Schlang in New York, USA. Pedlar studied at Cooper Union and the Art Students League in New York. She started her own firm in 1929 and for many years designed mass-produced lingerie under the name Iris. Pedlar was famous for gracious nightgowns and PEIGNOIRS and she popularized a short, CHEMISE–style nightdress. She used lace to trim and decorate many of her garments. Pedlar's lingerie designs were considered to be innovative and artistic. Christian DIOR and Hubert de GIVENCHY were just two couturiers who purchased her lines. She closed her business in 1970.

peep-toe Shoe style where the fabric of the shoe is cut away to expose the toe. Peep-toes have been popular since their introduction in the 1930s.

peg-top skirt Skirt that is cut to be very full over the hips and narrow at the ankle. A popular style during the 1920s. It was revived in the late 1960s and early 1970s as a style for eveningwear.

peg-top trousers Trousers which are cut to be extremely full over the hips and narrowing toward the ankle. Peg-top trousers were a fashionable style for men during most of the 19th century. They were adopted by women during the 1970s. The material is gathered into a series of folds at the waist for a narrow fit, which provides a contrast to the full hips and narrow ankles.

peignoir From the French *peigner*, 'to comb', the peignoir dates from the 16th century. It is worn by women in their private rooms before dressing. The peignoir has always been a loose gown, sometimes worn with a SHIFT underneath, with long or short sleeves, and generally falling to the ankles. In the 19th century, peignoirs were usually made of cotton or other lightweight fabrics and trimmed with lace and ribbons.

Elsa **Peretti**'s famous heart pendants in gold and diamond for Tiffany & Co.

The long-sleeved **pelisse** was usually worn three-quarter length over a dress or skirt and trimmed in a variety of simple or elaborate ways. Fashion plate from the *Courier des Dames*, 5 November 1845.

pelerine Fashionable CLOAK worn by women in the mid-19th century. The pelerine, based on an old pilgrim's cloak, had long ends at the front and a short back, usually waist-length. Worn as an outdoor garment, it was made of wool and other warm fabrics.

pelisse Nineteenth-century coat, CLOAK or MANTLE which was often fur-lined or padded. It was usually worn open, to reveal a dress or gown beneath.

pencil skirt Skirt cut in one straight line from the hips to the hem. It has been popular since the 1940s, when economical cloth measurements were in use, though it was not given its name until the 1950s.

Penn, Irving 1917–. Photographer. Born in Plainfield, New Jersey, USA. From 1934 to 1938 Penn studied under Alexey BRODOVITCH at the Philadelphia Museum School of Industrial Art. During the summers of 1937 and 1938 he worked as a graphic artist for Brodovitch, who was then art director of *HARPER'S BAZAAR*. During World War II Penn served with both the US and British armies and in

1943 was hired by Alex LIBERMAN to work in the art department of *VOGUE* in New York. Penn's job included creating covers for the magazine but he soon began to produce his own photographs. In 1944 he turned freelance, though he continued to work for *Vogue*. Penn's pictures are strong. Although they give the appearance of simplicity, they are often formal collections of something more complex. Penn has contributed a sober, sculptural quality to fashion photography. An artist whose brush is the camera, he is famous for his still-lifes, portraits and female nudes.

peplum *See* BASQUE.

Peretti, Elsa 1940–. Jewelry designer. Born in Florence, Italy. Peretti studied interior design in Rome and worked as a model in London and New York before turning to jewelry design in 1969. Her first success came when HALSTON and Giorgio SANT'ANGELO featured her work in their shows. Using horn, ebony, ivory and silver, Peretti creates simple, striking shapes. Since 1974 she has had a long association with TIFFANY, for whom she made asymmetrical heart pendants of gold and tiny diamonds. She also introduced 'Diamonds by the Yard' – affordable stones simply set on delicate chains.

permanent wave In 1904 a German hairdresser, Karl Nessler (later known as Charles

Nestlé), working in London, pioneered the use of an electric machine which permanently waved women's hair. Permanents did not become popular until the 1920s, when a steam process was invented. 'Home perms' came into use soon after World War II. The first home perm solutions created tight, crinkly curls. These became less fashionable in the years following World War II, when a looser, softer style was preferred.

Persian lamb *See* ASTRAKHAN.

Pertegaz, Manuel 1918–. Designer. Born in Aragon, Spain. At the age of twelve Pertegaz became a tailor's apprentice. After his family moved to Barcelona, he began making clothes for his sister and eventually, in 1942, he established a salon. Over the following twenty years Pertegaz became one of Spain's great couturiers, with houses in a number of Spanish towns,

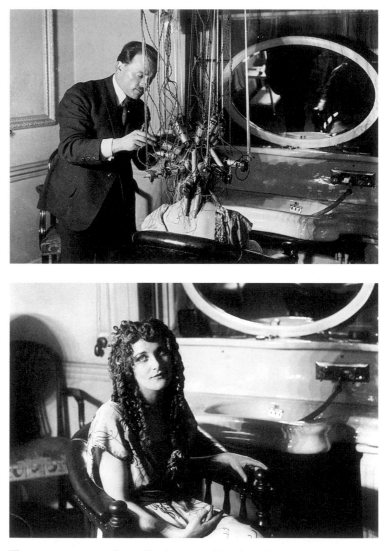

The **permanent wave** of 1921. *Top:* the process; *below:* the result.

Cotton brocade evening dress with matching sleeveless jacket by the Spanish couturier Manuel **Pertegaz**, 1964.

including one in Madrid. He is a classic designer of elegant clothes in the Spanish tradition of grand and stately garments. He was famous throughout Spain for his couture and ready-to-wear lines, despite the austerity of some of his designs.

Perugia, André 1893–1977. Shoe designer. Born in Nice, France. Perugia trained in his father's workshop and at the age of eighteen opened a shop in Paris where he sold handmade shoes. During the 1920s he made shoes for POIRET and later for FATH and GIVENCHY. His work was always associated with a high level of craftsmanship. He retired in 1970.

peter pan collar Flat, round collar, about two or three inches deep, sometimes stiffly starched, named after Peter Pan, the boy hero of J. M. Barrie's play of the same name of 1904. The peter pan collar was extremely popular with women during the 1920s, contributing to the boyish silhouettes of the decade. It has enjoyed revivals in subsequent periods.

petticoat From the Old French *petite côte*, a petticoat was originally a man's undershirt. By the Middle Ages it had become a woman's garment resembling a padded waistcoat or undercoat. As fashion replaced the undercoat with the CHEMISE, the petticoat became an underskirt, tied around the waist with ribbons or tapes. In the 19th century, the slim lines of the DIRECTOIRE necessitated the temporary abandonment of the petticoat, but by the 1840s it was again being worn, sometimes on view below skirts. In the 1860s support for Garibaldi's 'redshirts' created a vogue for red flannel petticoats. Throughout the 19th century, petticoats were generally made of linen, cotton, muslin or other fine fabrics. Warmer, heavier fabrics were worn in winter. By the early 20th century, petticoats were rarely visible. They became briefly popular in the 1970s when Ralph LAUREN showed cotton versions under denim skirts as part of his 'prairie look'.

Pfister, Andrea 1942–. Shoe designer. Born in Pesaro, Italy. As a child, Pfister moved to Switzerland, where he was educated. Later, he returned to Italy to study art and languages. In 1961 he took a course in shoe design in Milan and two years later moved to Paris and established himself as a designer for LANVIN and PATOU. Pfister showed his first collection of shoes in 1965 and in 1967 opened his first shoe shop. His shoes are colourful, stylish and amusing and have earned him an international reputation.

Picasso, Pablo 1881–1973. Painter. Born in Malaga, Spain. The 20th century's most famous artist, Picasso influenced fashion mainly through the work he did after meeting Georges BRAQUE in Paris in 1907. Their Cubist paintings inspired designs of sweaters and other garments in later years.

Picasso, Paloma 1949–. Jewelry designer. Born in Paris, France, the daughter of Pablo PICASSO and Françoise Gilot. Picasso was educated in Paris and attended the University of Nanterre. After completing her formal training in jewelry design in 1969, she became involved

Paloma **Picasso**'s multicoloured necklace of pearls with a rare hiddenite pendant, designed for Tiffany & Co.

in theatre and costume design. Using jeweled bikini strings from the Folies-Bergère, she fashioned exotic COSTUME JEWELRY which attracted a great deal of attention. In the same year, Yves SAINT LAURENT showed her jewelry with his collections. She launched her first collection of semi-precious and precious stones designed exclusively for TIFFANY in 1980. Picasso's designs are vibrant and imaginative. She is fond of unusual colour combinations and highly polished surfaces.

Picken, Mary Brooks 1886–1981. Teacher, writer. Born in Arcadia, Kansas, USA. Picken was taught to sew, spin and weave at an early age. After taking a dressmaking course in Kansas City, she studied design, tailoring and cutting in Boston and then became an instructor at the American College of Dressmaking in Kansas City, Missouri. From 1914 she wrote numerous books and articles, many under pseudonyms, on the practicalities of fashion: dressmaking, styling, tailoring and fabrics.

pierrot collar Smaller version of the large, stiff, ruffled collar of Pierrot, the French pantomime character, used on blouses during the 20th century.

Piguet, Robert 1901–53. Designer. Born in Yverdon, Switzerland. After training as a banker, Piguet went in 1918 to Paris, where he worked with REDFERN and POIRET. He found-

ed his own house in 1933. Until 1951, when he retired, he hired or used designs by BALMAIN, BOHAN, DIOR, GIVENCHY and GALANOS. He favoured dramatic gowns in a romantic style and created many costumes for the theatre, as well as well-cut suits and softly tailored dresses.

pillbox Small, oval hat with straight sides and a flat top, usually worn perched on the head at an angle. ADRIAN helped popularize the pillbox with a design made for Greta GARBO in *As You Desire Me* (1932) and the style remained in fashion into the 1940s. HALSTON's 1960s designs for Jacqueline Kennedy (*see* ONASSIS) brought the pillbox back into vogue. It was seen again briefly in the 1970s. *See* CASSINI.

pinafore *1.* Form of apron with a bib front, HALTER NECK and long skirt, that ties behind the waist. *2.* A 20th-century sleeveless dress with a low square-cut or SCOOP NECK which is often worn over a blouse (US: jumper).

Pinturier, Jacques 1932–. Milliner. Born in Auxerre, France. In 1949 Pinturier began

Sketch for a hat by the French milliner Jacques **Pinturier**, 1968.

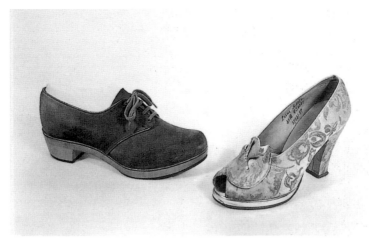

Platform soles from 1934 (*above*) and a more extreme 1970s version from Fiorucci (*below*).

working for his uncle, Gilbert Orcel, as a designer. In 1964 he joined CASTILLO and four years later opened his own business in Paris. Throughout his career Pinturier has worked with many couturiers. He treats his hats as art forms, so they often appear complex and futuristic in concept, but they are technically well thought out and have been widely influential.

Pipart, Gérard 1933–. Designer. Born in Paris, France. At the age of sixteen, Pipart began working for BALMAIN. He also worked for FATH, PATOU and BOHAN. After completing his military service he spent a short period as a freelance designer before being appointed in 1963 chief designer at Nina RICCI, where he has continued the house's style of sophisticated clothes for all occasions.

plaid *1. See* KILT. *2.* TARTAN or check cloth.

plastics Resin-like substances that are moulded by pressure and heat to create jewelry such as beads, stones and different settings. Plastics have been in use since the 1930s. They have also been employed to make garments. PVC, for example, was used for rainwear and outerwear in the 1960s.

platform soles Thick shoe sole introduced during the 1930s. Platform soles have been fashionable at some point in almost every decade,

notably the 1940s and 1960s. They were revived in the 1990s. *See also* ★FERRAGAMO.

playsuit Two-piece outfit of BLOOMERS and top, popular for beach attire during the 1950s.

plimsolls (US: sneakers) Rubber-soled canvas shoes popular since the 1870s for beach and sporting wear. The name was suggested by the introduction of the UK Merchant Shipping Act of 1876, sponsored by Samuel Plimsoll (1824–98), which required ships to display a line along their sides above which no vessel must sink into the water, thereby making overloading illegal.

Plunkett, Walter 1902–82. Costume designer. Born in Oakland, California, USA. Plunkett studied law at the University of California although he intended to be an actor. Later, working in Hollywood, he turned his skills to costume design and in 1926 was appointed head of the wardrobe department of FBO (later RKO) Studios. Apart from two years freelance work, he remained with the company until 1935. Then followed twelve years as a freelance until in 1947 Plunkett joined Metro-Goldwyn-Mayer, where he stayed until 1965. A respected costume designer, Plunkett contributed to hundreds of films, the most famous of which were *Gone with the Wind* (1938) and *Singin' in the Rain* (1951).

plus-fours KNICKERBOCKERS made of tweed or worsted, worn by Englishmen during the 1920s for sporting activities. The full cut permitted the fabric to fall four inches below the knee band, where it was gathered. Designers revived this garment as a fashion item for women during the 1970s. See *EDWARD VIII.

plush Cotton fabric with a velvet-like pile which was popular as a dress material in the 19th century.

pocketbook Small, flat HANDBAG which became popular during the late 19th century. In the 20th century, chiefly in the USA, the word can describe any small bag.

Poiret, Paul 1879–1944. Designer. Born in Paris, France. Poiret's father was a cloth merchant. In his teens Poiret became an umbrella maker's apprentice but his interests lay in fashion and he eventually sold some of his sketches to Madeleine CHERUIT at the house of Raudnitz Soeurs. In 1899 Poiret joined DOUCET, where his first design – a red cape – was extremely popular. In 1901 he moved to WORTH. Two years later Poiret decided to open his own house and was assisted in this by Doucet, who sent him Réjane, a famous actress

Paul **Poiret**'s models in his garden, showing their employer's talents. This back view reveals the exotic lines of Poiret's designs and his interest in fabric and silhouette. The headdresses range from a Greek-like bandeau to a large matinée hat.

Denise **Poiret**, Poiret's wife, photographed in 1913 wearing a grey tailored outfit with pink boots.

of the period. Under her patronage, Poiret was launched. In 1906 Poiret was responsible for loosening the formal silhouette of fashion and achieving a more relaxed shape by extending the CORSET to the hips and reducing the number of underclothes. In 1908 he published a brochure illustrated by Paul IRIBE entitled *Les Robes de Paul Poiret*. The drawings showed simple, elegant, softly fitted gowns, quite unlike the tightly corsetted, over-festooned dresses of the period. Poiret actually flirted with the basic shape created by the corset for many years, despite his claim to have freed women from its shackles. Nevertheless, this claim was not unfounded. He promoted the KIMONO shape in the early 1900s and was patronized by Isadora DUNCAN for his exotic, flowing garments. In 1909 Poiret featured TURBANS, AIGRETTES and HAREM PANTS – all inspired by the BALLETS RUSSES, which had provoked enormous interest in Eastern and oriental dress. Poiret fashioned garments of boldly coloured silks, brocades, velvets and lamé, simply constructed but rich in texture. In 1911 he commissioned another brochure, *Les Choses de Paul Poiret*, illustrated by Georges ★LEPAPE. In the same year he introduced a HOBBLE SKIRT which, while it freed the hips, confined the ankles. This fashion was not widely adopted and it attracted a great deal of attention and criticism. Poiret also established

the Ecole Martine, named after his daughter, where he employed untrained girls to design textiles and furnishings which were later made up by skilled craftsmen. Raoul DUFY worked with Poiret on many fabric designs for the textile company BIANCHINI-FERIER. Around this time Poiret produced one of his most famous shapes, 'the lampshade', created by wiring a TUNIC so that the hem stood out in a circle around the body. In 1912 he toured Europe with a group of models and followed this with a tour of the USA in 1913. Poiret made several attempts to promote the wearing of harem-type trousers below tunics. He was also noted for fur trimmings, scarves and hair ornaments. In 1914 he was instrumental in the creation of Le Syndicat de Défense de la Grande Couture Française, an attempt to protect member designers from piracy. At the outbreak of World War I, Poiret closed his business and joined the French army. Although he was active after the war, Poiret could not regain his former status. Postwar fashions were far more straightforward than his exotic garments.

poke bonnet Hood-shaped bonnet with a small crown at the back of the head and a wide brim at the front. It was tied under the chin so that the brim shielded the side of the face. Poke bonnets were popular in the 19th century, and eventually reached such exaggerated proportions that it was impossible to see the face except from the front. The vogue lasted until *c*.1860.

polka dot Pattern of evenly spaced dots printed on cotton, linen, silk, voile and mixed-fibre fabrics.

polo coat Coat first worn by attendants at sporting events, such as cricket and polo. Dating from the 20th century, the polo coat is a camel-hair or pale coloured light wool coat with a full skirt at the back, intended for casual wear. *See also* BROOKS BROTHERS.

polo collar White, round, starched shirt collar for men, popular at the turn of the 20th century. Later the name came to describe a soft, high, circular collar that turns down around the neck. Also known as a polo neck, it is often used on sweaters and casual sportswear attire.

Three popular hairstyles from the 1920s. *Left:* The sleek bob; *centre:* the **poodle cut**; and *right:* the crinkled lines of a marcel wave. The dress or jacket of the girl on the left has a deep peter pan collar, while the centre girl appears to be wearing a dress whose front section is patterned to resemble Egyptian heiroglyphics.

polo neck *See* POLO COLLAR.

polo shirt Originally a short-sleeved white PULLOVER made of knitted wool, with a turn-down collar which stayed in place during a polo game. From the 1930s the garment became integrated into leisurewear but in the latter part of the 20th century it was shown on runways as an alternative to a shirt under a suit.

polyester In 1941 J. F. Winfield and J. T. Dickson of the Calico Printer's Association introduced a polyester fibre composed mainly of ethylene glycol and terephthalic acid. By 1946 polyester fibres were used in home furnishings. In 1963 the DU PONT company launched Dacron in the US. Polyester fibre was used to make all kinds of fashion garments throughout the 1950s and it has continued to be one of the most frequently used man-made fibres in the manufacture of clothing. It is crease-resistant, dries quickly, and keeps its shape.

poncho From the Araucanian (a language of central Chile) word *pontho*, 'woollen cloth'. A poncho is a square or rectangular piece of woollen fabric, resembling a blanket, with an opening in the centre for the head. Ponchos are worn straight or diagonally. They originate in South America and are often woven with bright patterns and designs. They became popular in the USA during the late 1940s and the fashion

spread to Europe shortly after. The late 1960s fashions for ETHNIC clothes brought ponchos into vogue once again. *See* ★CASHIN.

pongee From the Chinese word *pen-chi*, 'home loom', pongee is a plain-woven fabric characterized by irregular cross-wise ribs and a dark ecru colour. It was originally a silk, but the 20th-century version is man-made, usually of a cotton mix. Both versions have been used for dresses and lingerie.

poodle haircut Hairstyle in which the hair is cut to about an inch and a half all over the head and curled. Popular in the late 1940s and 1950s.

poorboy Ribbed SWEATER with a slightly BATEAU NECKLINE and elbow-length sleeves. The poorboy became popular during the 1960s, when it was worn with skirts and trousers in summer and over blouses in winter.

pop over *See* MCCARDELL.

pop socks (US: pants stockings) Calf- or knee-length nylon STOCKINGS worn under trousers since the late 1960s.

poplin Strong, plain-woven fabric character-ized by cross-wise ribs that give it a corded effect. Originally made of a silk warp and wool weft, the name comes from the fabric *papalino*, made in the Papal town of Avignon in France,

Thea **Porter** sketch of a keyhole gypsy design in two voiles with flat gold braid trim, 1970s.

and the French fabric *popeline*, which was used for clerical vestments. The name poplin was common in England by the 18th century. Today poplin is made of combinations of silk, cotton, wool and man-made fibres. It is hardwearing and is used mostly for summer outerwear, such as jackets and coats.

Porter, Thea 1927–. Designer. Born in Damascus, Syria, of English parents. Porter studied English and French at London University from 1949 to 1950. Living in Beirut in 1953, she began painting. At the beginning of the 1960s she moved to London, where she opened a shop selling antique Turkish and Arabian carpets and silk textiles. By 1964 she was designing clothing, mainly based on Eastern and Middle-Eastern textiles. Porter's elegant CAFTANS attracted enormous attention. In 1968 she opened a store in New York, followed some six years later by one in Paris. She specialized in evening clothes of chiffon, crepe de chine, brocade, silk and velvet which were richly embroidered and decorated. Porter promoted the 1970s GYPSY styles with flounced chiffon dresses. Her clothes are sold worldwide, mostly in the Middle East. See *HIPSTER PANTS.

pouf A full short skirt often tucked up at the back, popularized by Christian LACROIX.

power suit Term coined in the 1980s to describe a skirt suit worn by businesswomen. The jacket resembled a man's suit jacket in cut but the shoulders were heavily padded and exaggerated.

Poynter, Charles In 1881 Charles Poynter took over the Parisian couture house established by John REDFERN. He continued to promote that firm's TROTTEUR as a fashionable outfit.

Prada Fashion house. Founded in 1913 in Milan, Italy. Originally established as Fratelli Prada, a manufacturer of high-quality leather goods, the company was successful until the 1970s. Its fortunes were revived when Miuccia Prada (b. 1949), granddaughter of the founder, Mario Prada, took over in 1978 and began producing accessories including a simple, black nylon BACKPACK fitted with leather straps. Backpacks and other accessory items made from nylon were stamped with the Prada name and quickly became desirable items which were widely copied. In 1988 Miuccia Prada introduced her first ready-to-wear line. She has become known for elegant streamlined clothing and for giving traditional garments a modern handling, for example, trimming nylon PARKAS with mink, and making TRENCHCOATS and TWINSETS out of silk faille. Her clothes, though often deceptively plain looking, have become widely influential.

prairie dress The prairie dress dates from the late 1880s. It was a long-sleeved calico or gingham dress with a frilled hem, reminiscent of the simple styles worn by the first women settlers in North America. In the 1970s, Ralph LAUREN produced a successful 'prairie look' which featured flounced white petticoats worn beneath denim skirts and cotton blouses trimmed with broderie anglaise.

Premet French fashion house which opened in 1911 and was particularly successful into the 1920s with its 'Garçon' and 'Gamine' models. GRES trained at Premet. The firm closed in 1931.

Princess line dresses for summer in the 1870s, showing the vertical seams that create the waist. Drawing by Jules David.

Preppie Style popular in North America in the late 1970s which imitated the dress of the IVY LEAGUE student. Essential ingredients of the Preppie look were the KILT or plaid skirt, BLAZER, tweeds, and Shetland or Fair Isle sweaters. These were worn with white blouses with short, frilly collars. Pastel shades were popular and the combination of red, white and blue was particularly fashionable. For men, the dress was corduroy trousers, madras trousers or shirts, and seersucker jackets. *See also* BROOKS BROTHERS.

prêt-à-porter French term for READY-TO-WEAR.

Price, Antony 1945–. Designer. Born in Bradford, England. Price attended Bradford School of Art and then studied fashion at the Royal College of Art, London, from 1965 to 1968. His first job was with manufacturer Stirling Cooper, with whom he remained until 1974 when he moved to Plaza. Price began designing under his own name in 1979, by which time he had already achieved a reputation as a designer on the rock music scene. His clothes were often theatrical and sexy, many of his designs harking back to Hollywood of the 1940s. Body-conscious, glamorous and often aggressive fashions are Price's hallmark. In the 1980s he became known for his shapely COCKTAIL DRESSES and party dresses.

princess line Sleek-fitting dress line achieved by making a garment without a waist seam. A popular style from the mid-19th century, the princess line was fitted over CRINOLINES and BUSTLES, with a gored skirt to create sufficient fullness. It was popular during the 1930s, 1950s and 1960s, in varying lengths. The princess line has often been designed to button up the front. Also known as fourreau style.

Pringle of Scotland Sock, hosiery and underwear company founded in 1815 by Robert Pringle. One of the largest companies specializing in the production of cashmere, lambswool, merino and shetland, Pringle is a subsidiary of Dawson International, the world's biggest processor of raw cashmere. During the 1920s and 1930s the name Pringle became synonymous with cashmere TWINSETS, CARDIGANS and sweaters. The company is also known for traditional INTARSIA sweaters, hand-inlaid with flower motifs and patterns.

The ballerina Margot Fonteyn, modelling a **Pringle** cardigan in the early 1960s.

Prussian collar High-standing, turn-down collar featured on the military greatcoats of Prussian officers in the 19th century. The Prussian collar has frequently been adapted to fashion garments.

psychedelic Irregularly patterned, brilliantly coloured clothes, often made of luminous cloth, which were popular in the 1960s and which originated in the HIPPIE movement. The colours and patterns were intended to represent the effects of taking hallucinogenic drugs.

Pucci Emilio 1914–92. Designer. Born Marchese Emilio Pucci di Barsento in Naples, Italy. Pucci spent two years at Milan University before moving to the University of Georgia in Athens, Georgia, USA, for a further two years study. In 1937, he enrolled at Reed College, Portland, Oregon, where he majored in social sciences and received his MA two years later. Returning to Italy, he spent the war years as a bomber in the Italian air force. He was awarded a doctorate in political science from the University of Florence in 1941. Pucci was a keen sportsman and as a high school student had been a member of the Italian Olympic ski team. After World War II, he was photographed by Toni FRISSELL of HARPER'S BAZAAR on the Italian ski slopes, wearing SKI PANTS of his own design. The magazine asked him to create some winter clothes for women which it subsequently published and which were put on sale in various New York stores. During the 1950s Pucci gained a reputation as a designer of sporting wear and relaxed daywear and contributed to the success of post-World War II Italian fashion design. He produced tapered trousers, CAPRI PANTS, shorts, resort dresses, brilliantly printed silk blouses and shirts, SLACKS and casual suits. His clothes were known for their bold patterns and colours. Pucci also designed ranges of underwear, sweaters and swimwear for US clothing manufacturers.

puff sleeves Short sleeves, gathered and set into the shoulders of garments to create a puffed effect. Worn since the 19th century on evening gowns, puff sleeves were also used on children's dresses and blouses. In the 20th century they have been a popular feature of summer clothes for women.

Pulitzer, Lilly dates unknown. Designer. Place of birth unknown. In 1958 Pulitzer founded a company in Palm Beach, Florida, USA. She could not sew, but was able to translate her ideas to seamstresses who made up her designs. She popularized a one-piece cotton housedress known as a 'Lilly'. The company sold A-LINE skirts and dresses in unusual colour combinations, such as pink and green. Colours like these and bold floral prints were Pulitzer's trademarks. Her clothes were popular with society women and she opened BOUTIQUES throughout the USA. She closed in 1984.

pullover Long-sleeved waist- or hip-length knitted SWEATER worn at the turn of the century for sporting activities. During World War I women knitted pullovers for the troops. They became fashionable in the 1920s in plain and patterned knit, with various necklines, and trimmed with contrasting fabrics – often fur. *See also* CHANEL *and* JUMPER.

pumps 1. Lightweight, flat, plain shoes originally worn by servants in the 18th century. In the late 19th century, black PATENT pumps became proper attire for men attending evening dances. In the 20th century, women adopted pumps made of plastic and leather for day, evening and leisurewear. 2. US term for COURT SHOES. *See also* CAPEZIO.

Punk Style of dress which first emerged in London, England, during the mid-1970s among teenagers, the unemployed and students. Hairstyles for both sexes included cropped hair, often shaved into strips, or longer hair, glued and backcombed to stick out at sharp angles and dyed red, green, purple or yellow. Faces were painted pasty white and eyes ringed in black. Punk dress was intended to attract attention and to frighten. Torn trousers exposed dirty flesh; skirts were short and split. Black leather jackets, often studded, dominated the scene. Chains were used to tie one trouser leg loosely to the other or were worn around the neck. T-SHIRTS were daubed with slogans. Other popular accessories included STRING VESTS and steel armlets. Safety pins held clothing together or were worn through the nose or ears. Pink and orange were favourite colours, often worn together. Many punk dress ideas found their way, in a more

Pyjama-style loungewear in the 1920s, typically made of satin and lace-trimmed.

refined manner, into ready-to-wear fashions of the 1980s. *See* WESTWOOD.

purse *See* HANDBAG.

PVC (polyvinyl chloride) Fabric originally developed in 1844 during experiments with oil-cloth. Chemically related to linoleum, PVC became fashionable during the 1960s when it was dyed bright colours and made up into outerwear, particularly hip-length 'scooter coats'.

pyjamas From the Hindi *paejama*, 'leg clothing'. In the 19th century pyjamas consisted of loose-fitting trousers and sashed jacket tops. By the turn of the century various forms of pyjamas existed, including lounging pyjamas, worn by men as elegant early evening attire. In the 1920s and 1930s women wore decorative evening pyjamas, and beachwear versions. The film *It Happened One Night* (1934), starring Claudette Colbert and Clark Gable, helped popularize pyjamas for women. Modern nightwear pyjamas evolved in the 1920s. *See also* GALITZINE.

Q

Quant, Mary 1934–. Designer. Born in London, England. Quant attended Goldsmith's College of Art in London from 1950 to 1953. In 1955 she spent several months with Erik, a London milliner, before leaving to open Bazaar, her first boutique, on the KING'S ROAD, with her future husband, Alexander Plunket Green, and Archie McNair. Quant began by selling young fashions by various designers but soon began to make up her own garments. She had little experience of fashion, but her low-priced, avant-garde clothes, geared to the teenage and young market, were an instant success and she became a household name. *Harpers & Queen* featured her spotted PYJAMAS. Quant's clothes were in perfect tune with the 1960s. Bright, simple and well-coordinated, they epitomized young British fashion in 'Swinging London'. She popularized the MINI SKIRT, coloured tights, SKINNY RIB sweaters, and low-slung HIPSTER belts. She created a 'wet' collection of PVC garments and sold vast numbers of waist-length, sleeveless crochet tops. Quant's clothes were classless and appealed to young and old alike. She turned her hand to every type of clothing from underwear and

Mary **Quant**, quintessential 1960s designer, wearing one of her own designs, photographed by David Bailey.

Mary **Quant** suit from 1959, not yet the mini. Photograph by Terence Donovan.

stockings to all-year-round fashions. In 1963 she started her wholesale design and manufacturing firm, Ginger Group. Quant was also a success in the USA, where she designed lines for the J. C. Penney store chain and the Puritan Fashions group In 1966 she established her famous and highly successful cosmetics line, with its striking daisy logo. Although she has continued to design, notably knitwear lines for the Japanese market, Quant's name will always be synonymous with the 1960s.

Quiana Nylon introduced by DU PONT in the late 1960s. Light and wrinkle-resistant, Quiana was knitted or woven into fabrics that were subsequently promoted as high-fashion materials.

quilting Cotton filling enclosed by two layers of fabric and held in place by stitching of regular or irregular decorative pattern. Quilting was popular for coats and jackets in the early 1920s and again in the 1970s. *See also* KAMALI.

R

Rabanne, Paco 1934–. Designer. Born Francisco Rabaneda y Cuervo in San Sebastian, Spain. Rabanne's mother was the chief seamstress at BALENCIAGA's Spanish branch. During the Spanish Civil War the family moved to France, where Rabanne was educated. He became a student of architecture at the Ecole des Beaux-Arts in Paris from 1952 to 1964. Rabanne's earliest contributions to fashion were his bold plastic jewelry and buttons which he sold to Balenciaga, DIOR and GIVENCHY. In 1965 he made his first plastic dress. A pioneer in the use of alternative materials for inventive fashions, Rabanne made dresses using pliers instead of needles and thread; metal discs and chains instead of fabric. His chainmail garments, constructed from small, geometric pieces, attracted a great deal of attention. Rabanne also designed dresses of crinkled paper, aluminium and jersey towelling seamed with Scotch tape. He attached chainlinks to knitwear and furs.

Man's short **raglan** coat, 1898.

Paco **Rabanne**'s innovative look for Autumn/Winter 1968–69 is constructed of South African ostrich plumes and aluminium panels.

Rabanne was in demand as a costume designer for the cinema, theatre and ballet. In 1966 he opened his own house, where he has earned an international reputation with his unusual jewelry, accessories and garments.

rabbit Long-haired fur of a rodent found in Europe, North and South America, China, Japan and Australia. Rabbit furs are dyed or marked to resemble other furs. The fur is usually cheap but seldom fashionable.

raccoon Small, carnivorous American mammal. Raccoon fur is long-haired, varying from silver and iron grey to blackish-brown tones with a dark stripe. It is hardwearing, and was very popular during the 1920s and 1930s, with a further vogue in the 1970s.

raglan Coat and sleeve named after Lord Raglan (1788–1855), British Commander during the Crimean War. A raglan sleeve extends from the neckline to the wrist. It is joined to the BODICE of a coat or dress by diagonal seams from the neck to under the arms, allowing for greater mobility of the arms and the body. Initially this

In the late 19th century, the **Rational Dress Society** favoured healthy garments that did not restrict the body. Rational dress styles were looser and more comfortable than the more stylized S-bend of the period.

sleeve was a feature of the short, woollen, raglan coat, but since the later 19th century it has been adapted to numerous other garments.

rah-rah skirt Short, frilly skirt worn by North American college cheerleaders in the 20th century. *See also* KAMALI.

Rahvis, Raemonde 1918–. Designer. Born in Cape Town, South Africa. Rahvis worked as a freelance designer in London from 1935 until 1941, when she opened a fashion house with her sister Dorothy, selling luxurious evening clothes and tailored daywear. She also designed costumes for a number of films.

raincoat Devised from the late-19th-century TRENCHCOAT, the raincoat was developed as a waterproof garment in the 20th century and is worn by both men and women. Military-style

versions with EPAULETS and a double YOKE at the shoulders were worn, collar turned up and loosely belted, by Hollywood film stars of the 1930s. This fashion endured into the 1980s. *See also* AQUASCUTUM *and* BURBERRY.

Rational Dress Society Founded in London in 1881, the Rational Dress Society endorsed Mrs BLOOMER's view of utilitarian fashions. Its members wore TURKISH TROUSERS and resisted on health grounds any attempt by fashion to restrict or deform the body. Active in dress reform, the society sold boneless STAYS and what it considered to be practical garments. Its publication, *The Gazette* (1888–89), condemned high heels and advocated the wearing of no more than seven pounds of underwear.

Ray, Man 1890–1976. Artist, photographer. Born Emmanuel Rudnitsky in Philadelphia,

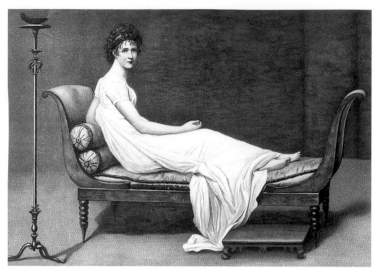

Madame **Récamier**, wearing the empire-line style of dress that she popularized in the early 19th century.

Pennsylvania, USA. Man Ray's family moved to Brooklyn, New York, in 1897. He graduated from school with a scholarship to study architecture but decided instead to take up painting. To finance his art, Man Ray opened a painting and photography portraiture studio. In 1921 he left for Paris and the following year was commissioned by Paul POIRET to photograph the latter's designs. Man Ray is best known for his work as a Surrealist and for his invention in the early 1920s of solarization, a photographic technique which has the effect of surrounding the subject with a thick outline of shadow. He worked as a fashion photographer for various magazines.

Rayne, Edward 1922–92. Shoe manufacturer. Born in London, England. The firm H. & M. Rayne was founded by Edward Rayne's grandparents in 1889. At the end of the century, H. & M. Rayne made shoes primarily for the theatre, counting many actresses among its private customers. In 1920, to provide interesting, decorative and fashionable shoes for a non-theatrical clientele, the company opened a shop in London's Bond Street which became highly successful. Edward Rayne joined the firm in 1940 and in 1951, on the death of his father, he took over as chairman and managing director. For some time H. & M. Rayne had been

closely associated with Herman DELMAN of Delman Shoes in the USA but in 1961 it was acquired by Debenhams Ltd, one of the largest department store groups in the UK. Rayne shoes are known worldwide and have extensive outlets in the UK and USA. Edward Rayne was responsible for finding and encouraging numerous shoe designers. He worked with couturiers such as AMIES, CAVANAGH and MUIR, and for VIVIER, the shoe designer. The firm also made shoes for DIOR. See *SLING BACKS.

rayon Named in 1924 by Kenneth Lord, Senior, after a competition to find a new name for artificial silk. Rayon is made from cellulose. It drapes well and has a high absorbency which allows it to dye well. In 1912 the first rayon 'silk' STOCKINGS were produced. In 1916 the first knitwear made of rayon came onto the market, and rayon outerwear soon followed. Rayon production increased dramatically in the 1920s and has continued at a high level. *See also* VISCOSE RAYON.

ready-to-wear (France: *prêt-à-porter*) Clothes which carry a designer's label but which can be bought ready-made off the peg.

Reboux, Caroline 1837–1927. Milliner. Born in Paris, France. In the 1860s Reboux's work came to the attention of Princess Metternich. By 1870 she was installed in a shop in Paris and by the 1920s she was one of the city's leading milliners. Reboux is associated with the popularization of the CLOCHE hat of the period. She worked with most of the major designers, providing hats for their collections.

Récamier, Juliette 1777–1849. Born Jeanne Françoise Julie Adelaide Bernard in Paris, France. Daughter and wife of bankers, Madame Récamier was a noted leader of French fashion in the early 19th century. She wore the high-waisted DIRECTOIRE line – also known in France as the RECAMIER – styled in soft, clinging fabrics.

Redfern, John 1853–1929. Born in England. In the 1850s Redfern worked as a tailor on the Isle of Wight. By 1871 he had extended his business to sell silk and MOURNING DRESS. When the town of Cowes became the centre of the yachting world at the end of the 19th century, Redfern began designing sports clothes for women. In 1879 he created a costume worn by Lillie LANGTRY – the Jersey Lily – and tailored serge outfits. In 1881 he established businesses in London and Paris, followed later by branches in Edinburgh and New York. His son, Ernest, took charge of the London and New York branches while Charles POYNTER looked after the Paris salon. By 1885 Redfern was producing yachting suits, travelling suits and riding habits. In 1888 he was appointed dressmaker to Queen VICTORIA. Redfern helped popularize the high-waisted, so-called Grecian style of 1908. In 1916 he created the first women's uniform for the Red Cross. Redfern closed his houses in the 1920s. See ★GAZETTE DU BON TON.

redingote From the English 'riding coat', worn by men in the 18th century, the mid-19th century redingote was a women's long-sleeved gown with a large, turn-down collar. Towards the end of the century it evolved into a tailored outdoor garment, cut in a PRINCESS LINE with a large, flat collar and full skirt which was worn open to reveal the dress beneath.

reefer Single- or double-breasted, thigh-length top coat worn by sailors during the 19th century. The semi-fitted garment was often

The **redingote** took a variety of forms in the 19th century, cut and adorned in different ways from decade to decade. From *Revue de la mode*, 1885.

trimmed with EPAULETS, pockets and brass buttons. In the second half of the 20th century the reefer became popular for casual wear, without decorative trim.

Reger, Janet *c.*1935–. Lingerie designer. Born in London, England. Reger attended Leicester College of Art and Technology. Throughout the 1970s she made a name for herself as a designer of glamorous, sexy underwear. In 1970 she produced TABARD-style nightdresses with slits at the sides. Silky nightdresses, satin PYJAMAS, and bra-and-pantie sets in black, white or pink with dyed lace inserts were popular items. In 1978 she created a beribboned WASPIE. Five years later her company was bought by BERLEI, but Reger returned to designing under her own name in 1984.

Rentner, Maurice 1889–1958. Manufacturer. Born in Poland. Rentner emigrated to the USA at the age of thirteen. He became a children's-wear salesman and eventually bought a glove manufacturing company. In the 1920s he began selling ready-to-wear clothing. He bought Paris models, notably by MOLYNEUX, which he copied and made up into off-the-peg clothes.

Simone de Beauvoir in **resortwear** by Hermès in 1938.

Rentner was one of the first manufacturers to hire and promote designers. *See* BLASS.

resortwear Term describing fashions worn in the fashionable resort areas of France during the 1920s and 1930s. Shorts, beach PYJAMAS, WRAPAROUND skirts and PLAYSUITS all fall into this category. By the latter part of the 20th century the word covered all kinds of lightweight garments for summer and cruisewear.

reticule Also known as a ridicule, this dainty 19th-century bag was originally made of network and served the function of a pocket. A cord was threaded through its neck and pulled tight and the reticule was carried around the wrist. Versions of the reticule were made in silk, velvet and other soft fabrics.

retro Word used to describe clothing from a previous era, usually at least twenty years earlier. Many designers feature retro garments in their collections. These clothes, though revisionist in attitude, are remade to work with current looks. During the 1990s flares and crochet, two significant items of 1960s fashion, reappeared in collections, but in a more sophisticated, mainstream style.

An afternoon suit by **Reville** in the 1920s featuring a cardigan jacket – a graphic fabric design on the sleeves matching that of the dress. The model carries an envelope bag and wears a slouch hat.

revers Wide LAPEL on jacket or coat.

Reville and Rossiter Couture house founded in London in 1906 by Mr William Reville, a designer, and Miss Rossiter, who was in charge of running the business. Both founders had previously worked for the London department store Jay's. In 1910 the company was appointed court dressmaker to Queen Mary and the following year it made the Queen's coronation robe. Reville and Rossiter specialized in formal gowns of EDWARDIAN STYLE and were patronized by members of the aristocracy. In 1936 Reville and Rossiter merged with WORTH.

rhinestones Glass or PASTE imitation stones, usually colourless or silvered. Rock crystal is also known as rhinestone. Rhinestones have been popular since the 1930s as dress and shoe decorations and jewelry.

Zandra **Rhodes** created this 'primavera' look for the summer of 1970 in handpainted silk chiffon trimmed with feather fronds.

A doll dressed in Nina **Ricci** for 1937.

Rhodes, Zandra 1940–. Designer. Born in Chatham, Kent, England. Rhodes studied textile printing and lithography at Medway College of Art, Kent, from 1959 until 1961, when she enrolled at the Royal College of Art, London. She graduated in 1966. Rhodes began by designing and printing highly individual textiles which she sold, made up into dresses, from a London shop. In 1968 she formed her own house. One of the most original talents to emerge since the 1960s, Rhodes has a unique way of mixing texture and pattern, handscreening many of her garments on chiffon and silks. Her exotic evening dresses often have uneven HANDKERCHIEF POINTS. Rhodes has produced felt coats with pinked edges, quilted TUNICS and embroidered satin garments. Her signatures are Art Deco motifs, zigzags, lipsticks, cacti plants, etc. In the late 1970s she added jersey to her collections and revived the CRINOLINE. Rhodes's fantastic creations are found worldwide. Her feminine, floating, chiffon dresses are favoured by movie stars and are particularly popular in the USA. See *PARKINSON.

rhodophane Mixture of cellophane and other synthetics developed in the 1920s by the French fabric company Colcombet. SCHIAPARELLI created several glass-like TUNICS of rhodophane in the 1930s.

Ricci, Nina 1883–1970. Designer. Born Maria Nielli in Turin, Italy. The Nielli family moved to Florence when Maria was five. She married a jeweler, Louis Ricci. After an apprenticeship with a couturier, Ricci opened her own house in Paris in 1932. Working directly from bolts of cloth, she created elegant, sophisticated clothes in classic styles. She was noted for her high standard of workmanship and became a popular designer for older women. Her son took over the management of the house in 1945. Jules François CRAHAY worked at Ricci until 1963 when Gérard PIPART became chief designer.

Riley, Bridget 1932–. Painter. Born in London, England. Riley studied at Goldsmith's College of Art and the Royal College of Art in London. Her early work was influenced by Impressionism but in the 1960s, after an extended visit to Italy, she became a noted figure in the OP ART movement. Although her mostly black and white paintings are static, the optic nerve reacts to give an impression of dazzle and movement. In the 1960s Op Art designs became popular for fabrics and Riley's paintings were used as the basis for dress fabric designs.

Rive Gauche See SAINT LAURENT.

Robb *c.*1907–. Illustrator. Born Andrew Robb in Leith, Scotland. Robb graduated from Edinburgh College of Art in 1926. After some years travelling, he joined a commercial art studio in London and worked during the 1930s for *VOGUE* and the *Daily Express*. He returned to the *Express* after the war to cover the Paris fashion shows. Robb was known for the boldness and economy of his illustrations. He worked often with Norman HARTNELL, making sketches of Hartnell's clothes for Queen Elizabeth II.

robe de style Dress style of the 20th century associated with Jeanne LANVIN. A *robe de style* has a close-fitting BODICE, a natural or lower waistline, and a full, bouffant skirt reaching to the calf or ankle.

Roberts, Patricia 1945–. Designer. Born in Barnard Castle, County Durham, England. Roberts studied at Leicester College of Art from 1963 until 1967, when she joined the knitting department of IPC Magazines in London. She became a freelance knitting pattern designer in 1972. Demand for her chunky, brightly coloured sweaters, jackets and cardigans was such that in 1976 she opened her first knitting shop selling handknitted clothes. Roberts's new, lively and exciting ideas contributed to the revolution in knitwear fashions during the 1970s. *See* ★KNITTING.

Rocha, John 1946–. Designer. Born in Hong Kong. The son of a Portuguese father and Chinese mother, Rocha went to London in 1970. After completing his studies at Croydon College of Design and Technology he opened a design business in Kilkenny, Ireland, in 1977. He later moved to Dublin and opened a boutique for which he designed sharply tailored linen suits. Rocha worked briefly in Milan between 1987 and 1989 before returning to Ireland. His fluid style, often influenced by oriental shapes, drew international attention and in 1994 he showed in Paris. He is also known for his sheer eveningwear, rich fabrics with hand-painted designs and crocheted knitwear.

Rochas, Marcel 1902–55. Designer. Born in Paris, France. Rochas opened his house in 1924. He was a strong, influential designer with an international reputation who anticipated many of the most prominent fashions of the 20th century. In 1933 his collection featured wide shoulders – a style generally attributed to SCHIAPARELLI. He favoured HOURGLASS silhouettes and foreshadowed the NEW LOOK by showing longer skirts in 1941, and BUSTIERS and GUEPIERES in 1943 and 1946. Rochas often worked with flower-patterned fabrics. He promoted the three-quarter-length coat and was one of the first designers to feature pockets in skirts. Rochas also specialized in separates and accessories which he sold from a BOUTIQUE in his salon.

roll-on Tightly elasticated GIRDLE without SUSPENDERS, worn in the 1960s when the popularity of trousers demanded unobtrusive underwear.

Ronay, Edina 1943–. Designer. Born in Budapest, Hungary. Ronay studied at St Martin's School of Art, London. Inspired by knitwear of the 1930s and 1940s, she began producing a range of handknitted sweaters which she sold through London markets.

The knitwear designer Edina **Ronay** models one of her own Fair Isle sweaters in 1981.

Known for her sportswear, Maggy **Rouff** was able to design evening gowns equally well. This early 1950s design is in black tulle with a sheer organdy long jacket – rather like a negligée – and silver choker necklace.

Shortly after, she was joined by Lena Stengard and by the late 1970s the firm of Edina and Lena was exporting sweaters worldwide. Ronay made her name with traditional Fair Isle patterns, motifs and bead decorations. With her numerous outworkers, she is one of the biggest UK handknit designers.

Rosenstein, Nettie dates unknown. Born in the USA. Rosenstein established her own business in 1917. She retired in 1927 but returned to work in 1931. Until the outbreak of World War II Rosenstein was well known both for her LITTLE BLACK DRESSES and for her evening gowns.

Rouff, Maggy 1896–1971. Designer. Born Maggy Besançon de Wagner in Paris, France. Rouff's parents were directors of the house of DRECOLL and it was there that Rouff began her design career. She opened her own house in 1928. Known for her lingerie and daywear, Rouff created wearable fashions in the haute couture tradition, though she achieved considerable success with her ready-to-wear lines. Rouff retired in 1948. The house remained open until the late 1960s.

rouleau Piece of material cut on the cross and made into a thin tube which acts as a belt or piping on hats and coats.

Russian In the fashion world, the term Russian describes several styles of dress, the overall image of each being a full-skirted, layered look, with fur often used as a trimming. After the Russian Revolution, Russian embroidery

experimented with seams (reversing them to the outside) and with asymmetrical cuts. In particular, she favours long, clinging sweaters or small cropped PULLOVERS, large rolled-back cuffs, and long shawls. Her outerwear often includes voluminous cape-like garments. Her colours are predominantly beige, grey, dark blue and charcoal. See ★TROUSER SUIT.

S

sable Lustrous fur from a member of the weasel family native to Canada and Russia. Lighter than mink, sable was popular in the 19th and early 20th centuries before it became prohibitively expensive.

sack Loose dress shape which tapered to below the knees, introduced by BALENCIAGA in the

Sonia **Rykiel** specializes in knitwear. The outfit shown here is from Spring/Summer 1986.

became popular in Paris. Grand Duchess Marie Pavlovna, daughter of Grand Duke Paul, organized a business which employed expatriate women to embroider traditional Russian PEASANT designs onto garments. The business was patronized by CHANEL and PATOU. There was a revival of Russian costume during the 1970s, when the ★COSSACK look included full, calf-length skirts; tall, baggy boots; high-collared jackets trimmed with braid; HEADSCARVES and shawls; and hats with circlets of fur.

Rykiel, Sonia 1930–. Designer. Born in Paris, France. Rykiel's first designs, in 1962, were of maternity dresses for herself. Shortly after, she created clothes for her husband's company, 'Laura'. In 1968 she opened her first BOUTIQUE. Specializing in knitwear, Rykiel is a first-rate designer creating elegant, fluid garments in soft wools, jersey, angora and mohair. A sensual outline is important to her garments and many are figure-hugging. She has also

Deep back pleats formed the 18th- and later the 19th-century **sacque**.

Left: Emanuel's 1984 version of the **sailor collar**, reversed onto the back, extra long, and finished with a bow. *Above:* Edward VIII in the original **sailor suit**, popular at the turn of the century.

mid-1950s but popularized by DIOR. Although the dress was loosely shaped, careful cutting was required to achieve the correct line. The sack created enormous controversy during the 1950s.

sacque *1.* Short, loose, sleeveless jacket worn with a petticoat or slip as a NEGLIGEE in the early 19th century. *2.* Deep back pleats that fall from the neck to the heels on 18th-century dresses, which were briefly popular again during the 19th century.

safari jacket Based on a man's loose shirt, the safari, or bush, jacket was worn by Europeans on safari in Africa. It was made of cotton, linen or water-repellent corduroy, often suede-finished and waterproofed, and featured breast, shell and hand pockets. It was belted and reached to below the hips. *See* SAFARI SUIT *and* ★SAINT LAURENT.

safari suit Made from heavy, waterproof material, the hip-length SAFARI JACKET had large PATCH POCKETS with buttoned flaps and a waist belt. Worn with short trousers, it was originally used in the African bush in the late 19th century. During the 20th century the style has been worn as summer attire with long or short trousers or a skirt.

sailcloth Heavy, plain-woven cotton, jute or linen which was originally used to make sails. Since the 1940s it has been made up into casual attire and clothes for sporting activities.

sailor collar Collar made of two thicknesses of a heavy fabric, sewn together and cut into a square which falls down the back and narrows to a point in front, where a bow is tied. It was a popular style for women in the 1920s. *See* SAILOR SUIT.

sailor suit Children's fashion first popular for boys in the 1840s when WINTERHALTER painted the five-year-old Prince Edward (who became EDWARD VII) in a naval uniform of a white suit with BELL BOTTOMS, SAILOR COLLAR, neckerchief and hat. The fashion was later adapted for girls and then for adults. It took various forms, the bell bottoms replaced by KNICKERBOCKERS, shorts or trousers. Usual fabrics were cotton or serge. In the 1920s and

Saint Laurent design for Dior in 1959: a wool and taffeta afternoon dress worn with a pearl choker.

Yves **Saint Laurent** at Christian Dior in 1953.

Some of Yves **Saint Laurent**'s influential designs: the famous knickerbocker suit of 1967 (*opposite top right*), the culottes of the following year (*above*) and the safari jacket of 1969 (*opposite bottom right*).

1940s sailor suits for women became popular, consisting of pleated skirts, sailor-collar blouses, BOATERS and REEFERS. Navy and white are the traditional colours.

Saint Laurent, Yves 1936–. Designer. Born in Oran, Algeria. Studying in Paris at the age of seventeen, Saint Laurent entered a competition sponsored by the International Wool Secretariat and won first prize for a COCKTAIL DRESS. Shortly after, he was hired by DIOR. When Dior died four years later, Saint Laurent took over the house. The collections of this precocious designer created considerable controversy: they were not what people had come to expect of the house of Dior. Saint Laurent's TRAPEZE of 1958 was a 'little girl' look: a narrow-shouldered dress with a semi-fitted BODICE and short, flared skirt. A year later he revived a shorter version of the HOBBLE SKIRT. In 1960 he showed black leather jackets, TURTLENECK sweaters and fur-trimmed hems.

The audience watched modern, street fashion redesigned in the hands of a couturier. In that same year Saint Laurent was called up to serve in the Algerian war. Some months later, discharged because of illness, he returned to Paris to find that Marc BOHAN had taken over as head designer at Dior. With business partner Pierre Bergé, Saint Laurent founded his own house in 1961. His first collection, in 1962, featured a successful gold-buttoned navy wool *PEA JACKET and workmen's SMOCKS in jersey, silk and satin. Year after year he made contributions to fashion. In 1963 his thigh-high boots were widely copied. In 1965 he welded art to fashion in his MONDRIAN dresses. He launched in 1966 the 'smoking' or *TUXEDO jacket for women – one of his most popular innovations. Also in 1966 Saint Laurent opened a string of ready-to-wear shops under the name Rive Gauche. Velvet KNICKERBOCKERS were an important feature of the 1967 collections. Nineteen-sixty-eight was the year he showed SEE-THROUGH blouses and the classic SAFARI JACKET; 1969 the year of the TROUSER SUIT; 1971, the year of the BLAZER. Throughout the 1970s Saint Laurent continued to reign in Paris. One of his most memorable collections, in 1976, variously nicknamed *COSSACK or RUSSIAN, featured exotic PEASANT costumes. The long, full skirts, BODICES and boots were widely influential, while the show made scarves and shawls permanent fashion fixtures. Saint Laurent is one of the most important post-World War II designers. From his early days at Dior, where he was part of the movement to rethink fashion without couture, Saint Laurent has been a leader. Until 1964 his outfits were basically for the young or young at heart but in the mid-1960s his designs became increasingly sophisticated. He put large numbers of women into trousers, adapted many garments from the male wardrobe – blazers, raincoats and overcoats – into female fashion items, and promoted black velvet so heavily that it came to be associated with him. Strict, tailored, yet tactfully cut, Saint Laurent's inspired garments were ideal for the EXECUTIVE woman emerging in the 1970s. Smart, stylish and casual, they reflected the feelings of the time. Yet he also showed considerable softness with his black COCKTAIL DRESSES, sweaters and billowing skirts. He is hailed today as the father of a whole new way of dressing.

salopettes French for OVERALLS, salopettes are long trousers with a sleeveless bib top and shoulder straps. In the second half of the 20th century, the garment has been adopted for casual wear and sports activities, particularly skiing.

Sanchez, Fernando 1934–. Designer. Born in Spain. After studying in Paris at the Ecole de la Chambre Syndicale de la Haute Couture (*See* HAUTE COUTURE) and winning a prize in the International Wool Secretariat competition of 1954, Sanchez worked for DIOR, creating most of the lines for the Dior BOUTIQUES, notably the sweater collections. He spent a brief period with the fur company Revillion before starting his own company in 1973, specializing in lingerie and loungewear. It is for his sexy, glamorous lingerie that he is chiefly remembered.

sandal The most primitive form of shoe, originally made of leather, sandals first became fashionable in the modern world in the 1920s, when it became permissible for women to show more of their feet. It was not until after World War II, however, that exposed toes, heels and insteps became entirely acceptable.

Sander, Jil 1943–. Designer. Born Heidemarie Jiline Sander in Wesselburen, Germany. Sander studied textile design in Germany before spending a year as an exchange student at the University of Los Angeles in California. She then became a journalist for American and German women's magazines before turning to freelance clothing design. In 1968 she opened her own boutique in Hamburg, showing her first collection six years later. Her MINIMALIST style gained popularity on the international market. She combines the simplicity of male garments with a feminine sense of luxurious fabrics.

Sant'Angelo, Giorgio 1936–89. Designer. Born in Florence, Italy. Sant'Angelo was brought up in Argentina and educated in Italy, where he studied law and architecture. He moved in 1962 to Hollywood to work as an animator for Walt Disney. In 1966 Sant'Angelo founded a ready-to-wear business and popularized the GYPSY styles of the late 1960s and early 1970s. During the 1980s he became well known for his beaded evening sweaters.

Jil **Sander**, one of Germany's most important designers, creates classic clothes with a contemporary feel. The design shown here is from her Autumn/Winter 1990–91 collection.

sari Length of fabric, forty inches wide by five to seven yards long, made of brilliantly coloured silk or cotton cloth, which constitutes the main outer garment of Indian women. The sari is worn over a short blouse and petticoat into which it is tucked and folded at the waist to form a skirt. The remaining end is draped over the shoulder.

sarong Piece of fabric, usually approximately five to seven yards long, which is wrapped around the body and tied at the waist or over the chest. The traditional dress of Balinese and Tahitian women, the sarong became popular in the 1940s for beach attire, a trend started by Dorothy LAMOUR, who wore sarongs in many of her films, including *The Jungle Princess* (1936) and *Road to Singapore* (1940). Sarongs emerged again in the early 1980s when the basic wrapped and knotted shape was adapted for summer fashions.

sash Long, wide piece of fabric worn around either the waist or the hips. Sashes made of luxurious fabrics were used on the waists of ball gowns during the 19th century. In the 20th century, they were used formally and informally, around both waist and hips.

Sassoon, David *See* BELLVILLE SASSOON.

Sassoon, Vidal 1929–. Hairdresser. Born in London, England. Sassoon was brought up in an orphanage. He trained under Raymond (Mr Teasie-Weasie) in the early 1950s and was soon patronized by pop stars and models. In 1959 he created 'The Shape', a layered cut that was tailored to the bone structure and designed for movement. It was a radical change from the BEEHIVE haircuts of the 1950s. In 1963 he cut the 'Nancy Kwan', a graduated bob, shorter at the back than in front. The following year he created the geometric 'Five-point Cut', in which the hair was cut into points at the nape of the neck and in front and back of the ears. In 1972, in an effortless move from the 1960s to the 1970s, Sassoon and his partner, Christopher Brooker, launched the 'brush cut', a soft style with the hair cut into a sphere and then brushed against the shape. Sassoon stopped cutting hair in 1974 but his salons continued to promote fashionable, up-to-the-minute hairstyles in tune with fashion's shapes. The 'Feather Cut' of 1977, with its wispy strands falling around the face, was extremely popular.

sateen Strong, lustrous fabric which is usually made of cotton with a satin weave. Sateen has been used for coat linings and, in the 20th century, for eveningwear.

satin Named after Zaytoun, China, where it was first made, satin was originally a glossy, lustrous fabric of closely woven silk. In the 20th century rayon and other synthetic fibres have taken the place of silk. A luxurious fabric, satin is mostly used for eveningwear.

sautoir Long chain or string of pearls. The sautoir became enormously popular and fashionable in the 1920s for evening wear.

S-bend silhouette Toward the end of the 19th century the S-bend shape became fashion-

Vidal **Sassoon**'s 1964 geometric '5-point cut', so different from the bouffant hairstyles of the 1950s.

able. It was achieved by wearing restrictive underwear which produced a large, overhanging, heavily padded bust, and a small, flat waist, which were balanced at the back by a projecting behind, culminating in full, flowing skirts, often gathered and raised on to a BUSTLE. The device which created the shape was a CORSET, cut to be worn low down on the bust and extended over the hips. When tightly laced, it narrowed the waist and pushed the body out at the bust and bottom. This style of dress was worn until the early 1900s. *See also* BEATON.

The crippling curves of the **S-bend**, the fashionable silhouette from the late 19th to the early 20th century.

Jean-Louis **Scherrer**'s dramatic approach to design is seen in 1985–86 in a taffeta and brocade evening dress and cape.

Scaasi, Arnold 1931–. Designer. Born Arnold Isaacs in Montreal, Canada. The son of a furrier, Scaasi (Isaacs spelt backwards) studied fashion design in Montreal before moving to Paris in the early 1950s to undertake an apprenticeship with PAQUIN. He worked briefly in New York with Charles JAMES before freelancing for Lilly DACHE, among others. In 1957 he opened a wholesale business, followed, five years later, by an haute couture line. He is noted in the USA for his tailored suits and glamorous eveningwear of COCKTAIL DRESSES and suits, often trimmed with feathers, fur and sequins, or embroidered.

Scavullo, Francesco 1929–. Photographer. Born in Staten Island, New York, USA. Scavullo was making home movies by the age of nine. On leaving school, he joined VOGUE for three years and was then apprenticed for a further three years to HORST. From 1948 Scavullo travelled and photographed for *Seventeen*, a new magazine aimed at teenagers. He created the hairstyle and makeup of the models, preferring a natural look generally considered unfashionable at the time. He worked for many women's magazines and during the 1950s became famous for his techniques using diffused lighting. Since 1965 his covers for *Cosmopolitan* reflect the unapologetic sexuality of the magazine.

Scherrer, Jean-Louis 1936–. Designer. Born in Paris, France. Unable to continue his dancing career after a fall at the age of twenty, Scherrer began to sketch. His talent took him to the House of DIOR, where he worked with Yves SAINT LAURENT. When Saint Laurent took over after Dior's death, Scherrer set up his own house. He produces both a couture and a ready-to-wear line. His clothes are classic, restrained and sometimes sombre and he is known for his sophisticated eveningwear.

Schiaparelli, Elsa 1890–1973. Designer. Born in Rome, Italy. Schiaparelli studied philosophy. She spent her early married life in Boston and New York and in 1922 moved to Paris. One of her first designs – a black sweater knitted with a white bow to give a TROMPE L'OEIL effect – was seen by a store buyer and subsequent orders

Elsa **Schiaparelli** in jazzy woollen mittens, scarf and hat, contrasting with the plainness of the coat, 1935.

Above: A **Schiaparelli** suit, inspired by Jean Cocteau.

Above right: **Schiaparelli**'s famous shoe hat designed with Salvador Dali. Dali was also the inspiration for the lips as pockets.

Right: Elsa **Schiaparelli**'s clear plastic necklace crawling with multicoloured insects.

put Schiaparelli in business. In 1927 she opened a shop called Pour le Sport. Her first full collection followed in 1929. Schiaparelli liked nothing better than to amuse, either by wit or shock. Her clothes were smart, sophisticated and often wildly eccentric, but she had a huge following. Her ideas, coupled with those she commissioned from famous artists, were carried out with considerable skill. She hired DALI, BERARD and COCTEAU to design fabric and accessories. Jean SCHLUMBERGER produced

COSTUME JEWELRY and buttons. CUBISM and SURREALISM influenced her designs. In 1933 she introduced the PAGODA SLEEVE, a broad-shouldered sleeve which determined the basic fashion silhouette until the NEW LOOK. Schiaparelli used tweed to make eveningwear and hessian for dresses. Her thick sweaters had padded shoulders. She dyed furs, put padlocks on suits, and created a vogue for TYROLEAN COSTUME. In 1935 she dyed the new plastic ZIPS the same colours as her fabrics and positioned them in exposed places rather than concealing them as dress closings, making their use both decorative and functional. She showed phosphorescent brooches and buttons like paperweights. The French firm Colcombet developed for her a fabric printed with newsprint, from which she made scarves. In 1938 her Circus collection featured *BUTTONS in the shape of acrobats diving down the front of a silk brocade jacket decorated with carousel horses. Schiaparelli embroidered zodiac signs onto her clothes and sold handbags that lit up or played a tune when opened. Two of her most famous hats were made in the shapes of ice cream cones and lamb cutlets. Schiaparelli's outrageous, irreverent chic was a great success. A brilliant colourist, she took one of Bérard's pinks, which she called 'Shocking Pink', and promoted it vigorously. In merging art with fashion, Schiaparelli gave women yet another option in dressing. During World War II she lectured throughout the USA and in 1949 opened a branch in New York. Schiaparelli held her last show in 1954.

Schlumberger, Jean 1907–87. Jewelry designer. Born in Mulhouse, Alsace, France. Schlumberger initially studied in Berlin for a career in banking but in the 1920s went to Paris where he began making pieces of jewelry, using china flowers. These were admired by Schiaparelli, who commissioned him to make BUTTONS and COSTUME JEWELRY. Schlumberger spent some time in the French army before emigrating to New York in 1940. Shortly afterwards, he opened his own business. Throughout the 1940s and 1950s he became well known for his designs of flowers, shells, starfish, birds and angels. In 1956 he joined TIFFANY & CO. as designer and vice-president. Over the following years he remained faithful to his early prefer-

ence for natural imagery. Sea-horses were Schlumberger's signature design.

Schnurer, Carolyn 1908–. Designer. Born Carolyn Goldsand in New York, USA. Schnurer trained as a teacher before turning to designing SPORTSWEAR in 1940 when she worked for her husband's bathing suit manufacturing company. In 1944 she introduced the 'cholo' coat, a loose-fitting, hip-length jacket with a high neck, based on an ancient garment worn by South American shepherds. Schnurer was noted for innovative fabric and used many textiles of her own design. In the 1950s she produced a wrinkle-resistant cotton tweed. She also used cotton for bathing suits and helped promote form-fitting, one-piece swimwear.

Schön, Mila 1919–. Designer. Born Maria Carmen Nustrizio Schön in Dalmatia, Yugoslavia. Schön's parents settled in Italy. In 1958, with no previous experience, she set up a dressmaking establishment in Milan. Her first couture collection, presented in 1965, was well-received in Italy and the USA. A ready-to-wear collection followed in 1971. Essentially a classic designer of dresses, suits and eveningwear, Schön, though not as well known as many of her colleagues, is one of the most respected names in Italian fashion and is noted for her sophisticated style and precise tailoring.

scoop neck Low, U-shaped neckline, popular throughout the 20th century for dresses, BODICES and T-SHIRTS.

Scott, Ken 1918–91. Designer. Born in Fort Wayne, Indiana, USA. After studying at Parsons School of Design in New York, Scott went to Guatemala to paint. He moved to Europe and at the end of the 1950s opened a salon in Milan, Italy. Scott was known for his highly coloured, boldly patterned flower-printed fabrics which in the 1960s were made up into CAFTANS and TUNICS. He also produced silky jersey BODYSTOCKINGS and was famous for his printed scarves.

seal Aquatic mammal found in colder regions of the world. Hair seals are hunted for their skins, and fur seals, found in the North Pacific, for their fur. Huge demand for the dense, shiny,

The master jeweler Jean **Schlumberger** drew inspiration from natural imagery. This shell design is from the 1940s.

weaving together fibres of different shrinkage capabilities. A popular fabric for summer attire during the second half of the 20th century.

see-through In 1968 Yves SAINT LAURENT introduced a blouse so sheer that the body was visible underneath it. See-through fashions appear periodically but are seldom popular.

Selincourt & Colman Wholesale MANTLE makers established in London by Charles de Selincourt in 1857. Joined by F. Colman, the company expanded to produce cloaks, shawls and children's wear. By the 1880s it had become one of Europe's leading wholesale furriers. It has exported worldwide since the 19th century and manufactures clothing for many stores.

but durable fur during the second half of the 19th century seriously depleted the seal herds. Seal fur was made into coats and hats. The fur of seal pups is considered particularly valuable.

seersucker Lightweight cotton, rayon or silk fabric with a crinkly striped surface created by

sequin French form of the Italian word *zecchino*, a Venetian gold coin. Sequins are small, shiny discs which used to be made of metal. Since the early 20th century they have been made of plastic and used as trimmings.

serge Even-sided, twill weave worsted fabric originally made of silk and/or wool which takes its name from the Italian word for silk, *serica*. By the 19th century, serge was used to make

The superbly tailored lines of a 1970s trouser suit by Mila **Schön**.

The **shawl** was an integral part of fashionable wear in the second half of the 19th century. Arthur Lasenby Liberty, who founded Liberty of London, started his career at Farmer and Rogers's shawl shop in London's Regent Street. This is an 1866 advertisement for the shop.

military uniforms and, in the latter part of the century, it was made up in various weights into dresses, bathing suits and outer garments. In the 20th century serge was usually made of wool blends and man-made fibres. It is most often used for suiting material.

Seventh Avenue Street in New York which has been the traditional base for the US ready-to-wear industry since the early 20th century.

shantung Hand-loomed silk originally produced in the Shantung province of China. Shantung is thin and soft, woven with uneven yarns to produce an irregular surface. In the 20th century shantung was usually made of silk mixed with cotton or rayon. This creates a heavier fabric than the original shantung, which is now rarely seen. Both fabrics have been traditionally used for eveningwear.

Sharaff, Irene c.1910–93. Costume designer. Born in Boston, USA. Sharaff is known for her costume designs for *The King and I* (1956) and *Funny Girl* (1968).

shawl Square or rectangular piece of cloth worn around the shoulders, loosely tied in front, over the bust. The first shawls worn as high fashion items reached Europe in the 18th century with British and French soldiers returning from the Indian wars. The patterns and designs of these shawls influenced European versions for the following one hundred years. In the UK, the weaving centres of Norwich and PAISLEY produced numerous shawls throughout the 19th century. In the early 1800s shawls were small, silk squares but from the 1830s they emerged as major fashion items. Skirts increased in width at this time and capes and MANTLES could no longer adequately cover the bulging silhouette. Shawls were the alternative, both for indoor and outdoor attire. They varied from the long, narrow STOLES of the 1830s and 1840s to the massive shawls of the 1850s and 1860s which were designed to envelope the

The **shawl** was an essential component of the 'granny style' of the 1970s.

The exaggerated **shawl collar** forms the bodice of a 1950s dress.

CRINOLINE. Indian shawls, especially those with the Kashmiri 'cone' motif (*boteh*), were particularly popular throughout the 19th century. Shops specialized in selling shawls made of cotton, lace, silk or wool; plain, printed, embroidered and often fringed. In the 20th century, shawls continued to be fashionable for both day and eveningwear.

shawl collar Coat or dress collar which is turned down to form a continuous line around the back of the neck to the front. It was popular in the 1930s, and again in the 1950s, when its shape was greatly exaggerated.

sheath Figure-hugging dress, usually with long sleeves, which has a tight, straight, ankle-length skirt. It was popularized by film actresses of the 1930s. The 1950s version was often made with a KICK PLEAT at the back. *See also* NORELL.

sheepskin Skin and wool of sheep found in Europe, North and South America, South Africa and Australia, which is shorn, combed, tanned, ironed and dyed before it is made into

jackets and coats. Hardwearing and warm, sheepskin outer garments are traditionally worn in cooler climates. They became fashionable for a brief period in the 1960s.

shell Sleeveless, WAISTCOAT-like top, often made of a lightweight fabric, such as silk, and worn under a jacket.

Sherard, Michael dates unknown. Place of birth unknown. London couturier who opened his house in 1946. Sherard was successful for a brief period, known for his tailored tweed day dresses and eveningwear. In 1964, after the demise of haute couture, he closed his salon.

shift Also known as a tank dress. The 19th-century shift was a white linen CHEMISE, smocked at the shoulders for fullness. Its simple shape was adopted as nightwear and by agricultural workers. The word shift now describes a simple, unstructured dress which opens at the front and which was popular in various lengths in the 1950s and 1960s.

Shilling, David 1953–. Milliner. Born in London, England. At the age of twelve Shilling designed a hat for his mother to wear to the annual race meeting at Ascot. Over the following years Mrs Shilling has continued to amuse and outrage race crowds with her son's extravagant creations. In 1969 Shilling began making hats for private buyers. Six years later he opened a hat shop in London. His early hats were pretty, highly trimmed affairs. They were widely copied to meet the demand created by a reawakened interest in hats. During the 1970s Shilling also produced disco hats. Later, he concentrated on dramatic shapes and silhouettes. *See also* ★DISCO.

shingle Short haircut popular during the 1920s which was shaped to a point at the nape of the neck. *See also* ANTOINE.

shirring Two or more rows of GATHERS used to decorate parts of garments, usually the sleeves, BODICE or YOKE.

shirtwaister 'Shirtwaist' was originally the word for a blouse, the feminine version of a man's shirt. By the 1940s the shirtwaister described a tailored, knee-length shirtdress which had long sleeves (buttoned at the cuff), a collar, and buttons to the waist, where it was often belted.

shorts Short trousers, originally part of male dress, have been worn by women since the 1920s in various lengths. They were associated with sporting gear and casual wear until the late 1970s, when designers showed suits of shorts and tailored jackets on the runways. They remain, however, a casual item of clothing.

Hat and printed silk scarf by the milliner David **Shilling,** Spring/Summer, 1984.

The shirtwaist blouse with starched front, from which the **shirtwaister** evolved, *Harper's Bazar*, 1894.

shoulder bag *See* HANDBAG.

shoulder pads Three-sided pads sewn into the shoulders of dresses, jackets, blouses and coats to give a broad-shouldered appearance. ADRIAN's use of wide, padded shoulders in his designs for actress Joan Crawford in the early 1930s started a vogue which continued into the 1940s. Shoulder pads were also employed by ROCHAS and SCHIAPARELLI in the late 1930s. They were briefly revived in the 1970s and used extensively in the early 1980s.

silk Natural fibre produced by the silkworm, a grub of the silkmoth (*Bombyx mori*), which feeds on mulberry leaves. The worms spin cocoons, exuding fine filaments which form a thread. Silk originated in China and was brought to Europe around the 12th century. Since it is expensive, it has always been considered a luxury fabric. In the 20th century massive silk production in Japan considerably reduced prices. Silk has been used throughout the 19th and 20th centuries for underwear, STOCKINGS, lingerie, blouses, dresses and eveningwear.

Simonetta 1922–. Designer. Born Duchesa Simonetta Colonna di Cesaro in Rome, Italy. In 1946 Simonetta opened a studio in Rome and signed her first collection as Simonetta Visconti, the name of her first husband. In 1953 she married Alberto FABIANI. The designers followed separate careers until 1962, when they embarked on a joint venture in Paris. Three years later Simonetta moved back to Rome, where she continued to design for several years. She was a popular international designer, famous for bouffant skirts and sprightly JUMPSUITS. She dressed many film stars in the late 1940s. She was also known for her knitwear and elegant COCKTAIL DRESSES. Simonetta retired in 1973.

Simpson, Adele 1908–95. Designer. Born Adele Smithline in New York, USA. After studying at the Pratt Institute, Simpson was made head designer in 1927 at Ben Gershel's, a ready-to-wear company. She then moved to Mary Lee Fashions where she designed under her own name and subsequently bought the business in 1949, changing its name to Adele Simpson Inc. In 1964 the company made GIVENCHY's special collection for Bloomingdale's. Simpson designed practical clothes, outfits which could be worn in layers and discarded to reveal eveningwear under daywear. In the 1950s she produced a CHEMISE DRESS with belts attached which could be tied at the front or back. Her blouse-and-suit, dress-and-jacket or coat-and-suit ensembles were extremely popular, especially with the wives of US politicians, and were widely copied.

siren suit One-piece OVERALL widely used during World War II. Based on the BOILERSUITS worn in the munitions factories of World War I, the siren suit had ample pockets and a large hood. It was zipped or buttoned from waist to neck. The siren suit was popularized by Winston Churchill, British Prime Minister from 1940 to 1945.

Sitbon, Martine 1951–. Designer. Born in Casablanca, Morocco. After studying at the Studio Berçot in Paris, Sitbon travelled extensively but returned to France to show her first collection in 1985. Fond of contrasts, Sitbon is a modernist whose clothes nonetheless have a

A charcoal coatdress with white shirt from the 1989–90 ready-to-wear collection of the Moroccan-born designer Martine **Sitbon** – a contemporary look but with historical overtones.

sense of history. Her long jackets and riding coats are rigorously cut, with narrow shoulders and softened waistlines. She also likes to design long skirts and trousers with a controlled flare at the lower leg. In 1988 she created her first collection for CHLOE.

ski pants Until *c.*1918 women wore long skirts or breeches on ski slopes. In the 1920s, PLUS FOURS became fashionable. After World War II, when women became used to wearing trousers, ski pants were worn. Made of wool, wool mixes and synthetic fibres, ski pants were ankle-length and tapered, secured by an elasticated strap under the instep. In 1952 stretch ski pants of wool and nylon mix were introduced. These were worn with brightly coloured poplin PARKAS. The ski pants shape was adopted in the 1950s as a casual trouser style. It reemerged in the 1980s and has remained popular.

skinny rib UK name for a figure-hugging, finely ribbed SWEATER worn in the 1960s.

slacks General name for sports trousers which were first worn by women in the 1920s.

A sleeveless 1965 version of the **skinny rib** sweater.

sling backs Shoe with an exposed heel, supported by a strap around the heel. Introduced in the 1920s, sling backs have been fashionable at some point in every decade. *See also* CHANEL.

Sloane Ranger Term first used by *Harpers & Queen* magazine in 1979 to describe a section of its readership. Sloane Rangers, who shopped or lived in the area around London's Sloane Square, wore white, ruffled cotton shirts with pleated skirts or sprigged cotton skirts from Laura ASHLEY, round-neck sweaters of cashmere or lambswool, navy blue or pale tights, low-heeled PUMPS, a short pearl necklace, and a utilitarian short, padded, sleeveless nylon waistcoat.

sloppy joe Baggy, hip-length, long-sleeved, knitted wool SWEATER with a round or V-neck, worn in the 1940s and 1950s, often teamed with tight trousers. The sloppy joe was distinguished by the extreme looseness of its fit.

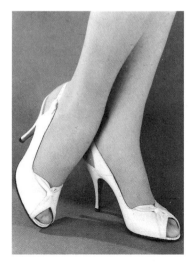

White calf and antelope **sling-back** peep-toe shoe designed by Rayne for 1960.

The milliner **Graham Smith** served as Design Director of Kangol from 1981 to 1991 and as Consultant Director from 1991 to 1998. These hats are from his Graham Smith at Kangol range for 1989.

slouch hat Hat associated with Greta GARBO, who wore it in *A Woman of Affairs* (1928). Based on but slightly larger than the CLOCHE of the 1920s, it was worn slanted at an angle and pulled down over the forehead. *See* ADRIAN.

Smith, Graham 1938–. Milliner. Born in Bexley, Kent, England. Smith attended Bromley College of Art from 1956 to 1957 and the following year studied at London's Royal College of Art. He spent 1959 in the millinery salon of Lanvin-Castillo, returning to London in 1960 to work for MICHAEL. In 1967 he set up his own business and made hats for Jean ★MUIR and other designers. He joined KANGOL in 1981 and successfully blended the company's traditional BERETS and CAPS with his own creations.

Smith, Paul 1946–. Designer. Born in Nottingham, England. Smith opened a boutique in Nottingham in 1970 selling designer clothes as well as garments he had made himself. In 1976 he showed his first menswear collection in Paris. Smith is best known for his signature shirts in offbeat colours and patterns. His label is successful worldwide, especially in Japan.

Smith, Willi 1948–87. Designer. Born in Philadelphia, Pennsylvania, USA. Smith studied fashion at the Philadelphia Museum College of Art and in 1964 won a scholarship to Parsons School of Design in New York. After graduating in 1968, he became a freelance knitwear designer. In 1976 he opened WilliWear, a SPORTSWEAR company. His oversized clothing anticipated the casual styles and attitudes of the following decades; baggy trousers and shorts, slouchy sweaters and generously proportioned shirts in colours and fabrics that could be easily mixed together. Many of his ideas were influenced by STREET STYLE.

smock The medieval smock, also known as a CHEMISE, was a loose, knee- or calf-length garment with a YOKE, made of cotton or linen and worn under gowns. In the 18th and 19th centuries it became a loose, yoked, shirt-like outer garment worn by agricultural workers. Most smocks had long sleeves and some had a large, flat collar. In the late 19th century women began wearing smock dresses made of fine cottons and lawn as an alternative to the period's

An example of **smocking** from 1881.

rigid, corsetted shapes. Smock dresses sold by LIBERTY from the mid-1880s were adopted by advocates of AESTHETIC DRESS. Since then smocks have been worn by artists. The 20th century smock was a loose, usually lightweight, sleeved garment. It was used as a fashion shape from the 1940s, and especially in the 1970s, when it was promoted by Laura ASHLEY.

smocking Panel or integral piece of material which is tightly gathered with decorative stitching. Traditionally seen on the YOKE of a child's dress, smocking can also be applied to the waist, hips or cuffs.

smoking jacket Man's silk, velvet or brocade long-sleeved, short jacket, decorated with buttons, which was worn at home in the second half of the 19th century. In the 20th century it described a man's silk robe, similar to a DRESSING GOWN. *Un smoking* is French for a TUXEDO. The 'smoking' for women will always be associated with Yves SAINT LAURENT.

sneakers US term for a rubber-bottomed shoe with canvas uppers and laces worn for sporting activities from the turn of the century. *See also* PLIMSOLLS.

The **snood** could be worn with or without a hat.

snood Knitted or openwork net which encases the hair at the back of the head. A snood can also be attached to a hat. An ADRIAN design for Hedy Lamarr in *I Take This Woman* (1939) helped popularize the snood. During the late 19th century and the 1930s and 1940s the snood was used to confine long hair.

Snow, Carmel 1887–1961. Magazine editor. Born Carmel White in Dublin, Ireland. In the 1890s, shortly after the death of Snow's father, Snow's mother moved the family to New York, where she opened a dressmaking establishment in Manhattan. After studying in Brussels and New York, Snow joined the family business. In 1921 she became a fashion writer on *VOGUE* and two years later was appointed fashion editor. In 1932 she was made editor of American *Vogue* but in the same year moved as fashion editor to rival publication *HARPER'S BAZAAR*, where she succeeded in improving the magazine's editorial content. She had great skill in spotting and promoting talent. Snow worked with art director Alexey BRODOVITCH and with some of the most revered names in fashion pho-

tography: Irving PENN, Martin MUNKACSI and Richard AVEDON. After her retirement in 1958, she continued to work as a fashion consultant in France and Italy.

sombrero Tall-crowned, wide-brimmed hat which has been worn for many centuries by men in Spain, Mexico and South America. Rarely used as a fashion shape, the sombrero is nonetheless a popular choice for summer headgear in hot climates.

Soprani, Luciano 1946–. Designer. Born in Reggiolo, Italy. Soprani studied agriculture before he joined the ready-to-wear firm of Max Mara in 1967. He became a freelance designer in 1975, and in the 1980s designed for GUCCI and Nazareno Gabrielli, though he was also associated with BASILE from 1981. Soprani has a lively approach to fashion, mixing disciplined tailoring with strong colours. He is a forceful Italian talent with his own line. He also continues freelance work.

sou'wester Rubber or canvas waterproofed hat with a wide brim which is longer at the back than the front. Since the 1950s, sou'westers have sometimes been worn as rainwear.

Space Age Name given to the 1964 collection of André *COURREGES which featured HIPSTER pants worn with sleeveless or short-sleeved dresses and jackets. Dresses were short and cut on clinically simple lines. Most outfits were worn with calf-length, square-toed boots usually made of soft, white leather. A large, HELMET-shaped hat topped the ensemble. Nearly all the clothes in this collection and subsequent derivative collections by other designers were made up in white fabric, colour being used sparsely and strategically.

Spade, Kate 1964–. Accessory designer. Born Katherine Brosnahan in Kansas City, Kansas, USA. Spade studied journalism before moving to New York and a job at *Mademoiselle* magazine where, in 1991, she became a fashion/accessories editor. Two years later she left the magazine to produce her first line of bags based on simple 'boxy' no-nonsense tote bags in six styles and three neutral colours. Other styles followed, such as knapsacks,

The 18th-century **spencer**, from which all other spencers derive.

Space-Age outfit by Pierre Cardin for Autumn 1966. The cut-out hole of the helmet is echoed by those on the bodice. Note the square-toed shoe of the period.

backpacks and utilitarian messenger bags, each with Spade's design philosophy of clean shapes. Spade uses fabrics such as nylon, burlap, madras, silk-satin and tweed in both subdued and brilliant colours. Her understated styles have become widely influential.

Spandex Man-made fibre with high stretch qualities which was first introduced in 1958 by DU PONT. Lightweight yet strong, it is used in swimwear, lingerie and hosiery.

Spanzelle Registered trademark for SPANDEX fibre made by the Firestone Tyre & Rubber Company.

spectator *See* CO-RESPONDENT SHOE.

spencer Originating in England in the 18th century, the spencer was a short, waist-length jacket, single- or double-breasted, worn by men. In the early 19th century it was adapted by women into either a short jacket reaching to just below the bust, worn as an outdoor garment, or an indoor evening jacket over a dress. At this time, it was sleeved or sleeveless, with a DECOLLETE neckline. In the late 19th century the spencer was a sleeveless garment made of wool or flannel which was usually worn under a jacket or coat for warmth.

Spook, Per 1939–. Designer. Born in Oslo, Norway. After studying at the School of Fine Arts in Oslo, Per Spook went in 1957 to Paris, where he enrolled at the Ecole de la Chambre Syndicale de la Haute Couture (*See* HAUTE COUTURE). He joined the house of DIOR for a number of years and also worked for FERAUD and SAINT LAURENT. Spook opened his own house in 1977. He had a lively approach to fashion, which was revealed in the bold clarity of his line and in his use of bright colours. The house closed in 1996.

George **Stavropolous** was known for his use of chiffon. This peach silk chiffon dress with its own capelet and scarf featured in his 1985 collection.

sportswear US term for daywear.

Sprouse, Stephen 1953–. Designer. Born in Ohio, USA. After attending the Rhode Island School of Design for only three months, Sprouse spent three years working as an apprentice for HALSTON, followed by a short stay at Bill BLASS. Sprouse became known in the late 1970s and the 1980s for his stage clothes for rock and roll stars. In 1983 he launched his first collection. Sprouse's clothes were inspired by 1960s fashions. He specialized in bright, Dayglo, fluorescent colours, especially 'hot' pink and yellow. He made MINI DRESSES, MINI SKIRTS shown with bare midriffs, graffiti dresses and stockings. Sprouse's clothes were unconventional and inspirational but by 1988 he was no longer in business.

squirrel Lightweight, soft, fluffy, short fur of the rodent of the same name found in almost every continent. Squirrel fur is naturally dark grey-blue or red but is frequently dyed pale brown. It is a serviceable fur and has been used since the late 19th century to make capes, coats and stoles.

Stavropoulos, George 1920–90. Designer. Born in Tripolis, Greece. In 1949 Stavropoulos opened a salon in Athens, where he became known initially for his couture tailored suits and coats. His most popular designs, however, were those based on the classical draped Greek silhouette. In 1952 DIOR invited him to work in Paris but Stavropoulos declined. Nine years later he moved to New York and set up a ready-to-wear and couture business. His first ready-to-wear collections were less favourably received than his elegant, understated couture clothes. By the mid-1960s his flowing chiffon evening gowns and coat-and-dress ensembles had become highly popular. The chiffon gowns were so widely copied that Stavropoulos created new, more innovative styles using chiffon mixed with lace or lamé.

stays Originally two pieces of stiffened fabric (a pair of stays) worn on the back and front of the body as foundationwear. The garment stems from the 17th century, when it was known as a 'body' and made of heavy linen or cotton, usually stiffened with WHALEBONE and short-waisted. In the 18th century stays were composed of rows of whalebone or cane sewn into a piece of fabric which was wrapped around the body and laced at the back. Fashions changed considerably in the early part of the 19th century but by the middle of the century the stiff, tightly laced shape was again popular and remained so until the early 20th century. During the second half of the 19th century the word CORSET began to replace the word stays.

Steichen, Edward 1879–1973. Photographer. Born in Luxembourg. Steichen's family emigrated to the USA in 1881. In 1894 he studied at the Milwaukee Arts Students League and shortly afterwards joined the American Fine Art Company as an apprentice photographer. He went to Paris in 1900 and studied at the Académie Julian. From then until 1914 he moved between Europe and the USA, painting and taking pictures. In 1911 he was encouraged

Victor **Stiebel**'s 1933 plaid evening dress of red, white and green, cut on the bias. The jacket has pleated sleeves and is lined in black chiffon.

by Lucien VOGEL to apply his talents to fashion photography. In 1914 he joined the US Army and served as a commander of a photographic division. After the war, Steichen settled in New York, gave up painting, and concentrated on advertising and fashion photography, taking photographs for American *VOGUE* and *Vanity Fair*, among others. In 1923 his supreme craftsmanship earned him the post of chief photographer for Condé NAST publications. His work is striking, independent and thoroughly modern in approach and content. His models confront the camera with their heads held high, posed in interiors and architectural settings which contribute texture and ambiance while providing a framework for fashion. Steichen worked best with one model, Marion Moorhouse, and used her frequently. In 1947 he left Condé Nast to become the Director of the Department of Photography at the Museum of Modern Art in New York.

Stiebel, Victor 1907–1976. Designer. Born in Durban, South Africa. Stiebel went to England in 1924 and as a student at Cambridge University he designed costumes and scenery for the Footlights revue. In 1929 he became an apprentice at REVILLE AND ROSSITER and in 1932 opened his own house. After serving in the British army during World War II, Stiebel moved in 1946 to Jacqmar, reopening his own house in the 1950s. He was known for his romantic clothes, which were worn by many actresses both on and off the stage. A member of the Incorporated Society of London Fashion Designers, Stiebel dressed members of the British Royal Family and designed uniforms for the WRENS and the WRAF. He favoured jersey and other soft fabrics and became famous for feminine evening dresses and for his outfits for the fashionable race meeting at Ascot.

Stile Liberty Italian term for ART NOUVEAU which derives from the association of the style with the London store of LIBERTY.

stiletto High, narrow heel which originated in Italy during the 1950s. It was made of nylon and plastic, which often covered a steel core.

stirrup pants Known as *fuseaux* in France, stirrup pants are similar to SKI PANTS. They taper towards the ankle and have a strap, often elasticated, around the instep and under the foot. Stirrup pants first became popular during the 1950s, when they were worn with large, baggy sweaters. They have been fashionable since the mid-1980s, made of lightweight knitted fabrics.

stockings Close-fitting coverings for the leg and foot which until the early 1600s were hand-knitted in silk, cotton or wool. During the 1600s, stockings were generally knitted by machine. The later 17th century saw both hand- and machine-knitted stockings but in the 18th century machine-knitted stockings became more and more popular – a trend that continued through to the 20th century. From the 1600s, stockings were made of silk, cotton or wool, as well as mixtures of these fibres. Throughout the 19th century there was a vogue for coloured stockings. Artificial silk stockings were popular from the end of the 19th century

Left: English **stockings** *c.* 1900, with a viper motif snaking round the leg. Turn-of-the-century stockings would have been completely covered by the dresses of the period.
Left, centre: Seamed stockings like these were the only option in the 1940s.
Left, bottom: Delicate Dior stockings with a rose motif, popular in the 1980s.

until 1940, when nylon stockings (NYLONS) were introduced. Nylons were classified into denier groups, a denier being the unit of weight by which the silk, rayon or nylon yarns are measured. Fifteen denier is a light, very sheer stocking, while 40 denier is thicker and more durable. During the early 20th century, as skirt lengths began to rise, patterned stockings enjoyed a brief vogue. Black stockings became fashionable in the 1920s, as did ribbed and patterned versions. Due to a shortage of materials during World War II, women were obliged to go without stockings and took to wearing ANKLE SOCKS. The flesh colours and suntan shades which had become *de rigueur* before the war retained their popularity in the postwar years. In the 1950s seamless stockings became generally available and knee-high stockings and PANTIEHOSE were also launched. Ten years later there was a trend for stockings and TIGHTS in stripes and lacy and geometric patterns as well as stockings with ankle motifs. In the more sober 1970s, dark tights, especially heavy ribbed versions, were common. In the 1980s stockings regained some of their popularity and there was a great deal of fashion interest in leg-wear. It was fashionable to wear highly coloured hose in PAISLEY patterns, checks, handpainted designs, and animal skin patterns. *See* TIGHTS.

stole Long, rectangular wrap which is usually worn around the shoulders and folded across the chest. It first became popular in the 1950s, worn over long evening dresses.

Strauss, Levi ?–1902. Born in Bavaria. Strauss arrived in San Francisco, California, during the goldmining boom of the 1850s. His first work trousers for miners were cut from brown tent canvas but several years later he began using DENIM, a French fabric which he dyed blue with indigo. In 1872 he took out a patent for these garments. Jacob Davis, a tailor from

Levi's from Levi **Strauss**, the most famous and lasting example of workwear moving into fashion.
Above: The real thing: two miners wearing their levi's.
Right: Levi's in 1982, with the worn-in look rather than the worn-out look of the 1960s.

Anna **Sui**'s designs often have a vintage flavour. The dress above is from her Spring 1997 collection.

Carson City, Nevada, joined Strauss in 1873 to patent a pair of trousers which had copper rivets at its stress points. After Strauss's death in 1902 the business continued as a family concern. In the USA the word 'Levi's' is synonymous with denim JEANS.

street style One of the most significant influences on designers in the second half of the 20th century, the term refers to clothing worn by young people – mostly teenagers – whose style is derived from low-budget clothing worn in such a way that it individualizes them from society in general but classifies them as part of a particular group or cult. Many couturiers and ready-to-wear designers incorporate elements of street style into their designs, refining and restructuring the clothing so that, in time, its source is unrecognizable.

string vest Loosely knit sleeveless cotton vest based on an undervest worn by men since the 19th century. It became popular as outerwear for a brief period during the 1960s and also in the late 1970s, as part of PUNK dress.

suede Suede is produced by buffing the flesh side of a tanned animal hide. The result is a velvet-like surface on one side of the leather. In the 20th century, especially after World War II, suede was used mainly for coats and jackets, though it has also been made into skirts, JERKINS, shoes and handbags.

suede fabric Man-made fabric made of knitted or woven cotton and other fibres, which is finished to resemble suede. A popular material in North America from the mid-20th century for dresses, coats, skirts and suits. *See also* HALSTON *and* ULTRASUEDE.

Sui, Anna 1955–. Designer. Born in Dearborn Heights, Michigan, USA. Sui studied at the Parsons School of Design in New York. After graduation she worked for a number of SPORTSWEAR companies and acted as a stylist for photographer Steven MEISEL. In 1980 she designed under her own name but it was not until 1991 that she became well-known. Drawing on a variety of cultural influences, and with considerable flair and humour, Sui gives a contemporary twist to many vintage styles such as BABY DOLL, FLAPPER and 1960s fashions. She also creates witty accessories.

sunglasses First produced in lightly tinted glass in 1885, sunglasses did not become a fashion accessory until the 1930s, when they were popularized by Hollywood's film stars. It was at this time that dark lenses became fashionable. The 1950s saw new, outlandish designs for sunglasses – star-spangled versions, glasses designed to resemble flowers, and wraparound glasses. This vogue continued into the 1960s. In the more sober, perhaps more status-conscious, 1970s, initialled 'designer' glasses became popular. In the 1980s black sunglasses – both lenses and frame – became fashionable as the trend for less conservative sunglasses re-emerged. This trend continued in the 1990s.

sunray pleats Fine pleats which radiate out from a central point on the waistband of a skirt or dress.

The loose **swagger coat,** known in the USA as a 'topper', was a popular fashion in the 1950s. These styles were advertised by Sears, Roebuck.

surah The original surah, from Surat in India, was a soft, lustrous fabric made from twilled silk. In the 20th century the name surah was given to a man-made fibre used in the manufacture of blouses and dresses.

Surrealism Movement in art and literature between the two World Wars which reacted against the rationalization and formalism of prevailing trends and concentrated on fantasy and the reconstruction of a dreamworld. Painters who were influenced by Surrealism included René Magritte, Salvador DALI, Pablo PICASSO and Joan Miró. The term Surrealism emerged in a fashion context in the late 1920s and was most often used during the 1930s to describe weird or psychologically suggestive garments. *See* SCHIAPARELLI.

suspenders *See* BRACES.

swagger coat (US: topper) Generously cut hip-length coat, often with a SHAWL COLLAR and large, turn-back cuffs, worn in the 1950s.

Swatch A contraction of 'Swiss' and 'watch', the Swatch was first produced in 1983 by a Swiss company. Intended to be colourful, durable and inexpensive, the ever-changing styles feature a round plastic face and plastic

A **sweetheart neckline** on a ruched bodice of 1943.

strap. Some models have become collectors' items. Swatch presents over two hundred new designs a year, mainly in their Spring/Summer and Autumn/Winter collections.

sweater Knitted woollen shirt worn by sportsmen in the late 19th century to encourage perspiration. In the 20th century the word sweater describes a sleeved, knitted woollen top reaching to the waist or longer. Evening sweaters trimmed with chiffon or crepe and embroidered with jewels were fashionable in the late 1930s. In the 1940s, short, waist-length versions were all the rage. During the late 1940s and 1950s, there were vogues both for tight sweaters (which gave their name to the 'sweater girls' of the period) and for long, baggy sweaters, a look which some women achieved by wearing men's sweaters. In the following decades sweaters of all lengths and styles have been acceptable fashion wear and this trend has continued, though since the late

1970s sweater designs have become more sophisticated.

sweatshirt *See* SWEATSHIRTING.

sweatshirting Thick, fleecy, cotton fabric worn with the fleecy side against the skin, usually used for casual SWEATERS and T-SHIRTS, known as sweatshirts. Sweatshirts have been worn by athletes since World War II for warm-up practice. Since the 1960s they have been popular for casual wear, often printed with the names of universities, brand-names and slogans. *See* KAMALI.

sweetheart neckline Neckline on dresses and blouses which is cut into two, almost semi-circular, curves which resemble a heart. The sweetheart neckline was popular throughout the 20th century.

swimsuit *See* BATHING SUIT.

T

tabard Dating from the Middle Ages, when it was worn as a military or ceremonial garment, the tabard is a hip-length, rectangular, sleeveless top, with a hole cut out for the head. It was a fashionable style during the 1960s. *See also* TUNIC.

tablier French for apron. A gown or skirt, designed with a front portion which resembles a decorative apron. Tablier skirts were fashionable in the 1860s and 1870s.

taffeta Fine, stiff fabric woven from real or artificial silk, with a glossy, iridescent sheen. Taffeta is believed to be named after the Persian fabric 'taftan'. It has been popular for eveningwear since the 19th century.

tailleur Tailored suit or ensemble which became popular during the second half of the 19th century.

tam o'shanter Round woollen cap named after the hero of the poem of the same name by

The **tailleur** or tailored suit belonged in every turn-of-the-century wardrobe. This model is from *Costumes Parisiens*, 1912.

the Scottish poet Robert Burns. It has a tight headband, a full, soft crown and is usually decorated with a centre pompon. In the late 19th century, women wore tam o' shanters for sporting activities. Also known as a Balmoral cap.

tango dress Dress worn to perform the tango, an Argentine dance popular in Europe between 1910 and the outbreak of World War II. An ankle-length dress, it was draped and split in the front or at the side to allow freedom of movement, and revealed part of the lower leg. The sleeves of the dress were cut loosely to allow for movement.

tango shoe Shoe which achieved popularity c.1910 as a result of the craze for tango dancing.

It was often made in white satin, with ribbon ankle straps, and had a small, curved heel.

tank top Short, sleeveless top with wide armholes, made from brightly coloured or patterned crochet or wool. It was popular in the 1960s and 1970s for casual wear.

tapestry Originally an ornamental woven cloth in which the design tells a story. In a fashion context, the word tapestry describes a heavy, figured fabric with a raised, often floral, design. Tapestry garments were briefly popular during the 1960s.

Tarlazzi, Angelo 1942–. Designer. Born in Ascoli Piceno, Italy. Tarlazzi studied political science in Rome but left at the age of nineteen to enter the house of CAROSA, where he spent four years designing ball gowns. In 1966 he went to Paris as an assistant to Michel GOMA at PATOU. He left in 1969 to work freelance, and spent 1971 and 1972 in New York. He eventually returned to Paris to take over the artistic direction of Patou. Tarlazzi opened his own house in Paris in 1978. He creates unconventional clothes for the conventional woman. His designs are generously cut and made of supple fabrics but they are always neat and sculpted.

Who would have thought that 18th-century gentlemen's combinations would be the basic silhouette for a marvellously supple and fluid garment such as this? By Angelo **Tarlazzi** for his 1984–85 collection.

The **tea gown** of 1888, featured in *Queen* – a more relaxed version of the well-constructed day dress.

tartan Closely woven woollen cloth which originated in Scotland, where different patterns are used to identify individual clans. The fabric is cross-banded with coloured stripes which create designs of various checked widths. In the 1840s Queen VICTORIA's frequent visits to her estate at Balmoral in Scotland stimulated a fashion for tartan garments. After World War II tartan KILTS and skirts became popular. In the 1980s tartan trousers were introduced by various designers and many subsequent winter collections have featured tartan fabric, often used in an unconventional manner. *See* PLAID.

Tassell, Gustave 1926–. Designer. Born in Philadelphia, Pennsylvania, USA. Tassell studied at the Philadelphia Academy of Fine Arts. In the late 1940s he joined Hattie CARNEGIE in New York, working first as a window dresser and later as a designer. After spending 1952 to 1964 in Paris, selling sketches to couture houses, he set up his own business in California. From the spare simplicity of his first collection,

Tassell went on to design other clean, elegant garments until 1972, when he moved to New York to take over Norman NORELL's house after Norell's death. He later resumed designing under his own name.

T-bar Woman's heeled shoe with a T-shaped strap cut from the uppers. It was introduced at the turn of the century and has remained a popular style, notably in the first half of the 20th century.

tea gown In the mid-19th century women wore pre-dinner gowns which were simply structured to allow CORSETS to be loosened or removed underneath. By the 1870s the tea gown was an elaborate affair, often long-sleeved, high-waisted and full at the back. It was made of chiffon, muslin, silk or satin and trimmed with lace ruffles and ribbons. Many tea gowns had elaborate TRAINS. In the 1920s, when women began to discard their corsets, and cut-away, slender COCKTAIL DRESSES became fashionable, the tea gown's popularity dwindled. It was replaced by the hostess gown of the 1950s. *See* LUCILE *and* PEIGNOIR.

teddy One-piece undergarment of unstructured BODICE and knickers which originated in the 19th-century CAMISOLE and knickers. The teddy first became popular in the 1920s when that era's slender, boyish shapes required minimal underwear.

tent dress In 1951 Cristobal BALENCIAGA introduced a woollen coat which flared from a low-standing collar into a widening A shape. Known as the tent, it was used for both dresses and coats. It was similar to the A-LINE but usually more exaggerated. *See also* MCCARDELL.

terry cloth *See* TOWELLING.

Terylene Man-made fibre developed by the Calico Printer's Association in 1941. It was produced by ICI and became the tradename for their fibre.

Thaarup, Aage 1906–87. Milliner. Born in Copenhagen, Denmark. Thaarup left school at sixteen to work in the ladies' hat department of Fonnesbeck's, a Copenhagen fashion store. From 1926 to 1932 he travelled to Berlin, Paris, London, Bombay and finally Delhi, where he set up a millinery business specializing in mourning hats. He opened a house in London in 1932, and his designs attracted much attention. One hat was decorated with tiny coloured safety pins; another – a white felt PILLBOX called 'Purl and Plain' – was trimmed with red and white knitting wool and two knitting needles. His other designs included peaked schoolboy caps; large 'halo' hats which broke with the current trend of TURBANS and BRETON HATS that sat deep on the head; and straw hats trimmed with plastic vegetables. After World War II, Thaarup designed 'Teen and Twenty' hats, a mass-produced line that sold worldwide.

The Gap *See* GAP.

Thomass, Chantal 1947–. Designer. Born in Paris, France. In 1967 Thomass sold dresses made from handpainted scarves to DOROTHEE BIS. In the same year, with her husband, she established a company, Ter and Bantine, to sell

Luxurious, highly trimmed underwear from the French designer Chantal **Thomass**.

young, off-beat clothes. The company was re-formed as Chantal Thomass in 1976. Since then Thomass has acquired a reputation for exotic underwear and theatrical, flirtatious clothes, made in sophisticated fabrics and often trimmed with frills and FLOUNCES. Her clothes are amusing, highly individual and distinctive.

ticking Heavy twill fabric, striped with coloured yarns and used for covering mattresses. In the second half of the 20th century it was used to make fashion garments. *See* BEENE.

tie Originally 'necktie', a wide band worn around the neck and elaborately draped or folded on the chest, worn by men in the 18th and 19th centuries. The tie, a narrow version of the above, usually worn under the collar of a shirt, evolved in the late 19th century and has been an essential item of formal menswear ever since. At the end of the 19th century women began wearing ties with blouses and

A popular garment of the 1960s: the **tie-dye** mini-dress.

Jacques **Tiffeau**'s 1964 jacket and matching tight trousers in dogstooth fabric.

skirts, though this was a trend rather than a longstanding fashion. Ties for women were again popular as part of the UNISEX fashions of the 1960s.

tie dye Method of dyeing fabric in which tiny pockets of the material are tied with thread to prevent the colour spreading to those areas, thus producing an irregular pattern. Tie-dye T-SHIRTS and casual shirts were popular in the 1960s.

Tiffany & Co. Company founded in New York City in 1837 by Charles Louis Tiffany (1812–1902) and John B. Young (dates unknown) as a stationery and fancy goods store. A third partner, J. L. Ellis, was taken on in 1841 and in the same year the firm began to buy important European jewelry collections. In 1853 Tiffany bought out the company, thereafter known as Tiffany & Co. The company merged in 1868 with a silversmith, Edward C. Moore & Co. – Moore had previously worked as a Tiffany designer. Louis Comfort Tiffany (1844–1933), son of the founder, and a champion of the Arts and Crafts Movement, joined the firm in 1900. Tiffany & Co. has an international reputation as a high class jewelers, dealing in gemstones and precious metals.

See also *PERETTI; *PICASSO, PALOMA; and SCHLUMBERGER.

Tiffeau, Jacques 1927–88. Designer. Born in Chenevelles, France. Tiffeau studied men's tailoring in the provinces and in Paris. After military service, he worked with a Parisian tailor until 1951, when he emigrated to New York. Hired as a pattern cutter by Maz Pruzan at the firm of Monte-Sano, Tiffeau soon became the firm's designer. In 1958 he and Pruzan's daughter, Beverly Busch, formed Tiffeau-Busch, a company specializing in young SPORTSWEAR. The firm closed in the late 1960s and Tiffeau returned to Paris where he worked for SAINT LAURENT in the early 1970s. In 1976 he was back in New York, designing freelance for Bill BLASS, among others.

tights Stretchable garment covering the feet, legs and body up to the waist. Associated with the theatre for several centuries, tights and pantiehose (a combination of panties and STOCKINGS) were introduced onto the fashion

TEXTURED TIGHTS AND PANTY-HOSE
for Misses and Girls

Essential wear with the 1960s mini skirt: **tights** and pantiehose advertised in the Sears, Roebuck catalogue.

market in the 1960s as an alternative to stockings. Although they were initially slow to catch on, most women had adopted them by the 1970s. Since then they have been made in almost every colour and pattern and have become an indispensable part of dress in both summer and winter. In the 1980s highly decorated and patterned tights appeared on the market. Lacy patterns have been popular since the 1960s. Other designs include multicolours, stripes, dots and even handpainted versions. Flesh-coloured tights, like stockings, are widely popular but black, grey and other neutral colours have often replaced them.

Tinling, Teddy 1910–90. Designer. Born Cuthbert Tinling in Eastbourne, England. At the age of twenty-one, Tinling opened a fashion house in London and during the 1930s his innovative designs for tennis star Suzanne LENGLEN attracted many other tennis clients. He joined the British army in 1939, reopening his house on his demobilization in 1947. Two years later his name became a household word when he designed a pair of frilly lace panties for Gussy Moran to wear at Wimbledon under her Tinling-designed tennis dress. Tinling was involved in tennis throughout his life, working for the Lawn Tennis Association and other tennis bodies, mostly in the field of public relations. From 1952 to

the 1980s he dressed most of the internationally famous women tennis stars both on court and off, using bizarre fabrics, such as crush resistant tweed, for some of his designs. In 1975 he moved his business to the USA.

tippet Piece of fabric, usually lace or lawn, wound like a small SHAWL around the neck, with the ends left hanging. A fashionable accessory for both day and eveningwear in the 19th century.

toggle Method of fastening a coat or jacket by looping a piece of cord or braid around a wooden or plastic peg.

toile *1*. Various simple twill weave fabrics. *2*. A model or pattern of a garment, made up in muslin for fitting or for making copies.

topless The most celebrated topless garment was the topless BATHING SUIT, designed in 1964 in California, USA, by Rudi GERNREICH. In a decade of considerable experimentation with dress and undress, the topless bathing suit was important as a symbol of freedom, though it never gained popularity as costume. The suit covered the body from the thighs to a high waist, where two thin straps crossed between the breasts and over the back.

topper US name for a usually short version of a *SWAGGER COAT.

toque Close-fitting brimless headdress, made from light wool, jersey or other fabrics with good draping qualities. An item of decoration, such as a FEATHER or jewel, adorned the centre of the toque. It was a popular style during the 1920s and 1930s.

toreador pants Tight trousers which lace at the knee, copied from the style worn by Spanish bullfighters. Toreador pants became popular during the mid-20th century.

tortoise-shell Translucent yellow and mottled brown material obtained from the shell of the hawk's-bill turtle. Tortoise-shell has been used for making jewelry since Roman times. Piqué tortoise-shell, inlaid with gold, silver or mother-of-pearl, was used from the 17th

In the late 19th century, getting dressed to go out was a complicated process. A hat was needed, as well as a muff and jacket, though it is unlikely that the wearer would feel cold in layers of bead-trimmed fabric and a long **train**. Photograph by Nadar.

century for haircombs, brooches and jewelry. The fashion for tortoise-shell peaked in the late 19th century and after World War I its popularity declined.

Toudouze, Anaïs 1822–99. Illustrator. Born in the Ukraine. Toudouze engraved fashion illustrations for more than thirty-five magazines, including *Monde élégant de 1850, Magazine des demoiselles, Modes de Paris de 1857* and *Moniteur de la toilette*. Her daughter, Isabelle Desgrange (1850–1907), was also a prolific fashion illustrator.

towelling (US: terry cloth) Cotton cloth woven with uncut loops on one side. Usually used for towels, it has been made up into beachwear since the 1950s.

tracksuit Two-piece outfit worn by athletes during the 20th century. Made of heavy cotton and/or synthetic fibres, the trousers are elasticated at waist and ankle. The top has long sleeves and an elasticated or drawstring waist. In the 1970s when exercisewear became fashionable, the tracksuit became popular casual attire for women.

train Long, rectangular piece of fabric which is attached to the back of a dress at the shoulders or waist. During the 19th century, trains were popular for formal evening attire but they had almost disappeared from the fashion scene by the turn of the century. *See also* WORTH.

trapeze line Launched by Yves SAINT LAURENT in 1958, the trapeze – short for trapezium, a quadrilateral shape with two parallel sides – was a wide, full, tent shape which reached to the knees. The bust was high and the back of the dress was cut to fall free from the shoulders.

Treacy, Philip 1967–. Milliner. Born in County Galway, Ireland. While a student at Dublin's National College of Art and Design, Treacy took a summer job with Stephen JONES in London. After winning a scholarship to the Royal College of Art, he returned to London to study fashion and millinery. While still a student, he continued to work for designers such as Rifat OZBEK and John GALLIANO. His degree show led to financial backing and in 1990 he opened his own business. Karl LAGERFELD and Marc BOHAN commissioned Treacy to create hats for their collections. Recognized early on as a milliner of outstanding technique and originality, Treacy creates hats which are often oversized and striking. He likes working with feathers, which he twists, curls and singes into fantastic shapes such as a huge, two-foot-high sailing ship, or into delicate feather bonnets which wrap around the face. Many of his hats resemble pieces of sculpture, with balance playing a key role. Treacy has created vast, concave straw discs which point skyward, huge basketweave platters attached to a tiny satin cap, and shirred satin in huge spirals and oyster shapes which frame the face. A mastercraftsman, Treacy blends elements of SURREALISM, mathematics and abstract art in his hatmaking.

trenchcoat Nineteenth-century military-style coat with EPAULETS and a double YOKE at the shoulders. In the 20th century, the civilian version of a World War I soldier's coat became known as a trenchcoat. Made of lightweight

Right: Philip **Treacy** is one of the world's most original and inventive milliners. His sculptural, fantastic creations have been commissioned by many major designers.

out by a group of US department store executives and she began producing ready-to-wear lines in the late 1940s. She works by cutting and draping bolts of fabrics. She is known for her crisp, tailored cuts and innovative ideas, particularly with outerwear. Credited with the introduction of removable scarves and collars from dresses and coats, Trigère has also created dresses with jewelry attached, sleeveless coats, reversible coats, and opera capes. One of her capes is made from black blanket wool and angora reversible to a shocking pink. Many of her coats are designed to be worn with two interchangeable dresses. Fur trims appear often in her collections. Trigère was one of the first designers to use wool for eveningwear.

Pauline **Trigère**'s red and black doubleface wool cape with angular closing, Autumn/Winter 1984.

wool or a cotton mix, it is worn as a RAINCOAT or topcoat.

tricorne Three-cornered hat with a turned up brim. Once part of military uniform, it was briefly popular with women in the 1930s.

tricot French for 'knitting'. Tricot is usually a woven or knitted cloth with fine lines on one side and cross ribs on the other. In the 20th century it was used for various garments, including sweaters, two-piece suits and dresses.

Trigère, Pauline 1912–. Designer. Born in Paris, France. Trigère knew how to operate a sewing machine by the age of ten and assisted her dressmaker mother. Her father was a tailor. After leaving school, she was employed as a trainee cutter at Martial et Armand in the Place Vendôme, Paris. She also worked as a freelance designer before moving in 1937 to New York, where she became assistant designer to Travis BANTON at Hattie CARNEGIE. Five years later she started her own house. Trigère's first small collection of custom-made dresses was bought

The fashionable **trilby** of the 1940s.

The International Wool Secretariat commissioned these *trompe l'oeil* outfits in 1965. Schiaparelli first set the vogue in the early 1920s. Note the Tyrolean hats in this picture – another Schiaparelli invention, this time of the 1930s.

trilby Soft felt hat with a plush-like texture, a dented crown and a flexible brim. A similar style, trimmed with a feather, is worn in the Austrian Tyrol. The trilby takes its name from the heroine of George du Maurier's novel *Trilby* (1894), who wore such a hat. It was a popular style in the 1930s and 1940s.

trompe l'oeil *Trompe l'oeil* is usually associated with painting and decoration but in fashion it refers to an optical illusion created by seaming or knitting a design into a garment. In the 1930s Elsa SCHIAPARELLI designed sweaters with *trompe-l'oeil* collars knitted into the overall design.

trotteur French for 'walking suit', an outfit introduced by John REDFERN in the 1890s. The trotteur consisted of a man's braid-trimmed jacket with buttons down the front and an ankle-length skirt which was flared at the back to permit easy walking. A highly popular suit, it was usually made of serge and wool.

trousers (US: pants) Outer garment which covers the body from the waist to the ankles in two separate leg sections. Trousers have been worn by men, in one form or another, since ancient times. Early-19th-century breeches, pantaloons and KNICKERBOCKERS are the closest relations to modern trousers. Straight, ankle-length trousers began to emerge in the 1800s but they were not considered acceptable attire for men until the late 19th century. Although actress Sarah Bernhardt appeared in trousers during the same period, they were not

Since the 1960s the **trouser suit** has become a staple of the female wardrobe. The suit shown here was part of Sonia Rykiel's ready-to-wear collection for Autumn/Winter 1997.

commonly worn by women until the 1920s. In the 1920s and 1930s CHANEL introduced 'yachting pants', and trousers – mostly baggy – were worn for the beach and for leisure activities. In the same period eveningwear trousers in elaborate fabrics became popular and there was a fashion for men to wear wide-legged OXFORD BAGS. During World War II women taking over men's work wore trousers in the factories and fields but after the war the only trousers that were fashionable were BERMUDA SHORTS, PEDAL PUSHERS and TOREADOR PANTS, all of which were worn as part of casual dress. The real trousers revolution came in the 1960s, with UNISEX fashions, though even at this time women wearing trousers were often refused entry to restaurants and the whole subject was one of heated debate. By the 1970s rules

and social attitudes had relaxed and trousers of many lengths and styles had become an acceptable part of female dress for both casual and formal attire. DRAINPIPE TROUSERS were worn by men during the 1950s and later adopted by women. CIGARETTE PANTS have been popular at various times since the 1950s. The women-in-trousers battle has been almost entirely won, though there is still resistance in some quarters to the idea of women wearing trousers to the office. *See also* BELL BOTTOMS *and* TROUSER SUIT.

trouser suit (US: pants suit) Women's two-piece suit of tailored trousers and jacket, a copy of the suit worn by men since the late 19th century. Although various women have worn men's suits since the early 1930s – the actress

Early-20th-century **tunic** dress of soft, fluid fabric, worn with a bandeau headdress of beads. For artistic effect, a garland of flowers is used as a boa.

Marlene Dietrich, for example – trouser suits for women did not become fashionable until the UNISEX vogue of the 1960s. They subsequently became a wardrobe staple.

T-shirt T-shaped, short sleeved, cotton shirts were worn by men under uniforms during World War I and were later adopted by labourers. Since the 1960s they have been widely popular in the West, printed with political slogans, logos, jokes, social comments or brandnames. Plain T-shirts, in cotton or cotton mix, are worn as summer attire. *See also* HAMNETT *and* PUNK.

tube Long, straight garment – a skirt, dress or vest – with two side seams and minimal decoration.

tulle Originally made of gauze or silk, tulle is a fine fabric of hexagonal mesh, used in dress trimmings, millinery and bridal gowns. In the 20th century it was often made of nylon. Tulle is believed to have originated in Tulle or Toul in France in the 18th century.

tunic Originally a short dress worn by ancient Greeks and Romans. Usually sleeveless and either tied about the waist or left untied, the tunic is a straight, tubular garment which has been adapted for many uses. In the 19th century it appeared as a coat-like garment worn over long skirts and dresses. The shape was also used by WORTH in his knee-length tunic dress of the 1860s. In the early 20th century Paul POIRET and other designers used the tunic as part of the long, slender lines of the prewar era. The shape became fashionable again in the 1960s when short tunic dresses were worn over slightly longer versions. The tunic has also been worn belted and unbelted over trousers.

turban Long scarf of fine linen, cotton or silk worn wound around the head. Turbans are commonly worn by Muslim and Sikh men. In the early years of the 20th century, Paul POIRET featured turbans with orientally inspired HAREM PANTS and TUNICS, made of lavish fabrics and exotically decorated. From 1910 to 1920 the turban became a popular hat style, preconstructed by milliners into the slightly pointed shape with which fashion is now familiar. In later decades, the turban became briefly popular for both day and eveningwear, notably in the 1930s, 1960s and 1980s.

Turbeville, Deborah 1937–. Photographer. Born in Medford, Massachusetts, USA. Turbeville went to New York in 1956 and spent two years with Claire MCCARDELL, as a model and assistant designer. From 1960 to 1972, she worked as a fashion editor on the *Ladies' Home Journal* and *Mademoiselle*. She then moved to London to work as a freelance photographer and during the 1970s travelled between London, Paris and New York, photographing for most of the major magazines. Turbeville's work is romantic and often eerie. Her women models look mysterious and elusive, as if they were acting out a scene in a play.

Turkish trousers *See* BLOOMERS *and* HAREM PANTS.

turtleneck High, close-fitting neckline on a knitted SWEATER or PULLOVER. Popular in the 1960s.

The original, single-breasted **tuxedo** for men, shown above in 1919. In 1966 Yves Saint Laurent created his version of the tuxedo for women, known as a 'smoking'. His sketch for this style is shown above right.

tuxedo Originally a semi-formal dinner jacket with silk lapels, generously cut in black or dark blue cloth, which took its name from the exclusive Tuxedo Club which opened in 1886 in Tuxedo Park, Orange County, New Jersey, USA. A similar dress coat without tails was popular in England at the same time. By the 1920s the tuxedo had become a double-breasted dinner jacket. It reverted to a single-breasted style after World War II. In France it is called a 'smoking.' Dinner jackets for women enjoyed a vogue in the late 1970s and 1980s. *See* SAINT LAURENT.

tweed The word tweed is thought to be a mis-reading of 'tweel', the Scottish pronunciation of twill. The fabric's association with the River Tweed, a large centre for the weaving industry in the 19th century, has helped perpetuate the error. Tweed is a rough-textured fabric, woven from wool in a variety of coloured patterns. It has been used since the end of the 19th century for coats and suits. It fell out of favour during the 1960s when lighterweight fabrics became popular, but re-emerged during the 1990s.

Twiggy 1949–. Model. Born Leslie Hornby in London, England. Under the guidance of entrepreneur Justin de Villeneuve, Twiggy was launched into the fashion scene in 1966. She was featured as a model in newspapers and magazines throughout the world, including *Elle* in France and *VOGUE* in the UK and USA. Dubbed 'Face of 1966', she swiftly became the symbol of the decade and her waif-like figure and wide-eyed looks were eagerly copied.

twill Fabric woven with diagonal lines of WEFT threads passing alternatively under and over WARP threads.

twinset Matching knitted CARDIGAN and SWEATER introduced in the 1930s. Originally worn during the day with a skirt or pair of trousers, the twinset has lost much of its conservative image and features in both casual-wear (slightly oversized and longer) and eveningwear, when the material may be woven with shiny threads and embroidered. *See* PRINGLE.

Tyrolean costume Costume worn in the Austrian Tyrol. Tyrolean garments were popularized by SCHIAPARELLI in the 1930s. Many are made of wool and embroidered. The male costume includes leather breeches with embroidered cloth BRACES, knitted woollen hose and a black leather jacket. Women wear full, embroidered skirts, PEASANT blouses and short jackets. Both sexes wear a TRILBY-like plush felt hat, trimmed with a feather. *See also* LODEN.

U

ulster Long, loose-fitting, calf-length woollen overcoat with a full or half belt which originated in the Irish province of Ulster. It was a popular coat for men and women from the late 19th to the early 20th century.

Ultrasuede Synthetic fabric of POLYESTER and polyurethane which is crease resistant and

The designer Richard **Tyler** created this glamorous evening outfit for his Autumn/Winter collection, 1996.

Tyler, Richard 1946–. Designer. Born in Sunshine, Australia. Tyler is the son of a dressmaker who also designed theatre and ballet costumes. At sixteen he left school to work for a Savile Row-trained tailor and two years later opened his own shop, Zippity-doo-dah, in Melbourne, designing clothes that were made by his mother. In the 1970s he became a designer for rock stars, moving in 1974 to Los Angeles. In 1988 he opened a menswear boutique in the city and in 1989 expanded into women's clothing. Tyler's celebrity clientele appreciated his exquisitely tailored clothes, many styled on updated 1940s fashions. Sophisticated, sculptured and somewhat theatrical, his designs – even his romantic eveningwear for women – are always rooted in masculine tailoring. He is famous for meticulously crafted jackets, lined with silk. From 1993 to the end of 1994 Tyler was head designer for Anne KLEIN. In 1996 he was made design director of BYBLOS.

The travelling **ulster**, featured in *Queen*, 1880.

Emanuel **Ungaro**'s velvet panne dress, with fabric from Abraham, for Spring/Summer 1984. The chic evening hat is by Maison Paulette.

machine washable. Ultrasuede is the trademark of the American Skinner Fabrics Division of Spring Mills Inc. *See also* SUEDE FABRIC.

umbrella From the Latin *umbraculum*, 'a shady place', the umbrella was originally used as protection against both rain and sun. In the 16th century it was made of leather and then of increasingly lighter fabrics up to the introduction of the soft lace and tulle confections of the 19th century. It was at this time that the distinction was made between the PARASOL, a lightweight accessory used by women for protection against the sun, and the umbrella, a sturdier object carried by both men and women to shield them from rain. In the late 19th century lightweight umbrellas specially designed for

women began to appear. Umbrellas are usually functional but they have been fashionable items at certain points in most decades, made with carved or decorated handles. In the 1960s and 1970s they became a more prominent fashion accessory and were produced in bright colours.

Ungaro, Emanuel 1933–. Designer. Born in Aix-en-Provence, France, to Italian parents. Ungaro was trained initially to be a tailor in the family business but in 1955 he went to work in Paris and after a brief period with a small tailoring firm he joined BALENCIAGA. In 1961 he moved to COURREGES and four years later opened his own business. He specialized in futuristic, angular, tailored coats and suits; short, sharp A-LINE dresses; lace SEE-THROUGH

SKETCHES IN LOWER ROW CONTRAVENE OUR AUSTERITY RULES BY POINTS NOTED IN CAPTIONS

Maggy Rouff's dinner dress, row of buttons as ornamentation only	Lelong's wool dress Double row rouleau at neck. Cuffs turned back	Molyneux suit. Turn-back cuffs and but-toned flap on pockets	Piguet. Wool dress shoulder buttons as ornament, not fastening	Lelong. One too many buttons and used as ornamentation only

The **Utility Scheme** set up by the British Board of Trade during World War II instituted strict guidelines regarding the conservation of materials. Here certain designers are given a dressing down for wasteful use of fabric and buttons.

dresses; deeply cut armholes on dresses and coats; shorts and matching BLAZERS; thigh-high BOOTS; over-the-knee socks; and metal garments. Many of his clothes were made from special fabrics designed by Sonja Knapp. Ungaro produced his first ready-to-wear lines in 1968. During the 1970s his work became softer and less rigid. His clothes are most often made in the rich, boldly printed fabrics that have become his hallmark. He pays great attention to detail in order to enhance the colours, patterns and texture of the cloth.

unisex Clothes designed to be worn by either sex, popular in the 1960s and 1970s. Unisex garments included trousers, jackets, waistcoats and shirts. The unisex look emerged as men took to wearing floral patterns and women adopted men's garments. Although novel at the time, the idea has been accepted in fashion since the early 1980s.

Utility Scheme In 1941, because of the exi-gencies of World War II, clothes were rationed in the UK. The following year Hardy AMIES, Norman HARTNELL, Edward MOLYNEUX, Digby MORTON, Victor STIEBEL, Bianca MOSCA

and Peter Russell cooperated with the Board of Trade to design Utility clothes made of a pre-scribed yardage of material and number and manner of trimmings. The designers produced coats, suits, dresses and OVERALLS to Board of Trade requirements. Rationing ceased after the war but fabrics remained in short supply until the end of the 1940s.

V

Valenciennes A type of bobbin lace characterized by a background of diamond-shaped mesh. Originally made in the town of Valenciennes, on the French/Flemish border.

Valentina 1909–89. Designer. Born Valentina Nicholaevna Sanina in Kiev, Russia. After a sojourn in Paris during the Russian Revolu-tion, Valentina moved in 1922 to New York where, four years later, she started her own dressmaking business. Trained for the stage and interested in theatre, she made costumes for many stage productions, and her clothes were popular with actresses for off-stage wear. She

Valentino

designed along architectural lines, producing dramatic clothes, including TURBANS, VEILS, swirling capes and evening gowns. She was a successful designer until her retirement in 1957.

Valentino 1932–. Designer. Born Valentino Garavani in Voghera, Italy. Valentino studied in Milan at the Accademia Dell'Arte and in Paris at the Ecole de la Chambre Syndicale de la Haute Couture (*See* HAUTE COUTURE). He then spent almost ten years in Paris, working first with DESSES, from 1950 to 1955, and then with LAROCHE. He returned to Italy in the late 1950s and in 1959 opened a couture house in Rome. He showed his first collection in 1960 but it was with his 1962 collection, shown in Florence, that his name became internationally known. Probably Italy's most famous designer, Valentino makes clothes that are elegant, glamorous and gracefully cut. His dramatic yet tasteful touches and accessories have been widely copied: big bows, embroidered stockings, and the initial V worn as buttons and at the neckline. He is as well known for his daywear as for his evening-wear. Valentino's confident, stylish designs are made of quality fabrics. His clients include many international socialites and in Italy his name is a household word.

Italian elegance from **Valentino** for 1964.

van den Akker, Koos 1939–. Designer. Born in The Hague, Holland. In 1955, with no prior formal training, van den Akker enrolled at the Royal Academy of Art in The Hague. His first work in fashion was with Christian DIOR in Paris but he returned after several years to Holland and opened his own BOUTIQUE. In 1968, with a portable sewing machine in his luggage, he moved to the USA and set up a temporary shop on a Manhattan sidewalk which attracted a great deal of attention. His first designs were quilted garments with inserts of lace. By 1970 he had opened the first of several stores in the city. Taking his inspiration from fabric, van den Akker creates clothes that are highly individual and boldly coloured statements in collage and PATCHWORK.

vandyke Large, white, lace-trimmed collar which fans out over the shoulders, named after Sir Anthony Van Dyck (1599–1641), the Flemish painter, in whose portraits the collar was often shown. *See* LITTLE LORD FAUNTLEROY.

Multi-fabric drop-waist dress with bright floral collage from Koos **van den Akker**, Autumn/Winter 1985–86.

The Belgian designer Dries **van Noten** has built an international reputation since the mid-1980s. These eveningwear designs are from his Spring/Summer 1997 collection.

van Noten, Dries 1958–. Designer. Born in Anvers, Belgium. After studying fashion at Antwerp's Royal Academy of Arts, van Noten started his own company in 1985. A MINIMALIST who favours spare lines and dark colour palettes, he built up a large following in Belgium before he attracted international attention. He uses figure-defining fabrics such as jersey and silk knits and is known for layering jackets over dresses and trousers. He also produces sleek suits with jackets buttoned on the diagonal, long DUSTER COATS, and matte sequined evening dresses.

vareuse Fisherman's SMOCK from Breton, France. A loose garment with a standaway collar, which is cut to hang to the hips. In his 1957 collections, Christian DIOR included variations of the vareuse, made up in a variety of fabrics.

Varon, Jean *See* BATES.

Varty, Keith *See* BYBLOS.

Vass, Joan 1925–. Designer. Born in New York, USA. Vass was educated at Vassar College and studied philosophy at the University of Wisconsin, graduating in 1942. She worked in New York as an editor before joining the Museum of Modern Art as an assistant curator. In 1974 she began a non-profit-making company helping knitters market their skills. Vass created designs for hats and sweaters, which she supplied to knitters. Two years later she was designing woven garments, adding coats and daywear to her collection. Known mostly for her sweaters knitted from chenille, alpaca, angora and other fine quality wools, Vass has also established a reputation for her clothing lines, which are distinguished by their lack of both shoulder pads and applied decoration. Her most popular line is called Joan Vass USA.

veil Thin piece of fabric that falls over the eyes and/or face, partially concealing them. Tulle or lace veils attached to BONNETS were popular throughout the 19th century. Toward the end of that century, there was a vogue for motoring

Hat and **veil**, trimmed with a bird, late 1950s.

veils, worn over a hat and tied under the chin with a curtain at the back to keep out the dust. Other versions resembled a bag with a slot for the eyes. Veils can be made in many lengths and fabrics. In the 1890s veils sprinkled with chenille dots were briefly fashionable. Heavy crepe mourning veils were worn throughout the 19th century. During the 20th century veils gradually declined in favour, though short veils that just covered the eyes were popular until the 1940s. The fashion for long, white, bridal veils has endured since the 19th century.

velour French for velvet. A smooth, soft, closely woven fabric with a short, thick pile, which can be made of cotton, mohair, wool or synthetic fibres. Velour was used in the 20th century for many garments, notably TRACK-SUITS and leisurewear.

velvet From the latin *vellus*, 'fleece', velvet has been known in Europe since the Middle Ages. It is a closely woven fabric with a short, dense pile which produces a soft, rich texture. In the 19th century velvet was made in part or completely of silk but in the 20th century it was made from acetate and rayon. Commonly used in the 19th century for dresses and jackets, since

the early 20th century velvet has been considered a luxury fabric and has usually been reserved for eveningwear, though there was a vogue in the late 1960s and early 1970s for velvet skirts and trousers for daywear.

velveteen Twill or plain-woven cotton with a short weft pile made to imitate velvet. It has been in use since the early 20th century.

Venet, Philippe 1931–. Designer. Born in Lyons, France. At fourteen, Venet became an apprentice to Pierre Court, a well-respected couturier based in Lyons. He moved to Paris in 1951, working first for SCHIAPARELLI and two years later for GIVENCHY. In 1962 Venet opened his own house, achieving fame with his finely tailored coats, suits and eveningwear. The house closed in 1996.

Venetian lace Needlepoint lace with a distinctive circular pattern, which has been made in Venice since the 15th century.

vent Slit or open section in a jacket or coat which gives fullness and width, used by dressmakers since the 19th century.

Vernier, Rose ?–1975. Milliner. Place of birth unknown. Brought up in Vienna, Austria, Vernier established a millinery business in Poland before moving to London in 1939. After World War II, she became a popular London milliner, patronized by society figures and by the British royal family. She worked closely with AMIES, CREED, MORTON and MATTLI, producing designs for their collections. She retired in 1970.

Versace, Gianni 1946–97. Designer. Born in Calabria, Italy. Versace worked with his dressmaker mother before moving to Milan. He swiftly established a reputation as a skilled designer and created suede and leather collections for GENNY and evening clothes for the firm of Complice. In 1978 he opened his own business. Versace was one of the most important Italian designers of the 1980s and 1990s, famous for his strong colour sense and clean lines. He liked to wrap the female form, often with BIAS CUT clothes and fluid silks. Many of his ideas were audacious but all were carried out to a

Gianni **Versace**, always a master cutter of leather, displayed his talents in this luminous, striking and supple jacket, part of his Spring/Summer collection for 1982.

high level of technical achievement. Versace viewed his clothes as powerful statements which were executed with unfailing confidence. Almost always the body was swathed or the garment wrapped in some manner. In Versace's clothes, classical historical references blend with bold geometric shapes and complex textures in brilliant colours. His designs are unmistakable; he enjoyed working with leather and experimenting with new fabrics and trimmings. Versace's designs for the theatre and ballet undoubtedly influenced his fashion work.

Vertès, Marcel 1895–1961. Illustrator. Born in Ujpest, near Budapest, Hungary. Vertès studied to become an aviation engineer, but turned instead to drawing and painting. In the early 1920s he went to Paris, where he worked for the satirical magazine *Rire*, and for the GAZETTE DU BON TON, studying in his spare time at the Académie Julian. Vertès illustrated books and designed costumes and sets for films, the theatre and musicals. He worked briefly for *Vanity Fair* in New York before going to London to illustrate for SCHIAPARELLI perfumes. After World War II he worked as a book and magazine illustrator. His hallmarks were his light, graceful and witty watercolour sketches of high fashion and high society.

Victor, Sally 1905–77. Milliner. Born Sally Josephs in Scranton, Pennsylvania, USA. Victor acquired her training as a milliner by working in her aunt's New York shop. At the age of eighteen she joined the millinery department of Macy's store and after two years moved to a New Jersey department store as head millinery buyer. In 1927 she married Sergiv Victor, the head of Serge, a wholesale millinery company, and soon became the company's chief designer. In the early 1930s she sold hats under her own name and in 1934 opened her own millinery store. From the 1930s to the early 1950s, Victor was one of the most influential and innovative milliners in the USA. She wove and dyed fabric on her own premises, experimenting with felt and denim as well as more exotic fabrics. She produced chessmen-shaped PILLBOXES, collapsible BONNETS, a SAILOR HAT and hats based on Chinese lanterns, geisha bonnets, Ali Baba topknots and Native American headdresses. Victor was a popular designer with the wives of American political figures, as well as with stage and screen actresses, all of whom wore her less controversial hats. She retired in 1968.

Victoria, Queen 1819–1901. Born Alexandria Victoria in London, daughter of Edward, Duke of Kent, and Princess Victoria Mary Louisa of Saxe-Coburg-Gotha. In 1837 Victoria became Queen. In 1840 she married Albert of Saxe-Coburg-Gotha, her cousin. Her wedding gown was made of Spitalfields silk and her veil of Honiton *LACE. Although Victoria was not herself a figure of fashion, she was responsible for many vogues. Her affection for her Scottish estate at Balmoral, for example, produced a trend for garments named after the house, and for TARTAN in general. Her adoption of MOURNING DRESS, on the death of her consort in 1861, made such dress *de rigueur* for widows and caused a dramatic increase in the production of suitable fabrics.

vicuna Wool from the vicuna, a small animal of the llama family found in the Andes mountain range of South America. One of the finest fibres, vicuna is soft, strong and expensive to produce – a dozen animals are required to make one piece of cloth. Naturally cinnamon brown or fawn in colour, vicuna was a popular material in the 20th century for coats, capes, jackets and suits.

Vionnet, Madeleine 1876–1975. Designer. Born in Aubervilliers, France. Apprenticed to a seamstress at the age of eleven, Vionnet worked in the Paris suburbs in her late teens before joining Kate O'Reilly, a London dressmaker, in 1898. In 1900 she returned to Paris and was employed by Mme Gerber, the designing member of CALLOT SOEURS. Vionnet joined DOUCET in 1907 and remained with him for five years. In 1912 she opened her own house, closing during World War I and reopening shortly after. Greatly favoured by pre-World War I actresses Eve Lavallière and Réjane, Vionnet was one of the most innovative designers of her day. She conceived her designs on a miniature model, draping the fabric in sinuous folds. Mistress of the BIAS CUT, she commissioned fabrics two yards wider than usual to accommodate her draping. She dispensed with the CORSET and used diagonal seaming and FAGGOTING to achieve her simple, fluid shapes. Many of Vionnet's clothes looked limp and shapeless until they were put on. In the late 1920s and early 1930s she reached the height of her fame. She was credited with the popularization of the COWL and HALTER NECK. She favoured crepe, crepe de chine, gabardine and satin for evening dresses and day dresses, which were often cut in one piece, without armholes. Suits had gored or BIAS-CUT skirts; WRAP-

Vionnet at work on her miniature model in 1935.

Vionnet's expertly cut dress of 1933.

AROUND coats were made with side fastenings, and many garments fastened at the back or were pulled on over the head without a fastening of any kind. Bands of grosgrain often acted as lining and support for the insides of fine crepe dresses. Vionnet used striped fabrics but she was not a colourist. A smooth shape and fit were her main aims in achieving the ultimate in dress designs – a dress that fits sympathetically to the body. No other designer has equalled her enormous technical contribution to haute couture. Vionnet retired in 1939.

viscose Man-made cellulose fibre derived from wood pulp. In 1905 COURTAULD's began production of viscose rayon. Viscose is used in sweaters, dresses, coats, blouses and leisurewear.

viscose rayon The most common of the various types of rayon production, viscose rayon was invented by three British chemists, Cross, Bevan and Beadle, in the late 19th century. It was patented in 1892. Viscose rayon fibres have been used in most types of garments since the turn of the century, though major production did not begin until after World War II.

Vivier, Roger 1913–. Shoe designer. Born in Paris, France. Vivier studied sculpture at the Ecole des Beaux-Arts in Paris until an invitation from friends to design a collection of shoes for their shoe factory interrupted his studies. In 1936 he worked for other shoemakers before opening his own house the following year. Vivier designed for many major shoe manufacturers: Pinet and Bally in France, Miller and DELMAN in the USA, RAYNE and Turner in the UK. Delman turned down one of his designs, a Chinese-style platform shoe – which was subsequently taken up by SCHIAPARELLI.

Roger **Vivier**, one of the 20th century's greatest shoe designers, created this jeweled shoe for 1963–64.

Georgina **von Etzdorf**'s luxurious handprinted velvet scarves and other accessories of the late 1980s and 1990s were widely influential.

A jeweled, heeled mule, 18th century in style but entirely modern in construction, created by the master shoemaker Roger **Vivier** in 1964.

In 1938 Vivier agreed to work exclusively for Delman in the USA, but the completion of his contract was prevented by his mobilization in 1939. One year later he was out of the army and off to New York where he worked with Delman until 1941. In 1942, having studied millinery, Vivier opened a shop with Suzanne Remi, a well-respected Parisian milliner who was living in New York. In 1945, back with Delman, he produced several collections, one of which included his 'crystal shoes'. He returned to Paris in 1947 and worked freelance until Christian DIOR opened a shoe department in his salon in 1953 and appointed Vivier as designer. During his stay at Dior, Vivier designed some of the most influential shoes of the period. He translated 18th-century MULES into evening shoes, COURT SHOES and day boots. In 1957 he created a stacked, leather-heeled, chisel-toed shoe which became very popular. He made circular DIAMANTE heels, wedge shoes (*See* WEDGIES) and bead-embroidered shoes. In the 1960s he designed African SANDALS and a shoe with a mother-of-pearl, TORTOISE-SHELL or silver buckle. A nonconformist master craftsman who rarely falters, Vivier is noted for his skill in positioning and balancing innovative heels and for his imaginative use of texture. He reopened his business in 1963 in Paris and continues to produce two collections a year.

Viyella Tradename established in 1894 by William Hollins & Company for its woven fabric of wool and cotton. Viyella was used in the late 19th century for men's nightshirts and underwear but in the 20th century it gradually became a popular fabric for all the family, made into pyjamas and nightgowns. Soft, warm and hardwearing, the cloth has maintained its appeal. In the 1960s and 1970s Viyella shirts were popular, often printed with a Tattersall check.

Vogel, Lucien 1886–1954. French magazine publisher. Vogel founded the *GAZETTE DU BON TON* in 1912 and encouraged such artists as DRIAN, BARBIER, LEPAPE, IRIBE, MARTY and

MARTIN to produce elegant hand-coloured plates. In 1922 he launched LE JARDIN DES MODES (which was purchased by Condé NAST), and he also became the editor of VOGUE. He created a magazine entitled Vu in 1928. After spending the years of World War II in the USA, he returned to France in 1945 and edited Le Jardin des modes until his death.

Vogue Magazine started in the USA in 1892 as a fashion weekly catering to society women. In 1909 Vogue was purchased by Condé NAST and became twice monthly in 1910. British Vogue was added to the American stable in 1916. French, Australian, Spanish and German Vogue followed, though Spanish Vogue lasted only from 1918 to 1920 and German Vogue survived only a few issues in 1928. Vogue was transformed by Nast from a small weekly paper into the 20th century's most influential fashion magazine. Devoted to fashion, society and the arts, it has successfully promoted art, photography, illustration and literature through its pages. See also CHASE, LEPAPE, VOGEL and VREELAND.

voile Fine, sheer, semi-transparent plain-woven fabric of tightly twisted yarns, made of cotton, silk, wool or, in the 20th century, man-made fibres. Voile has been used since the 19th century for making blouses and dresses.

Vollbracht, Michaele 1947–. Designer, illustrator. Born in Kansas City, Missouri, USA. At age seventeen Vollbracht enrolled at Parsons School of Design in New York. After graduation he worked for Geoffrey BEENE and Donald BROOKS before joining Norman NORELL, with whom he stayed until 1972. Vollbracht also created a number of illustrations for the New York store Bloomingdale's. In the 1970s he started his own business, selling garments made of hand-printed silks. This company was closed down and a new one opened in 1981.

von Etzdorf, Georgina 1955–. Textile designer. Born in Lima, Peru. Von Etzdorf attended Camberwell School of Art in London. In 1981 she started a company with two art school friends, producing distinctive, handprinted textile accessories and clothing, particularly scarves of deep rich velvets and chiffons which have been widely influential.

Diane **von Fürstenberg** created her best-selling jersey wraparound dress – a modern classic – in 1976.

Von Fürstenberg, Diane 1946–. Designer. Born Diane Michelle Halfin in Brussels, Belgium. Von Fürstenberg majored in economics at the University of Geneva. In 1969 she became an apprentice to Angelo Ferretti, an Italian textile manufacturer, and using silk jersey prints she produced a line of clothes, mostly TUNIC dresses in varying lengths and BIAS-CUT SHIRTWAISTERS. In 1972 she opened her own business in New York. In the 1970s she created a WRAPAROUND dress which became a bestseller. It had long sleeves, a fitted top, and a skirt which wrapped around the body to tie at the waist. Von Fürstenberg favours jersey and often uses geometric prints.

Vreeland, Diana 1906–89. Magazine editor. Born Diana Dalziel in Paris, France. Vreeland moved to New York at the age of eight. In 1937 she joined HARPER'S BAZAAR in New York, becoming fashion editor in 1939. In 1962, after twenty-five years with Harper's Bazaar, Vreeland left and became associate

Vuokko's fresh and simple dresses for Scandinavian summers. The designs date from the mid-1970s, the fabrics from the early 1980s. An uncomplicated approach contributes to Vuokko's success.

editor of VOGUE the following year. Soon after, she was appointed editor-in-chief and stayed with *Vogue* until 1971. From the late 1930s Vreeland was an arbiter of fashion and style. Her keen eye for talent promoted numerous models, photographers and designers. Her own sense of personal style, which she never hesitated to reveal, not only inspired others but also made her famous. She edited *Vogue* during the 1960s with flamboyance and flair. In 1971 Vreeland became a consultant to the Costume Institute of the Metropolitan Museum of New York and was responsible for many of the museum's exhibitions on fashion and style.

Vuokko 1930–. Designer. Born Nurmesniemi Vuokko in Finland. Vuokko studied dressmaking at the Ateneum in Helsinki and then took a course in ceramics at Helsinki's Institute of Industrial Design. She graduated in 1952 and worked for various textile companies, for MARIMEKKO, and in industrial and houseware

design before forming Vuokko in 1965. Her fashion garments are based on simple shapes; she uses cotton and jersey in clear, bright colours and the patterns in her fabrics are an integral part of the overall design. During the late 1960s and early 1970s she produced various lines but was particularly noted for prints designed with swirling circles and stripes.

W

Wainwright, Janice 1940–. Designer. Born in Chesterfield, England. Wainwright studied at Wimbledon School of Art, Kingston School of Art and the Royal College of Art, London. From 1965 to 1968 she worked for the company Simon Massey, creating many lines under her own name. Then followed six years of freelance designing before Wainwright established her own company in 1974. Her interest in fab-

Janice **Wainwright**'s pagoda-style dress of 1976.

rics was evident from her long, lean shapes, sinuous seaming, and use of the BIAS CUT. She favoured matte jersey, crepe and soft wools, which she manipulated into swirling, spiralling outfits that were often full-shouldered.

waist cincher *See* WASPIE.

waistcoat Man's waist-length, sleeveless garment worn under a jacket and over a shirt. Often made from silk or heavily embroidered fabrics, the waistcoat buttons at the front and usually has two small pockets. Women adopted waistcoats in the late 19th century and wore them with skirts and blouses into the early 20th century. In the 1960s, as part of the general fashion explosion, women often wore waistcoats borrowed directly from a man's wardrobe, favouring in particular pin-striped versions. During the 1970s and 1980s the waistcoat, made of many different fabrics, was absorbed as another item of female dress, often worn with tailored suits. It was also adopted as casualwear, cut in exaggerated proportions, as STREET STYLE entered mainstream fashion. *See* EXECUTIVE.

Warner Bros Co. In 1874 two American brothers, Lucien G. and I. de Ver Warner – both doctors – established a company to manufacture and promote health CORSETS. In 1914 they bought the patent to the backless bra (*See* BRASSIERE) from Mary Phelps Jacob (Caresse Crosby). In 1932 the company introduced ROLL-ONS and in 1935 cup fittings for bras. The

A design from Vivienne **Westwood**'s influential Buffalo collection of Autumn/Winter 1982–83.

From **Westwood**'s 'Vive la Cocotte' collection, Autumn/Winter 1995–96.

From **Westwood**'s 'Vive la Cocotte' collection, Autumn/Winter 1995–96.

Promotion for **Warner**'s 'Rust-Proof' corset on a showcard of 1902. Rust stains on underwear were the most troublesome corset problem of the late 19th century.

Warner's Birthday Suit of 1961 – a close-fitting, smoothly lined pantie-corselette made with Lycra – was an innovation in its field.

warp Loom threads which stretch lengthwise and are interwoven with the WEFT or filing threads.

waspie Also known as a waist cincher or *guêpière*, the waspie is an abbreviated CORSET constructed of bone and elastic inserts, and laced at the back or front to draw in the waist. Marcel ROCHAS was one of the first designers to introduce the *guêpière* in 1946. It was worn under the NEW LOOK fashions of the post-World War II period. In the 1980s wide, laced belts, resembling the waspie, were briefly fashionable. *See* BUSTIER *and* CORSET.

Watteau Name given to a dress style of the late 19th century that resembled gowns in early 18th-century paintings by Jean Antoine Watteau (1684–1721). A Watteau-style dress has a SACQUE back and a tightly fitted front BODICE.

Weber, Bruce 1946–. Photographer. Born in Greensburg, Pennsylvania, USA. While not strictly a fashion photographer in the traditional

sense, Weber's work has been highly influential. His photographs for advertisements and on the editorial pages of magazines portray a lifestyle and attitude in which the clothes appear to be incidental. Yet his naturalistic, uncluttered settings serve to enhance the clothing, so that the secondary message – that of what the models are wearing – actually becomes the most important.

wedgies Shoe with a wedge-shaped sole. Wedgies have varied in height and style since their introduction in the 1930s.

weft Crosswise threads woven into fabric on a loom. *See* WARP.

Westwood, Vivienne 1941–. Designer. Born Vivienne Isabel Swire in Glossop, Derbyshire, England. Westwood spent one term at Harrow Art School before leaving to train as a teacher. In the late 1960s she and Malcolm McLaren opened a shop in the KING'S ROAD, London. During the 1970s both the McLaren-managed pop group, the Sex Pistols, and Westwood's shop attracted a great deal of attention. Representing an anarchic urban youth culture, the shop, which was known by a variety of names, sold leather and rubber clothes to people with interests in PUNK, bondage and fetishism. Although they were shocking in 1976, when she produced her 'Bondage' collection of studded, buckled and strapped clothing, many of Westwood's ideas, watered down, have filtered into mainstream fashion. A totally uncompromising designer, she is unquestionably one of the most influential figures of her time. Her alliance with street culture, her anti-establishment views and her insistence on promoting clothes that suggest aggressive sex, guarantee her enormous press coverage. Westwood's clothes are criticized as being unwearable yet her designs are widely copied throughout the world, and her shows raided for ideas. In 1981 she began showing in Paris. Her 'Pirate' and 'New Romanticism' looks of the 1980s brought her to the attention of the fashion world, although the huge swirling petticoats, buckles, ruffles, pirate hats and baggy boots set fashions that were a decade ahead of their time. Instrumental in the vogue for underwear worn as outerwear, with bras worn over dresses, in the mid-1980s Westwood showed CORSETS and CRINOLINES (staples of a 19th-century woman's wardrobe), and claimed them to be not restrictive but sexy. Her shoes are extreme in height and decoration. The 'Savages' collection of 1982, and later the 'Hoboes', prefaced GRUNGE, and contained many elements – torn clothing, exposed seams – that were simultaneously emerging with the DECONSTRUCTIONISTS. Later designs, in the 1990s, focused on traditional garments which she reinvents and exploits, creating in the onlooker an unease in the new connotations she presents between garments, styles and cuts. Her clothes have a unique personality.

wet look *See* CIRE.

whalebone Horny substance from the upper jaw of the whale. A whaling industry was established in the Bay of Biscay in the 12th century. By the 17th century demand had moved the industry to Greenland. Whalebone was generally used for CORSETS and STAYS. In the years *c.*1855 to 1866, when the CRINOLINE was popular, the demand for whalebone was so great that whales were threatened with extinction. In the late 19th century, elastic fibres and metal replaced whalebone as elements of body shaping and support.

windbreaker *See* WINDCHEATER.

windcheater Waist-length jacket with a fitted waistband which was adapted from British RAF flying jackets in the late 1940s and early 1950s. Made from wool, gabardine or nylon, the windcheater is usually waterproof and zips or buttons from waist to neck. It is worn for sporting activities and casual attire. *See also* ANORAK *and* PARKA.

wing collar High, stiff collar of a shirt or blouse with upper corners that turn down. It was a popular shirt style for men's formal wear in the late 19th and early 20th centuries. Women briefly adopted the shirt style in the 1920s and it was revived in the 1970s.

Winterhalter, Franz Xaver 1806–73. Painter. Born in the Black Forest, Germany. Winterhalter became the court painter in

The **wing collar** of the 1890s was worn almost exclusively by men until the 1920s, when it was briefly adopted by women (*top*).

A portrait by **Winterhalter** of the Empress Eugénie and her maids of honour, *c.* 1860.

Karlsruhe in 1828. During the 1850s and 1860s he travelled and worked in Paris and London, returning to Germany in 1870. Winterhalter is known for his famous portraits of European royalty, including the Empress EUGENIE and Queen VICTORIA, whose full-skirted, off-the-shoulder gowns he painted in such detail that this style of dress has been linked with his name.

Women's Wear Daily (***WWD***) Originally a journal for the clothing industry, *Women's Wear Daily* was successfully converted to a popular magazine appealing both to the trade and to the public by John FAIRCHILD, who became its publisher in 1960. The magazine reported trade goings-on as well as fashion shows. It also covered parties and charity functions, describing the clothes of the guests and passing on gossip. Fairchild gave space to first-rate fashion artists. In 1973 he launched *W*, a bi-weekly journal printed on paper heavy enough to allow him to reproduce good quality photographs.

Wonderbra *See* BRASSIERE.

wool Mass of strong and flexible fibres which makes up the fleece of sheep. The outer cells of the coiled fibre repel water while the inner cells absorb moisture, thus making the cloth very warm. In use since the Stone Age, wool has been made up into almost every kind of garment. In the late 19th century it was used for underwear and swimwear as well as indoor and outdoor clothes. The main areas of wool production are Australia, New Zealand, South Africa and Argentina. Woollen yarns are pliable and less expensive than the harder, smoother and stronger worsted yarns. *See* BOTANY, LAMBSWOOL, MELTON *and* WORSTED.

worsted Hardwearing woollen fabric made of smooth yarn, which takes its name from Worstead in Norfolk, England, where it was originally made. Serge and gabardine worsteds have been popular since the late 19th century for suits and outer garments.

The Englishman Charles Frederick **Worth** *(above)* is considered to be the founder of haute couture. He opened his house in Paris in 1858 and dressed both society and the demi-monde until his death in 1895. Worth dominated the scene from the mid-19th-century crinoline *(opposite top)* to the bustle *(left)*, to the more slender lines of the late 19th century *(top left and right)*. After his death, the house of Worth was continued by his sons, Gaston and Jean-Philippe.

Worth, Charles Frederick 1825–95. Designer. Born in Bourne, Lincolnshire, England. Worth started work at the age of twelve in a draper's shop in London and a year later began a seven-year apprenticeship at the haberdasher's Swan & Edgar's, selling shawls and dress materials. After moving to the silk mercer's Lewis & Allenby for a brief period, he left for Paris in 1845. His first job in the French capital was at Maison Gagelin, where he sold MANTLES and shawls. Five years later he opened a dress-making department at the store. In 1858 Worth went into partnership with a Swedish businessman, Otto Bobergh, and opened his own house. He was soon a favourite of the Empress EUGENIE, and her influence and patronage were instrumental in his success. In the 1860s he introduced the TUNIC dress, a knee-length gown worn with a long skirt. In 1864 he abolished the CRINOLINE and pulled skirts up and back into a TRAIN. Five years later he raised the waistline and created a BUSTLE behind. In 1870, when the Second Empire collapsed, Worth closed his business, only to reopen the following year. Although there was less demand for court trains and crinolines,

261

Worth, Gaston

Worth continued as the top Parisian couturier, dressing actresses Sarah Bernhardt and Eleonora Duse and patronized by European royalty and international society. He handled rich materials in a sensitive manner, using simple designs and creating clothing on flattering lines. Much of his work is associated with the movement to redefine the female form and fashionable shape by removing excessive RUFFLES and frills, altering BONNET shapes by pushing them back off the forehead, and reshaping the crinoline and the bustle. Worth's copious use of luxurious fabrics throughout the second half of the 19th century inspired the silk manufacturers of Lyons to weave more and more interesting textiles. For some of his clients he designed a complete collection of clothes for every occasion. Worth's customers enjoyed being 'created' by the master and were happy to trust him to enhance their finer points by his skilful cutting of cloth. Although he designed restrained travelling clothes and walking garments, he was most famous for his evening gowns, often of white tulle. Worth was a gifted designer who, in retrospect, seems to have had a clear understanding of the times in which he lived. He was able to dress both society and the demi-monde with equal good, though obviously affluent, taste. After his death in 1895, Worth's sons, Gaston and Jean-Philippe, continued the business, which passed through four generations before it was taken over by the house of PAQUIN in 1953. *See* ★DECOLLETE.

Worth, Gaston 1853–1924. Born in Paris, France, son of Charles Frederick WORTH. In 1874, Gaston Worth began working at his father's couture house. On his father's death the following year, he took over the business with his brother, Jean-Philippe. Gaston Worth was the business administrator and commercial mind behind the company. He was also the first president of the Chambre Syndicale de la Haute Couture (*See* HAUTE COUTURE), an organization set up to protect designers from piracy. He retired from the house of Worth in 1922. *See also* WORTH, JEAN PHILIPPE.

Worth, Jean–Philippe 1856–1926. Designer. Born in Paris, France, son of Charles Frederick WORTH. Jean-Philippe Worth was instrumental in the House of Worth's smooth transition

The **wraparound** style has been popular for tops, skirts and dresses since the 1950s. The wraparound top shown above is by the American designer Vera Maxwell.

from the late 19th century to the early 20th century without altering the style set by its founder. Strongly influenced by his father, Jean-Philippe Worth was particularly well known for his eveningwear. He designed until the late 1900s. *See also* WORTH, GASTON.

wraparound The term wraparound refers to a style whereby clothing is fastened by wrapping around the body rather than by the use of buttons or other fastenings. It can be used in dresses, skirts or tops. The wraparound skirt is a 20th-century style which originated with the SARONG. The skirt section, made of a rectangular piece of fabric, is wrapped once around the body, the front panel overlapping to fasten at the waist. Wraparound tops were especially popular in the early 1980s as part of the vogue for exercise wear. In general, wraparound garments are popular for casual wear, beach attire, and – in ankle-length versions – for eveningwear. *See* ★VON FURSTENBERG.

Y

Yamamoto, Kansai 1944–. Designer. Born in Yokohama, Japan. Yamamoto studied English at Nippon University. After working briefly for a designer, he opened his own house in 1971. The presentation of Yamamoto's shows made him famous: dramatic clothes shown in an exciting environment. By blending the vigorous, exotic and powerful designs of traditional JAPANESE dress with Western day-wear, he achieves a unique, abstract style.

Yamamoto, Yohji 1943–. Designer. Born in Japan. Yamamoto graduated from Keio University in 1966 and then attended Bunka Fukuso Gakuin, the Japanese college of fashion, for two years. After working as a freelance designer, he formed his own company in 1972 and his first collection was shown in Japan in 1976. Yamamoto is an uncompromising, nontradi-tionalist designer. He swathes and wraps the body in unstructured, loose, voluminous garments, similar in style and philosophy to those of Rei KAWAKUBO. Many of his clothes have additional flaps, pockets and straps.

Yantorny, Pietro dates unknown. Shoe-maker. Born in Russia. One of fashion's legends, Yantorny was at one time curator at the Cluny Museum, Paris. In the early years of the 20th century he had a shoe shop in Paris and was known for his high prices, for the length of time it took him to make shoes – often several

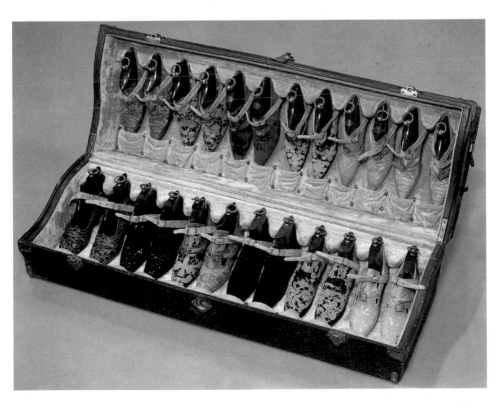

The shoes in the trunk shown above are the work of the designer Pietro **Yantorny**. Yantorny was the curator of the Cluny Museum and he made shoes for a few select clients in his spare time. Those shown here were created *c.* 1914–18 for the society hostess Rita de Acosta Lydig.

years – and for the high-handed manner in which he treated his clients.

Yéyé French version of the Beatles' 'Yeah, Yeah, Yeah' refrain, used to describe the clothing of the early 1960s.

Y-line Line of Christian DIOR's 1955 collection which showed a slender body with a top-heavy look achieved by large collars that opened up into a V-shape. The Y could also be inverted in the form of long TUNICS with deep slits at each side.

yoke Traditionally an integral portion of a SMOCK, a yoke is the upper part of a garment, usually fitted across the bust and around the back between the shoulders. Pleated, gathered or plain, it supports the rest of the garment. A yoke can also be the oversize waistband of a skirt, curved downwards, from which the rest of the skirt hangs. Yoked skirts were particularly popular during the 1930s and again in the early 1970s when fashions based on rural dress and PEASANT costumes were in vogue.

yoked skirt *See* YOKE.

Yuki 1937–. Designer. Born Gnyuki Torimaru in Mizki-Ken, Japan. After training as a textile engineer, Yuki left Japan in 1959 for London. He studied English for three years, then history of architecture at the Art Institute of Chicago, returning to London in 1964 to attend the London College of Fashion. After graduating in 1966 he worked for Louis FERAUD and MICHAEL as well as HARTNELL before spending three years in Paris with CARDIN. He opened his own company in 1973 and became famous for his sculpted, one-size, draped jersey dresses which are designed to fall away from the body as it moves, then resume their intended shape and position.

Z

zazou suit French version of the ZOOT SUIT, worn by a small group of young French men and women in the early 1940s. For female 'zazous' the look consisted of a wide-shouldered zoot jacket, short pleated skirt and platform shoes.

zip (US: zipper) In 1893 W. Litcomb Judson of Chicago, USA, patented a clasp locker system of fastening which was constructed of a series of hooks and eyes with a clasp lock for opening and closing. In 1913 Gideon Sundback, a Swede working in the USA, developed Judson's ideas and produced a hookless fastener with interlocking metal teeth. This fastener was first used on money belts and tobacco pouches and in 1917 members of the US navy were issued with windproof jackets with clasp-lock fasteners at the front. It was B. G. Worth of B.F. Goodrich Co. who gave the name 'zipper' to a fastener that was used at the time for closing shoes. In the early 1930s SCHIAPARELLI was one of the earliest designers to use zips on fashion garments. By the mid-20th century the zip had been further refined and was composed of two strips of metal or plastic at each side of an

The rustic smock was the source for this 1970s yoked blouse and matching skirt with **yoke**.

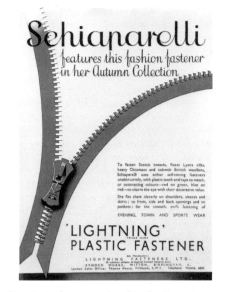

On 4 September 1935, when this advertisement appeared, the words **zip** and zipper were not yet in general use.

The **zoot suit** found its way from South to North America in the early part of the 20th century. It was most popular in the 1940s and 1950s.

opening, to which are attached two rows of metal teeth which lock in one direction and open in the other.

zipper *See* ZIP.

zoot suit Suit worn mainly by Mexican-Americans and African-Americans in the USA in the 1940s and 1950s. It consisted of a wide-shouldered jacket with a narrow waist and a drape which fell deep into the back. Often knee-length, the jacket tapered to baggy trousers which were still wide at the knee but narrowed at the bottom. The zoot suit was usually made of brightly coloured fabric.

Zoran 1947–. Designer. Born Zoran Ladicorbic in Belgrade, Yugoslavia. Zoran graduated from the University of Belgrade with a degree in architecture. In 1971 he moved to New York. His first collection in 1977 attracted a great deal of interest. He is a MINIMALIST designer, cutting luxurious fabrics into precise, simple shapes and avoiding where possible the use of fastenings, decorations and accessories. He has produced a capsule wardrobe consisting of trousers, a cardigan, a top, four T-shirts and several skirts of different lengths, which is intended to answer all travel requirements. Cashmere is one of his favourite fabrics. He restricts his use of colour to a basic palette of red, black, grey, cream and white.

zouave jacket Collarless, waist-length, braid-trimmed, BOLERO-style jacket with three-quarter-length sleeves. It is named after the Zouaves, a regiment of French soldiers attached to the Hussars, who in the 1830s adopted an Arab-style costume which incorporated such a jacket. During the 1860s women wore zouave-style jackets for indoor and outdoor wear.

SOURCES OF ILLUSTRATIONS

a: above; b: bottom; c: centre: l: left; r: right; t: top.

© ADAGP, Paris and DACS, London: pp. 60r, 82, 83l, 83r, 88, 89, 111t, 146, 153t. ©Aquascutum Ltd: p. 16. Courtesy Giorgio Armani: p. 17. Courtesy David Bailey/*Sunday Times*: p. 20. ©David Bailey: p. 194b. Courtesy Archives Balenciaga, Paris: p. 22t. Courtesy Balmain. Drawings René Gruau.: pp. 23b, 24t. Courtesy Jeff Banks: p. 24b. Courtesy Geoffrey Beene: p. 29t. ©Courtesy Bellville Sassoon: p. 29b. Courtesy Elio Berhanyer: p. 31. Courtesy Manolo Blahnik: p. 34. Courtesy of Bill Blass, Ltd. Archives: p. 35. Courtesy Body Map: p. 38t. The Brooklyn Museum, Millicent Rogers Collection: p. 211b. Courtesy Brooks Bros.: p. 45. Courtesy Liza Bruce: p. 46. Caisse Nationale des Monuments Historiques et des Sites, Paris: pp. 36l, 36r, 79, 128, 236, 241, 261b. Courtesy Calman Links: pp. 50, 105. Calouste Gulbenkian Foundation Museum, Lisbon: p. 146. Courtesy Pierre Cardin: p. 223l. ©Cartier. Photo Louis Tirilly: p. 54b. Courtesy Bonnie Cashin: p. 55. Courtesy Oleg Cassini: p. 56. Courtesy Nino Cerruti: p. 58. Courtesy Hussein Chalayan. Photo Chris Moore: p. 59t. ©Courtesy Chanel: p. 59. Courtesy Caroline Charles: p. 61. Courtesy Central Museum, Northampton: pp. 69, 187t. Courtesy Clements Ribeiro. Photo Tim Griffiths: p. 66b. Courtesy Cluett, Peabody and Co.: p. 18. *Collier's Weekly*, New York, 1904: p. 113. Chateau Compiègne: p. 259. Courtesy Sybil Connolly: p. 68. Stuart Cosgrove Collection: p. 265r. *Costumes Parisiens*, 1912: p. 231l. Courtesy Courrèges: p. 72. Courtesy Patrick Cox: p. 73t. Courtesy Wendy Dagworthy: p. 77. Courtesy Oscar de la Renta: p. 78. Courtesy Ann Demeulemeester. Photo Marleen Daniëls: p. 80. Courtesy Archives Christian Dior: p. 226b. Courtesy Dolce & Gabbana: p. 85. Courtesy Edina & Lena: p. 202. Courtesy Perry Ellis: p. 92. ©Courtesy Emanuel: pp. 93t, 205l. European Silk Commission: p. 210l. Courtesy Fendi. Photo Peter Lindbergh: p. 98. Courtesy Ferragamo: p. 99. Courtesy Fiorucci: p. 187b. Fotomas Index: pp. 22b, 23t, 58, 245. Courtesy Gina Fratini: p. 104. Drawings ©Jean-Paul Gaultier. Courtesy Jean-Paul Gaultier: pp. 109, 110. Courtesy Rudi Gernreich: p. 111b. Courtesy Ghost: p. 112l. Courtesy Bill Gibb: 112r. Courtesy Givenchy: pp. 32b, 115. Courtesy Andrew Grima: p. 117. Courtesy Gucci: p. 118. Courtesy Norman Hartnell Ltd: p. 121. Courtesy Hermès. Photos

Philippe Peraldi: p. 123. Courtesy Carolina Herrera: p. 124l. Courtesy Peter Hope Lumley: pp. 14, 52b, 219b. Courtesy Barbara Hulanicki: pp. 42, 127. Hulton Getty Picture Library: pp. 15, 21, 26, 33, 38b, 40, 57, 60l, 62, 63, 66t, 67t, 70t, 75, 91, 108, 124r, 134, 151r, 159, 172, 174t, 184, 190, 192t, 194t, 200r, 225, 234l, 242l. *I Was Lord Kitchener's Valet* by David Block, 1970s: p. 43. *Illustrated London News* Picture Library: pp. 12, 175. ©International News Photos. Photo Stuart Heydinger: p. 13. Courtesy Betty Jackson. Photo Martin Brading: p. 129l. Courtesy Betty Jackson. Photo S. Karadia/Spoon: p. 129r. Jaeger Archives: pp. 130, 134r. Drawings © courtesy Betsey Johnson: p. 132. Courtesy Stephen Jones: p. 133t. Courtesy Charles Jourdan: p. 133b. *Journal des jeunes personnes*, 1850s: p. 260. Courtesy Norma Kamali: p. 135l. Courtesy Kangol Hats Ltd: p. 135r. Courtesy Donna Karan: p. 136. Courtesy Kenzo. Photo Peter Lindbergh: p. 137. Courtesy Kenzo. Photo ©O. Toscani: p. 138. Courtesy Calvin Klein: p. 140r. Courtesy Roland Klein. Photo Chris Moore: p. 141t. Diana Korchien: p. 103 Courtesy Lacoste: p. 143b. Courtesy Christian Lacroix. Photo Guy Marineau: p. 144tl. Courtesy Christian Lacroix. Photo Joe Dorsey: p. 144tr. Drawing courtesy Christian Lacroix: p. 144b. Drawing courtesy Karl Lagerfeld: p. 145 tl. Courtesy Karl Lagerfeld. Photos ©Pascal Thermé: p. 145. Courtesy Helmut Lang: p. 147r. ©Lanvin Estate: p. 148. Courtesy Guy Laroche: p. 149. Courtesy Ralph Lauren: p. 150. Pierre Le Tan Collection, Paris: p. 213t. Courtesy Hervé Léger. Photo: Guy Marineau: p. 151l. Courtesy François Lesage: p. 153b. Courtesy Levi Strauss: p. 227. Courtesy Liberty & Co.: p. 10. Mansell Collection: pp. 32t, 52t, 120t, 197, 203, 205r, 209b, 214, 221, 226c. Drawing Courtesy Vera Maxwell: pp. 160, 262. Photos ©Niall McInerney: p. 107. Courtesy Alexander McQueen: p. 161. The Metropolitan Museum of Art, New York. Gift of Capezio Inc.: p. 263. Courtesy Simone Mirman: p. 163r. *Missonologia*, Electa, 1994. Courtesy Missoni: pp. 164tl, 164tr. Courtesy Missoni: pp. 164bl, 164 br. Courtesy Issey Miyake Inc.: p. 165. Courtesy Moschino: p. 168. Courtesy Thierry Mugler: p. 169. Courtesy Jean Muir: p. 170. Musée du Louvre, Paris: p. 198. Musée de la Mode et du Costume, Paris: pp. 152, 166, 251r. Photo Tabard. Musée de la Mode et du Textile, Paris. ©UFAC Collection: p. 251l. *New York Herald*, Paris, 17 May 1896: p. 93b. Courtesy Bruce Oldfield: p. 173. Photo ©Norman Parkinson. Courtesy Zandra Rhodes: p. 176. Courtesy Mollie Parnis: p. 178. Courtesy Jean

Patou: p. 179. *Patricia Roberts' Second Knitting Book*, 1983: p. 141b. Drawings by John Peacock: pp. 37, 120b, 196t, 204r, 215r, 222, 223r, 230, 258, 264. Thierry Perez, Courtesy Azzedine Alaïa: p. 11. Photo Source: p. 163l. Courtesy Jacques Pinturier: p. 186b. Collection Poiret – de Wilde: pp. 188, 189. Popperphoto: p. 39. Courtesy Thea Porter: pp. 125r, 191. Courtesy Pringle of Scotland: p. 192. Courtesy Mary Quant. Photo Terence Donovan: p. 195. Courtesy Paco Rabanne. Photo J. W. T. Paris: p. 196b. Courtesy Nina Ricci Archives: p. 201r. Royal and Ancient Golf Club, St Andrews/ Colnaghi & Co. Ltd: p. 90b. Courtesy Sonia Rykiel: pp. 204l, 240. Courtesy Yves Saint Laurent: pp. 71, 181, 206tr, 206bl, 206br, 207, 242. ©Courtesy Jil Sander: p. 208. Courtesy Vidal Sassoon: p. 209t. Courtesy Mila Schön: p. 213b. Courtesy Sears, Roebuck and Co.: pp. 65, 95, 229, 235. Courtesy David Shilling: pp. 84, 216. Courtesy Martine Sitbon: p. 218. Courtesy Caroline Smith: p. 248. Courtesy Graham Smith and Kangol Hats Ltd.: p. 220. Photo courtesy L. J. Smith Ltd, Sandwick, The Shetlands: p. 96. Courtesy Paul Smith: p. 73b. Courtesy George Stavropoulos: p. 224. Courtesy Anna Sui: p. 228. *Sunday Times* Costume Research Institute: pp. 106, 111b, 119, 140l, 182l, 185, 201l, 206tl, 219t, 234r, 239, 246t. Courtesy Angelo Tarlazzi: p. 231r. Courtesy Chantal Thomass: p. 233. Courtesy Tiffany & Co.: pp. 183r, 186t. Courtesy Philip Treacy. Photos Robert Fairer: p. 237. Courtesy Pauline Trigère: p. 238t. Courtesy Richard Tyler: p. 243t. Courtesy Emanuel Ungaro: p. 244. Courtesy Verdura Inc.: p. 81. Courtesy Dries van Noten: p. 247. Courtesy Gianni Versace: p. 249. By courtesy of the Board of Trustees of the Victoria and Albert Museum, London: pp. 49, 51, 97, 143tl, 143tr, 226t, 260b. *Victorian Fashions and Costumes from Harper's Bazar, 1867–1898*, Dover Publications, 1974: pp. 27, 41, 182, 261tl, 261tr. Visual Arts Library: pp. 125l, 200l, 210r. Courtesy Roger Vivier: p. 251b. Courtesy Roger Vivier. Photo: Erica Lennard: p. 252l. Courtesy Georgina von Etzdorf: p. 252r. Courtesy Diane von Fürstenberg: p. 253. Courtesy Vuokko: p. 254. Courtesy Janice Wainwright: p. 255. Courtesy Warners and Co.: p. 257. Weidenfeld and Nicholson Archives: pp. 70b, 70t, 139, 147l, 156. Courtesy Vivienne Westwood. Photos: Niall McInerney: p. 256. Courtesy Vivienne Westwood. Photo Patrick Fetherstonhaugh: p. 47.

The publishers would like to thank all the designers and companies who generously made available original sketches and photographs from their archives, and in particular:

Azzedine Alaïa, Aquascutum Ltd, Giorgio Armani, Jeff Banks, Geoffrey Beene, Bellville Sassoon, Elio Berhanyer, Manolo Blahnik, Bill Blass, Body Map, Brooks Bros., Calman Links, Pierre Cardin, Cartier, Bonnie Cashin, Oleg Cassini, Nino Cerruti, Hussein Chalayan, Chanel, Caroline Charles, Clements Ribeiro, Cluett, Peabody & Co., Sybil Connolly, Courrèges, Patrick Cox, Wendy Dagworthy, Oscar de la Renta, Ann Demeulemeester, Christian Dior, Dolce & Gabbana, Edina & Lena, Perry Ellis, Emanuel, Fendi, Ferragamo, Fiorucci, Gina Fratini, Jean-Paul Gaultier, Bill Gibb, Givenchy, Andrew Grima, Gucci, Norman Hartnell, Carolina Herrera, Hermès, Barbara Hulanicki, Betty Jackson, Jaeger, Betsey Johnson, Charles Jourdan, Norma Kamali, Kangol Hats Ltd, Donna Karan, Kenzo, Calvin Klein, Roland Klein, Lacoste, Christian Lacroix, Karl Lagerfeld, Helmut Lang, Lanvin, Guy Laroche, Ralph Lauren, Hervé Léger, François Lesage, Liberty & Co., Vera Maxwell, Simone Mirman, Missoni (with thanks to Gai Pearl Marshall), Issey Miyake Inc., Claude Montana, Moschino (with thanks to Gai Pearl Marshall), Jean Muir, Thierry Mugler, Bruce Oldfield, Mollie Parnis, Jacques Pinturier, Jean Patou, Thea Porter, Pringle of Scotland, Mary Quant, Paco Rabanne, Zandra Rhodes, Patricia Roberts, Nina Ricci, Sonia Rykiel, Yves Saint Laurent, Jil Sander, Vidal Sassoon, Mila Schön, Sears Roebuck & Co., David Shilling, Martine Sitbon, Graham Smith, George Stavropoulos, Levi Strauss, Anna Sui, Angelo Tarlazzi, Chantal Thomass, Tiffany & Co., Philip Treacy, Pauline Trigère, Richard Tyler, Emanuel Ungaro, Koos van den Akker, Dries van Noten, Georgina von Etzdorf, Verdura Inc., Versace, Diane von Fürstenberg, Vuokko, Janice Wainwright, Warners and Co., Vivienne Westwood, Whitmore-Thomas.

Special thanks to John Peacock.

Every effort has been made to trace the copyright owners of the illustrations included in this *Dictionary*. Any further information would be welcomed by the publishers.

BIBLIOGRAPHY

General fashion references

Arnold, Janet, *A Handbook of Costume*, London, 1973.
Batterberry, Michael and Ariane, *Mirror, Mirror: A Social History of Fashion*, New York, 1977.
Black, J. Anderson and Garland, Madge, *A History of Fashion*, London, 1953.
Boucher, François, *A History of Costume in the West*, London, 1967.
——, *20,000 Years of Fashion*, New York, 1982.
Bradfield, Nancy, *Costume in Detail, 1730–1930*, London, 1968.
Brooke, Iris, *A History of English Costume*, London, 1937.
Chenoune, Farid, *A History of Men's Fashion*, London, 1993.
Crawford, M. D. C., *The Ways of Fashion*, New York, 1941.
Cunnington, C. W. and Phillis, *Handbook of English Costume in the 19th Century*, London, 1959.
Cunnington, Phillis, *Costume*, London, 1966.
Davenport, M., *The Book of Costume*, 2 vols, New York, 1948.
De Marly, Diane, *Fashion for Men: An Illustrated History*, New York, 1985.
Ewing, Elizabeth, *History of 20th Century Fashion*, London, 1974.
Garland, Madge, *Fashion*, London, 1962.
Glynn, Prudence, *In Fashion: Dress in the Twentieth Century*, London, 1978.
Godey's Lady's Book(s), Philadelphia, 1872.
Gurell, Lois M. and Beeson, Marianne S., *Dimensions of Dress and Adornment*, Iowa, 1977.
Kempner, Rachel H., *Costume*, New York, 1977.
Khornak, Lucille, *Fashion 2001*, New York, 1982.
Laver, James, *Taste and Fashion*, London, 1937.
——, *Costume*, New York and London, 1963.
——, *Fashion*, London, 1963.
——, *Style in Costume*, London, 1949.
——, *Modesty in Dress*, London and Boston, 1969.
—— and de la Haye, Amy, *Costume and Fashion*, London and New York, 1995.
Mansfield, Alan and Cunnington, Phillis, *Handbook of English Costume in the 20th Century, 1900–1950*, London, 1973.
Martin, Richard, *Fashion and Surrealism*, London and New York, 1989.
McCrum, Elizabeth, *Irish Fashion Since 1950*, Ulster, 1996.
Milbank, Caroline Rennolds, *Couture*, London and New York, 1986.

Monserrat, Ann, *And The Bride Wore*, London, 1973.
Moore, Langley Doris, *The Woman in Fashion*, London, 1949.
Peacock, John, *The Chronicle of Western Costume*, London and New York, 1991.
——, *Costume 1066–1990s*, London, 1994.
——, *Twentieth Century Fashion: The Complete Sourcebook*, London and New York, 1993.
Picken, Mary Brooks, *Dressmakers of France*, New York, 1956.
Polhemus, Ted, *Streetstyle*, London, 1994.
——, *Style Surfing*, London and New York, 1996.
Rubin, Leonard G., *The World of Fashion*, San Francisco, 1976.
Russell, Douglas A., *Costume History and Style*, New Jersey, 1983.
Wilcox, R. Turner, *Mode in Costume*, New York, 1947.
Yarwood, Doreen, *English Costume*, London, 1952.

Fashion dictionaries and encyclopaedias

Anthony P. and Arnold, J., *Costume: A General Bibliography*, 2nd edition, London, 1974.
Calasibetta, Charlotte, *Fairchild's History of Fashion*, New York, 1975.
Houck, Catherine, *The Fashion Encyclopedia*, New York, 1982.
Ironside, Janey, *A Fashion Alphabet*, London, 1968.
Martin, Richard, *The St. James Fashion Encyclopedia*, Detroit, 1997.
McDowell, Colin, *McDowell's Directory of Twentieth Century Fashion*, London, 1984.
Picken, Mary Brooks, *The Fashion Dictionary*, New York, 1939.
Stegemeyer, Anne, *Who's Who in Fashion*, New York, 1980.
Watkins, Josephine Ellis, *Who's Who in Fashion*, 2nd edition, New York, 1975.
Wilcox, R. Turner, *Dictionary of Costume*, New York, 1969.
Yarwood, Doreen, *Encyclopedia of World Costume*, New York, 1978.

Books about fashion and costume designers

Baillen, Claude, *Chanel Solitaire*, London, 1973.
Barillé, Elisabeth, *Lanvin*, London, 1997.
Baudot, François, *Alaïa*, London, 1996.
——, *Chanel*, London, 1996.
——, *Christian Lacroix*, London, 1997.

——, *Elsa Schiaparelli*, London, 1997.

——, *Poiret*, London, 1997.

——, *Yohji Yamamoto*, London, 1997.

——, *Thierry Mugler*, London, 1998.

Benaïm, Laurence, *Issey Miyake*, London, 1997.

Bergé, Pierre, *Yves Saint Laurent*, London, 1997.

Bourhis, Katell Le, *et al.*, *Emilio Pucci*, Geneva, 1997.

Brooklyn Institute of Arts and Sciences, *The Age of Worth*, New York, 1982.

Casadio, Mariuccia, *Missoni*, London, 1997.

——, *Moschino*, London, 1997.

——, *Versace*, London, 1998.

Charles-Roux, Edmonde, *Chanel*, London, 1976.

——, *Chanel and Her World*, London, 1981.

Chenoune, Farid, *Jean Paul Gaultier*, London, 1996.

Chierichetti, David, *Hollywood Costume Design*, New York, 1976.

De Graw, Imelda, *25 Years/25 Couturiers*, Denver, 1975.

De Marly, Diana, *Worth, Father of Haute Couture*, London, 1980.

Demornex, Jacqueline, *Vionnet*, London, 1991.

Deslandres, Yvonne, *Poiret*, London, 1987.

Desveaux, Delphine, *Fortuny*, London, 1998.

Galante, Pierre, *Mademoiselle Chanel*, Chicago, 1973.

Giroud, Françoise, *Dior: Christian Dior 1905–1957*, London, 1987.

Grand, France, *Comme des Garçons*, London, 1998.

Haedrich, Marcel, *Coco Chanel, Her Life, Her Secrets*, London and Boston, 1972.

Jouve, Marie-Andrée, *Balenciaga*, London, 1997.

Kamitsis, Lydia, *Vionnet*, London, 1996.

Keenan, Brigid, *Dior in Vogue*, London and New York, 1981.

Krell, Gene, *Vivienne Westwood*, London, 1997.

Latour, Anny, *Kings of Fashion*, New York, 1956.

Laynam, Ruth, *Couture, An Illustrated History of the Great Paris Designers and Their Creations*, New York, 1972.

Lee, Sarah Tomerlin, ed., *American Fashion: The Life and Lines of Adrian, Mainbocher, McCardell, Norell, Trigère*, New York, 1975.

Leese, Elizabeth, *Costume Design in the Movies*, London, 1976.

Madsen, Axel, *Living for Design: The Yves St Laurent Story*, New York, 1979.

Martin, Richard, *Gianni Versace*, New York, 1997.

——, *Charles James*, London, 1997.

—— and Koda, Harold, *Christian Dior*, New York, 1997.

Mauriès, Patrick, *Christian Lacroix: The Diary of a Collection*, London and New York, 1996.

Morris, Bernadine, *Valentino*, London, 1996.

Mulassano, Adriana and Custaldi, Alfa, *The Who's Who of Italian Fashion*, Florence, 1979.

New York City Metropolitan Museum of Art, *The World of Balenciaga*, New York, 1973.

Osma, Guillermo de, *Fortuny, Mariano Fortuny: His Life and Work*, London, 1980.

Perkins, Alice K., *Paris Couturiers and Milliners*, New York, 1949.

Piaggi, Anna, *Karl Lagerfeld: A Fashion Journal*, London and New York, 1986.

Pochna, Marie-France, *Dior*, London 1996.

Saunders, Edith, *The Age of Worth*, London, 1954.

Sischy, Ingrid, *Donna Karan*, London, 1998.

Vercelloni, Isa Tutino, *Missonologia: The World of Missoni*, Milan, 1994.

White, Palmer, *Poiret*, London and New York, 1973.

Williams, Beryl, *Fashion Is Our Business: Careers of Famous American Designers*, Philadelphia, 1945.

Books by fashion designers, milliners, costume designers, etc.

Amies, Hardy, *Just So Far*, London, 1954.

Antoine, *Antoine by Antoine*, New York, 1945.

Balmain, Pierre, *My Years and Seasons*, London, 1964.

Cardin, Pierre, *Past, Present and Future*, London, 1990.

Creed, Charles, *Made to Measure*, London, 1961.

Daché, Lilly, *Talking Through My Hats*, London, 1946.

Dior, Christian, *Christian Dior and I*, New York, 1957.

——, *Dior by Dior*, London, 1957.

Etherington-Smith, Meredith, *Patou*, London, 1983.

Ferragamo, Salvatore, *Shoemaker of Dreams*, London, 1957.

Gordon, Lady Duff, *Discretions and Indiscretions*, London, 1932.

Greer, Howard, *Designing Male*, New York, 1951.

Hartnell, Norman, *Royal Courts of Fashion*, London and New York, 1971.

Head, Edith and Ardmore, Jane K., *The Dress Doctor*, Boston, 1959.

Hulanicki, Barbara, *From A to Biba*, London, 1984.

Klein, Bernat, *Eye for Colour*, London, 1965.

Lacroix, Christian, *Pieces of a Pattern: Lacroix by Lacroix*, London and New York, 1992.

Leiber, Judith, *The Artful Handbag*, London and New York, 1995.

Links, J. G., *How to Look at Furs*, London, 1962.

Bibliography

Moschino, Franco and Castelli, Lydia, *Moschino: X Years of Kaos!*, Milan, 1993.

Poiret, Paul, *En Habillant l'Epoque*, Paris, 1930.

——, *King of Fashion: The Autobiography of Paul Poiret*, Philadelphia, 1931.

——, *Revenez-y*, Paris, 1932.

Quant, Mary, *Quant by Quant*, London, 1965.

Schiaparelli, Elsa, *Shocking Life*, London and New York, 1954.

Sharaff, Irene, *Broadway and Hollywood: Costumes Designed by Irene Sharaff*, New York, 1976.

Thaarup, Aage, *Heads and Tails*, London, 1956.

Tinling, Teddy, *Sixty Years in Tennis*, London, 1983.

Worth, Jean-Philippe, *A Century of Fashion*, Boston, 1928.

Fashion illustrators and illustration

Barbier, Georges, *The Illustrations of Georges Barbier in Full Colour*, New York, 1977.

Brunelleschi, Umberto: Fashion Stylist, Illustrator, Stage and Costume Designer, New York, 1979.

Delhaye, Jean, *Affiches Gravures Art Deco*, London, 1977.

Drake, Nicholas, *Fashion Illustration Today*, London and New York, 1994.

Erté, *Things I Remember: An Autobiography*, London and New York, 1975.

Gallo, Max, *L'Affiche miroir de l'histoire*, Paris, 1973.

Ginsburg, Madeleine, *An Introduction to Fashion Illustration*, London, 1980.

Kery, Patricia Franz, *Great Magazine Covers of the World*, New York, 1982.

McDowell, Colin, *The Man of Fashion*, London and New York, 1997.

Moore, Doris Langley, *Fashion Through Fashion Plates 1771-1970*, London, 1971.

Packer, William, *The Art of Vogue Covers*, New York, 1980.

——, *Fashion Drawing in Vogue*, London, 1984.

Petersen, Theodore, *Magazines in the Twentieth Century*, Chicago, 1965.

Ramos, Juan, *Antonio*, London and New York, 1995.

Schaw, Michael, *J. C. Leyendecker*, New York, 1974.

Vertès, Marcel, *Art and Fashion*, New York and London, 1944.

Fashion photographers and photography

Beaton, Cecil, *Photobiography*, New York, 1951.

——, *The Glass of Fashion*, London, 1954.

——, *Selected Diaries, 1926–54*, London, 1954.

Devlin, Polly, *Vogue Book of Fashion Photography*, New York, 1979.

Ewing, William A., *Blumenfeld: A Fetish for Beauty*, London and New York, 1996.

Hall-Duncan, Nancy, *The History of Fashion Photography*, New York, 1979.

Kery, Patricia Franz, *Great Magazine Covers of the World*, New York, 1975.

Nickerson, Camilla and Wakefield, Neville, *Fashion Photography of the 90s*, London, 1997.

Packer, William, *The Art of Vogue Covers*, New York, 1980.

Ross, Josephine, *Beaton in Vogue*, London, 1986.

Steichen, Edward, *A Life in Photography*, New York, 1963.

Vreeland, Diana and Penn, Irving, *Inventive Paris Clothes, 1909–1939*, London, 1977.

World of magazines

Ballard, Bettina, *In My Fashion*, New York and London, 1960.

Chase, Edna Woolman and Ilka, *Always in Vogue*, New York and London, 1954.

Garland, Ailsa, *Lion's Share*, London, 1970.

Petersen, Theodore, *Magazines in the Twentieth Century*, Chicago, 1965.

Seebohm, Caroline, *The Man Who Was Vogue*, New York, 1982.

Snow, Carmel, *The World of Carmel Snow*, New York, 1962.

White, Cynthia L., *Women's Magazines 1693–1968*, London, 1970.

Yoxall, H. W., *A Fashion of Life*, London, 1966.

Department stores and retailing

Adburgham, Alison, *Shops and Shopping*, London, 1964.

Brady, Maxine, *Bloomingdales*, New York, 1980.

Daves, Jessica, *Ready-Made Miracle: The American Story of Fashion for the Millions*, New York, 1967.

Jarnow, Jeanette and Judelle, Beatrice, *Inside the Fashion Business*, 2nd edition, New York, 1974.

Levin, Phyllis Lee, *The Wheels of Fashion*, New York, 1965.

Marcus, Stanley, *Minding the Store*, Boston, 1974.

Pope, Jesse, *The Clothing Industry in New York*, New York, 1970.

Roscho, Bernard, *The Rag Race*, New York, 1963.

Haute-couture and ready-to-wear

Allen, Agnes, *The Story of Clothes*, London, 1955.
Bertin, Celia, *Paris à la mode*, London, 1956.
——, *La Couture, terre inconnue*, Paris, 1956.
Daves, Jessica, *Ready-Made Miracle: The American Story of Fashion for the Millions*, New York, 1967.
De Marly, Diana, *The History of Haute Couture 1850–1950*, London and New York, 1980.
Halliday, L., *The Makers of Our Clothes*, London, 1966.
Ley, Sandra, *Fashion for Everyone: The Story of Ready-to-Wear 1870s–1970s*, New York, 1976.
Lynam, Ruth, ed., *Couture*, New York, 1972.
Richards, Florence, *The Ready-to-Wear Industry, 1900–1950*, New York, 1951.
Riley, R. and Vecchio, W., *The Fashion Makers*, New York, 1967.

Accessories, make-up, hairstyles

Baynes, Ken and Kate, *The Shoe Show: British Shoes since 1790*, London, 1979.
Becker, Vivienne, *Antique and 20th-Century Jewellery*, London, 1980.
Braun, Ronsdorf M., *The History of the Handkerchief*, Leigh-on-Sea, England, 1967.
Buck, Anne, *Victorian Costume and Costume Accessories*, London, 1961.
Castelbajac, Kate de, *The Face of the Century: 100 Years of Make-up and Style*, London and New York, 1995.
Clabburn, Pamela, *Shawls*, Buckinghamshire, England, 1981.
Crawford, T. S., *A History of the Umbrella*, New York and Devon, 1970.
Epstein, Diana, *Buttons*, New York, 1968.
Foster, Vanda, *Bags and Purses*, London, 1982.
Ginsburg, Madeleine, *The Hat*, London, 1990.
Grass, Milton E., *History of Hosiery*, New York, 1953.
Houart, V., *Buttons: A Collector's Guide*, London, 1977.
Kennett, Frances, *The Collector's Book of Twentieth Century Fashion*, London, 1983.
Mauriès, Patrick, *Jewelry by Chanel*, London, 1993.
McDowell, Colin, *Hats*, London and New York, 1992.
——, *Shoes*, London and New York, 1989.
Mirabella, Grace, *Tiffany & Co.*, London, 1997.
Nadelhoffer, Hans, *Cartier*, London, 1984.
O'Keeffe, Linda, *Shoes*, New York, 1996.

Sallee, Lynn, *Old Costume Jewellery 1870–1945*, Alabama, 1979.
Snowman, A.K., *The Master Jewelers*, London, 1990.
Swann, June, *Shoes*, London, 1982.
Wilcox, R. Turner, *The Mode in Hats and Headdresses*, New York, 1959.
Wilson, Eunice, *The History of Shoe Fashions*, New York, 1969.

Underwear

Cunnington, C. W. and Phillis, *The History of Underclothes*, London, 1951.
Ewing, Elizabeth, *Dress and Undress*, London and New York, 1978.
Fontanel, Béatrice, *Support and Seduction: A History of Corsets and Bras*, London, 1990.
St Laurent, Cecil, *The History of Ladies' Underwear*, London, 1968.
Waugh, Norah, *Corsets and Crinolines*, London, 1954.
Yooll, Emily, *The History of the Corset*, London, 1946.

Textiles

American Fabrics Magazine, ed., *Encyclopedia of Textiles*, New York, 1972.
Earnshaw, Patricia, *The Dictionary of Lace*, Buckinghamshire, England, 1981.
——, *The Identification of Lace*, Buckinghamshire, England, 1982.
Kleeburg, Irene Cumming, *The Butterick Fabric Handbook*, New York, 1982.
Linton, George E., *The Modern Textile and Apparel Dictionary*, New Jersey, 1973.
Luscombe, S., *The Encyclopedia of Buttons*, New York, 1967.
Picken, Mary Brooks, *The Fashion Dictionary*, New York, 1939.
Simeon, Margaret, *The History of Lace*, London, 1979.

General history

Adburgham, Alison, *A Punch History of Manners*, London, 1961.
Howell, Georgina, *In Vogue*, London, 1975.
Keenan, Brigid, *The Women We Wanted to Look Like*, New York, 1977.

Period history

Arlen, Michael, *The Green Hat*, London, 1924.
Battersby, Martin, *The Decorative Twenties*, London, 1969.

Bibliography

———, *The Decorative Thirties*, London, 1971.

Bennett, Richard, *A Picture of the Twenties*, London, 1961.

Bernard, Barbara, *Fashion in the 60s*, London and New York, 1958.

Brough, James, *The Prince and the Lily*, London, 1975.

Brunhammer, Yvonne, *Lo Stile 1925*, Milan, 1966.

Dorner, Jane, *Fashion in the Forties and Fifties*, London, 1957.

Garland, Madge, *The Indecisive Decade*, London, 1968.

Garrett, Richard, *Mrs Simpson*, London, 1979.

Goldring, Douglas, *The Nineteen Twenties*, London, 1945.

Haney, Lynn, *Naked at the Feast*, London, 1981.

Hillier, Bevis, *The World of Art Deco*, Minneapolis, 1971.

Jenkins, Alan, *The Twenties*, London, 1974.

Lardner, John, *The Aspirin Age 1914–1941*, London, n.d.

Laver, James, *Between the Wars*, London, 1961.

———, *The Jazz Age*, London, 1964.

Margueritte, Victor, *La Garçonne*, Paris, 1922.

Melinkoff, Ellen, *What We Wore*, New York, 1984.

Ridley, Jasper, *Napoleon III and Eugénie*, London, 1979.

Roberts, Cecil, *The Bright Twenties*, London, 1970.

Robinson, Julian, *Fashion in the 40s*, London and New York, 1976.

———, *Fashion in the 30s*, London, 1978.

Seaman, C. C. B., *Life in Britain between the Wars*, London, 1970.

Stevenson, Pauline, *Edwardian Fashion*, London, 1980.

The fashion scene

Adburgham, Alison, *View of Fashion*, London, 1966.

Bender, Marilyn, *The Beautiful People*, New York, 1967.

Brady, James, *Super Chic*, Boston, 1974.

Carter, Ernestine, *20th Century Fashion, A Scrapbook 1900 to Today*, London, 1957.

———, *With Tongue in Chic*, London, 1974.

———, *The Changing World of Fashion*, London and New York, 1977.

———, *Magic Names of Fashion*, London, 1980.

de Wolfe, Elsie, *After All*, London, 1935.

Fairchild, John, *The Fashionable Savages*, New York, 1965.

Flanner, Janet, *Paris Was Yesterday*, New York, 1979.

Kelly, Katie, *The Wonderful World of Women's Wear Daily*, New York, 1972.

Lambert, Eleanor, *The World of Fashion, People, Places, Resources*, New York, 1976.

Morris, Bernadine and Walz, Barbara, *The Fashion Makers*, New York, 1978.

Spanier, Ginette, *It Isn't All Mink*, New York, 1960.

Psychology and sociology of fashion

Anspach, Karlyne Alice, *The Why of Fashion*, Amos, Iowa, 1968.

Baines, Barbara, *Fashion Revivals*, London, 1981.

Bergler, Edmund, *Fashion and the Unconscious*, New York, 1953.

Delbourg-Delphis, Marylene, *Le Chic et Le Look*, Paris, 1981.

Dorner, Jane, *The Changing Shape of Fashion*, London, 1974.

Flügel, John C., *The Psychology of Clothes*, London and New York, 1966.

Garland, Madge, *The Changing Form of Fashion*, London, 1970.

Gernsheim, A., *Fashion and Reality 1840–1914*, London, 1963.

Hawes, Elizabeth, *Fashion Is Spinach*, New York, 1938.

———, *It's Still Spinach*, Boston, 1954.

———, *Why Is a Dress?*, New York, 1954.

Hollander, Anne, *Seeing through Clothes*, New York, 1978.

Horn, Marilyn J., *The Second Skin: An Interdisciplinary Study of Clothing*, 2nd edition, Boston, 1975.

Hurlock, Elizabeth B., *The Psychology of Dress*, New York, 1929.

Konig, Rene, *The Restless Image: A Sociology of Fashion*, London, 1973.

Laver, James, *How and Why Fashions in Men's and Women's Clothes Have Changed during the Past 200 Years*, London, 1950.

Lurie, Alison, *The Language of Clothes*, London and New York, 1981.

Pritchard, Mrs Eric, *The Cult of Chiffon*, New York, 1902.

Roach, Mary Ellen and Eicher, Joanne B., *Dress, Adornment and the Social Order*, New York, 1965.

Rosencrantz, Mary Lou, *Clothing Concepts: A Social-Psychological Approach*, London, 1972.

Ryan, Mary S., *Clothing: A Study In Human Behaviour*, New York, 1966.

Young, Agatha Brooks, *Recurring Cycles of Fashion*, New York, 1937.